Utilizing Green Finance for Sustainable Development

Karima Toumi Sayari
Al Zahra College for Women, Oman

Revenio Jalagat
https://orcid.org/0000-0002-8878-3825
Al Zahra College for Women, Oman

Rafat Al Batayneh
Al Zahra College for Women, Oman

IGI Global
Scientific Publishing
Publishing Tomorrow's Research Today

Vice President of Editorial	Melissa Wagner
Director of Acquisitions	Mikaela Felty
Director of Book Development	Jocelynn Hessler
Production Manager	Mike Brehm
Cover Design	Jose Rosado

Published in the United States of America by
IGI Global Scientific Publishing
701 East Chocolate Avenue
Hershey, PA, 17033, USA
Tel: 717-533-8845 | Fax: 717-533-7115
Website: https://www.igi-global.com E-mail: cust@igi-global.com

Library of Congress Cataloging-in-Publication Data

Names: Sayari, Karima, 1978- editor. | Jalagat, Revenio, 1978- editor. | Al-Batayneh, Rafat, 1982- editor.
Title: Utilizing green finance for sustainable development / [edited by] Karima Toumi Sayari, Revenio Jalagat, Jr., Rafat Al-Batayneh.
Description: Hershey, PA : IGI Global Scientific Publishing, [2026] | Includes bibliographical references and index. | Summary: "This book aims to explore the nexus of green finance and sustainable development"-- Provided by publisher.
Identifiers: LCCN 2025020206 (print) | LCCN 2025020207 (ebook) | ISBN 9798337312408 (hardcover) | ISBN 9798337312415 (paperback) | ISBN 9798337312422 (ebook)
Subjects: LCSH: Economic development--Economic aspects. | Finance--Environmental aspects. | Sustainable development.
Classification: LCC HD75.6 .U86 2026 (print) | LCC HD75.6 (ebook)
LC record available at https://lccn.loc.gov/2025020206
LC ebook record available at https://lccn.loc.gov/2025020207
CIP Data
British Cataloguing in Publication Data
A Cataloguing in Publication record for this book is available from the British Library.

Table of Contents

Detailed Table of Contents

This study explores the synergy between Fintech and Green Finance. It employed quantitative research methodology through bibliometric analysis, highlighting the performance analysis of data and providing a scientific map of previous studies related to the topic. Key findings based on performance analysis showed that 2024 marked the highest publication of Fintech and Green Finance, most sources from journals. The top university publishing in this area is the University of Hongkong specializing in Finance and Economics, and China produced the most manuscripts. Bibliometric analysis revealed that the top three keywords are green finance, China, and economic development. While co-authorship assessment showed the highest link strength by Fahad Taghzadeh-hesary and the most bibliographically coupled documents are those manuscripts that are published in Environmental Science and Pollution Research, and Sustainability Journals. More studies on Fintech and green finance are highly recommended to fill the gap in the body of knowledge and foster environmental and economic sustainability.

Global initiatives for economic development started with the Industrial Revolution. However, it caused serious environmental issues. It necessitated to focus on eco-friendly developmental projects. Accordingly, the sustainable development paradigm has evolved to balance both environmental and developmental models. Although the UN affirmed sustainable development from 1987 onwards, its scope was elaborated with MDGs and SDGs. The declaration of SDGs in 2015 provided a framework for a global sustainable future. However, developing countries face financial hurdles in responding positively to the demands of SDGs that prioritize sustainable development and environmental protection. The OECD (2021) notes that developing countries experience 2.5 to 3.7 trillion dollars shortfall to meet the demands of SDGs. To address this complexity, developed countries, international institutions, and multinational and transnational corporations promoted green finance. From this perspective, this chapter critically evaluates the scope and functioning of green finance in light of a sustainable future.

The purpose of this chapter is to identify and compare the main topics addressed by the indicators performance indicators of microfinance institutions (MFIs), which are discussed in literature and used by some of the main rating agencies, in three dimensions of sustainability (financial, social and environmental), according to the Triple Bottom Line perspective. The indicators were identified in the literature (Scopus and Web of Science databases) and in 12 specialized rating agencies. Literature and rating agencies converge on topics like structured financial planning, social impacts, and mitigation of environmental risks. The rating agencies reflect the microfinance market practices with focus on financial factors (such as profitability and productivity) coupled with the MFIs social and environmental objectives. Divergently, literature emphasizes the importance of the accessibility and diversity of microfinance services.

This chapter explores the burgeoning field of green finance and its crucial role in aligning financial markets with sustainable development objectives. It examines how incorporating environmental, social, and governance (ESG) factors influences traditional risk and return profiles, presenting both opportunities and challenges for investors and financial institutions. We delve into innovative financial instruments and strategies designed to mobilize capital towards environmentally sound and socially responsible projects. Furthermore, the chapter critically analyzes the evolving concept of fiduciary responsibility in the context of sustainability, arguing for a broader interpretation that encompasses long-term value creation and planetary well-being. By bridging the gap between financial imperatives and sustainability goals, this chapter underscores the transformative potential of integrating responsibility into the core of financial decision-making for a more resilient and equitable future.

Green finance has emerged as a critical enabler in promoting sustainable development by directing financial flows towards environmentally responsible and climate-friendly initiatives. This paper explores the pathways through which green finance supports economic growth while ensuring environmental protection, such as through green bonds, sustainable loans, and renewable energy investments. It examines key challenges including regulatory inconsistencies, limited market awareness, and risk-return trade-offs that hinder widespread adoption. At the same time, the study highlights significant opportunities, such as policy innovations, technological advancements, and global commitments to climate action, which can accelerate the integration of green finance into mainstream economic planning. By addressing these challenges and leveraging available opportunities, green finance can play a transformative role in achieving long-term sustainability goals and climate resilience.

Green orientation as a strategic tool in achieving sustainability in SMEs has turned out to be an imperative and conscious shift towards business processes that strive to be environment friendly. The study attempts to explore the green orientation tools, challenges and the possible outcomes when employed as a strategy in SMEs. The study gives an idea about some of the main elements and factors that would ease the achievement of sustainability through green orientation in SMEs and the factors that could hinder or act as a barrier in achieving the sustainability through the employment of green orientation. The study investigates the probable challenges exclusively faced by the small and medium enterprises and businesses like financial restraints, lack of expertise and lack of the desire to adapt to changes in the concerned corporate culture. The study also gave the recommendation for SMEs who are interested in implementation of green orientation as a strategy in achieving and ensuring the long-term sustainability of their businesses.

The purpose of this chapter is to show how firms can theoretically be both profitable and socially responsible by examining the main motivations (economic and ethical) for adopting Equator Principles. A study, by theme and by principle, of the main contributions of version IV of the Equator Principles compared to version III, makes it possible. This chapter presents a literature review of the main studies examining the degree of integration of sustainability issues in the governance systems of banks. Through this theoretical as well as empirical literature review, this study attempts to assess the relevance of Equator Principles as a tool for implementing Corporate Social Responsibility in the banking sector and to clarify the stakes of an evolution towards a socially and environmentally responsible project financing policy. There are many questions surrounding the actual impacts of Equator Principles and whether they can produce the desired results. The answers to these questions allow for truly informed decisions to be made. However, providing an answer is a rather complex task and such an evaluation would be well beyond the scope of this research.

Present study investigates the impact of Green Finance and CO2 emissions on GDP per capita of four Asian OECD economies controlling for Expenditure on Education, and Foreign Direct Investment using panel data for the time-period 2015 to 2023, applying pooled OLS, Fixed Effects, and Random Effects Models, and ultimately selecting the Fixed Effects Model based on robust statistical tests (Hausman and Breusch-Pagan LM), revealing that Green Finance significantly enhances GDP per capita, Expenditure on Education unexpectedly hinders it in the short term, and both CO2 emissions and Foreign Direct Investment lack statistically significant effects within countries, thereby underscoring the importance of internal structural factors and advocating for tailored, sustainability-driven, and context-sensitive economic growth strategies.

Climate change leads to extreme weather conditions, which produce economic disruption, financial instability, and sector risk. Financial institutions stand to face greater losses should they neglect the risks. Network for Greening the Financial System (NGFS), established in 2017, advocates for sustainable finance. Central banks greenlight green investment and environmental management of risk. Green finance drives capital into green energy and climate-friendly projects and connects growth and climate objectives. India's net-zero by 2070 will need 2.5% of GDP invested every year by 2030. The Reserve Bank of India (RBI) facilitates green finance with policies, refinancing, and green bonds. Green finance needs to be strengthened for a low-carbon, resilient economy, with central banks taking the lead.

The increasing urgency of addressing climate change has spurred the rise of green consumer finance products, designed to promote sustainable consumption and investment. This chapter explores green loans, credit cards, insurance, and investment options that prioritize environmental sustainability, analyzing their drivers consumer demand, government policies, and financial institutions' roles. The benefits, including environmental impact, financial savings, and social responsibility, while acknowledging challenges such as low awareness, accessibility barriers, and cost concerns. Through case studies and best practices, the chapter showcases successful initiatives and outlines the future of green finance, emphasizing innovation and cross-sector collaboration. Aimed at policymakers, investors, and financial institutions, it provides insights into aligning financial strategies with sustainable development goals to foster a greener economy. By addressing barriers and leveraging opportunities, green consumer finance can play a pivotal role in advancing global sustainability efforts.

The chapter comprehensively discusses the impact of European green finance policies on sustainable development. As an important tool for addressing climate change and promoting the green transformation of the economy, green finance has become a core component of the European policy system. First, the chapter points out that the impact of climate change and environmental pollution on the economic system is becoming increasingly prominent, including physical risks and transition risks. Secondly, the chapter elaborates on the green finance practices of major European countries through case analysis, covering the innovation and application of tools such as green bonds, green credit, and carbon trading markets. These policies have effectively promoted the development of renewable energy and significantly improved the competitiveness of the green economy. At the same time, green finance policies promote the green transformation of the economy through mechanisms such as internalizing environmental costs and promoting technological innovation.

Preface

INTRODUCTION

The urgent global agenda to achieve sustainable development has placed unprecedented emphasis on the role of financial systems in promoting environmental stewardship and inclusive economic growth. Traditional financial mechanisms, while instrumental in fostering industrial expansion and modernization, have also inadvertently contributed to ecological degradation and resource depletion. As global economies transition toward greener paradigms, the notion of *green finance*—the integration of environmental, social, and governance (ESG) considerations into financial decision-making—has emerged as a critical catalyst for sustainable development. This volume, *Utilizing Green Finance for Sustainable Development*, offers an in-depth exploration of the conceptual, empirical, and policy dimensions of green finance and its transformative role in the global sustainability movement.

Green finance serves as a vital bridge between economic ambition and environmental responsibility. By channeling capital flows toward low-carbon technologies, renewable energy projects, and environmentally responsible industries, it creates a foundation for long-term economic stability that is both resilient and equitable. However, the practical implementation of green finance is complex and context-specific, shaped by regional regulatory frameworks, market dynamics, and socio-political priorities. This book brings together leading scholars and practitioners to present diverse perspectives on how green finance is being deployed across different economies to balance growth with ecological preservation.

At the heart of this book lies the conviction that finance must evolve beyond profit maximization to become an engine of sustainability. The contributions within this volume collectively illuminate the intersections of innovation, policy, and ethical responsibility, demonstrating how financial instruments and institutions can drive meaningful progress toward the Sustainable Development Goals (SDGs). Through a multidisciplinary lens, the chapters examine not only the mechanisms of green finance but also the barriers, challenges, and opportunities it presents in shaping a sustainable global future.

CHAPTER OVERVIEW

Chapter 1, *"Unveiling Synergies Between Fintech and Green Finance: A Bibliometric Analysis"* by Revenio Jalagat, Karima Sayari, and Rafat Al-Batayneh, investigates the convergence of financial technology and green finance using bibliometric methods. The chapter maps global research trends, identifies influential authors and institutions, and highlights the growing prominence of this intersection as a driver of sustainability and innovation.

Chapter 2, *"Prospects of Green Finance for a Sustainable Future: A Critical Study"* by Jipson Joseph, contextualizes green finance within the framework of the United Nations Sustainable Development Goals. It emphasizes the financial disparities between developed and developing economies and explores how green finance can bridge the gap to achieve a more inclusive global future.

Chapter 3, *"Microfinance Performance Indicators Under Sustainability Perspective"* by Renan Payer, Elaine Araújo, Hélder Costa, and Luciano de Souza, compares the approaches of academic literature and rating agencies in evaluating microfinance institutions. The study applies the Triple Bottom Line framework to reveal how financial, social, and environmental dimensions intersect within the microfinance sector.

Chapter 4, *"Integrating Sustainability into Financial Markets: Risk, Return, and Responsibility"* by Ananya Pandey, examines how ESG integration reshapes investment paradigms. It explores the recalibration of fiduciary responsibility to include long-term ecological and social considerations, emphasizing the ethical evolution of financial decision-making.

Chapter 5, *"Utilizing Green Finance for Sustainable Development: Pathways, Challenges, and Opportunities"* by Rishikaysh Kaakandikar, Shital Newase, and Manasi Gujrathi, analyzes the mechanisms, limitations, and prospects of green finance in fostering sustainable growth. The authors present actionable insights into the development of regulatory and market frameworks that can enhance the global adoption of green financial practices.

Chapter 6, *"Green Orientation Strategies: An Imperative for Enhancing SMEs Sustainability in Digital Age"* by Shweta Jaiswal, Nishtha Agrawal, and Shafqat Ali, focuses on the unique challenges faced by small and medium enterprises in integrating sustainability into their business models. The chapter provides strategic guidance on implementing green orientation tools and overcoming financial and cultural barriers.

Chapter 7, *"The Contribution of the Equator Principles to Sustainable Finance"* by Syrine Ben Romdhane, investigates the Equator Principles as a global standard for responsible project financing. The chapter critically evaluates the evolution of these principles and their influence on corporate social responsibility within the banking sector.

Chapter 8, *"Leveraging Green Finance for Sustainable Development: An Empirical Analysis of Economic Growth and Environmental Sustainability of Asian OECD Economies"* by Pragti Dixit, Mukul Bhatnagar, Rajinder Kaur, Nikhil Varghese, and Vibhuti Jain, provides a rigorous empirical assessment of green finance's role in driving economic growth in Asia. Using advanced econometric modeling, it underscores the structural importance of sustainability-driven financial policies.

Chapter 9, *"Fostering Sustainable Finance Through Green Initiatives by the Reserve Bank of India"* by Neetu Ahmed and Gurleen Kaur, explores the role of central banking in advancing sustainable finance. The chapter details how the Reserve Bank of India promotes environmental risk management, green bond markets, and low-carbon investment strategies aligned with national climate commitments.

Chapter 10, *"The Role of Green Consumer Finance Products in Advancing Sustainable Development"* by Jyoti Rani, Shashiranjan Yadav, and Bhaskar Mitra, turns attention to consumer-facing financial products such as green loans and investment portfolios. It examines how individual financial behaviors contribute to systemic sustainability outcomes through innovation and awareness.

Chapter 11, *"European Green Financial Strategies and their Role in Sustainable Growth"* by Weirong He and Sameer Kumar, concludes the volume with a comparative exploration of Europe's pioneering role in green financial systems. Through policy analysis and case studies, it highlights how European nations are leveraging green finance to lead the global transition toward sustainable growth.

CONCLUSION

Collectively, the chapters in this volume present a comprehensive panorama of how green finance serves as a linchpin for sustainable transformation across sectors and geographies. The insights reveal that while the frameworks and instruments may differ across economies, the underlying goal remains consistent: to align financial systems with environmental imperatives and social progress. By advancing awareness and action in this field, the contributors illuminate pathways for policymakers, academics, and practitioners to mobilize capital for a more sustainable future.

As editors, we recognize that the success of green finance depends not only on the innovation of financial instruments but also on the collective will to redefine the purpose of finance itself. Green finance challenges traditional notions of value, urging stakeholders to view profitability through the lens of ecological balance and long-term resilience. The chapters herein demonstrate that the transition toward sustainability is not only possible but essential for the continued prosperity of global economies.

We extend our deepest gratitude to the contributing authors, reviewers, and institutions whose intellectual rigor and commitment to sustainability have made this work possible. It is our hope that *Utilizing Green Finance for Sustainable Development* will serve as both a scholarly reference and a practical guide for future research, policy development, and global collaboration in building an equitable, resilient, and environmentally responsible financial future.

Chapter 1

Unveiling Synergies Between Fintech and Green Finance: A Bibliometric Analysis

Revenio Cabanilla Jalagat
https://orcid.org/0009-0007-5535-6919
Al Zahra College for Women, Oman

Karima Sayari
https://orcid.org/0000-0001-7564-022X
Al Zahra College for Women, Oman

Rafat Al Batayneh
Al Zahra College for Women, Oman

ABSTRACT

This study explores the synergy between Fintech and Green Finance. It employed quantitative research methodology through bibliometric analysis, highlighting the performance analysis of data and providing a scientific map of previous studies related to the topic. Key findings based on performance analysis showed that 2024 marked the highest publication of Fintech and Green Finance, most sources from journals. The top university publishing in this area is the University of Hongkong specializing in Finance and Economics, and China produced the most manuscripts. Bibliometric analysis revealed that the top three keywords are green finance, China, and economic development. While co-authorship assessment showed the highest link strength by Fahad Taghzadeh-hesary and the most bibliographically coupled documents are those manuscripts that are published in Environmental Science and

DOI: 10.4018/979-8-3373-1240-8.ch001

Pollution Research, and Sustainability Journals. More studies on Fintech and green finance are highly recommended to fill the gap in the body of knowledge and foster environmental and economic sustainability.

INTRODUCTION

Quite a number of financial institutions and firms have been encouraged to develop green financial mechanisms and devices to fund eco-friendly projects and investment in green bonds. The UN in 2010 through its UN Climate Change Conference (COP 16) for example, conducted the 16th Annual Summit held in Mexico to urge the leaders from developed nations to pledge together in the mobilization of USD 100 billion yearly starting 2020 to help developing countries resolve climate challenges by availing climate bonds (Kwong et al., 2023). Driven by the outcome of this event, firms from different nations have embraced the development of green bonds that provide impact on environmental, social, and governance (ESG) investment and performance. According to Yale Program on Climate Change Communication (YP-CCC, 2022), the global climate change has alarmed 33% of Americans contributing into 15% growth rate as compared to the figures in 2017. The United Nations (UN) has formulated 17 sustainable development goals wherein included in the goals is to foster environmental protection, sustainability, and climate change resolutions.

The increasing awareness in environmental conservation and preservation by corporations have led to the development of initiatives on how firms and corporations can financially be supported in promoting eco-friendly activities through green financing in response to the 2021 UN Climate Summit (COP26), requiring nations worldwide to implement sustainable development initiatives and help corporations or firms launch green sustainable projects that will combat climate change at the global scale (Kwong et al., 2023). Many organizations have responded with the UN requirements by strategizing means to counter the adverse effects of climate change in line with the UN's sustainable development goals and have been pioneered by central banks of some nations with their introduction of the Central Banks and Financial Supervisors Network for Greening the Financial System (NGFS) and the Sustainable Banking and Finance Network (SBFN) (Durrani et al., 2020).

Moreover, recent changes globally are centered on sustainable development motivated by the implementation of green finance, emphasizing sustainable environment by investing on climate resilience programs, eco-friendly projects, and carbon reduction (Taghizadeh-Hesary & Yoshino, 2019). Along with green finance is the increasing global attention on financial technology (Fintech) as a reckoning force in transforming the financial industry by modifying the offering of financial services related digital banking, blockchain technology, and artificial intelligence

(Arner et al., 2016).The integration of Fintech and green finance have become a rapidly growing topic of interest for the industry and in the academe which labeled as Green Fintech. Lin and Hong (2022) stressed that the intersection of Fintech and green finance provides a novel resolution to environmental problems by capitalizing Fintech devices to promote efficiency, transparency, and sustainable financial systems. For instance, the application of blockchain technology is undertaken to track green bond usage, while Artificial Intelligence (AI) is being utilized to evaluate Environmental, Social, and Governance (ESG) risks correctly (Rabbani et al., 2020).

Moreover, many countries have undergone remarkable advancements in integrating Fintech invention and technology into green finance to foster sustainable communities. In Europe for instance, the Green Digital Finance Alliance and the Swiss Green Fintech Network disclosed the Green Fintech taxonomy launching on November 30, 2021 at the global level. The seven platforms include green digital payment and account solutions, green digital investment solutions, digital ESG data and analytics solutions, green digital crowdfunding and syndication platforms, green digital risk analysis and insure-tech, greenal digital deposit and lending solutions, and green digital asset solutions. On December 2020, a Greenprint project was established by the Monetary Authority of Singapore in order to leverage Fintech in enhancing green finance system, fund accumulation, supervise sustainability commitments, and assess its impact. The Greenprint initiative has proven to dispense ESG data, accumulate data, store ESG information in blockchain-driven register, and create an open marketplace to structure Fintech firms with green investors and issuers. The increasing attention towards Fintech and green finance in various fields have also led to the development of popular themes in academic discourse however, there is still scarcity in literature that provides comparison and analysis specifying the intersection between Fintech and green finance that prompted the researchers to conduct an extensive review of the topics that clarify the two different constructs. Academicians have explored the connection between Fintech and green finance by integrating actual experiences and practices into research yet previous literature related to these two domains are fragmented, hence requires holistic understanding on how Fintech and green finance be applied consistently in an integrated manner.

RESEARCH GAP

Even with the increasing importance of Fintech and green finance in the different fields, there is still limited systematic assessment and evaluation of its intellectual viewpoints. According to Kwong et al. (2023), too limited exploration of academic investigation towards Fintech and green finance or green Fintech and only five published papers are available in the Web of Science database which warrants a further research inquiry. Academically, investigations on Fintech and green finance have received increasing academic attention as individual constructs but integration of these two remain scarce and rarely examined. For instance, in the study of Hu et al. (2025), they stressed that many studies have been conducted addressing Fintech and green finance as parallel but fragmented areas resulting into difficulty of conceptualizing how technological advancements can reinforce sustainable financial ecosystems. This disintegration between Fintech and green finance according to Challoumis (2024) poses a problem considering the increasing regulations in the use of digital tools to enhance green investment and environmental impact tracking. Furthermore, limited investigations were conducted that explore the nexus of Fintech and green finance but rather narrowly focusing on technological feasibility, undermining the importance of dealing with governance, scalability, and others such as blockchain's carbon footprint and other digital infrastructures (Bakkensen & Ma, 2020; John-Mathews, 2021a).

In addition, Malamas et al. (2023) ironed out that limited studies were performed in emerging economies that restrain the penetrability of current insights and the development of inclusive and wide utilization of relevant strategies reflecting the synergy of Fintech and green finance. The lack of vivid, rigorous, and interdisciplinary investigation platforms that evaluate both the trade-offs and synergies between Fintech and green finance, lawmakers and organizations faced the risk of advancing counterproductive initiatives (El Hasanah, 2025). Hence, current studies and literature inadequately provide direction on how to apply Fintech-driven green finance instruments at scale, across various regulatory and socioeconomic environments.

To fill this gap, this paper utilizes bibliometric analysis to create scientific mapping of the literature as a quantitative approach to bring out trends, evolving themes, influential authors, and core publications (Donthu et al., 2021). The use of bibliometric approach is appropriate for evaluating quickly emerging interdisciplinary fields including the Fintech and green finance wherein theoretical limits are flexible and research outcome is distributed over various journals and disciplines. Because of the lack of attempts in investigating Fintech and green finance in the past, this paper tries to address the following questions: (1) What are the trends on Fintech and green finance related to the following areas such as researches performed overtime, publication sources, top universities conducting studies related to the topic, top fields or disciplines, most active countries, and top journals performing studies on Fintech and green finance; (2) How does keyword co-occurrence indicate semantic similarity or thematic clustering in different text genres? (3) Can co-authorship networks be used to predict research impact or future collaborations? And, (4) How has the structure of research in a specific field evolved over time based on bibliographic coupling networks?

The chapter is structured according to the sequence provided. Introduction which highlights the basic concepts of Fintech and green finance, the extent of application of the two in other countries, literature and previous studies that affirm or argue the studies already examined. It is followed by the research methodology that portrays the methodology and tools used in conducting the study and graphical presentations using VOSviewer. Thirdly, the findings and discussions section wherein the results are interpreted and relate it with recent available studies in the field. It is concluded by conclusion, recommendation, and avenues for future research directions.

METHODOLOGY

The quantitative research methodology was employed in this investigation with bibliometric analysis. With the use of VOSviewer, researchers were able to portray the scientific mapping of gathered information, substantiate the knowledge-generation and connect it with the varied disciplines and specializations, countries, institutions, scholars, etc. (Zupic & Carter, 2015). Apart from the different quantitative analytical tools, the VIOSveiwer is one of the most used tools by various researchers as it makes them easier to map out literature and previous researches and other collected data to find out research gaps and future studies (Paul & Criado, 2020). Bibliometric analysis enhances advanced meta-analyses to showcase visualization which is appropriate and adequate complement to systematic literature reviews. As applied in the study, bibliometric approach was mainly used to analyze previous studies from journals, book chapters, books, and other related sources. To employ the bibliometric analysis, the VIOSviewer software analyze the topic "Unveiling Synergies Between Fintech and Green Finance: A Bibliometric Analysis" wherein it was undertaken for important justifications. Firstly, it provides readers a guide in evaluation and analysis through scientific mapping and visualization, and secondly, it establishes a knowledge map that helps users in acquiring data from various sources.

In analyzing the collected data, performance analysis was performed from different sources such as journals, books, chapters, etc. It encompasses assessing the trends on Fintech and green finance related to the following areas such as researches performed overtime, publication sources, top universities conducting studies related to the topic, top fields or disciplines, most active countries, and top journals performing studies on Fintech and green finance. Then, biblimetric analysis was performed to determine visual maps on co-occurrences and keywords; co-authorship, and bibliographic coupling. Leydesdorff and Vaughan (2006) stressed that the employment of keywords and co-occurrences are important in identifying key trends of the studies and documents related to the discipline under investigation and it offers key features of co-occurrences in data science including co-citation, co-word, and co-link. Co-authorship according to Ullah et al. (2022) evaluates collaborative contribution by scholars networks among nations, institutions, teams, as conjoint publications among organizations and in various nations through representative participation in research endeavors or activities. While bibliographic coupling assesses the affinity of two documents by using common or related citations (Taşkın & Aydinoglu, 2015).

Furthermore, the data collected from this study are sourced from Lens database centered on the synergy between Fintech and green finance. The researchers prefer to use the Lens database because it is accessible and open for data sourcing compared to databases like Web of Science and Scopus where it require subscription. It is also transparent, enabling reproducibility and encompasses broad information content, and is integrated with other sources including Crossref, PubMed, etc. Lastly, Lens has interdisciplinary coverage that allows wide scope of fields promoting cross-domain for bibliometric investigations. The search process started with determination of the title, abstract, and keywords such as "Green Finance" OR "Fintech" OR "Financial Technology" OR "Green Finance and Fintech". Only manuscripts written in English are considered for analysis purposes. After screening, 33,240 papers were determined and considered for analysis as they are within the scope and complied with the predetermined criteria.

FINDINGS AND DISCUSSIONS

Collected data are analyzed and interpreted in this section. Section 1 presents the performance analysis of the trends reflecting Fintech and green finance according to studies conducted from 1970-2025, sources of publications, top Universities performing research related to the topic, top field or discipline of study, most active countries performing the research on Fintech and green finance, and top journals. Section 2 depicts the visualization and scientific mapping reflecting co-occurrences and keywords, co-authorship, and bibliographic coupling.

Figure 1. Study performed from 1970 to 2025

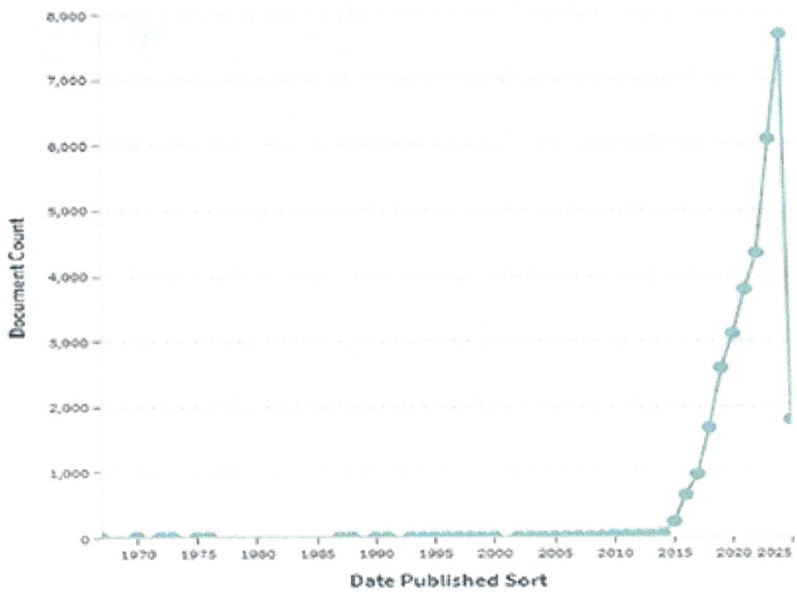

Figure 1 shows that 2024 has the highest published documents (7,681), followed by 2023 (6,083) documents. The year 2022 has accounted for 4,334 documents; 2021, 3,783 documents; and 2020 with 3101 documents. Moreover, a remarkable ascending trend in academic investigations of Fintech and green finance between 2020 to 2024 considering a growing scholarly attention in the interchange of Fintech and sustainability. It also paves the way to innovation acceleration, increasing engagement to environmental, social, and governance (ESG) frameworks, increasing awareness on Fintech and green finance, climate change integration, policy adaptation and implications, and others. With the advancement of technologies, the intensity of applying financial technologies and green finance significantly increased.

Figure 2. Sources of publications

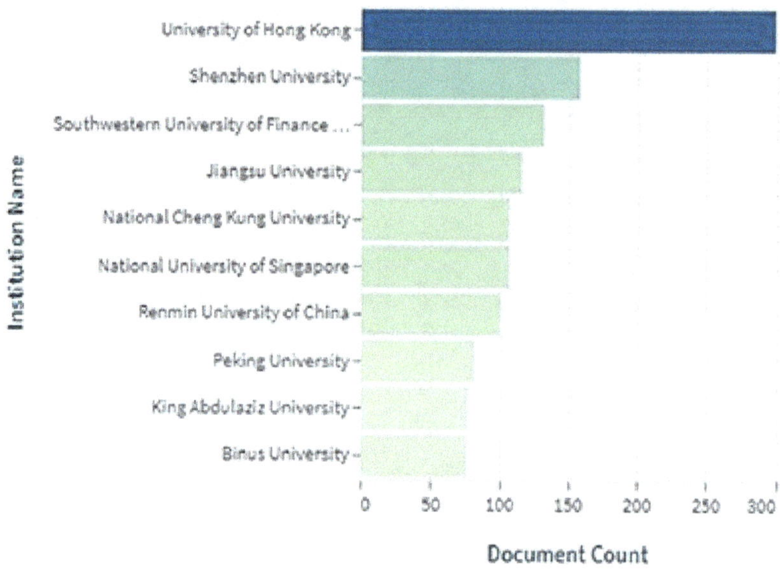

The published documents utilized in this study encompasses different sources wherein mostly derived from journal article (21,032 documents), book chapters (4,784 documents), unknown sources (3,166), conference proceedings (1,180), preprint (772), and others. The study is mainly supported by manuscripts from journal publications which can make the findings reliable and credible in terms of the research outcome. Propositions and arguments that are sourced from journals add value to the influence of the findings in the body of knowledge.

Figure 3. Top Universities Performing Research

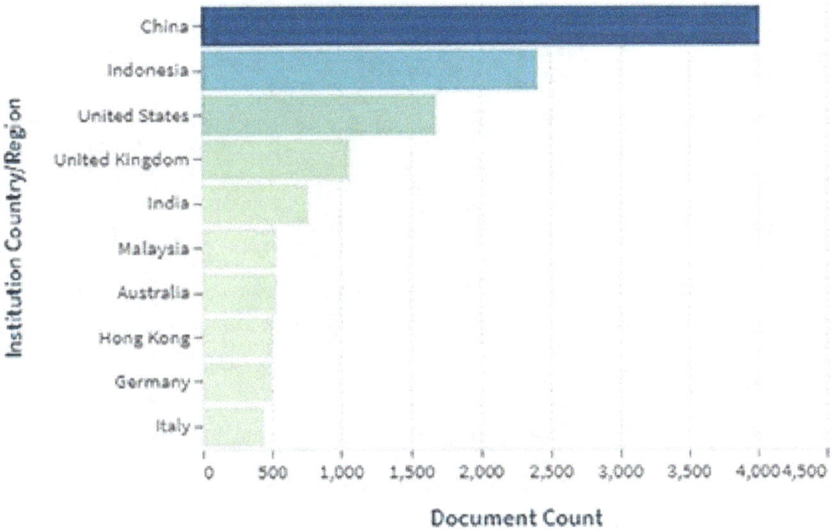

The top 10 universities that conducted studies on green finance and Fintech include University of Hongkong (299 papers), Shenzhen University (158 papers), Southwestern University of Finance and Economics (132 papers), Jiangsu University (116 papers), National Cheng Kung University (107 papers), National University of Singapore (107 papers), Renmin University of China (101 papers), Peking University (82 papers), King Abdulaziz University (77 papers), and Binus University (76 papers). Remarkably, China has the highest number of Universities in the top 10 with 6 universities listed belonging to China and all these universities in the top 10 are Asian universities. The China's commitment to the advancement of technological financial innovations enabled the country to become a major contributor to investigations in Fintech and green finance highlighting sustainability in the financial sector. This is also inspired by the blending of a firm and strong government policy, growing commitment to carbon neutrality, and speedy improvement in digital infrastructure (Wang & Liu, 2024; Zhang et al., 2022). Chen et al (2023) added that, China's supremacy in this field justifies not only a domestic concentration on green technological progression but also an opportunity to establish global frameworks and standards for sustainable finance. Moreover, Fintech platforms with green finance developed by China driven by strategic investments can be utilized as financial model for other developing countries (IMF, 2023).

Figure 4. Top Field of Study

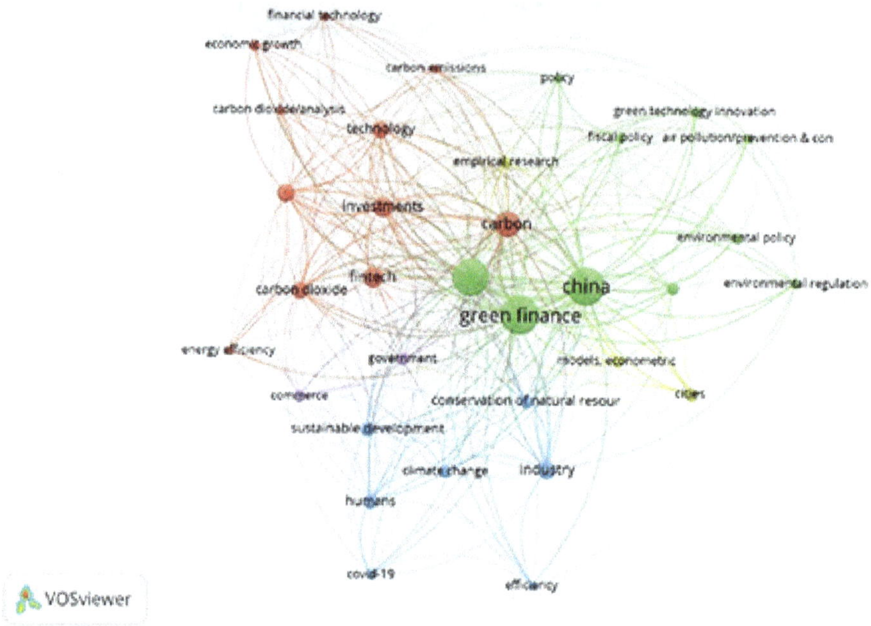

It can be seen in Figure 4 that the Finance field occupied the highest study areas with 11,325 documents and seconded by Economics field with 10,322 documents. Third in the list is Computer Science (9,220 documents), Political Science (7,570 documents), and Law with 6,022 documents. Finance and Economics are the two major fields in the application of fintech and green finance wherein the focus dealt more on sustainable environment and climate change resolutions. Emphasis on these two domains potentially change the financial and economic landscape of the countries and businesses taking into consideration the integration of environmental factors in the way businesses operate. For instance, Li et al. (2023b) explained that Fintech platforms utilize financial algorithms to evaluate credit risk and mechanize investment decisions which make finance as major player in designing programs for cost-effective capital allocation and risk management in Fintech and green finance. On the other hand, finance enables the promotion of green finance by utilizing financial tools such ESG funds and green bonds to generate capital for sustainable environmental programs (Kashif et al., 2025). In the aspect of implementing climate-driven projects, finance aids innovation such as the green crowdfunding that enables investors sponsor climate-related undertakings (Jokhio et al., 2025).

Economics on the other side promotes the proliferation of Fintech and green finance as it provides policies and foundations to understand how fintech and green finance be effectively managed. The growing significance of economics in Fintech and green finance contributes to the promotion of savings and investments by utilizing the user-centered system of Fintech platforms (Pavlidis, 2025).

Figure 5. Most Active Countries/Regions

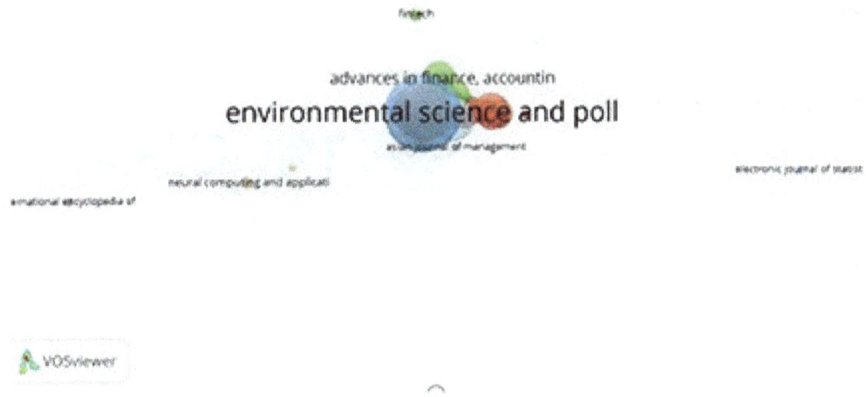

In descending order, Figure 5 depicts that China (4,025 papers) is the most active in research related to green finance and Fintech. Indonesia is in second spot with 2,410 papers, United States (1,684 papers), UK (1,073 papers), India (774 papers), and Malaysia (539 papers). Moreover, in seventh place is Australia (538 papers), Hongkong (510 papers), Germany (500 papers), and Italy with 448 papers. These results may imply that developing countries are equally competing with developed countries in the exploration of Fintech and green finance concerning environmental upgrading and development. Moreover, Asian countries are evidently raising awareness in financial technologies enhancements that can be instrumental in economic development such as India, Malaysia, and Indonesia.

Further analysis of the findings showed that China, United Kingdom and United States including Indonesia have demonstrated an active contribution in Fintech and green finance reflecting the robustness of research undertakings. Debrah et al. (2022) stressed that China led in total publications and citation impact in green finance while the UK with relatively lower outputs but posted a high citation per article (Kou et al., 2021). The United States according to Boubaker et al. (2023) propelled in both industry-driven fintech and academic theory specifically in fields such as AI in Finance, blockchain employment, and ESG investing.

For policy implications, advancement of researches in Fintech and green finance such as China, US, UK, and others are instrumental in implementing green finance policies internationally in relation to achieving cross-border Fintech infrastructure and automated finance regulations. In parallel, emerging economies that excel in the field of Fintech and green finance such as India, Malaysia, and Indonesia may aid in the democratization of financial innovation wherein more collaborative effort of these countries will enhance global presence and recognition as well as enhance the opportunities for context-specific solutions to sustainability and financial inclusion (Li et al., 2024).

Figure 6. Top 10 Journals

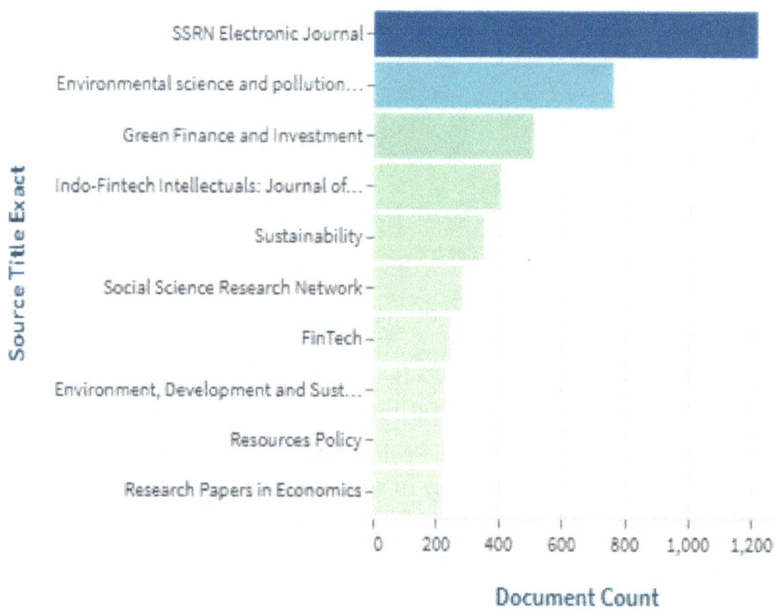

Figure 6 depicts the top journals that perform studies on green finance and Fintech. SSRN Electronic Journal tops the list with 1,217 documents and followed by Environmental Science and Pollution Research International, 763 documents. The third rank to 10th rank consist of Green Finance and Investment, 510; Indo-Fintech Intellectuals: Journal of Economics and Business, 406; Sustainability, 354; Social Science Research Network, 283; Fintech, 245; Environment Development and Sustainability, 228; Resources Policy, 228; and Research Paper in Economics, 220. These findings indicate that the research agenda which deals with Fintech and green finance is becoming a priority in terms of regulatory innovation; environmental, social influence; and related topics. These journals may also set the pace for citations in policy consultations and discussions in central banks and other government agencies for policy implications and for cross-disciplinary collaborations wherein it promotes integration between technology, finance, economics, and environmental science. For financial markets and institutions, the development of new products may rely on insights from journals as well as in dealing with financial risk management wherein models from journal published materials are helpful and relevant. For instance, financial performance indicators can be sourced from peer-reviewed publications and Fintech analytics (Manoharan et al., 2024). Furthermore, the findings help business start-ups determine evolving trends and successful commercial models, gauge Fintech solutions for sustainable development and financial inclusion in developing markets (Mhlanga, 2024).

BIBLIOMETRIC ANALYSIS

Data utilized in the study was further analyzed through bibliometric mapping starting with the co-occurrence analysis of 470 keywords with a minimum occurrence of 5. From 470, 33 keywords met the threshold and are interconnected, resulting into 5 clusters, 303 links, and total link strength (TLS) of 1,194. Specifically in Table 1 Figure 7, the extracted keywords from the most occurred keywords to the least include green finance, China, economic development, carbon, investments, Fintech, renewal energy, industry, carbon dioxide, technology, humans, sustainable development, cities, conservation of natural resources, environmental pollution, commerce, government, climate change, green technology innovation, and economic growth. The study of Kozar and Wodnicka (2024) confirmed these findings by identifying the keywords extracted from Scopus and Web of Science databases the same words such as green finance, climate change (Wan et al., 2023), sustainable development, economic growth, carbon dioxide (Udeagha & Muchapondwa, 2023), renewal energy (Delina et al., 2023), and Fintech. The increasing attention to the field of green finance and Fintech is indeed evident particularly in promoting environmentally friendly financing activities and programs. The top 5 keywords that accounts for high TLS comprise of green finance, China, economic development, carbon, and investments. China is instrumental in the development of green finance and Fintech which align with Figure 5 detailing that China is the most active country performing studies in the field.

Furthermore, the study of Nhung and Hang (2024) on green finance shows similar findings in co-occurrence and keywords analysis generated from Web of Science (WOS) database reflecting same keywords such as green finance, renewal energy, economic growth, investment, sustainable development and green innovation. This may mean that these keywords are the most topics that draw the attention of the academicians and scholars in the field.

Table 1. Co-occurrences and keywords

Seq. No.	Keyword	Occurrences	Total Link Strength (TLS)
1	Green Finance	79	304
2	China	74	308
3	Economic Development	73	341
4	Carbon	36	167
5	Investments	21	106
6	Fintech	21	59
7	Renewal Energy	18	98
8	Industry	18	81
9	Carbon Dioxide	16	83
10	Tehnology	15	80
11	Humans	12	53
12	Sustainable Development	12	47
13	Cities	10	45
14	Conservation of Natural Resources	10	43
15	Envronmental Pollution	9	40
16	Commerce	8	47
17	Government	8	40
18	Climate Change	8	30
19	Green Technology Innovation	7	36
20	Economic Growth	7	32

Figure 7. Network visualization of Co-occurrences and Keywords.

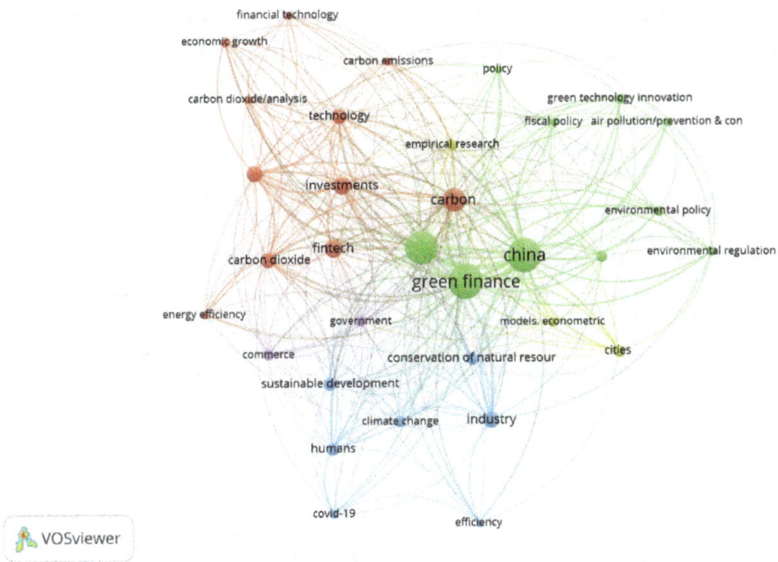

Visual mapping to determine Co-authorship was also performed in examining local and global collaboration of authors. Using the VOSviewer, data processing proceeds with a minimum number of documents per author of 1 and minimum number of citations of an author is 1 to gain wider coverage of the documents. The analysis was made to determine the trends in co-authorship as shown in Table 2 and Figure 8. The VOSviewer was run with minimum number of 25 authors per document, minimum number of documents of an author is 1, and minimum number of citations of an author is 5 resulting into 1,246 documents and 67 documents meeting the threshold. There are 26 items, 5 clusters, and 75 total link strenght (TLS). The top 10 co-authors ranked by TLS comprised of Fahad Taghzadeh-hesary (TLS=11); Huaping Sun (TLS=10); Linnam Yan (TLS=7); Tadiwanashe Muganyi (TLS=7); Xinmeng Tang (TLS=6); Ruoyu Zhong (TLS=6); Xiaoguang Zhou (TLS=6); Ruoyu Zhong (TLS=6); Shuangliang Yao Lars (TLS=4); and Homuf (TLS=3). The ranking according to citations was also considered when authors have the same TLS. These results can be explained that while many studies conducted focusing on investigating green finance and Fintech separately, still few studies explore the synergy between these two domains. The scarcity of co-authorship in this field is evident with the highest TLS of only 11 and can be a venue for more collaborative studies from different parts of the world. However, these findings also showcase the increasing attention of scholars and researchers in interdisciplinary topics and global cooperation through publishing in international peer-reviewed and high impact journals. Undeniably, China has gained the highest recognition in this research field of Fintech and green finance surpassing United States and other highly developed countries (See also Figure 5). Hence, the need for more investigation on Fintech and green finance integration can help improve the nations' sustainability outcomes.

Table 2. Co-Authorship according to the TLS.

Seq.No.	Author	Documents	Citations	Total Link Strength (TLS)
1	Fahad Taghzadeh-hesary	4	714	11
2	Naoyuki Yoshino	1	566	1
3	Xinmeng Tang	4	542	6
4	Xiaoguang Zhou	3	542	5
5	Huaping Sun	3	503	10
6	Rui Zhang	1	480	2
7	Lars Homuf	2	479	3
8	Linnam Yan	2	478	7
9	Tadiwanashe Muganyi	2	478	7
10	Charistian Haddad	1	468	1
11	Guangyou Zhou	1	405	2
12	Jieyu Zhu	1	405	2
13	Sumei Luo	1	405	2
14	Thomas Puschmann	1	392	0
15	Mohd Zaini Abd Karim	1	384	1
16	Muhammed Saeed Meo	1	384	1
17	Ruoyu Zhong	3	381	6
18	Ginglong Shao	1	371	2
19	Xuedi Ren	1	371	2
20	Shuangliang Yao	2	357	4

Figure 8. Visualization of Co-authorship.

Table 3 and Figure 9 shows the mapping of bibliographic coupling. In analyzing further through bibliographic coupling, a minimum number of citation of a document of 1 and a minimum number of citations of a source of 1 resulting to 426 items, interconnected items of 213, 17 clusters and TLS of 68,287. Results showed that the top cases of bibliographic coupling of authors are on documents published in Environmental Science and Pollution Research (TLS=22,960); followed by Sustainability (TLS=11,824); third, Frontiers in Environmental Science (TLS=9,651); Fourth in rank, Environment, Development and Sustainability (TS=5,839); then, Resources Policy (TS=3,481); Journal of Risk and Financial Management (TS=2,598); Discover Sustainability (TS=2,520); Advances in Finance, Accounting, and Economics (TS=2305); Financial Innovations (TS=2,212); and completing with the tenth place is Sustainable Development with the TLS of 2,088. The TLS shows a strong connection and co-citation of authors in many papers published in the journals ranked hereunder which is an evidence that studies concerning topics on Fintech and green finance considerably growing as a field of study.

Table 3. Bibliographic coupling of documents by TLS.

Seq.No.	Source	Documents	Citations	Total Link Strength (TLS)
1	Environmental Science and Pollution Research	84	2318	22960
2	Sustainability	46	1353	11824
3	Frontiers in Environmental Science	26	225	9651
4	Environment, Development and Sustainability	17	118	5839
5	Resources Policy	15	856	3781

continued on following page

Table 3. Continued

Seq.No.	Source	Documents	Citations	Total Link Strength (TLS)
6	Journal of Risk and Financial Management	7	71	2598
7	Discover Sustainability	10	8	2520
8	Advances in Finance, Accounting, and Economics	15	124	2305
9	Financial Innovations	19	937	2212
10	Sustainable Development	4	67	2088
11	Heliyon	9	119	2039
12	SSRN Electronic Journal	26	23	2029
13	Emerging Markets Finance and Trade	4	54	1893
14	Economic Research-Ekonomska Istrazivanja	5	121	1871
15	Electronic Commerce Research	12	175	1848
16	Energies	5	148	1819
17	Journal of Environmental Management	6	80	1788
18	Economic Change and Restructuring	9	88	1605
19	Plos One	6	22	1594
20	Future Business Journal	4	10	1377

Figure 9. Scientific Mapping of Bibliographic Coupling by TLS..

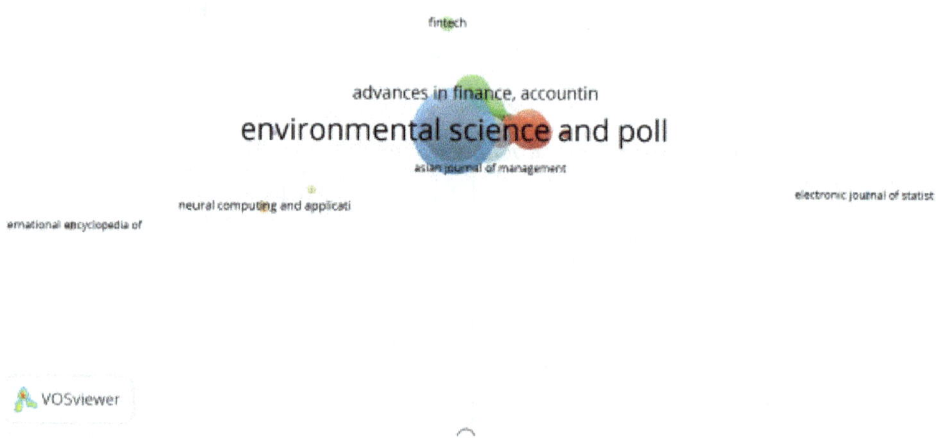

CONCLUSION AND RECOMMENDATIONS

Undertaking a bibliometric study focusing on Fintech and green finance showcases a changing and rapidly emerging picture wherein technological innovation and sustainability objectives progressively diverge. The interlink between these two constructs account both the academic and application of theories that adress climate change while upgrading financial platforms. In this paper, it can be observed that there is increasing trend of research attention on Fintech and green finance wherein China dominates the literature showing their active role in regulations and frameworks directed towards digital innovation and green finance.

The study aimed at investigating the synergy between the Fintech and green finance by performing bibliometric analysis. It evaluate the trends of studies on Fintech and green finance as a separate investigation and the publications that integrates the two constructs in terms of the studies conducted from 1970-2025, sources of publications, top Universities performing research related to the topic, top field or discipline of study, most active countries performing the research on Fintech and green finance, and top journals. Figure 1 shows that 2024 has the highest published documents (7,681), followed by 2023 (6,083) documents. Figure 2 depicts that the two top sources of publications are mostly derived from journal article (21,032 documents), book chapters (4,784 documents). The top universities undertaking research on the topic include the University of Hongkong (299 papers), Shenzhen University (158 papers), Southwestern University of Finance and Economics (132 papers), Jiangsu University (116 papers), National Cheng Kung University (107 papers). Figure 4 revealed that the Finance field occupied the highest study areas with 11,325 documents and seconded by Economics field with 10,322 documents. Figure 5 depicts that China (4,025 papers) is the most active in research in green finance and Fintech. Indonesia is in second spot with 2,410 papers, United States (1,684 papers), UK (1,073 papers), India (774 papers), Malaysia (539 papers). Figure 6 depicts the top journals that perform studies on green finance and Fintech. SSRN Electronic Journal top the list with 1,217 documents and followed by Environmental Science and Pollution Research International, 763 documents.

It can also be summarized that the most occurred keywords to the least include green finance, China, economic development, carbon, investments, Fintech, renewal energy, industry, carbon dioxide, technology, humans, sustainable development, cities, conservation of natural resources, environmental pollution, commerce, government, climate change, green technology innovation, and economic growth. For co-authorship, the top 10 co-authors ranked by TLS comprised of Fahad Taghzadeh-hesary (TLS=11); Huaping Sun (TLS=10); Linnam Yan (TLS=7); Tadiwanashe Muganyi (TLS=7); Xinmeng Tang (TLS=6); Ruoyu Zhong (TLS=6); Xiaoguang Zhou (TLS=6); Ruoyu Zhong (TLS=6); Shuangliang Yao Lars (TLS=4); and Homuf (TLS=3). Finally, assessing the bibliographic coupling based on the citations and TLS by a journal, the top three journals with bibliographic coupling of authors are on documents published in Environmental Science and Pollution Research (TLS=22,960); followed by Sustainability (TLS=11,824); third, Frontiers in Environmental Science (TLS=9,651).

The findings have drawn different implications for the body of knowledge. Firstly, the study reveals the need of literature that focused on harmonizing standards, digital governance, and green finance to ascertain that technological innovations and developments support sustainability goals. Secondly, encourage more financial innovations like the offering of the mechanisms and tools such as blockchain for green bonds, artificial intelligence (AI) in finance, and others to enhance accountability, transparency, and scale in sustainable finance. In relation to the sustainable development goals (SDG), the findings help enhance the integration of green finance and Fintech as important mechanisms in attaining SDG considering that the goals are emphasized on clean energy and climate action.

The main contribution of this paper is that, the outcome in the determination of the trends of investigation with integration of Fintech and green finance will open more avenues for wider investigations quantitatively and qualitatively for more robust studies in the field. Secondly, it addresses the scarcity of literature and more application of cases and scenarios that reflect the synergy between Fintech and green finance. It is therefore recommended that wider studies can be undertaken considering the keywords explored in this study, more collaborative efforts or co-authorship from different nations and backgrounds to increase cooperation among various authors, increase visibility of research outputs, and enhance bibliographic coupling of documents.

The bibliometric standpoint of Fintech and green finance contemplate a paradigm transformation in global financial content from profit-centered to sustainability- and innovation-driven finance. Though Fintech and finance have grown in parallel, their intersection turns into a auspicious opportunities for remodeling capital markets and enabling climate-resilient economic growth. Nevertheless, sound integration and more empirical validation are required to fully leverage Fintech as a means for sustainable finance.

REFERENCES

Arner, D. W., Barberis, J., & Buckley, R. P. (2016). The evolution of fintech: A new post-crisis paradigm? *Georgetown Journal of International Law*, *47*(4), 1271–1319.

Bakkensen, L. A., & Ma, L. (2020). Sorting over flood risk and implications for policy reform. *Journal of Environmental Economics and Management*, *104*, 102362. DOI: 10.1016/j.jeem.2020.102362

Boubaker, S., Karim, S., Naeem, M. A., & Rahman, M. R. (2023). On the prediction of systemic risk tolerance of cryptocurrencies. *Technological Forecasting and Social Change*, *198*, 122963. DOI: 10.1016/j.techfore.2023.122963

Challoumis, C. (2024, October 3-4). *Financial Literacy in an AI-Driven World: What you need to know* [Presentation]. *16th International Scientific Conference*, Philadelphia, USA.

Chen, M., Liang, Y., Zhu, J., & Zheng, S. (2023). A DEA-based ESG performance evaluation framework for sustainable supply chain finance. *Sustainability*, *15*(2), 723.

Debrah, C., Darko, A., & Chan, A. P. C. (2022). A bibliometric-qualitative literature review of green finance gap and future research directions. *Climate and Development*, *15*(5), 432–455. DOI: 10.1080/17565529.2022.2095331

Delina, L.L, Lam, Rainbow, Y.H.,Tang, W.S., & Wong, K.Y. (2023). Mapping the actor landscape of a future fintech-funded renewable energy ecosystem in Hong Kong. *Journal of Environmental Studies and Sciences*, *13*(3), 419–427.

Donthu, N., Kumar, S., Mukherjee, D., Pandey, N., & Lim, W. M. (2021). *H*ow to conduct a bibliometric analysis: An overview and guidelines. *Journal of Business Research*, *133*, 285–296.

Durrani, A., Rosmin, M., & Volz, U. (2020). The role of central banks in scaling up sustainable finance—What do monetary authorities in the Asia-Pacific region think? *Journal of Sustainable Finance & Investment*, *10*, 92–112.

El Hasanah, L. N. (2025). Exploring Green Research Opportunities Within the Fintech Landscape for Sustainable Growth. *Start-Up and Financial Technology*, *1*(1), 44–56. DOI: 10.70764/gdpu-sft.2025.1(1)-04

Hu, H., Jia, Z., & Yang, S. (2025). Exploring FinTech, green finance, and ESG performance across corporate life-cycles. *International Review of Financial Analysis*, *97*, 103871. DOI: 10.1016/j.irfa.2024.103871

IMF. (2023). *Fintech and the Sustainable Finance Agenda: Policy Considerations for China and Beyond.* International Monetary Fund. https://www.imf.org/en/Publications

John-Mathews, J. (2021a). Some critical and ethical perspectives on the empirical turn of AI interpretability. *Technological Forecasting and Social Change, 174*, 121209. DOI: 10.1016/j.techfore.2021.121209

Jokhio, S. M., Fuzail, M., Murtaza, M., Anwar, A., Lodhi, K., & Asif, T. (2025). *FinTech and Green Finance: Assessing the Impact of Financial Technology Adoption on Sustainability Performance in Emerging Economies*. https://www.researchgate.net/publication/392164574

Kashif, M., Pinglu, C., Ullah, A., & Qian, N. (2025). The Impact of Green Finance and Fintech Mechanisms on Financial Stability: Evidence from advanced emerging economies. *China Finance Review International*. Advance online publication. DOI: 10.1108/cfri-07-2024-0393

Kou, G., Akdeniz, Ö. O., Dinçer, H., & Yüksel, S. (2021). Fintech investments in European banks: A hybrid IT2 fuzzy decision-making approach. *Financial Innovation*, *7*(1), 1–23. DOI: 10.1186/s40854-020-00218-x PMID: 35024283

Kozar, L. K., & Wodnicka, M. (2024). FinTech and Green Finance: Bibliometric Analysis. *Procedia Computer Science*, *246*, 2080–2089. DOI: 10.1016/j.procs.2024.09.643

Kwong, R., Kwok, M. L. J., & Wong, H. S. M. (2023). Green FinTech Innovation as a Future Research Direction: A Bibliometric Analysis on Green Finance and FinTech. *Sustainability*, *15*, 14683. DOI: 10.3390/su152014683

Leydesdorff, L., & Vaughan, L. (2006). Co-occurrence matrices and their applications in information science: Extending ACA to the Web environment. *Journal of the American Society for Information Science and Technology*, *57*, 1616–1628. DOI: 10.1002/asi.20335

Li, B., Liu, Z., Jia, X., & Ma, F. (2024). Digital finance, financing constraints, and green technological innovation: A spatial analysis. *Global Finance Journal, 61*, 100988. DOI: 10.1016/j.gfj.2024.100988

Li, J., Gong, Y., Ho, K., & Zhang, C. (2023b). Trust and price efficiency. *Journal of International Financial Markets, Institutions and Money*, *89*, 101855. DOI: 10.1016/j.intfin.2023.101855

Lin, L., & Hong, Y. (2022). Developing a Green Bonds Market: Lessons from China. *European Business Organization Law Review*, *23*(1), 143–185. DOI: 10.1007/s40804-021-00231-1

Malamas, V., Dasaklis, T. K., Arakelian, V., & Chondrokoukis, G. (2023). A blockchain framework for digitizing securities issuance: The case of green bonds. *Journal of Sustainable Finance & Investment, 14*(3), 569–595. DOI: 10.1080/20430795.2023.2275212

Manoharan, G., Nithya, G., Razak, A., Sharma, S., & Ashtikkar, S. P. (2024). Challenges and Opportunities in Green Finance: Overcoming Barriers and Scaling up Sustainable Investments. In Misra, S., Jadeja, R., & Mittal, M. (Eds.), *Practical Approaches to Agile Project Management* (pp. 398–413). IGI Global Scientific Publishing., DOI: 10.4018/979-8-3693-3318-1.ch022

Mhlanga, D. (2024). FinTech and Inclusive Economic Development in Africa. *Africa Growth Agenda, 21*(4). https://hdl.handle.net/10520/ejc-afgrow_v21_n4_a3

Nhung, D. T. H., & Hang, T. T. T. (2024). Research on Green Finance: A Bibliometric Analysis. *RESEARCH REVIEW International Journal of Multidisciplinary, 9*(7), 01–07. https://doi.org/DOI: 10.31305/rrijm.2024.v09.n07.001

Paul, J., & Criado, A. R. (2020). The art of writing literature review: What do we know and what do we need to know? *International Business Review, 29*(4). Advance online publication. DOI: 10.1016/j.ibusrev.2020.101717

Pavlidis, G. (2025). Empowering sustainable finance with artificial intelligence: a framework for responsible implementation. In Lee, J., & Darbellay, A. (Eds.), *A Research Agenda for Financial Law and Regulation* (pp. 23–38). Edgar Online., DOI: 10.4337/9781803929996.00009

Rabbani, M. R., Khan, S., & Thalassinos, E. I. (2020). FinTech, blockchain and Islamic finance: An extensive literature review. *International Journal of Economics and Business Administration, 8*(2), 65–86.

Taghizadeh-Hesary, F., & Yoshino, N. (2019). The way to induce private participation in green finance and investment. *Finance Research Letters, 31*, 98–103.

Taşkın, Z., & Aydinoglu, A. U. (2015). Collaborative interdisciplinary astrobiology research: A bibliometric study of the NASA Astrobiology Institute. *Scientometrics, 103*(3), 1003–1022.

Udeagha, M. C., & Muchapondwa, E. (2023). Green finance, fintech, and environmental sustainability: Fresh policy insights from the BRICS nations. *International Journal of Sustainable Development and World Ecology, 30*(6), 633–649.

Ullah, M., Shahid, A., Din, I. U., Roman, M., Assam, M., Fayaz, M., Ghadi, Y., & Aljuaid, H. (2022). Analyzing Interdisciplinary Research Using Co-Authorship Networks. *Complexity, 2022*, 1–13. DOI: 10.1155/2022/2524491

Wan, S., Lee, Y. H., & Sarma, V. J. (2023). Is Fintech good for green finance? Empirical evidence from listed banks in China. *Economic Analysis and Policy, 80,* 1273–1291.

Wang, H., & Liu, F. (2024). Digital finance and enterprise innovation efficiency: Evidence from China. *Finance Research Letters, 59,* 104709. DOI: 10.1016/j.frl.2023.104709

YPCCC. (2022). Global Warming's Six Americas, September 2021. https://climatecommunication.yale.edu/publications/global-warmings-six-americas-september-2021/

Zhang, A., Wang, S., & Liu, B. (2022). How to control air pollution with economic means? Exploration of China's green finance policy. *Journal of Cleaner Production, 353,* 131664. DOI: 10.1016/j.jclepro.2022.131664

Zupic, I., & Cater, T. (2015). Bibliometric Methods in Management and Organization. *Organizational Research Methods, 18,* 429–472. DOI: 10.1177/1094428114562629

Chapter 2
Prospects of Green Finance for a Sustainable Future:
A Critical Study

Jipson Joseph
https://orcid.org/0009-0005-1795-5051
Christ University, India

ABSTRACT

Global initiatives for economic development started with the Industrial Revolution. However, it caused serious environmental issues. It necessitated to focus on eco-friendly developmental projects. Accordingly, the sustainable development paradigm has evolved to balance both environmental and developmental models. Although the UN affirmed sustainable development from 1987 onwards, its scope was elaborated with MDGs and SDGs. The declaration of SDGs in 2015 provided a framework for a global sustainable future. However, developing countries face financial hurdles in responding positively to the demands of SDGs that prioritize sustainable development and environmental protection. The OECD (2021) notes that developing countries experience 2.5 to 3.7 trillion dollars shortfall to meet the demands of SDGs. To address this complexity, developed countries, international institutions, and multinational and transnational corporations promoted green finance. From this perspective, this chapter critically evaluates the scope and functioning of green finance in light of a sustainable future.

DOI: 10.4018/979-8-3373-1240-8.ch002

1 INTRODUCTION

From the Industrial Revolution onwards, the globe witnessed enormous economic growth (Qian, 2024). This became crucial in the aftermath of the Second World War due to the insecurities and financial crises of the time. Most countries prioritized economic development at any cost, believing that it would reduce poverty and inequality and promote welfare. However, together with industrial growth, development, and economic benefits, environmental degradation also emerged. The increasing presence of polluting substances in the air, water, and soil caused severe health and existential hazards to human beings. This necessitated an emphasis on environmental protection (Khan, 2023). Various environmental movements proposed interesting ideas for eco-friendly developmental aspirations. With the Brundtland Report of 1987, the UN officially proposed sustainable development, affirming that developmental aspirations should prioritize environmental concerns (WCED, 1987). This paradigm called for social, economic, and environmental sustainability, confirming the importance of the triple bottom line. Thereafter, the ecological concerns became more vivid.

Compared to mere developmental projects, the globe requires sustainable development projects. The Paris Agreement and other international agreements, conferences, and treaties demand the positive involvement of national and international agents for environmental protection. Sustainable development methods and environment protection programs require proper planning and more financial and human resources investment. Lack of financial support has been one of the serious drawbacks of the growing acceptance of sustainable development (Hu & Gan, 2025). Green finance and sustainable development are intimately connected. Green financing focuses on increasing the financial flow from the public, private, and other sectors to sustainable development priorities (Zhang et al., 2019). It revolves around three poles: government, business people, and citizens. Green finance denotes financial investments in sustainable development and eco-friendly projects, plans, and policies. It tries to prioritize the environmental needs of the society. It facilitates the green projects of society. A sustainable future will be realizable only in the context of appropriate green finance programs. However, there are various limitations and challenges to the wide implementation of green finance.

From this perspective, this chapter examines green finance in the context of sustainable development. It analyses green finance's role in ensuring an eco-friendly society that affirms environmental security, economic growth, and a sustainable future. It also explores the influence of green finance in the global attempts towards realizing Sustainable Development Goals (SDGs) and evaluates its various challenges and drawbacks. Based on the critical study, the chapter puts forward specific policy guidelines for the global acceptance and implementation of this inspirational program of action, green finance.

2 CONCEPTUAL FRAMEWORK

This chapter revolves around four basic concepts: environmental degradation, sustainable development, sustainable future, and green finance. Ecological degradation, resulting from imprudent exploitation of natural resources and throwaway culture, caused the globe to design a developmental program that does not negate environmental concerns. The concept of sustainable development evolved in this context. The United Nations (UN) prioritizes the sustainable future of all people and the ecosystem by declaring sustainable development goals (SDGs) as specific objectives of the sustainable development paradigm. The realization of these goals, especially that of a sustainable environment, may not be possible without adequate funding. Green Finance is a viable option for addressing this complex issue.

2.1 Ecological Degradation

The whole globe was predominantly an agrarian society before the Industrial Revolution. The entire globe's religious, philosophical, and cultural capital affirmed the importance of environmental protection. Many cultures ascribed divine nature to the ecosystem and demanded reverence. However, with the Industrial Revolution, people prioritized profit over ecological concerns. Authors like Balsalobre-Lorente et al. (2019) criticize economic expansion as it causes uncontrollable environmental degradation. Industries discharge vast amounts of CO_2 and greenhouse gases (GHG), which cause unpredictable damage to the ecosystem (Qian, 2024). History testifies to the negative correlation between economic growth and environmental security. The massive polluting energy outflow from the industrial sector caused environmental changes, global warming, and health issues for all living organisms (Khan, 2023). The globe faces food scarcity, species extinction, resource depletion, increasing waste generation, and extreme weather events, endangering the security of all living beings (Sahhbaz & Sinha, 2019). Economic growth has adversely affected the environmental quality by increasing the emission of pollutants (Khan, 2023). Since the income from the industrial sector was higher than that of the agricultural sector, many people migrated to industrial areas. This led to increasing urbanization. The significant population shift from farming to the urban industrial sector caused many environmental problems (Qian, 2024). Both industrialization and urbanization are vital components of economic growth. However, both of them cause lasting insecurities in the ecosystem. Their preference for improving the living conditions of people through economic growth does not address their genuine need for a healthy environment. Until the last quarter of the 20th century, the world prioritized economic development regardless of environmental protection. This preference led to a massive increase in environmental degradation. Increasing ecological degradation is a constant threat to human development.

2.2 Sustainable Development

Economic growth and environmental preservation are prime concerns of the present global society. This movement started in the second half of the 20th century. The developed countries have reached the present stage of welfare through industrialization and economic growth. It instigated the developing countries to prioritize industrialization and ensure people's well-being. As a result, the entire globe faces the problem of environmental degradation. In such a scenario, the World Commission on Environment and Development (WCED, 1987) proposed sustainable development to advance the sustainability of the environment and economy for the present and future generations (Khan, 2023). The globe wanted to address the inconsistency between economic development and environmental degradation for the ecosystem's survival. It tried to propose a model of development that revolves around the thinking of "how industry can both produce products to meet needs and generate wealth in ways which do not degrade the environment" (Roy, 1996, 36). However, the Brundtland Commission report did not limit its conceptualization of development to the concerns of the present generation but insisted that it should be a "development that meets the needs of the present without compromising the ability of future generations to meet their own needs" (WCED, 1987, no.27). Sustainable development is thus a developmental paradigm that stands for intragenerational and intergenerational justice, prioritizing both development and environmental protection.

Sustainable development is not an antagonist of economic growth. On the other hand, it provides a suitable framework for economic growth revolving around human survival and sustainable human progress without degenerating the environment and denying the possibilities for the future generation's meaningful life (WCED, 1987). While the existing developmental models advocated economic growth without addressing other vital concerns, the sustainable development model affirmed that the developmental aspirations should be inclusive to ensure the welfare of people and the ecosystem in the present and future generations. Although sustainable development is discussed chiefly within environmental protection, its ultimate objective is to ensure a developmental paradigm for economic growth that respectfully considers the ecological needs of the present and coming generations. Sustainable development is concerned with the future of humanity and the ecosystem. It reminds policymakers and other actors that humans have no future without a healthy environment (Kingsbury et al., 2004).

Sustainable development was proposed to ensure inclusive growth and to confront people's profit-oriented interactions. As a policy model, it insisted that national and international policymakers promote a developmental design without undermining environmental concerns. It affirmed that when the sustainability drive is absent in a developmental model, it complicates people's economic, social, and environmental interests. It promotes genuine welfare by balancing economic development, social well-being, and environmental justice (Kingsbury et al., 2004). Sustainable development, thus, is the suitable policy framework for the sustainable future of humanity and the ecosystem.

2.3 Sustainable Future

The concept of a sustainable future evolved from the discussions on sustainable development that prioritized economic, social, and environmental sustainability. The ecological movements of the second half of the 20th century provided a required framework. The 1973 UN Conference on Environment in Stockholm took up sustainability demands to the international level, which became finalized through the Brundtland Report of 1987. The 1992 UN Conference on Environment and Development furthered international action for sustainability drive. However, the terminology sustainable future became a slogan of global and national policy frameworks only in the 21st century. The UN Millennium Declaration that framed the Millennium Development Goals (MDGs) did not explicitly use the term sustainable future. But it implicitly refers to the ideals and values of a sustainable future. The UN initiated a program of action in 2015 called Sustainable Development Goals (SDGs) to realize a sustainable future for the whole world. However, it did not explicitly use the term sustainable future, but "better future for all people" (UN General Assembly, 2015, no. 50).

A sustainable future argues that all developmental aspirations should be sustainable and maintain equilibrium between economic growth and conservation of natural resources. It promotes the protection of different ecosystems, advances social equity, and improves all people's quality and value of life (Roy et al., 2023). Sustainable future objectives demand national and international governments to cooperate in designing and implementing well-framed industrial models and policies affirming environmental protection, fostering innovation and competitiveness, ensuring people's welfare, creating more employment opportunities and economic diversification, underlining people's security, and achieving inclusive growth through SDGs that emphasize a progressive vision (Qian, 2024). With the 2030 Agenda for Sustainable Development, the aspirations for a sustainable future have become a global objective. The growing interconnectedness between nations affirms that the globe should strive for a sustainable future for all people and ecosystems. The experience of COVID-19 was a reminder for the world to promote cooperation and partnerships to achieve a sustainable future without any limits.

2.4 Green Finance

Green finance originated in the last decade of the 20th century with the contributions of the United Nations Environment Program (UNEP). It represents the global financial network's one of the first systematic and structured attempts to make financial performances for addressing environmental challenges (Berrou et al., 2019). Green finance evolved to address threats like climate change and environmental degradation (Bhatnagar & Sharma, 2022). One of the first attempts that promoted the requirement of financing global environmental programs started with the Club of Rome's report "Limits to Growth" (1972) (Le et al., 2024). The 1980 discussions on green economy also triggered the movement towards green finance. The idea of a green economy originated in the developed world, where people were more aware of the threatening impact of industrial growth on the environment. Their interest in green and sustainable economic development slowly led to the origin of green financing (Bhatnagar & Sharma, 2022). Establishing the Global Environment Facility (GEF) in 1991 was a decisive moment in the history of green finance. It is a multilateral trust fund that provides financing and grants to developing countries to address various environmental issues. It is the primary funding source for the United Nations Framework Convention on Climate Change (UNFCCC) and the United Nations Convention on Biological Diversity (UNCBD). It works with 183 countries and partners with the World Bank, UN agencies, and NGOs to make better results for environmental sustainability. Since its primary beneficiaries are developing countries, it functions as a catalyst for global environmental protection. The 1992 Rio Summit also advocated the importance of supporting the eco-friendly projects of developing countries (Le et al., 2024). The UNEP Finacial Initiative (UNEP FI), launched in 1992, was another significant step. Currently, it has over 275 banks as signatories, covering almost 45% of the global banking assets, supporting sustainable practices and green finance (Hu & Gan, 2025). The Kyoto Protocol's Clean Development Mechanism (CDM) provided financial incentives based on calculating carbon credits (Le et al., 2024). One of the first attempts at green financing was associated with issuing green bonds to fund environmentally friendly projects. The European Investment Bank issued the first green bond in 2007. Green bonds are designed to finance projects like renewable energy, sustainable use of natural resources, clean transport, sustainable waste management, and control and prevention of pollution with environmental impact (Berrou et al., 2019). But, Flaherty et al. (2017) argue that similar forms of green finance were present even before. The formation of the Green Climate Fund (GCF) in 2010 is the immediate reason for the widespread use of green finance in policymaking and academic circles. One hundred ninety-four countries established the GCF to offer financial support to developing countries in their attempts to reduce GHG emissions and mitigate climate change (Zhang et al., 2019).

Green finance is interchangeably used with many terms like climate finance, carbon finance, environmental finance, green investment, and sustainable finance (Hu & Gan, 2025). Although climate finance is actively used as a substitute for green finance, it has only a limited scope compared to the larger scope of green finance. Climate finance is specifically focused on addressing the issues related to climate change. Sustainable finance has a larger scope than green finance as it includes not only environmental issues (Dziwok & Jäger, 2024). However, on a broader ambit, all these terms refer to environmental degradation and its aftereffects. It intersects the financial sector, environmental protection, and economic growth. It includes many core elements like green credit, securitization, green bonds, equator principles, green industrial funds, green banks, green insurance, and many other things that provide financial support to greening projects (Bhatnagar & Sharma, 2022). Inspired by various authors, Hu and Gan (2025) state that green finance should include three core elements: financial system components that promote green investment, funding for public policies to complete eco-friendly projects and efforts and people's adaptation strategies, and financing environment protection-oriented private and public investments. Green finance is defined as "financing of investments that provide environmental benefits in the broader context of environmentally sustainable development." It includes a wide range of public and private financial institutions that prioritize the possibilities for effectively managing environmental risks. The benefits of green finance include reducing pollution, reducing carbon and GHG emissions, improving energy efficiency, promoting sustainable development, and mitigating and adapting to climate change (G20 Green Finance Study Group, 2016, p.3).

Hu and Gan (2025) argue that the globe needs to prioritize green finance since it is essential for tackling ecological degradation, ensuring the progress of SDGs, preserving sustainable resources, and promoting a sustainable future. Green finance can function as a strong foundation for long-term growth and sustainable development, affirming a sustainable future (Bhatnagar & Sharma, 2022). Green finance needs to be updated on time, along with the changes and developments in policy, technology, and market dynamics. Integrating the latest digital technologies like blockchain and artificial intelligence in green finance can enhance transparency and efficiency (Le et al., 2024).

3 LITERATURE REVIEW

Green finance is one of the new fields in academic research, particularly became popular with the UN-initiated sustainable development paradigm of 1987. However, a lot of literature is available that emphasizes the importance of green finance. Bhatnagar and Sharma (2022) explain the evolution of green finance in response to the growing global demand for environmental protection. It analyzes the Scopus-indexed literature from 1997 to 2021 to show the development of the areas. Zakari and Khan (2022) investigate the role of green finance in achieving sustainable development. They analyze the data of 11 countries and affirm that green finance helps to increase environmental sustainability. Fu et al. (2023) examine the relationship between green finance and sustainable development. They specifically focus on how green finance can be used to combat climate change and achieve climate neutrality. Dogan et al. (2023) claim that the energy transition from non-renewable to renewable is vital for realizing sustainable development goals. Conventional energy sources increase global warming and cause climate change, adversely affecting the global economy. Green finance methods can support the implementation of renewable energy sources, ultimately benefitting global economic growth. Yildirim (2023) critically examines greenwashing techniques in the context of sustainability. According to her, greenwashing has both positive and negative effects. It can be used to escape from the demands of sustainability drive or to move slowly towards sustainability. Roy et al. (2023) argue that waste management has an intimate relationship with sustainable development goals. The aspirations for a sustainable future can be realized only through properly managing waste. Dziwok and Jäger (2024) give a critical overview of green finance. They explain the meaning and emergence of green finance, underlying the implications of its different forms like neoliberal green finance, transformative green finance, and reformist green finance. Hu and Gan (2025) explore how green finance has grown over the decades. They show the latest trends in green finance using a bibliometric analysis of recent literature. Zhang et al. (2025) investigate the impact of green finance on rural green development and claim that green finance has a significant role in developing countries. Cojoianu et al. (2025) state that market-based and institutional factors have been the main drivers for the growth of green finance policies. The above-stated literature deals with many areas of green finance, like its evolution, relevance, and energy efficiency. However, only a few studies have undertaken that critically examine green finance in connection with SDGs for a sustainable future.

4 GREEN FINANCE AND SUSTAINABLE DEVELOPMENT: AN ANALYSIS

Finance is the energizer for development. Green finance is essential for institutions, industries, and other actors to prioritize sustainable development. Many sustainable developmental objectives become unrealized due to insufficient financial resources. The institutions that promote sustainable developmental aspirations, especially of developing and underdeveloped countries, must assist them with financial support. Although the international framework of sustainable development was introduced in 1987, it still has not been fully realized due to a steady increase in environmental footprints and a lack of funds for the endeavors of developing countries (Kihombo et al., 2021). The following points examine how green finance can contribute towards sustainable development.

4.1 Green Finance and Economic Growth

The globe cannot think of surviving except through economic growth as its benefits have strongly impacted the present well-being in most parts of the world. Many countries have reached a reputable position in economic growth, which helps them emphasize and implement sustainable development models underlying the importance of ecological balance. Hu and Gan (2025) state that green finance originated as an aftermath of economic development. When people's per capita income increases, they become more aware of environmental sustainability and demand green products and investments. Economic development provides the financial capacity and infrastructure to support green finance strategies. However, developing countries fail to ensure quality economic growth due to investment difficulties, lack of scientific and technological advancements, low productivity, low GDP per capita, and a solid institutional framework (Khan, 2023). Raza et al. (2021) argue that there is a positive correlation between economic growth and institutional quality. The national institutional framework should promote the concerns of its people over the profit-making interests of multinational and transnational corporations. These financial giants can contribute to increasing the country's GDP. But, they may not address the issue of environmental degradation. If the government and its institutions do not have a quality governance and value system, they may sacrifice their people's concerns for financial motives. Such things have happened in many developing countries. Those authorities claim that the government requires income for infrastructure development and economic growth, which can be achieved only through increased foreign investment. It necessitates deregulating specific measures and policies in favor of them (Jerbi, 2009). Many of these foreign investors prefer developing countries as the environmental commitments are so stringent in the developed world. Compromising environmental concerns for economic growth will not do any long-term benefits. They should protect the ecosystem by imposing severe carbon taxes and legal principles like the polluter pays principle. Preparing the circumstances for foreign investment to advance economic development does not mean repudiating its environmental concerns (Khan, 2023). Economic growth is mandatory for any country that becomes vibrant with increased foreign investment. But, if those investors are causing alarming insecurities in the ecosystem, the government should have other financial sources to address such a precarious situation. Green finance can assist governments in promoting eco-friendly developmental projects.

4.2 Green Finance, Carbon Emissions, Renewable Energy, and Economic Growth

Economic growth through industrialization and other methods is vital for human development. Energy has a crucial role in the economic development of any country. However, the type of energy is an important area of concern. Most industries use non-renewable energy and emit CO_2, which causes global warming and many insecurities. Zhang et al. (2019) note that "maintaining the 2^0C temperature threshold of the Paris Agreement requires $53 trillion in energy-related investments by 2035." Energy consumption and carbon emissions are closely related. Carbon emissions are reduced if renewable energy sources are used, whereas if non-renewable energy is used, carbon emissions are drastically increased (Dogan et al., 2020). Until recently, the world largely depended on non-renewable and fossil fuel energy sources, which harmed the ecological balance and reduced the quantity of natural resources. The globe can reduce carbon emissions only if it concentrates more on renewable energy sources like solar and wind. Renewable energy reduces carbon emissions and increases energy efficiency (Khan, 2023). Dong et al. (2020) affirm that renewable energy usage reduces emissions in middle- and high-income countries. It is a misconception that reducing the use of non-renewable sources will adversely affect economic growth. However, Countries like China, the US, Japan, Germany, and India have taken effective steps to increase the use of solar energy (Pourasl, 2023) and affirm that economic growth is possible through renewable energy sources. China's total renewable energy generation (from solar and wind sources) amounts to 3,749TWh, and the US ranks second with 1,493TWh, showing a difference of 2256 TWh (Derrick, 2024). Since China is one of the fastest-growing economies in the world, its focus on renewable energy sources is an encouragement for the whole world.

The interest in renewable energy "can balance energy requirement and economic growth" (Khan, 2023, p. 123399). Its increased use can promote the aspiration for sustainable development, enhance an eco-friendly life, endorse global interests in the green economy, encourage sustainable attempts for the conservation of natural resources, and control the side effects of carbon emission (Dogan et al., 2023). Developing countries must also focus on reducing carbon emissions and increasing renewable energy usage for economic growth. Khan (2023, pp. 123399-12400) states, "There is a need to adopt best practices that encourage renewable energy, green innovation, energy efficiency, carbon finance, adaptive innovation, and sustainable development." Adoption of these best practices is not relatively easy for the developing countries. If they have a sound governance system that supports technological innovation, it can increase their energy efficiency and reduce the percentage of emissions (Li et al., 2023). They must initiate various programs and policies like subsidies, tax credits, and other incentives for increasing the use and improvement of renewable energy (Khan, 2023). However, even a welfare-oriented government requires massive funding for installing and developing renewable energy plants, which they cannot easily generate since they also need to fund other activities from their limited financial resources. In such a situation, green finance would be a perfect solution to empower developing countries' attempts to widen renewable energy usage.

4.3 Green Finance and Technological Advancements

Scientific and technological advancements have a decisive role in the sustainable development of any country (Kihombo et al., 2021; Jafri et al., 2021). The availability and accessibility of the latest technologies indicate how fast an economy can grow (Khan, 2023). There are differences of opinion concerning the impact of technological advancement on the environment. Salman et al. (2019) claim it positively contributes to ecological degradation. They argue that the latest technologies emit more GHG and cause alarming insecurities. But, Danish et al. (2019), Dong et al. (2018), and Khan (2023) argue that they reduce the risk of environmental degradation. The globe is required to reduce CO_2 and promote a green economy, which is possible only through the support of the latest technologies (Churchill et al., 2019). The economic growth of the developed countries affirms the importance of technological advancement. It "enhances the energy efficiency, automates the processes, and reduces the fossil fuel consumption" (Khan, 2023, p. 123398). The latest technologies reduce time, energy, and human involvement in hazardous labor and increase production and profit. Churchill et al. (2019) argue that society can decrease emissions of polluting elements and stimulate the pace of sustainable development through effective technological advancements. Scientific and technological growth requires massive funds for research and development. Developing countries may be unable to accommodate such a situation. Their research and developmental aspirations are minimal due to their insignificant financial position. Green finance can strengthen poor countries' research and development wing to activate their green economy aspirations. The efficient use of technology and the evolution of new ideas, with the help of green finance, can enable sustainable development objectives. Furthermore, present-day consumers strongly demand green products, which forces enterprises to innovate such products. The innovation and marketing of those products face high uncertainties and relatively lower returns. Some industrialists cheat the customers by greenwashing (Yildirim, 2023). But, others may face financial constraints, requiring novel financing forms like green finance (Hu & Gan, 2025). They can make technological advancements and better green products with the support of green finance.

4.4 Green Technology, Environmental Security, and Sustainable Future

Proper developmental policies can resolve ecological insecurities. The present developmental framework is closely associated with technological growth. Many argue that increased technological outbreaks can cause serious environmental issues, as analyzed above. However, the latest model of green technology provides a significant framework for eco-friendly technological advancements. Various terminologies like Clean Technology, Greentech, and Cleantech also refer to green technology. It is a developmental model that uses little or zero non-renewable resources and creates less waste than conventional development settings (Kim, 2011; Samad & Manzoor, 2011). Green technology is an umbrella term that includes various activities like reducing carbon emissions and pollution, enhancing resource and energy efficiency, preventing biodiversity loss, and promoting equitable and improved human welfare without increasing environmental risks (UNEP, 2011). Human well-being and societal welfare require technological advancements and environmental security. Both are essential components of economic growth as well. Sidelining environmental security demands for the growing technological advancements has done enough damage in the past. Many scholars, thus, insisted on making radical changes in technology to ensure ecological stability (Kemp, 1994). Green technology or ecotechnology evolved within this context. It is "environmentally benign technology, including systems that operate with a minimum impact on species and habitat" (Jørgensen, 2001, 6393). It prioritizes technologies that do not harm the ecosystem. It does not demand compromising the developmental or environmental concerns but calls for justice (Ong, 2012). Compared to the other three Industrial Revolutions, the Fourth Industrial Revolution actively employs green technology for sustainable development

(Siekmann et al., 2023). The Fifth Industrial Revolution is believed to follow the same to ensure a sustainable future.

The Industrial Revolution, technological advancements, and economic development caused alarming environmental insecurities by decreasing natural resources, generating large amounts of non-biodegradable waste, and emitting polluting substances. Since green technology focuses on low-carbon emissions and efficient use of resources, it can substantiate the demands of environmental security (Cheberyako et al., 2021). Estonia is the world's greenest country, with an Environmental Performance Index (EIS) score of 75.3, due to its extensive eco-friendly policies, sustainable practices, commitment to protecting non-renewable resources, and effective waste management system (World Population Review, 2025). Increased installation of green technology is not easy as it requires huge investment. Global environmental security and a sustainable future will only be realizable when the world shifts to green technology. However, this is a herculean task for the developing countries as they face economic instability. The developed world must assist the developing world's greening attempts as the environmental issues are not limited to specific boundaries (Cheberyako et al., 2021). Green finance has the potential to address this requirement. The global financial actors should finance eco-friendly projects in the developing world so that these low- and middle-income can prioritize their greening attempts and ensure environmental security for the sustainable future of the whole globe. To achieve this objective, affluent people should come out of their individual and national interests to global interests, affirming intragenerational and intergenerational demands of justice.

4.5 Green Finance and Circular Economy

The industrial sector played a crucial role in global economic development. The demand for goods and services increased along with population growth. This growing demand led to the development of a linear model of production and consumption. It had the advantage of satisfying people's growing needs. But, it will not be a suitable model in the long run, as it causes depletion of natural resources, waste accumulation, and environmental degradation. Both production and consumption demands need to be responsible, as affirmed by SDG 12, for realizing a sustainable future. This necessitated redesigning consumption and production methods with new technologies and methods. From this perspective, the concept of a circular economy evolved. It revolves around resource efficiency, waste reduction, and environmental protection (Hegab et al., 2023). Although some scholars attribute the origin of this concept to the 1970s with the global environmental movements and the Stockholm Conference, it received the attention of policymakers, specifically in the 21st century (Geissdoerfer et al., 2017). Korhonen et al. (2018) argue that the wide use of the circular economic model can provide more than $1000 billion in annual benefits to the global economy. Geissdoerfer et al. (2017) define the circular economy as "a regenerative system in which resource input and waste, emission, and energy leakage are minimized by slowing, closing, and narrowing material and energy loops." They argue that it can achieved with a systematic long-term design, timely maintenance, "repair, reuse, remanufacturing, refurbishing, and recycling." Against the drawbacks of the linear economy, it puts forward a model of sustainability and endurance. It also enlarges the scope of circular design without being limited to the traditional 'repair and reuse' concept alone.

A circular economy is emphasized as an economic growth model that perfectly aligns with environmental protection and economic development demands (Korhonen et al., 2018). The circular economy and sustainable development emphasize intergenerational and intergenerational commitments to economic growth and environmental protection. Since the circular economy affirms a global vision and program of action, it also follows the same functioning model of sustainable development (Geissdoerfer et al., 2017). One of the most significant advantages of this economic model is that it shifts the role of the public from consumers to users (Corvellec, 2022) by promoting a development model with durable goods and services so that the exploitation of natural resources and the accumulation of waste would be less. However, this is not an easy task as it requires huge initial investments to make durable goods and services that satisfy the needs and interests of people. As stated above, this model can provide many benefits to environmental protection programs, but it requires proper mechanisms to ensure the quality of products and the functioning of the circular economy. When the quality of production is increased, it may affect its quantity. It also advances concerns regarding the massive investment in quality raw materials and skilled workers. All these affirm the importance of adequate funding for promoting the circular economy model. The developing world, multilateral institutions, and multinational and transnational corporations should take the initiative to financially and technically support the production of quality and durable goods and services by the industrialists of developing countries to support the efforts for environmental protection and sustainable development through a circular economy model.

5 GREEN FINANCE AND SUSTAINABLE DEVELOPMENT GOALS

The UN Sustainable Development Summit (2015) was a historic moment in the history of the sustainable development movement. It evaluated the results of the MDGs and suggested the need to adopt the 2030 Agenda to transform the world (UN,

2015). The 2030 Agenda is a highly acclaimed policy guideline "to end extreme poverty, fight inequality, foster peace and justice, and protect our planet" (Carpentier & Braun, 2020, p. 14) and stands as a "global reference point for the transition to sustainable development" (Weiland et al., 2021, p. 91). It revolved around six core elements: people, dignity, planet, prosperity, justice, and partnership (Shi et al., 2019). Global partnership is the energizer for this inspirational Agenda, and the UN prioritized overcoming the South-North divide in developmental and environmental politics through this model (Weiland et al., 2021). However, it did not prefer to make rules; instead, it underlined "governance through goals" (Kanie & Biermann, 2017). The 2030 Agenda functions through a framework of SDGs with 17 goals and 169 targets. The universal agreement on SDGs is regarded as a significant step towards the sustainable development drive (Stafford-Smith et al., 2017). The declaration of SDGs proposed an all-inclusive developmental approach (Shi et al., 2019). The 17 SDGs focus on establishing peace in the world revolving around its other four pillars: people (SDGs 1, 3, 4, 5, 11, & 16), planet (SDGs 2, 6, 7, 13, 14, &15), prosperity (SDGs 8, 9, 10, &12), and partnership (SDG17) (UN, 2015).

The Sustainable Bank Network's (SBN) Global Progress Report 2018 claims that the globe requires an annual investment of seven trillion dollars to achieve the SDGs by 2030 (Hu & Gan, 2025). Such massive funding is not an easy task for the developing world. Accordingly, policymakers, academics, and practitioners have emphasized the relevance of green finance. This realization is visible in the global scenario as there are more publications on the scope of green finance after the declaration of SDGs in 2015 (Zhang et al., 2019). However, Arora and Sarker (2023) argue that the COVID-19 scenario slowed down the growth rate of both advanced and emerging economies. The OECD (2021) reported that the developing countries' financial shortfall in meeting the SDGs increased from $2.5 to $3.7 trillion after the pandemic. This has increased the finance gap between the developed and developing countries. The UNCTAD (2024) notes that Global Foreign Direct Investment (FDI) fell by 2% in 2023 due to economic slowdown and geopolitical tensions. This trend may continue as the US has changed its foreign aid policies. The OECD (2021, p. 3) states, "A shift of only 3.7% of the USD 100 trillion of assets held globally by institutional investors towards sustainable activities in developing countries would be sufficient to fill the USD 3.7 trillion gap." The SDGs are realizable for developing countries only if there is adequate financial support from global institutions and developed countries. Green finance is the best option for channeling funds to developing countries' sustainable development projects. It shows that developing world and international institutions should prioritize SDGs in their funds allocation to ensure a sustainable future.

6 GREEN FINANCE AND SUSTAINABLE FUTURE: A CRITIQUE

Green finance has all the capacity to lead the entire globe to a sustainable future. However, it also has limitations and challenges that limit its operational efficiency. The definition of green finance lacks clarity and universal acceptance. The problem with green finance is that each financial provider frames its definition, complicating the entire scenario of greening efforts (G20 Green Finance Study Group, 2016). The scope and full potential of green finance have not been fully defined, which affects the execution of strategies for its implementation. The globe lacks specific policy guidelines for promoting green finance. Inconsistency and insufficient policy framework are significant obstacles to its advancement. It also lacks products and services that can assist investors in assessing green finance's value. The effectiveness of green finance on environmental protection is not yet fully realized, affecting further funding possibilities (Hu & Gan, 2025). Although there has been some progress in the financing of green projects, it is still insignificant. The coordination between public and private actors is less effective than its requirement. The national banks are asked to provide green loans to strengthen eco-friendly developmental projects. But, they very rarely offer such assistance (G20 Green Finance Study Group, 2016). Greenwashing is a crucial challenge regarding green finance. Many industries receive green finance funding and claim their production process and products are green, masking their true identity (Yildirim, 2023). The actual impact of green finance cannot be assessed in such a misleading process. They misuse the green finance funds, causing transparency and accountability issues. Besides, the risk possibilities of green finance, like any other investment options, cause insecurities in investors to make significant investments. The returns from green finance are comparatively low, which forces the investors to opt for other better options. Furthermore, weak institutional governance, corruption, and poor implementation initiatives cause troubles to the full-fledged functioning of green finance (Zakari & Khan, 2022). All these above-mentioned challenges and drawbacks do not negate the value of green finance for the future but affirm that if they are significantly addressed, it can function as a strong framework for realizing a sustainable future.

7 A POLICY FRAMEWORK FOR AN EFFICIENT GREEN FINANCE SYSTEM

The globe requires a proper and systematic functioning of green finance to address the systemic failures in environmental protection due to an increased concentration on profit-oriented economic development. Policymakers urgently need an immediate program of action when confronted with the issue of ecological degradation (Hu &

Gan, 2025). Although developing countries are more in need of a proper eco-friendly developmental policy framework, they lack the appropriate financial capacity to take up such an inspirational project. Developed countries, multinational and transnational corporations, NGOs, and affluent individuals should assist these projects to ensure a sustainable future. They must identify strategies to make sustainable investments to support environmentally sustainable projects (Fu et al., 2023). Their ultimate objective should be to support the developing world's developmental projects that do not negate environmental aspirations. It is a *quid pro quo* strategy by which the developed world financially assists the green projects of developing countries so that their developmental initiatives would not destroy the ecosystem.

To achieve an effective green finance system, all the leading actors should collaborate to develop, improve, and implement green finance principles and values applicable globally. They must promote capacity-building projects and knowledge-sharing among the countries to obtain global support for green finance. Facilitation of cross-border investments in green bonds is also essential. A proper mechanism should be instituted to measure green finance's financial and environmental risks and beneficiary projects (G20 Green Finance Study Group, 2016). Measuring ecological externalities is a complicated task requiring proper policies. Committed policies and regulatory frameworks can address the difficulties in assessing adaptation gains and pricing inactivity (Hu & Gan, 2025). International agencies like the UN institutions on environment protection (UNEP, GEF, IPCC, UNFCCC, and UNDP) should instigate developed countries and other actors to increase their share in green finance and monitor the implementation of such funded projects to ensure transparency and accountability. The World Bank, International Finance Corporation, Asian Development Bank, multilateral organizations, and international and national development banks must prioritize developing countries' access to affordable finance mechanisms for eco-friendly projects (Suri, 2023). International institutions should compare the various green finance initiatives to promote the best models and strategies that can be applied globally (Fu et al., 2023).

7.1 Green Finance and Corporate Social Responsibility

The current economic growth can be equated with corporate culture. Multinational and transnational corporations have emerged in almost all fields. Although the concept—corporate social responsibility (CSR)—appeared in the 1950s, it got its attention in the last decades of the 20th century (Mariani et al., 2021). Milton Friedman promoted the idea of Corporate Social Responsibility (CSR) in the 1970s, contributing financial assistance to sustainable development programs (Hu & Gan, 2025). Enlarging the scope of CSR, Freeman (1984) affirmed the responsibility of multinational and transnational corporations to all stakeholders. CSR is defined as "actions that further some social good, beyond the interests of the firm and that which is required by law" (McWilliams & Siegel, 2001, p. 117). It is also defined as "the responsibility of enterprises for their impacts on society" (European Commission, 2011). CSR functions in two different perspectives: from the perspective of customers, it focuses on availing quality, healthy, and ecofriendly products; and from the perspective of all stakeholders, it emphasizes undertaking projects of sustainable development for sharing a portion of the economic benefits with the vulnerable sections of society (McWilliams & Siegel, 2001).

CSR is a self-regulation process for industrialists and business people to encourage them to share some percentage of their annual profits for some philanthropic activities (Kasturi Rangan et al., 2015). These contributions can provide financial assistance to various projects in society. Only through policy designs like CSR can the triangular relationship between economic, environmental, and social dimensions of sustainability be achieved. It affirms that affluent people and industrialists are obliged to the needs of people and the planet. Industries function in a society using many resources and are obliged to return a share of the profit to the society for its welfare. (Schwartz & Carroll, 2007). To satisfy consumers' interests and respond to CSR assignments, corporate giants contribute a portion of their profits to eco-friendly programs and initiatives (Hu & Gan, 2025).

Green finance requires massive investment and funding from various actors. The developed countries alone cannot be held responsible. It requires the involvement of multinational and transnational corporations, industrial owners, business people, and affluent people. The CSR fund of the industries and multinational and transnational corporations is a suitable mechanism for increasing the investment options in green finance. They must prioritize eco-friendly projects and sustainable development programs to ensure their responsibility towards the planet. The CSR fund providers to green finance need to monitor the implementation process of the funded projects to affirm that they are sustainably used. The CSR fund can act as a model of national and international collaborative green finance systems for strengthening global attempts toward sustainable development aspirations.

7.2 A way forward

The globe cannot survive long with this slow process of environmental protection. The global attempts at sustainable development and ecological protection lose their effectiveness mainly because of the poor financial conditions of the developing world. Green finance can reduce this gap and promote the globe towards a sustainable future. However, its functioning needs to be strengthened with more positivity and openness. The funds allocated to sustainable environmental projects must reach the deserving people, and a proper mechanism should coordinate and monitor the flow and implementation of funds. Decentralization of funds and the establishment of green banks have a significant role in this context.

Developed nations aim to guarantee that over $100 billion reaches developing countries annually to address climate change and strengthen environmental protection strategies. The main channel of this fund flow is the GCF, providing direct access to developing countries (Chaudhury, 2020). However, the present scenario is not appealing to green finance. The US government has decided to retrieve from the responsibilities of the Paris Agreement. It adversely affects their financial support to developing countries and eco-friendly projects. Global environmental protection attempts will be curbed if other developed countries follow the same *modus operandi*. The UN and other international institutions should devise specific guidelines to ensure that the change of a state government will not affect its international responsibilities, which will affect the larger public. Besides, the allocated funds must reach the deserving people. The role of intermediaries should be controlled for the effective functioning of such funds. Various governments have used the decentralization architecture to create subnational climate change funds, allocating national and international funds to community-prioritized public goods investments to increase local resilience to climate change (Hesse, 2016). Such decentralized functioning should be promoted globally for better results in green finance for a sustainable future.

Green banks are mission-oriented financial institutions created to address ecological degradation and climate change, accelerating the shift towards clean energy and net-zero emissions (Bhushan & Singh, 2024). They finance a wide range of activities, which focus on reducing carbon and GHG emissions, generating eco-friendly employment opportunities, improving local communities, and promoting the realization of SDGs by leveraging private capital with public funds (Griffith-Jones et al., 2022). The mission-oriented financial institution can strengthen sustainable environment and development projects and programs. The financial support from these banks can leverage the developing world's developmental projects with a spirit of sustainability.

8 CONCLUSIONS

From the second half of the 20th century, the globe seriously concentrated on environmental protection. Industrial development was necessary for economic growth, but policymakers and ecological activists demanded not to disregard environmental concerns. Accordingly, the sustainable development paradigm emerged in the academic circle. It received universal acceptance with the Brudtland Report of 1987. Thereafter, various conferences and international initiatives enhanced the framework of sustainable development. Global initiatives became more meaningful by promoting environmental protective developmental policies towards the end of the 20th century. The 3rd Millennium began with an inspirational move of the UN that declared MDGs for advancing global attempts at sustainable development and environmental protection. This move was strengthened by the announcement of SDGs in 2015 to continue and enlarge the mission of MDGs. The 17 SDGs set the global march towards a sustainable future. However, developing countries face financial hurdles in achieving the SDGs significantly. On the one hand, they cannot ignore industrial development as they barely need economic growth; on the other hand, they also must promote strategies for environmental protection. They require financial assistance from powerful actors to address this complexity and subscribe to the sustainable development model.

Green finance evolved to balance developing countries' developmental aspirations with environmental protection. It encourages investments in developing countries to assist their eco-friendly developmental projects. It brings together various actors like developed countries, international financial institutions, multinational and transnational corporations, NGOs, and affluent people to boost global efforts for a sustainable future by being involved in the sustainable development attempts of the developing world. It underlines the rationale of SDG 17, encouraging collaborative efforts for better results.

Although green finance faces various challenges and limitations, it has the potential to function as a perfect supporting system for realizing the SDGs and a sustainable future. The criticisms on green finance do not undermine its value but recommend focusing on solving the limitations for efficient functioning. It strengthens the developing world's efforts for economic growth by assisting them in reducing carbon emissions, focusing on renewable energy, advancing technological updates, switching to green technologies, and promoting the circular economy model. The SDGs will become easily realizable across the globe through this initiative. However, international institutions and national governments must focus on establishing a proper policy framework for the smooth functioning of green finance. The responsible utilization of CSR funds, designing effective implementation mechanisms, and ensuring transparency and accountability are essential for enlarging the scope of green finance. Since globalization has opened a world of interconnectedness, the issues in any part of the globe have repercussions in other parts. This necessitates global efforts to support the developmental and environmental needs of the developing world. Accordingly, green finance would be a perfect model for global endeavors toward a sustainable future despite all the limitations and challenges.

REFERENCES

G20 Green Finance Study Group. (2016). G20 Green Finance Synthesis Report. https://g20sfwg.org/wp-content/uploads/2021/07/2016_Synthesis_Report_Full_EN.pdf

Arora, R. U., & Sarker, T. (2023). Financing for Sustainable Development Goals (SDGs) in the Era of COVID-19 and Beyond. *European Journal of Development Research, 35*, 1–19. https://link.springer.com/article/10.1057/s41287-022-00571-9 PMID: 36620200

Balsalobre-Lorente, D., Driha, O. M., Bekun, F. V., & Osundia, O. A. (2019). Do Agricultural Activities Induce Carbon Emissions? The BRICS Experience. *Environmental Science and Pollution Research International, 26*, 25218–25234. https://link.springer.com/article/10.1007/s11356-019-05737-3 PMID: 31256399

Berrou, R., Dessertine, P., & Migliorelli, M. (2019). An Overview of Green Finance. M. Migliorelli & P. Dessertine (Eds.), *The Rise of Green Finance in Europe: Opportunities and Challenges for Issuers, Investors, and Marketplaces* (pp. 3-19). Palgrave Macmillan.

Bhatnagar, S., & Sharma, D. (2022). Evolution of Green Finance and Its Enablers: A Bibliometric Analysis. *Renewable & Sustainable Energy Reviews, 162*, 112405. https://www.sciencedirect.com/science/article/abs/pii/S1364032122003136

Bhushan, M., & Singh, R. (2024). Talent Management Facilitates Net-Zero Transition through Employee Green Behavior. In Singh, R., Khan, S., Kumar, A., Luthra, S., & Chokshi, H. (Eds.), *Net Zero Economy, Corporate Social Responsibility and Sustainable Value Creation: Exploring Strategies, Drivers, and Challenges* (pp. 117–129). Springer.

Carpentier, C. L., & Braun, H. (2020). Agenda 2030 for Sustainable Development: A Powerful Global Framework. *Journal of the International Council for Small Business, 1*(1), 14–23. https://www.tandfonline.com/doi/full/10.1080/26437015.2020.1714356

Chaudhury, A. (2020). Role of Intermediaries in Shaping Climate Finance in Developing Countries—Lessons from the Green Climate Fund. *Sustainability, 12*(14), 5507. https://www.mdpi.com/2071-1050/12/14/5507

Cheberyako, O. V., Varnalii, Z. S., Borysenko, O. A., & Miedviedkova, N. S. (2021). "Green" Finance as a Modern Tool for Social and Environmental Security. IOP Conference Series: Earth and Environmental Science. https://iopscience.iop.org/article/10.1088/1755-1315/915/1/012017

Churchill, S. A., Inekwe, J., Smyth, R., & Zhang, X. (2019). R&D Intensity and Carbon Emissions in the G7: 1870-2014. *Energy Economics*, *80*, 30–37. https://www.sciencedirect.com/science/article/abs/pii/S0140988318305024?via%3Dihub

Cojoianu, T. F., French, D., Hoepner, A. G. F., Sheenan, L., & Vu, A. (2025). On the Origin of Green Finance Policies. *Journal of Financial Stability*, *79*, 101418. https://www.sciencedirect.com/science/article/pii/S1572308925000476

Corvellec, H., Stowell, A. F., & Johansson, N. (2022). Critiques of the Circular Economy. *Journal of Industrial Ecology*, *26*, 421–432. https://onlinelibrary.wiley.com/doi/pdf/10.1111/jiec.13187?trk=public_post_comment-text

Danish, B. M. A., Mahmood, N., & Zhang, J. W. (2019). Effect of Natural Resources, Renewable Energy, and Economic Development on CO_2 Emissions in BRICS Countries. *Science of the Total Environment,* 678, 632-638. https://www.sciencedirect.com/science/article/abs/pii/S004896971932039X?via%3Dihub

Derrick, M. (2024). Top 10: Countries Using Renewable Energies. *Energy Digital*. https://energydigital.com/top10/top-10-countries-using-renewable-energies

Dogan, E., Luni, T., Majeed, M. T., & Tzeremes, P. (2023). The Nexus between Global Carbon and Renewable Energy Sources: A Step Towards Sustainability. *Journal of Cleaner Production*, *416*, 137927. https://www.sciencedirect.com/science/article/abs/pii/S0959652623020851?via%3Dihub

Dong, K., Sun, R., Jiang, H., & Zeng, X. (2018). CO_2 Emissions, Economic Growth, and the Environmental Kuznets Curve in China: What Roles Can Nuclear Energy and Renewable Energy Play? *Journal of Cleaner Production*, *196*, 51–63. https://www.sciencedirect.com/science/article/abs/pii/S095965261831624X?via%3Dihub

Dziwok, E., & Jäger, J. (2024). A Critical Overview of Green Finance. In Jäger, J., & Dziwok, E. (Eds.), *Understanding Green Finance: A Critical Assessment and Alternative Perspective* (pp. 2–17). Edward Elgar., https://www.elgaronline.com/edcollchap/book/9781803927558/book-part-9781803927558-8.xml

Flaherty, M., Gevorkyan, A., Radpour, S., & Semmler, W. (2017). Financing Climate Policies through Climate Bonds — A Three Stage Model and Empirics. *Research in International Business and Finance*, *42*, 468–479. https://www.sciencedirect.com/science/article/abs/pii/S0275531916301003?via%3Dihub

Freeman, R. E. (1984). *Strategic Management: A Stakeholder Approach*. Pitman Publishing.

Fu, C., Lu, L., & Pirabi, M. (2023). Advancing Green Finance: A Review of Sustainable Development. *Digital Economy and Sustainable Development,* 1(20), 1-19. https://link.springer.com/article/10.1007/s44265-023-00020-3

Geissdoerfer, M., Savaget, P., Bocken, N. M., & Hultink, E. J. (2017). The Circular Economy—A New Sustainability Paradigm? *Journal of Cleaner Production, 143*, 757–768. https://www.sciencedirect.com/science/article/abs/pii/S0959652616321023

Griffith-Jones, S., Marodon, R., Rochon, L. P., & Xu, J. (2022). Introduction: Unleashing the Potential of Public Development Banks for Achieving Sustainable Development Goals. In *Development and Public Banks* (pp. 1-4). Routledge.

Hegab, H., Shaban, I., Jamil, M., & Khanna, N. (2023). Toward Sustainable Future: Strategies, Indicators, and Challenges for Implementing Sustainable Production Systems. *Sustainable Materials and Technologies,* 36, e00617. https://www.sciencedirect.com/science/article/abs/pii/S2214993723000520

Hesse, C. (2016). Decentralizing Climate Finance to Reach the Most Vulnerable. *International Institute for Environment and Development*. https://www.iied.org/g04103

Hu, D., & Gan, C. (2025). Green Finance Development and its Origin, Motives, and Barriers: An Exploratory Study. *Environment, Development, and Sustainability*. https://link.springer.com/article/10.1007/s10668-024-05570-w

Jafri, M. A. H., Liu, H., Usman, A., & Khan, Q. R. (2021). Re-evaluating the Asymmetric Conventional Energy and Renewable Energy Consumption-Economic Growth Nexus for Pakistan. *Environmental Science and Pollution Research International, 28*(4), 37435–37447. https://link.springer.com/article/10.1007/s11356-021-13131-1 PMID: 33713265

Jerbi, S. (2009). Business and Human Rights at the UN: What Might Happen Next? *Human Rights Quarterly, 31*(2), 299–320. https://www.jstor.org/stable/20486754

Jørgensen, U. (2001). Greening of Technology and Ecotechnology. In Smelser, N. J., & Baltes, P. B. (Eds.), *International Encyclopaedia of the Social and Behavioural Sciences* (pp. 6393–6396). Elsevier.

Kanie, N., & Biermann, F. (Eds.). (2017). *Governing through Goals: Sustainable Development Goals as Governance Innovation*. MIT Press.

Kasturi Rangan, V., Chase, L., & Karim, S. (2015). The Truth about CSR. *Harvard Business Review, 93*(1/2), 40–49. https://hbr.org/2015/01/the-truth-about-csr

Kemp, R. (1994). Technology and the Transition to Environmental Sustainability: The Problem of Technological Regime Shifts. *Futures*, *26*(10), 1023–1046. https://www.sciencedirect.com/science/article/abs/pii/001632879490071X

Khan, Q. R. (2023). From Industrialization to Dehumanization: Understanding the Deriving Forces of Environment and Implications for Sustainable Development. *Environmental Science and Pollution Research International*, *30*, 123396–123411. https://link.springer.com/content/pdf/10.1007/s11356-023-30983-x.pdf PMID: 37981608

Kihombo, S., Ahmed, Z., Chen, S., Adebayo, T. S., & Kirikkaleli, D. (2021). Linking Financial Development, Economic Growth, and Ecological Footprint: What is the Role of Technological Innovation? *Environmental Science and Pollution Research International*, *28*, 61235–61245. https://link.springer.com/article/10.1007/s11356-021-14993-1 PMID: 34170468

Kim, H. -E. (2011). *The Role of the Patent System in Stimulating Innovation and Technology Transfer for Climate Change: Including Aspects of Licencing and Competition Law*. Nomos Verlagsgesellschaft mbH.

Kingsbury, D., Remenyi, J., McKay, J., & Hunt, J. (2004). *Key Issues in Development*. Palgrave Macmillan.

Korhonen, J., Honkasalo, A., & Seppälä, J. (2018). Circular Economy: The Concept and Its Limitations. *Ecological Economics*, *143*, 37–46. https://www.sciencedirect.com/science/article/abs/pii/S0921800916300325

Le, D. A., Truong, T. H., & Dang, T. C. (2024). *Green Finance Tools Education in Vietnam: A Mixed Method Study*. Vin University.

Li, G., Gao, D., & Shi, X. X. (2023). How Does Information and Communication Technology Affect Carbon Efficiency? Evidence at China's City Level. *Energy & Environment*, *35*(8), 4272–4293. https://journals.sagepub.com/doi/10.1177/0958305X231156405

McWilliams, A., & Siegel, D. (2001). Corporate Social Responsibility: A Theory of the Firm Perspective. *Academy of Management Review*, *26*(1), 117–127. https://www.jstor.org/stable/259398

OECD. (2021). *Mobilizing Institutional Investors for Financing Sustainable Development in Developing Countries: Emerging Evidence of Opportunities and Challenges*. OECD Publishing. https://one.oecd.org/document/DCD(2021)11/en/pdf

Ong, P. (2012). Environmental Justice and Green-Technology Adoption. *Journal of Policy Analysis and Management*, *31*(3), 578–597. https://www.jstor.org/stable/41653815

Pourasl, H. H., Barenji, R. V., & Khojastehnezhad, V. M. (2023). Solar Energy Status in the World: A Comprehensive Review. *Energy Reports*, *10*, 3474–3493. DOI: 10.1016/j.egyr.2023.10.022

Qian, L. H. (2024). An Empirical Study on the Relationship between Urbanization, Transportation Infrastructure, Industrialization, and Environment Degradation in China, India, and Indonesia. *Environment, Development and Sustainability*, •••, 1–27. https://link.springer.com/content/pdf/10.1007/s10668-024-05773-1.pdf

Roy, S. (1996). Development, Environment, and Poverty: Some Issues for Discussion. *Economic and Political Weekly*, *31*(4), 29–41. https://www.epw.in/journal/1996/4/review-political-economy-review-issues-specials/development-environment-and-poverty

Roy, S., Rautela, R., & Kumar, S. (2023). Towards a Sustainable Future: Nexus between the Sustainable Development Goals and Waste Management in the Built Environment. *Journal of Cleaner Production*, *415*(20), 137865. https://www.sciencedirect.com/science/article/abs/pii/S0959652623020231

Salman, M., Long, X., Dauda, L., & Mensah, C. N. (2019). The Impact of Institutional Quality on Economic Growth and Carbon Emissions: Evidence from Indonesia, South Korea, and Thailand. *Journal of Cleaner Production*, *241*, 118331. https://www.sciencedirect.com/science/article/abs/pii/S0959652619332019

Samad, G., & Manzoor, R. (2011). Green Growth: An Environmental Technology Approach. *Pakistan Development Review*, *50*(4), 471–490. https://thepdr.pk/index.php/pdr/article/view/2480

Schwartz, M. S., & Carroll, A. B. (2007). Integrating and Unifying Competing and Complementary Frameworks: The Search for a Common Core in the Business and Society Field. *Business & Society*, *47*(2), 148–186. https://journals.sagepub.com/doi/10.1177/0007650306297942

Shi, L., Han, L., Yang, F., & Gao, L. (2019). The Evolution of Sustainable Development Theory: Types, Goals, and Research Prospects. *Sustainability*, *11*, 7158. https://www.mdpi.com/2071-1050/11/24/7158

Siekmann, F., Schlör, H., & Vengaus, S. (2023). Linking Sustainability and the Fourth Industrial Revolution: A Monitoring Framework Accounting for Technological Development. *Energy, Sustainability and Society*, *13*(26). https://energsustainsoc.biomedcentral.com/articles/10.1186/s13705-023-00405-4

Stafford-Smith, M., Griggs, D., Gaffney, O., Ullah, F., Reyers, B., Kanie, N., Stigson, B., Shrivastava, P., Leach, M., & O'Connell, D. (2017). Integration: The Key to Implementing the Sustainable Development Goals. *Sustainability Science*, *12*, 911–919. https://pmc.ncbi.nlm.nih.gov/articles/PMC6086249/ PMID: 30147763

Suri, A. (2023). A Comprehensive Framework for India's Climate Finance Strategy. *Carnegie Endowment for International Peace*. https://carnegieendowment.org/research/2023/03/a-comprehensive-framework-for-indias-climate-finance-strategy?lang=en

UN General Assembly. (2015). Transforming Our World: The 2030 Agenda for Sustainable Development. A/RES/70/1. https://docs.un.org/en/A/RES/70/1

UNCTAD. (United Nations Conference on Trade and Development). (2024). World Investment Report 2024. https://unctad.org/publication/world-investment-report-2024

UNEP (United Nations Environment Program). (2011). *Towards a Green Economy: Pathways to Sustainable Development and Poverty Eradication*. UNEP.

WCED (World Commission on Environment and Development). (1987). *Report of the World Commission on Environment and Development: Our Common Future*. United Nations.

Weiland, S., Hickmann, T., Leder, M., Marquardt, J., & Schwindenhammer, S. (2021). The 2030 Agenda for Sustainable Development: Transformative Change through the Sustainable Development Goals? *Politics and Governance*, *9*(1), 90–95. https://www.cogitatiopress.com/politicsandgovernance/article/view/4191

World Population Review. (2025). Greenest (Most Eco-friendly) Countries 2025. https://worldpopulationreview.com/country-rankings/greenest-countries

Yildirim, S. (2023). Greenwashing: A rapid escape from sustainability or a slow transition? *LBS Journal of Management & Research,* 21(1), 53-63. https://www.emerald.com/insight/content/doi/10.1108/lbsjmr-11-2022-0077/full/html

Zakari, A., & Khan, I. (2022). The Introduction of Green Finance: A Curse or Benefit to Environmental Sustainability? *Energy Research Letters*, 3(3). https://erl.scholasticahq.com/article/29977-the-introduction-of-green-finance-a-curse-or-a-benefit-to-environmental-sustainability

Zhang, D., Zhang, Z., & Managi, S. (2019). A Bibliometric Analysis on Green Finance: Current Status, Development, and Future Directions. *Finance Research Letters*, *29*, 425–430. https://www.sciencedirect.com/science/article/abs/pii/S1544612319300765?via%3Dihub

Zhang, D., Zhao, N., & Yang, Z. (2025). The Impact of Green Finance on Rural Green Development: Theory and Evidence. *Finance Research Letters*, *107648*, •••. https://www.sciencedirect.com/science/article/abs/pii/S1544612325009079

KEY TERMS AND DEFINITIONS

Climate Finance: Climate finance is a limited concept compared to green finance. Climate finance provides financial assistance to various programs and policies addressing climate change.

Green Finance: Green fiance means providing financial assistance for environment-friendly projects and policies. It prioritizes sustainable development by reducing environmental risks. Its prime objective is to ensure financial support for the eco-friendly developmental programs of developing countries.

Green Technologies: Green technologies are those innovations that aim to reduce human-induced environmental risks. By reducing waste and pollution, green technologies promote ecological sustainability.

Greenwashing: Greenwashing is nothing other than cheating the customers. Some industries use this deceitful practice to claim that their products, services, and policies are eco-friendly, which is not true.

Sustainable Development: Sustainable development is the global policy framework that aims to ensure the developmental aspirations of the present generations without denying the environmental ambitions of future generations.

SDGs: SDGs are the internationally accepted 17 goals for realizing sustainable development.

Sustainable Future: A sustainable future is the ultimate objective towards which the global community is marching. It is the process of balancing between the social, economic, and environmental aspects of sustainable development for the well-being of present and future generations.

Chapter 3
Microfinance Performance Indicators Under Sustainability Perspective:
Comparing Rating Agency Practices Against Academic Approaches

Renan Carriço Payer
https://orcid.org/0000-0002-0417-082X
Universidade Federal Fluminense, Brazil

Elaine Aparecida Araújo
https://orcid.org/0000-0001-7522-6889
Universidade Federal Fluminense, Brazil

Hélder Gomes Costa
https://orcid.org/0000-0001-9945-0367
Universidade Federal Fluminense, Brazil

Luciano Azevedo de Souza
https://orcid.org/0000-0001-5091-9769
Universidade Federal Fluminense, Brazil

ABSTRACT

The purpose of this chapter is to identify and compare the main topics addressed by the indicators performance indicators of microfinance institutions (MFIs), which

DOI: 10.4018/979-8-3373-1240-8.ch003

are discussed in literature and used by some of the main rating agencies, in three dimensions of sustainability (financial, social and environmental), according to the Triple Bottom Line perspective. The indicators were identified in the literature (Scopus and Web of Science databases) and in 12 specialized rating agencies. Literature and rating agencies converge on topics like structured financial planning, social impacts, and mitigation of environmental risks. The rating agencies reflect the microfinance market practices with focus on financial factors (such as profitability and productivity) coupled with the MFIs social and environmental objectives. Divergently, literature emphasizes the importance of the accessibility and diversity of microfinance services.

1. INTRODUCTION

The emancipation of the poor and excluded ones from traditional financial systems has been the subject of much debate in recent years. In this debate, it is understood that sustainable financial relationships are relevant to the development of a country or region. In this scenario, microcredit and microfinance are essential instruments for the most vulnerable population. They help provide greater financial inclusion, but at the same time, these financial services need to be financially solid to serve the public with few guarantees (Pattnaik et al., 2024; Sierra et al., 2024).

Microfinance institutions (MFIs) have been successful in providing credit at affordable interest rates to those who are the neediest and, at the same time, have reported low levels of default (Khan et al., 2025). This has attracted the attention of investors, who are looking for opportunities for socially responsible investments (Ayayi and James, 2018; Hermes and Hudon, 2018). Microcredit may be understood as a simplified loan with less paperwork, destined for investments in productive activities, generating income and working for microentrepreneurs (Ayal et al., 2025). In turn, microfinance refers to a more comprehensive set of financial services that incorporate savings, insurance, money transfers, and others besides microcredit (Bourlès and Cozarenco, 2018).

Since they focus on a more socially vulnerable audience, microcredit and microfinance are often given a relevant social role (Bourlès and Cozarenco, 2018). MFIs need to achieve financial self-sufficiency and, at the same time, ensure that the social outreach is broad (number of clients served, for example) and deep (reaching the population with a critical socio-economic situation and high poverty level) (Diaz-Serrano and Sackey, 2018).

Despite advances in research on microfinance performance, there are still several important gaps that hinder a more complete understanding of the subject. One of the main challenges lies in the fact that microfinance institutions (MFIs) have two objectives at the same time: on the one hand, they want to promote the financial inclusion of people in vulnerable situations; on the other, they need to ensure their own financial sustainability (Chekenya and Mundava, 2025). However, there is still a lack of studies on standardized indicators to measure the performance of these institutions. Financial indicators—such as rate of return or default—are well established and widely used. Social indicators, which measure things such as client empowerment, impact on communities, or improvement in quality of life, are still underdeveloped and vary widely between studies. Indicators on environmental aspects are also scarce and underdeveloped, making it difficult to compare different institutions and contexts. Thus, this chapter addresses this gap and is guided by the following question: "How can a set of microfinance performance indicators be structured from the perspective of economic (financial), social, and environmental sustainability?"

Given these essential demands for MFI maintenance, a notion of microfinance performance measurement is inaugurated, a subject increasingly addressed in the literature (Marfo et al., 2025). Some potential benefits suggested by the literature are improvement of management practices and evaluation methods (Hermes and Hudon, 2018); greater competitiveness, with an improvement of weaknesses and leveraging of strengths (Bibi et al., 2018); attractiveness towards investors, receiving higher investment volumes (Hamdani and Ibenrissoul, 2017; Ben Abdelkader and Mansouri, 2019).

Emphasis is given to institutional management. In this way, MFIs' performance indicators become relevant for managers to focus on meeting the requirements of such indicators, improving management practices and, consequently, institutional performance (Ullah et al., 2025). Thus, when using these indicators appropriately to improve management practices and assessment methods, MFIs managers will be watching over the MFIs own survival and perpetuity (Hermes and Hudon, 2018).

The performance appraisal study assumes a practical relevance for microfinance rating agencies. Rating agencies are organizations in the microfinance field specialized in assessing the overall performance, risks, and market positioning of MFIs. Based on an exhaustive assessment, the agencies issue an opinion or note (called *rating*) on the MFIs' long-term viability and credibility (Donou-Adonsou, 2025). As previously mentioned, MFIs are special financial institutions. As in most cases, they have a financial nature combined with a main social function. Thus, a pertinent discussion regarding performance in microfinance concerns the need to take financial and social aspects into account (Thrikawala et al., 2017).

Moreover, the environmental issue increasingly demands the attention of MFIs, according to Hudon and Allet (2015). For the authors, it is necessary to pay attention to the environmental impacts of the activities of MFIs and their customers. It is also necessary to consider the standards and investors' growing concern for the environment. In short, MFIs need to consider, in addition to financial and social factors, also the environmental aspect (Donou-Adonsou, 2025). With this multidimensional objective as the main guide, the results and MFIs' organizational performance need to be analyzed considering three dimensions (financial, social, and environmental) that, taken together, characterize the perspective of sustainability and the Triple Bottom Line (Golesorkhi et al. 2019).

Regarding the importance of the subject, studies on microfinance performance under the prism of sustainability are very recent and in small number, constituting an emerging topic (Chen and Wang, 2024). The literature presents several models with indicators to assess performance in the financial and social dimensions singly or together (Timbula and Marvadi, 2023; Grigoryan et al., 2025). However, when it comes to evaluating the MFIs performance under the prism of the three dimensions of sustainability (financial, social, and environmental), there are few articles available in the academic literature (Donou-Adonsou, 2025).

For the reasons explained in the paragraphs above, this chapter focuses on MFIs performance according to the perspective of the three dimensions of sustainability (financial, social, and environmental) and the Triple Bottom Line. More specifically, the paper aims, on one hand, to identify the financial, social, and environmental performance indicators of MFIs, those discussed by academic studies and those used by some of the major rating agencies; and, on the other hand, to compare the identified indicators in terms of approach trends to point out convergences and divergences in both fields (rating agencies and literature).

This chapter presents a division of indicators into large groups within each sphere (social, financial, and environmental). The purpose of this division into groups is to systematize a distribution of indicators into more relevant factors or criteria within each sphere to offer research possibilities for future studies and important items to be considered by rating agencies.

Furthermore, for each of the spheres and group of indicators, possible convergences in the indicators considered both by rating agencies and in the literature were analyzed. At the same time, possible divergences between indicators restricted to literature and those restricted to rating agencies were also discussed. These comparisons made it possible to point out some approaches for future research to be explored in literature and to suggest some themes for indicators that could be included in the instruments used by rating agencies. In other words, the analysis of performance indicators used by rating agencies can help identify research gaps that have not yet been studied in microfinance literature. On the other hand, rating agencies can expand and enrich their methodologies by incorporating indicators used exclusively by studies in literature.

This chapter is organized and oriented as follows:

1. Introduction
    - Contextualization of microfinance and its role in financial inclusion.
    - Challenges of the financial and social sustainability of MFIs.
    - Gaps in the literature on performance indicators.
    - Justification and objective of the chapter.
2. Concepts and Literature Review
    - Origins and Evolution of Microfinance
    - Theoretical Aspects of Microfinance
    - Recent Microfinance Performance Research
3. Theoretical Foundations on Performance Evaluation
    - Traditional Finance Theory
    - Stakeholder Theory
    - Theory of Sustainable Development
    - Double Bottom Line (Armendáriz & Morduch)
    - Triple Bottom Line (Elkington)
4. Categories of indicators to measure performance in microfinance
    - Microcredit vs. Microfinance
    - Indicator categories: financial, social and environmental
5. Articles Identified in the Literature and Rating Agencies Considered
    - SLR (Kitchenham & Charters) methodology
    - Application of the PRISMA protocol
    - Databases and selection criteria
6. Microfinance Performance Indicators
    - Financial Indicators
    - Social Indicators
    - Environmental Indicators
7. Convergences and Divergences between Literature and Rating Agencies
    - Comparisons by indicator group
    - Summary tables by dimension (financial, social, environmental)
8. Future Approaches
    - Thematic map (Biblioshiny)
    - Suggestions for indicators for agencies and literature
    - Tables of topics to explore
9. Conclusions
    - Summary of findings
    - Theoretical and practical contributions
    - Limitations of the research
    - Implications for future research
10. References

2. CONCEPTS AND LITERATURE REVIEW

2.1 Origins and evolution of microfinance Microfinance has very ancient origins, rooted in community savings and lending practices that have existed for centuries. In different parts of the world—such as chit funds in India, hui in China, and susu or tontines in Africa—communities created informal credit systems based on mutual trust and reciprocity (Grigoryan et al., 2025). These arrangements functioned as alternatives to the traditional banking system, especially for people living on the margins of the formal economy. The modern version of microfinance began to take shape in the 19th century, with initiatives such as rural credit cooperatives in Germany, led by Friedrich Wilhelm Raiffeisen and Hermann Schulze-Delitzsch (Donou-Adonsou, 2025). But it was in the 1970s that the concept gained global prominence, thanks to the work of Muhammad Yunus in Bangladesh. With Grameen Bank, Yunus introduced an innovative approach: granting small loans without formal guarantees, focusing on women and low-income communities. This model spread around the world and inspired several other initiatives (Mohamed and Elgammal, 2023). In the 1990s, the sector underwent a phase of rapid growth, driven by NGOs, specialized banks, and public policies. In 2005, the UN officially recognized the importance of microfinance by declaring that year the International Year of Microcredit, highlighting its role in the fight against poverty. With this expansion, different types of Microfinance Institutions (MFIs) emerged, such as NGOs, cooperatives, banks, and non-bank financial institutions. These organizations began to offer a wider range of services, including micro-savings, micro-insurance, and money transfers, expanding the reach and complexity of the sector (Khan et al., 2025). Despite these advances, microfinance faces significant criticism and challenges. One of the main challenges is the difficulty of accurately measuring the socioeconomic impact of loans (Wirasedana et al., 2024). This is because the funds are often used for both household consumption and productive activities, which makes it more complex to evaluate the results. In addition, there are debates about the real effectiveness of microfinance in reducing poverty, especially in contexts where access to credit is not accompanied by financial education or technical support (Beisland et al., 2023). On the other hand, the sector has reinvented itself with the use of digital technologies, such as mobile banking platforms and fintechs, which help expand the reach of MFIs and reduce their operating costs. Another positive point is the increase in the presence of women in operational positions, which has had significant social impacts and contributed to the strengthening of institutions (Chekenya and Mundava, 2025).

2.2 Theoretical aspects of microfinance Microfinance has emerged as a concrete alternative to address a persistent challenge: the financial exclusion of millions of people who live on the margins of the traditional banking system. Rather than being limited to credit, this model offers a range of services—such as savings, insurance, and transfers—that help low-income families and small entrepreneurs organize their finances, invest in their businesses, and improve their quality of life. The central idea is simple and powerful: access to credit should be a basic right and can be an effective way to combat poverty (Adem and Dsouza, 2024). One of the most striking aspects of microfinance is that it is based on trust. Instead of requiring material guarantees, many institutions rely on solidarity groups, where the participants themselves take responsibility for each other (Sarpong-Danquah et al., 2023). This logic not only reduces the risk of default but also strengthens the bonds between community members. In addition, there is a significant social impact, especially among women, who gain more autonomy, self-esteem, and a voice in family and social decisions. The model, therefore, goes beyond economics: it can promote inclusion and social transformation (Mia, 2024). For these institutions to continue functioning and expand their reach, it is essential that they be sustainable. This means finding a balance between social commitment and financial viability. The so-called "dual objective" approach seeks precisely that: to offer affordable credit without compromising the financial health of the organization (Beisland et al., 2023). To achieve this balance, it is necessary to set fair interest rates, diversify services—such as financial education and insurance—and maintain efficient management. Economic theory applied to the sector reinforces the importance of models that allow for growth without losing sight of the social mission (Lu and Zhang, 2025). Microfinance is seen as a strategic tool for local development. It encourages entrepreneurship, creates jobs, and drives economies that are often ignored by large banks. However, it must be recognized that the model is not perfect (Marfo et al., 2025). There are risks, such as over-indebtedness, and difficulties in accurately measuring the real impacts on poverty. For this reason, researchers have sought more comprehensive forms of assessment, combining quantitative and qualitative data. In addition, well-structured public policies and a favorable regulatory environment are essential to ensure that microfinance fulfills its role in a responsible and sustainable manner (Hussain et al., 2025). This sustainability plays an essential role because it is a broad concept that seeks to balance environmental, social, and economic dimensions to ensure that current development does not compromise the future of the next generations. This idea gained momentum with the Brundtland Report in 1987, which introduced the term "sustainable development" as a proposal for responsible growth (Hossain et al., 2025). Since then, several theoretical approaches have been developed to understand how this balance can be put into practice. In this context, models such as the Triple Bottom Line have emerged, which propose that companies and organizations should measure their performance not only by profit (financial bottom line), but also by the social and environmental impact of their activities (Chai et al., 2025). In practice, this means rethinking how we use natural resources, how we produce, and how we consume. Environmental sustainability is based on the principle that the planet's resources are limited and must be used responsibly, respecting their capacity for regeneration. In the economic sphere, the idea is that growth should be inclusive and lasting, considering the social and environmental costs of business decisions (Timbula and Marvadi, 2023). This is where the concept of ESG (Environmental, Social, and Governance) comes in, which has been gaining prominence in the corporate world. It guides companies to adopt responsible practices in relation to the environment, society, and governance to generate sustainable value and attract conscious investors (Vranovci, 2025). Finally, the social dimension of sustainability reinforces the importance of ensuring decent living conditions, promoting equity, and strengthening citizen participation. Theories such as participatory governance and social capital show that community involvement in resource management and public decision-making is essential to building lasting solutions. Sustainability, therefore, is not an isolated concept, but an integrated vision that requires collaboration between governments, businesses, and civil society. By adopting principles such as ESG and the Triple Bottom Line, it is possible to transform sustainability into a concrete practice capable of generating real and lasting positive impacts (Peñarreta Quezada and Chavez Alvear, 2025).

2.3 Latest Research on Microfinance Performance The most recent research on the performance of microfinance institutions (MFIs) has brought important advances but also reveals challenges that remain present in the sector (Abera et al., 2025). One of the main points observed is that in many regions—such as Southern Africa—financial efficiency still takes precedence over social efficiency. This shows that many MFIs are more concerned with their sustainability and organizational growth than with the direct impact they have on the lives of the people they serve (Grigoryan et al., 2025). One aspect that has been gaining attention is the role of women within these institutions. Studies show that when women hold operational positions, such as credit officer, the social performance of MFIs tends to improve (Ullah et al., 2025). However, when it comes to leadership positions or participation in administrative councils, the presence of women has shown a negative correlation with financial results. This data raises important questions about structural and cultural barriers that still need to be better understood and addressed (Donou-Adonsou, 2025) Another factor that strongly influences the performance of MFIs is the financial environment of the countries where they operate. Institutions operating in more developed financial systems tend to perform better, both in terms of efficiency and reach. In these contexts, it is common for loans to be of lower value per client but with a higher total volume, which may indicate a more cautious and effective risk management strategy (Khan et al., 2025). The way these institutions are organized also makes a difference. NGOs and non-bank financial institutions (NBFIs), for example, tend to be more efficient than credit unions and traditional banks. This advantage may be linked to the greater operational flexibility and stronger social focus of these entities (Hussain et al., 2025). These findings show how complex and multifaceted the microfinance sector is. The balance between generating social impact and maintaining financial viability remains one of the major challenges (Ayal et al., 2025). At the same time, studies point to promising ways to improve institutional practices and develop more integrated evaluation models that consider local realities and the needs of the communities served (Chekenya and Mundava, 2025).

3. THEORETICAL FOUNDATIONS ON PERFORMANCE EVALUATION IN MICROFINANCE

Assessing the performance of microfinance institutions (MFIs) requires a multidimensional theoretical approach that reflects the complexity of their objectives and impacts (Hossain et al., 2025). Traditionally, the analysis of economic and financial efficiency in these institutions is grounded in classical finance theories, which prioritize indicators such as profitability, liquidity, leverage, and operational sustainability (Afriyie, 2022). This perspective aims to ensure that MFIs can maintain long-term viability, even when operating in high-risk, low-income environments. However, unlike conventional financial institutions, MFIs operate with an explicit social mission, which calls for expanding evaluation criteria beyond financial performance (Grigoryan et al., 2025).

In this context, the social responsibility of MFIs is assessed through stakeholder theory, which posits that organizational success depends on the ability to meet the expectations of various groups—including clients, communities, employees, and social investors. The social mission thus becomes a central axis in performance analysis, measured by indicators such as financial inclusion, empowerment of vulnerable populations (especially women), and impact on local development (Mohamed and Elgammal, 2023). This dimension requires institutions to balance efficiency with equity, promoting ethical and responsible access to credit without compromising the autonomy of beneficiaries (Sarpong-Danquah et al., 2023).

Environmental sustainability, although historically less emphasized in microfinance assessments, has gained importance considering sustainable development theory (Mkhitaryan, 2022). This approach recognizes that institutional performance must account for the ecological impact of operations, encouraging practices that respect environmental limits and contribute to the preservation of natural resources (Beisland et al., 2023). The inclusion of environmental criteria—such as financing sustainable productive activities, responsible waste management, and environmental education—aligns microfinance with ESG (Environmental, Social, and Governance) principles and the Triple Bottom Line framework, which advocates for integrated evaluation based on three pillars: profit, people, and planet (Timbula and Marvadi, 2023). Consequently, a multidimensional analysis enables a more comprehensive and ethical understanding of the role of microfinance in sustainable development (Messomo Elle, 2021).

The theoretical analysis of MFIs has evolved to incorporate multiple dimensions beyond financial efficiency, reflecting the complexity of their social and environmental goals (Rohmana and Wulandari, 2025). A key reference is the microfinance theory developed by Armendáriz and Morduch, which introduces the concept of the Double Bottom Line. According to this framework, MFIs should be evaluated not only for their financial sustainability but also for the social impact they generate (Hossain et al., 2025). This approach acknowledges that while economic viability is essential for operational continuity, the core purpose of microfinance is to promote financial inclusion and reduce poverty, particularly among vulnerable populations (Armendáriz & Morduch, 2010).

Building on this perspective, Elkington proposed the Triple Bottom Line concept, which expands organizational evaluation criteria to include environmental sustainability alongside financial and social performance. This framework is especially relevant for MFIs engaged in local development, where credit can support sustainable productive practices. The Triple Bottom Line suggests that organizations should be assessed based on three pillars: profit, people, and planet—fostering an integrated vision that links economic responsibility, social justice, and environmental stewardship. This approach aligns with the growing adoption of ESG principles in the financial sector (Elkington, 1994).

Another foundational theoretical pillar is stakeholder theory, formulated by Freeman, which argues that organizational performance should consider the interests of all groups affected by the institution's activities, not just shareholders or investors. In the microfinance context, this means recognizing the active role of clients, communities, employees, governments, and partner organizations in creating social value (Freeman, 2010). Finally, sustainable development theory provides a conceptual foundation for integrating economic, social, and environmental dimensions into long-term strategies (Fersi and Boujelbène, 2022). It emphasizes that development is only sustainable when it promotes equity, respects ecological boundaries, and ensures the continuity of benefits for future generations. Evaluating MFIs through a multidimensional lens thus reveals their potential as agents of social, economic, and environmental transformation (Basha et al., 2021).

Some studies specifically contribute to a broader and more integrated understanding of the performance of microfinance institutions (MFIs) in diverse contexts by addressing different dimensions—financial, social, and environmental—but converge in advocating a multidimensional approach to assessing the effectiveness and sustainability of these institutions. Marachto & Baruani (2024) highlight the importance of integrating the Triple Bottom Line discourse—which simultaneously considers financial, social, and environmental results—into the practices of Congolese MFIs. The research shows that offering green financial products not only contributes to environmental sustainability but also improves financial performance, suggesting that there is not necessarily a trade-off between these dimensions.

This perspective is complemented by Deh and Khouma (2023), who analyze the determinants of the financial performance of MFIs in Senegal and Côte d'Ivoire. The authors identify factors such as institutional size, liquidity, and capital structure as crucial for financial viability, but also recognize that this viability is essential for MFIs to fulfill their social mission. Singh (2024) deepens the discussion on social performance, using panel data to assess how institutional practices affect indicators such as financial inclusion and women's empowerment. The study reinforces that the social effectiveness of MFIs is directly linked to the quality of services provided and the ability to adapt to the needs of beneficiaries.

Finally, Djoufouet and Nzongang (2020) explore governance mechanisms and their influence on the performance of MFIs in Cameroon. The authors demonstrate that diverse and well-structured administrative boards, especially with female representation, can improve both social and financial performance, highlighting the interdependence between governance and institutional results. Together, these studies point to a theoretical convergence: the performance of MFIs cannot be assessed in isolation by financial indicators. It is necessary to incorporate social, environmental, and governance dimensions, aligning with the principles of the Triple Bottom Line. This integrated approach allows not only for more accurate measurement of results but also for guiding more effective and sustainable institutional strategies.

4. CATEGORIES OF INDICATORS TO MEASURE PERFORMANCE IN MICROFINANCE

Microcredit designates small loans to low-income individuals and informal microentrepreneurs. They are traditionally excluded from the regular financial system mainly due to their low indebtedness, capacity and insufficiency or absence of real guarantees. The aspects that distinguish microcredit from traditional credit are solidarity groups (beneficiaries who take responsibility for reimbursement of credits together); granting consecutive loans with increasing amounts according to the punctuality of the borrowers; and monitoring of financed projects (Lu and Zhang, 2025).

Microfinance includes financial services in general (insurance, savings, general credits, etc.), whereas microcredit covers credit modalities, getting into the scope of microfinance (Shettima et al., 2018). An important attribute that distinguishes microfinance institutions from others is what came to be called a "double mission," which is the balance between a social agenda (or social impact) with its financial objectives (Marfo et al., 2025). Microfinance has a diversified target audience such as needy families, small entrepreneurs, social insurance companies, etc. Microfinance is a relevant economic instrument with a clear social objective in the context in which it operates, as it contributes to greater social inclusion (Bibi et al., 2018).

Therefore, the role of microfinance is significant for many individuals who crave better living conditions. Thus, it is also important to discuss MFIs' performance, whose evaluation is relevant to guarantee the mission of these institutions. This process brings many benefits to MFIs, such as improving performance, reducing costs, and improving their image (Nawaz, 2010). MFIs' financial dimension has its results evaluated by financial performance that expresses the measure of how efficient they are in using resources and transforming them into services. For this to happen, the institution must generate enough income to reimburse the costs of all inputs and goods as a minimum (Wirasedana et al., 2024).

It is possible to obtain a good level of financial performance in microfinance mainly through operational self-sufficiency, which happens when the operating revenues are at least sufficient to defray operating expenses (Adem and Dsouza, 2024). However, financial performance also involves aspects such as a high-quality and well-managed credit portfolio; fair profitability in credit operations; adequate balancing of assets and liabilities, and credit portfolio management to minimize negations (Gaganis, 2016; Chikalipah, 2018). In 2003, a team of microfinance assessment agencies, donors, banks, voluntary organizations, and corporations established some guidelines on the definitions of financial terms, indicators, and adjustments for microfinance. The indicators fall into four categories: asset quality, profitability, efficiency and productivity, and financial management (Chikalipah 2018). Figure 1 shows these categories.

Figure 1. Major categories (groups) of financial indicators

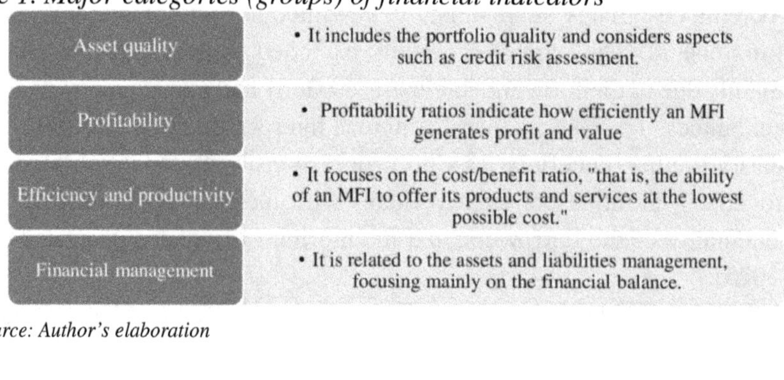

Source: Author's elaboration

The social performance is directly related to the objectives and social mission of the MFI, linked to the provision of quality and adequate financial services to needy, socially vulnerable, and excluded people (Gul et al. 2017; Nasrin et al., 2018). From the social perspective, a good social performance implies offering quality and adequate financial and assistance services to reach needy individuals. In this sense, the microfinance social outreach covers the number of clients served and their socioeconomic profile, such as poverty level. Thus, we have, respectively,the breadth and depth dimensions of social outreach (Ledgerwood, 1999; Golesorkhi et al., 2019; Donou-Adonsou, 2025).

In 2005, Accion, a global non-profit organization committed to financial inclusion projects, developed a structure of social performance indicators on microfinance that was addressed in several studies (D'Espallier et al., 2017; Golesorkhi et al., 2019; Ullah et al., 2025). Such indicators cover six principles: social outreach, association with the community, clients, employees, social mission, and transparency (Figure 2).

Figure 2. Social performance indicators by Accion (SOCIAL).

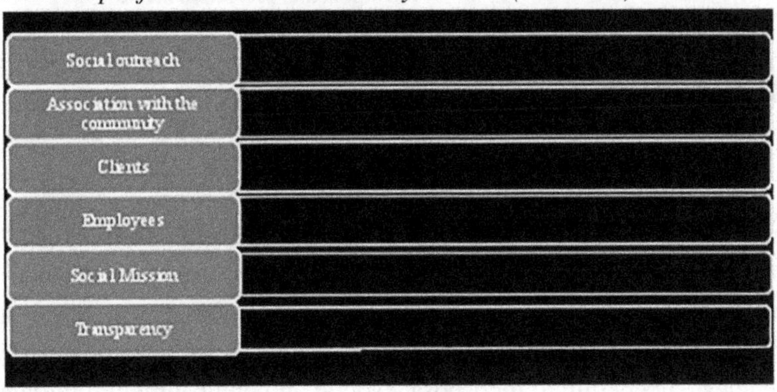

Source: Author's elaboration

Concerning the environmental perspective, it is important to look at MFIs' performance in this sphere as microfinance must be presented, as a way of protecting the environment (Allet, 2014). MFIs committed to environmental results can enjoy greater timely payments from customers, more investments, greater appreciation from stakeholders, and better assessments by rating agencies (Kazemian et al., 2016). It is possible to evaluate environmental performance under two approaches. The first one analyzes quantitative and indicators aspects, measuring results such as energy consumption, material inputs, solid waste, atmospheric emissions, etc. The second one focuses on the efforts made by senior management to influence the environmental operational performance (results) of the business (Hudon and Allet, 2015).

Additionally, environmental performance in microfinance implies internal (environmental policy and ecological footprint) and external (green loans, environmental non-financial services, and environmental risk-assessment factors (Khan et al., 2025). With that in mind, Allet (2014) developed a tool to measure MFIs' environmental performance: the "Microfinance Environmental Performance Index" (MEPI). This tool is based on five dimensions (groups), as shown in Figure 3.

Figure 3. MEPI's environmental performance indicators.

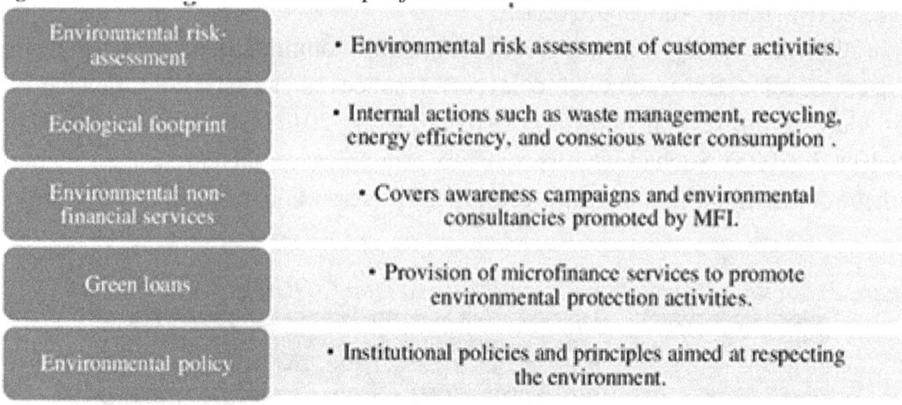

Source: Author's elaboration

The growing integration of ESG (Environmental, Social, and Governance) criteria into institutional assessment practices has significantly transformed the way in which the performance of organizations, including microfinance institutions (MFIs), is analyzed (Ayal et al., 2025). Traditionally focused on financial metrics, rating agencies have begun to incorporate social and environmental indicators into their methodologies, reflecting a more holistic view aligned with the principles of sustainable development. Tools such as SPI4, developed by CERISE, have played a key role in this process. This tool allows for a comprehensive assessment of MFIs' social performance, aligning with the Universal Standards for Social Performance Management, which guide institutions to place clients at the center of their strategic and operational decisions (Adem and Dsouza, 2024).

In this context, the concept of triple bottom line, proposed by Elkington (1994), has gained wide acceptance, especially among impact investors and development finance institutions. This approach proposes that organizational success should be measured not only by financial profit, but also by the social and environmental impact generated by the organization's activities (Timbula and Marvadi, 2023). In the microfinance sector, this perspective is particularly relevant, as these institutions operate in contexts of social and environmental vulnerability, where credit can be an instrument of transformation. Impact investors, in turn, have increasingly sought out organizations that demonstrate commitment to these three pillars, recognizing that the generation of sustainable value depends on a balanced integration of economic results, social justice, and ecological responsibility (Lu and Zhang, 2025).

The adoption of these theoretical and practical benchmarks represents a paradigm shift in how the role of MFIs in development is understood. By incorporating ESG criteria and the concept of triple bottom line into their strategies and evaluation systems, these institutions not only reinforce their social mission, but also increase their attractiveness to financiers and partners committed to sustainability (Sarpong-Danquah et al., 2023). This evolution points to a future in which organizational performance will increasingly be measured by its ability to generate positive and lasting impacts across multiple dimensions (Vranovci, 2025).

5. ARTICLES IDENTIFIED IN THE LITERATURE AND RATING AGENCIES CONSIDERED

The present chapter identifies the MFIs' financial, social, and environmental performance indicators pointed by the literature and those used by the main rating agencies. A presente pesquisa adota a abordagem de Revisão Sistemática da Literatura (SLR) conforme os princípios metodológicos estabelecidos por Kitchenham e Charters (2007), que estruturam o processo em três etapas principais: planejamento, execução e relatório. O objetivo central da revisão foi identificar os indicadores de desempenho financeiro, social e ambiental utilizados pelas instituições de microfinanças (IMFs), tanto na literatura acadêmica quanto nas metodologias aplicadas por agências de classificação.

Na fase de planejamento, foram definidos os objetivos da revisão, os critérios de inclusão e exclusão, as fontes de dados e os termos de busca. A pesquisa concentrou-se em artigos publicados entre 2015 e 2025, indexados nas bases SCOPUS e Web of Science, utilizando os descritores "Microfinance" e "Performance". Para garantir rigor metodológico e transparência no processo de seleção, foi adotada uma adaptação do protocolo PRISMA (Preferred Reporting Items for Systematic Reviews and Meta-Analyses), conforme proposto por Moher et al. (2015). A adaptação considerou três critérios principais: Identificação, Triagem e Inclusão, conforme representado no fluxograma da Figura 4.

Figure 4. PRISMA flowchart.

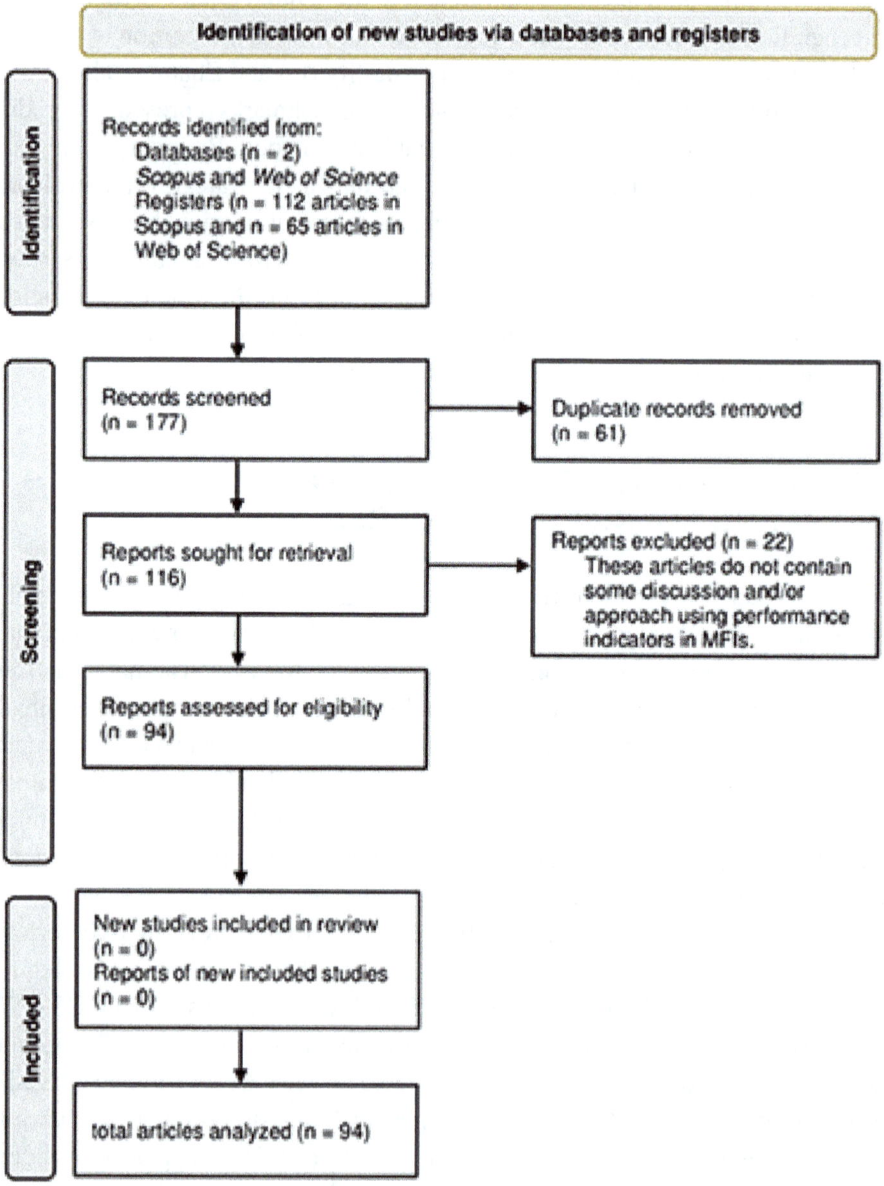

Source: Author's elaboration based on Moher et al. (2015).

During the execution, 112 articles were identified in the SCOPUS database and 65 in the Web of Science, of which 61 were duplicates. After removing the duplicates, 116 articles were analyzed, of which 94 presented discussions or approaches related to performance indicators in MFIs. These articles were selected for indicator extraction. At the same time, a search was conducted for assessment methodologies used by rating agencies, focusing on three dimensions: financial, social, and environmental. For the financial dimension, the methodologies of Microfinanza Financial Rating, World Bank, MicroRate, and TheMix Market were considered. For the social dimension, the approaches of TheMix Social, SPI4 CERISE, Accion International, and Microfinanza Social were included. For the environmental dimension, the methodologies of Green Index, Mix Green, and SPI4 CERISE were used, aligned with Allet's (2014) Microfinance Environmental Performance Index (MEPI).

In the final stage (report), the identified indicators were compiled, organized, and systematized, allowing for a comparison between those used in the literature and those employed by rating agencies. A total of 74 financial, 54 social, and 29 environmental indicators were obtained. The analysis revealed convergences between the academic and practical fields, as well as conceptual and terminological divergences. Some indicators appeared simultaneously in different methodologies and articles, while others, although named differently, had equivalent meanings. The systematization allowed the indicators to be grouped according to categories established by the literature and agencies, contributing to a broader and more integrated understanding of MFIs' performance from the perspective of triple bottom line and ESG criteria, which are increasingly valued by impact investors and development finance institutions.

6. PERFORMANCE INDICATORS IN MICROFINANCE

6.1. Financial performance indicators

The compilation of financial performance indicators resulted in 74 indicators. From them, it was observed that 37 indicators are both covered by the rating agencies and the literature simultaneously. It was also found that eight indicators are addressed exclusively by the literature and 29 indicators are used strictly by the rating agencies. These 74 indicators were grouped, as described in the methodology, according to the indicator categories defined by Chikalipah (2018): efficiency and productivity; asset quality; profitability and financial management (Figure 5).

It was observed that half of the indicators are addressed by the rating agencies and the literature simultaneously (Figure 5). Among the four groups of indicators, the "profitability" group has the largest number of indicators present simultaneously both in the literature and rating agencies. The "profitability" group is important both in the academic sphere and in the microfinance market. Many studies in literature address this factor as a relevant item in financial performance in microfinance. Due to the importance to investors, different profitability indicators are used by rating agencies. Since detailed financial information is often difficult to obtain, researchers usually use indicators such as "Return of assets," "Return on equity," and "Financial self-sufficiency" as financial performance measures. (Wirasedana et al., 2024).

It is important to note that in the "Efficiency and productivity" group, all indicators are covered by rating agencies. The indicators highlight staff productivity and the efficiency of MFIs. Golesorkhi et al. (2019) point out that the cost per borrower indicator, for example, illustrates well the relationship between efficiency and productivity in an MFI.

Regarding the "Financial management" group, it is known that MFIs are institutions aimed at a vulnerable public with few guarantees. Ayayi and James (2018) explain that MFIs need to plan and execute good financial management. In Figure 5, it is noticed that there are many indicators unique to the rating agencies, which in practice signal a concern with this issue (Beisland et al., 2023). Borrowers' default is another issue that permeates the discussion in MFIs. That is why it is necessary to establish some indicators on the quality of assets, such as "Portfolio at risk > 30 days." The "Asset quality" group brings these indicators. Vranovci (2025) explains that an MFI needs to organize financial reserves and promote policies to avoid and deal with default cases.

Figure 5. Financial performance indicators grouped

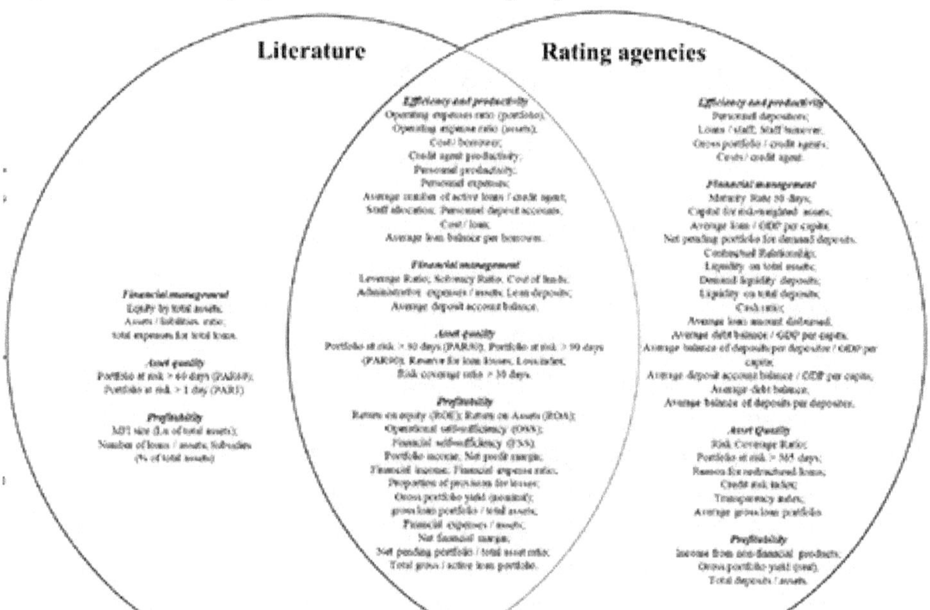

Source: Author's elaboration

6.2. Social performance indicators

The compilation of social performance indicators resulted in 54 indicators. Of the total, it was observed that 27 indicators are covered by the rating agencies and the literature simultaneously. It was also found that three indicators are addressed exclusively by the literature and 24 indicators are used strictly by the rating agencies. Half of the indicators are contained in the intersection region. As described in the methodology, the 54 indicators were grouped according to the categories of indicators proposed by Accion International: social outreach, association with the community, clients, employees, social mission, and transparency (Figure 6).

Figure 6. Social performance indicators gouped.

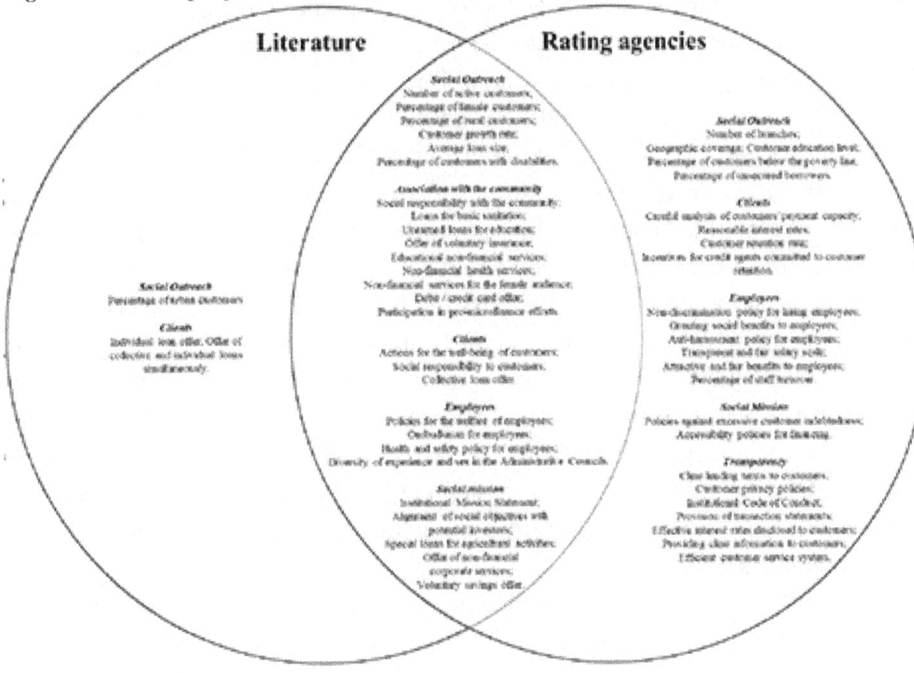

Source: Author's elaboration

A total of nine indicators relate to the "association of MFIs with the community." All of them are addressed by the rating agencies and the literature simultaneously, which indicates the subject relevance, both in the academic approach and in the MFIs' day-to-day (Figure 6). This group includes indicators that refer to primary social issues: health, education, and basic sanitation. Such factors are essential for a community to enjoy decent conditions and have greater hope for a promising future (Rohmana and Wulandari, 2025).

The social mission of MFIs can be understood as a specific social goal of these institutions, and it needs to be clearly defined through the institutional mission statement (Messomo Elle, 2021). The indicators classified within this group emphasize the importance of social mission as an essential item to be considered by investors. This importance is reflected through several variables (Casselman et al., 2015). Siti-Nabiha and Siti-Nazariah (2011) understand that MFIs need to provide non-financial services such as social assistance, health promotion, educational services, among others, to such audience.

There is also an emphasis on the MFIs' social outreach, with indicators reflecting both the depth and breadth of social outreach in the intersection region. The "Number of active customers" indicator, for example, is widely used as a breadth measure of social outreach because it indicates the number of borrowers benefited by MFIs (Hermes and Hudon, 2018). It is observed in the "Clients" group that only three of the nine indicators belong to the region of intersection. The indicators of this intersection region, "Actions for the well-being of clients" and "Social responsibility with clients," almost literally, depict the role of MFIs concerning clients. Siti-Nabiha and Siti-Nazariah (2011) show that MFIs need to be customer-centered to incorporate their needs into their strategies (Chen and Wang, 2024).

Also, regarding the "Clients" group, four indicators are specific to the ratings and are focused on customer retention or their ability to pay. On the other hand, the two indicators in the literature encompass the issue of the offer of individual and collective loans by MFIs as an important factor to facilitate access to loans. All ten indicators of the "Employees" group are covered by the rating agencies. It is noticed that the ratings' own indicators bring the issue of social and salary benefits to employees as a factor of satisfaction, in addition to the question of their moral integrity. Maintaining employee satisfaction has been considered an important criterion among the various items considered for social performance in microfinance (Beisland et al., 2023).

The transparency issue includes the largest number of indicators among those addressed only by the rating agencies. Transparency indicators address the clarity and organization of the information in MFIs, as well as their availability whenever customers need them (Grigoryan et al., 2025). The confidentiality, integrity, and availability of information must be aligned with each other (Bibi et al. 2018). An important document is the institutional Code of Conduct, which goes through the criteria of transparency. Bibi et al. (2018) explain that it clearly needs to include rules to guide and discipline the MFI's conduct according to its social principles.

6.3. Environmental performance indicators

The compilation of environmental performance indicators resulted in a total of 29. Of this number, it was observed that 16 indicators are covered by the rating agencies and the literature simultaneously. It was also found that five indicators are addressed exclusively by the literature, and eight indicators are used strictly by the rating agencies. Only over half of the indicators (55.2%) are contained in the intersection region. As described in the methodology, these 29 indicators were grouped according to the categories proposed by the "Microfinance Environmental Performance Index" (MEPI): environmental risk-assessment, ecological footprint, environmental non-financial services, green loans, and environmental policy addressed by the rating agencies and the literature simultaneously (Figure 7).

There are five indicators that address different aspects of environmental policy, encompassing not only factors internal to MFI (such as its policies and its employees) but also external factors (such as customers and investors) (Grigoryan et al., 2025). The environmental policy can help an MFI identify the environmental objectives it wants to pursue more precisely to attract more investment, as many investors are concerned with the environmental issue (Agathou and Schuite, 2015).

The environmental policy subject has the highest number of environmental performance indicators. The "ecological footprint" group has all the indicators covered by the rating agencies, with three of these indicators being addressed simultaneously by the literature and the rating agencies. They portray the issue of specific goals for the MFI to reduce its ecological footprint, which means internal activities that cause direct or indirect damage to the environment (Mia, 2024).

Figure 7. Environmental performance indicators grouped.

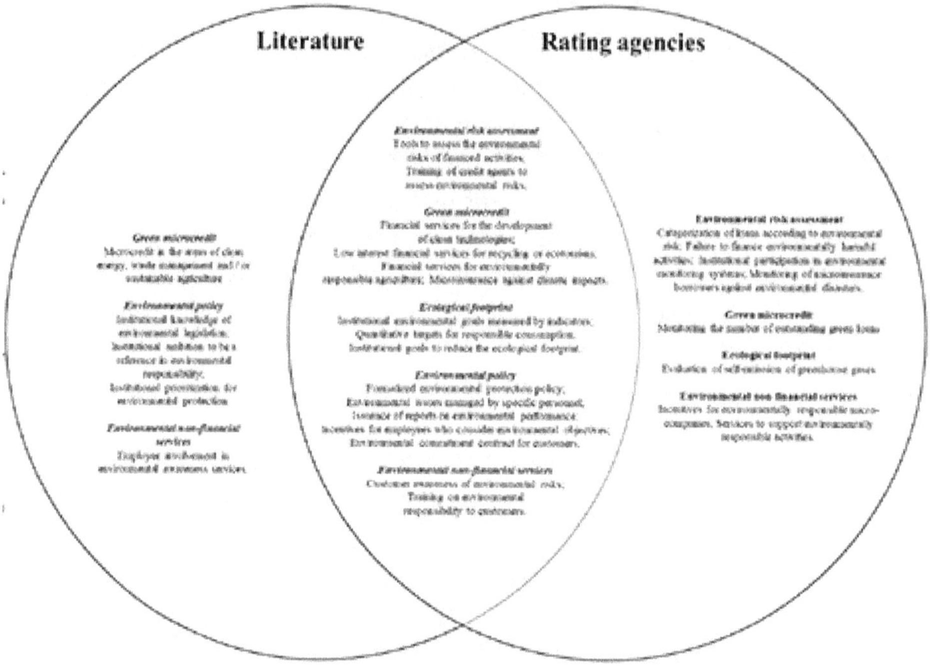

Source: Author's elaboration

The "green microcredit" group has a single indicator found strictly in the literature. This indicator portrays the importance of microcredit in the areas of clean energy, waste management, and/or sustainable agriculture (Agathou and Schuite, 2015). The only indicator found only in the rating agencies seems to give importance to the need to monitor financial issues in these green loans. Hudon and Allet (2015) argue that microcredit aimed at enterprises that promote environmental preservation must be financially viable to guarantee self-sufficiency.

The "Environmental non-financial services" group has a good distribution of indicators between the literature and the rating agencies (Grigoryan et al., 2025). Certainly, it is important for an MFI to offer support, training, and environmental education to its customers (Basha et al., 2021). Customers can achieve better environmental commitment if an MFI offers adequate training or support for the activities to be financed (Agathou and Schuite, 2015).

The "Environmental risk assessment" group is strongly emphasized by the rating agencies, indicating that an MFI needs to consider the direct and indirect environmental risks in the financed projects, in addition to monitoring them (Adem and Dsouza, 2024). In fact, environmental risk can be defined as the "actual or potential threat of adverse effects on living organisms and the environment by effluents, emissions, wastes, resource depletion, etc." Allet (2014) recalls that various measures can be taken by MFIs to minimize environmental risks, such as training, risk analysis tools, registration systems, list of risk activities not financed, among others.

7. CONVERGENCES AND DIVERGENCES IN THE APPROACH OF LITERATURE VERSUS RATING AGENCIES

After the previously descriptive analysis, it is possible to discuss convergences and divergences between the explanation undertaken by the literature and the performance evaluation methodologies implemented by the rating agencies.

In the financial sphere, literature and rating agencies have a common approach to managing expenses, optimizing the MFIs staff, and planning MFI financial activities. In addition, financial and operational self-sufficiency are important factors for both the literature and rating agencies. The rating agencies prioritize the financial performance of the MFIs. The issue of financial income has a special role in evaluating the performance of MFIs. For the author, the microfinance sector needs to think of several strategies to guarantee financial income, as loans are granted at low-interest rates.

The profitability and efficiency/productivity of MFIs are well addressed by the literature and rating agencies. Together, these subjects make up 70.3% of the financial performance indicators number in the intersection region. The profitability factor is relevant because, according to Hermes and Hudon (2018), many studies in the literature address this factor as an important item in the financial performance of microfinance. In addition, many ratings aimed at assessing the financial performance of MFIs use different indicators related to profitability, as this item has been increasingly concerning for investors, as pointed out by Kar and Swain (2018) and Basha et al. (2021)

The rating agencies, in general, focus on the MFIs' financial performance operations, the productivity of credit agents, the financial liquidity of MFIs, and the ability of MFIs to recover from the impacts generated by the portfolio at risk. Meanwhile, the literature focuses more on factors such as preventing customer over-indebtedness and managing MFIs assets. This difference can be explained by the fact that the literature explores further the discussion of internal and external aspects that may have some influence on the performance of MFIs.

Several researchers developed indicators using the variable "total assets." Ayayi and James (2018), for example, used the "MFI size (Ln of total assets)" indicator in their work on the relationship between performance and structure of the MFI's boards of directors. Golesorkhi et al. (2019) addressed the indicator "Number of loans/assets" in their article on the institutional culture of MFIs, and Basha et al.

(2021) used the "Subsidies (in% of total assets)" indicator in their work on influences capital structure of MFI in its financial performance. Other indicators highlight the relevance of the MFIs' financial management, focusing on the indebtedness issue (such as the "liability/assets" ratio) and emphasizing the relation between profitability and MFIs assets (Lu and Zhang, 2025).

Table 1 contains a summary of the main points of convergence and divergence between the scope of financial performance indicators adopted by the literature and rating agencies. The main points of convergence and divergence are organized according to the groups of indicators.

Table 1. The main points of convergence and divergence of financial performance indicators

Group	Main convergence points	Main divergence points
Profitability	Use of traditional financial indicators, such as ROA, ROE, FSS, and OSS. Commonly, the relevance of financial income measured on financial variables is explored.	The literature explores the variable "asset size," which is more accessible to researchers. Rating agencies, however, use more specific variables, such as gross portfolio yield.
Asset quality	Use of common financial indicators, such as PAR30 and PAR90. Commonly, they explore the importance of financial reserves to cover financial risks.	Literature adapts some indicators using PAR1 and PAR60. Rating agencies mainly explore the issue of financial transparency differently from the literature.
Financial management	Both consider important financial variables such as solvency and leverage.	Literature uses variables "assets" and "liabilities" typical of MFIs. Rating agencies, however, bring macroeconomic variables into financial performance indicators.
Efficiency and productivity	Consider operating expenses in MFIs' performance indicators and relevant factors such as productivity and other expenses with employees and customers.	The productivity of credit agents is seen exclusively by the rating agencies' indicators as a key factor in the performance of MFIs.

Source: Author's elaboration

On the social side, literature and rating agencies have in common the fact that both consider the relevance of collective loans, the well-being of customers, and attention to the needs of employees (benefits, ombudsmen, promotion, etc.) (Grigoryan et al., 2025). Literature and rating agencies also converge on the approach of aligning the social mission with the expectations of investors and, also, on the MFIs' engagement with communities exercising their differential roles in them (Siti-Nabiha and Siti-Nazariah, 2011). The rating agencies and literature focus on the social outreach, the maintenance practices of MFI's clientele, the dignity of employees, accessibility to the services offered by MFIs, and the transparency of information provided to clients. Both the literature and the rating agencies address the situation of the most vulnerable people. The "Percentage of female customers" indicator is an example that has been widely used because, according to Kar and Swain (2018), many women are in a position of social vulnerability.

Another common approach is the fact that an MFI must be present in the community. In fact, the MFIs must be in contact with the local community, accompanying borrowers and promoting activities for well-being. Thus, MFIs need to engage in activities for the social development of the community, job and income generation, among others. (Beisland et al., 2023). A common subject to literature and rating agencies is the MFIs' social mission. Five indicators focus on offering financial and non-financial services committed to the fulfillment of the institutional social mission and address the relevance of an institutional declaration of social mission aligned with the interests of investors.

Alternatively, some divergences are observed. The literature focuses more on the importance of serving urban clients by MFIs. Lu and Zhang (2025) highlight that the role of microfinance is also relevant for clients who live in peripheral areas of large cities, either to finance their own businesses or for individual or family consumption. The authors also point out that many urban clients aim to develop micro-enterprises as a form of income.

The literature has discussed the internal effects on the social performance of the MFI. One of these discussions revolves around employee well-being, as the study by Amersdorffer et al. (2015) and Basha et al. (2021), for example. According to the authors, valorization policies and assistance to the employees of the MFIs can contribute to improving the performance of the MFI. The literature discusses the importance of offering collective individual loans. It is notorious when an MFI offers individual and collective loans to borrowers without guarantees and on a trust basis. Thus, fulfilling one of the roles that distinguish them from conventional financial institutions (Piot-Lepetit and Tchuigoua, 2022).

In general, rating agencies show significant concern for MFIs' customers. One of these concerns is the care of customers' personal and financial information (Chai et al., 2025). It is also given considerable importance to retain customers and follow them so that they can honor their commitments. Siti-Nabiha and Siti-Nazariah (2011) explain that clients are valuable to an MFI and caring for them is a fundamental issue for the longevity of these institutions.

Another important point is the issue of moral integrity and policies against various types of harassment highlighted in the indicators of rating agencies. Golesorkhi et al. (2019) explain that in a corporate environment where employees are respected, the organizational climate tends to be respectful and serious. For the authors, these ingredients are essential in an MFI (Beisland et al., 2023). Other points addressed with more emphasis by the rating agencies are the precaution of over-indebtedness of clients and the promotion of social inclusion services. Kazemian et al. (2016) argue that the microfinance differential is to monitor the borrower. In this way, MFI agents can learn about the enterprise or activity to be financed, offer specialized training or consultancy, and infer the borrowers' ability to pay.

Table 2 contains the main points of convergence and divergence between the scope of social performance indicators adopted by the literature and rating agencies. The main points of convergence and divergence are organized according to the groups of indicators.

In the environmental sphere, literature and rating agencies have in common the discussion on financial services for environmental preservation activities and goals to reduce the ecological footprint of MFIs. In addition, both the literature and the rating agencies emphasize the environmental awareness of clients, the institutional tools for assessing environmental risks, and the structuring of an environmental policy that is also capable of attracting more investment to the MFI (Timbula and Marvadi, 2023).

Another common approach between the literature and the rating agency indicators is around the fact that MFIs have specific financial services for ventures that promote environmental preservation, such as recycling and clean technologies. This suggests that green microcredit has been considered a kind of microfinance service that aims to stimulate entrepreneurship in activities directly related to the conscious use of environmental resources. Then again, there are also divergences in the environmental sphere. The rating agencies focus more on the viability of environmental services and the maintenance of MFIs' environmental policies in the face of MFIs' financial demands. Meanwhile, the literature emphasizes the importance of green loan diversity and the construction of an institutional culture aimed at environmental preservation (Grigoryan et al., 2025).

Table 2. The main points of convergence and divergence of social performance indicators

Group	Main convergence points	Main divergence points
Social Outreach	Literature and rating agencies consider indicators that consider vulnerable clients such as rural citizens, women, and people with disabilities.	Different from the literature, rating agencies contemplate indicators that take into account other broader variables such as poverty line, education level of clients, and geographic coverage of MFIs.
Association with the community	Both the literature and the rating agencies consider the indicators that reflect the community reality: basic sanitation, education and, health. Basic needs covered by the indicators	There aren't performance indicators exclusive to the literature or rating agencies.
Clients	Two factors are central: customer well-being and social responsibility. The client needs to be seen as a target of the MFIs' social objective, and it is also necessary to safeguard their well-being and their personal and citizen evolution.	The literature proposes the challenge of offering individual and collective credit. However, rating agencies place more emphasis on collective credits based on joint and several guarantees and effective credit risk analysis measures.
Employees	Both the literature and the rating agencies take into account the well-being of employees, as well as health, safety, professional development policies, and democratic progression to hierarchical grades in the MFIs.	Exclusively, the rating agencies consider indicators that address the issue of employee benefits and anti-discrimination policies.
Social mission	The literature and the rating agencies portray a central aspect of the indicators: The institutional mission aligned with social objectives and the perspective of investors.	Uniquely, while considering accessibility to credit important, rating agencies also focus on measures to mitigate excessive indebtedness.
Transparency	There aren't performance indicators on transparency contemplated simultaneously by the literature and by rating agencies	Exclusively, the transparency indicators are only considered by the rating agencies and assume variables such as availability of information, clarity, and accessibility of data.

Source: Author's elaboration

In the literature, the subject "environmental policy" is highlighted and is approached based on the principle that environmental responsibility is part of an institutional culture committed to the environment. Many MFIs that wish to improve their environmental outcomes need some specific environmental policy or guidance (Hudon and Allet, 2015). The literature also highlights the fact that MFI employees are involved in environmental responsibility activities. Allet (2014) argues that it is important that MFI employees are engaged in the environmental cause and belong to environmental projects. In this way, they will know in practice the importance of the environmental issue in microfinance activities (Vranovci, 2025)

On the other hand, the rating agencies have performance indicators aimed at measuring the emission of self-emission of greenhouse gases. Allet (2014) explains that it is important to use this indicator if the MFI has this data, above all, to monitor its ecological footprint. In general, the rating agencies value this subject as investors expect that the MFI considers the direct and indirect environmental risks that exist in the financed ventures and be able to monitor them (Rohmana and Wulandari, 2025). The author also emphasizes the importance of registration systems for environmentally harmful activities, and the relevance of a list of risk activities not financed, among others.

Table 3 contains the main points of convergence and divergence between the scope of environmental performance indicators adopted by the literature and rating agencies. The main points of convergence and divergence are organized according to the groups of indicators.

Table 3. The main points of convergence and divergence of environmental performance indicators

Group	**Main convergence points**	**Main divergence points**
Environmental risk assessment	Emphasize the importance of assessing environmental risks through appropriate tools or training credit agents.	The rating agencies have exclusivity in the indicators that involve the issue of environmental monitoring.
Green microcredit	Relevant variables are considered in the indicators such as clean technologies, recycling, ecotourism, responsible agriculture, and climate impacts.	The rating agencies have exclusivity in the indicator that aims to monitor green credit. The literature, however, has exclusivity when working with other variables such as clean energy, waste management, and sustainable agriculture.
Ecological footprint	There is a common use of quantitative indicators to measure the ecological footprint considering the reduction of pollution and responsible consumption.	In particular, rating agencies consider the indicator that includes the assessment of self-emission of greenhouse gases.
Environmental policy	Indicators measure items considering environmental commitment and responsibility at an institutional level and also in funded activities.	Literature exclusively values institutional knowledge of environmental legislation aimed at environmental protection.
Environmental non-financial services	They focus on indicators that turn to customers as protagonists of social responsibility when carrying out activities with low or negligible environmental impact	The literature considers important the involvement of employees in environmental awareness services, but rating agencies place more emphasis on incentives for clients to undertake environmentally responsible activities

Source: Author's elaboration

8. FUTURE APPROACHES

Figure 8 shows the thematic map based on the analysis and grouping of word networks. The thematic map describes two parameters: centrality and density, which characterize the themes in a two-dimensional space. Centrality measures the extent to which a word network interacts with other networks. The theme's centrality represents the strength of its external connections with another thesis and can be used as an indicator to measure its influence throughout the field of research. Density classifies the strength of internal loops between all keywords within a topic. Therefore, the density of a given theme represents its development (Aria et al., 2022).

Based on their centrality and density, the themes are distributed in four quadrants, defined by the following four categories:

1. Motor themes in the upper right quadrant. These themes are fully developed and vital to the research field.
2. Specialized and peripheral themes (Niche themes) in the upper left quadrant. Since these themes have a relatively higher density but less centrality, they are isolated and have limited influence in the field, despite their distinct internal development.
3. Emerging or declining topics in the lower left quadrant. The themes of this category are underdeveloped and marginal to the field of research.
4. Basic and cross-sectional topics in the lower right quadrant. They are not yet fully developed but have a distinctly prominent position in the field of research.

According to the diagram in Figure 8 generated from the article's abstract, we can observe 3 (three) main themes with different levels of density and centrality. Among the most developed motor themes in the literature are microfinance, performance, and institutions with centrality and density above the midline, indicating that such subjects are well developed in literature and are relevant for understanding the topic.

The words 'provide' 'period' and 'development' point to thematic with low centrality (relevance) but median density (development). Based on the word 'development' it is possible to state that the microfinance sector contributes to expansion as it seeks to aggregate people excluded from traditional financial systems.

The terms 'outreach', 'countries' and 'MFIs' appear with low density and medium relevance, indicating that the terms related to research themes and can be further explored by the literature, such as the social theme outreach that refers to the engagement of microfinance services to the most vulnerable clients.

Figure 8. Thematic map

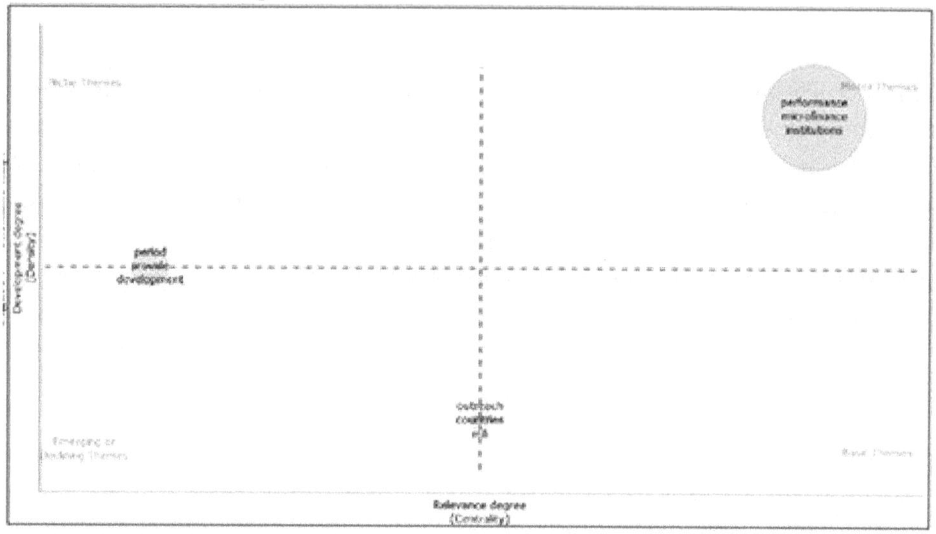

Source: Author's elaboration with Biblioshiny.

8.1 Suggestions for Future Approaches To Indicators In The Literature And Rating Agencies

From the explanations made previously, it is noted that 16 indicators, among the 157 identified, are cited exclusively in the literature. These 16 indicators represent potential themes that can be added to the evaluation methodologies used by the rating agencies to possibly expand the scope of these MFIs' performance evaluation methodologies.

In the financial sphere, the rating agencies could develop or improve indicators on financial management considering the MFIs' indebtedness. The high MFI indebtedness levels can lead the institution to stagnation and consequently have its social role overshadowed (Grigoryan et al., 2025). The rating agencies could also enrich their evaluation methodologies by addressing other topics on profitability, such as the relation between the number of loans granted and the MFI total assets. Regarding the item "asset quality," the rating agencies could incorporate more portfolio at-risk indicators (> 60 days and > 1 day, for example).

In the social sphere, rating agencies could address the issue of offering individual loans. If MFIs establish effective measures to monitor individual borrowers and propose specific measures to assess individual credit risk, it may be possible to make this type of credit feasible (Mohamed and Elgammal, 2023). Regarding the social outreach subject, rating agencies could address the issue of urban clients, portraying, in addition to quantitative factors, aspects related to the activities most performed by these borrowers and their social impacts on the urban environment (Wirasedana et al., 2024). The results of many surveys, such as Thomas and Kumar (2016) and Hermes and Hudon (2018), show that social outreach indicators provide a satisfactory explanation of social performance, as social outreach not only reflects the demands of the most vulnerable but also how these demands change their level of well-being.

In the environmental context, the rating agencies could use indicators on green loans in the areas of clean energy, waste management, and/or sustainable agriculture. In addition, the rating agencies could analyze the possibility of considering the incentives that MFIs give to green loan borrowers in their performance evaluation methodologies (Grigoryan et al., 2025). Another potential issue to be explored by the rating agencies is the importance of MFI employees getting involved with environmental responsibility activities and services (Fersi and Boujelbène, 2022). Besides, rating agencies could better explore the relationship between environmental responsibility and institutional culture. This relation was addressed exclusively in literature by some authors, such as Hudon and Allet (2015), for example. Table 4 contains a systematization of the issues that can be considered by the rating agencies.

Table 4. Systematization of issues to be explored by the rating agencies.

Financial	*Profitability*: **Relation between loans granted and MFI's total assets.** *Asset quality*: **Portfolio at-risk indicators.** *Financial management:* **MFIs indebtedness.**
Social	*Clients*: Offer of loans based on collective guarantees. *Social outreach*: Urban customers and their demands
Environmental	*Green microcredit*: Financing of activities beneficial to the environment. *Environmental non-financial services*: Employee support for environmental projects. *Environmental policy:* Institutional culture focused on environmental responsibility.

Source: Author's elaboration

A total of 61 indicators, among 157 identified, are addressed exclusively by the rating agencies considered. These 61 indicators represent potential subjects that can be used by academics to broaden and possibly deepen the discussion in the academic literature on MFIs' performance.

In the financial sphere, the financial liquidity of MFIs is managed exclusively by rating agencies. For this reason, academics could discuss further studies on the topic, for example, how the financial liquidity of MFIs can contribute to the perpetuity of these institutions. Academic researchers could also carry out studies on the need to maintain financial reserves to cover possible losses with portfolios at risk.

In this sense, two indicators could be used: "Financial risk coverage ratio," measured by the financial reserve for loan losses regarding the portfolio at risk for more than 30 days, and the "Percentage of loans recovered," measured by the percentage of loans defaulted that were recovered. Another potential issue to be addressed in the literature is the issue of profitability concerning assets. Profitable MFIs are considered successful in the microfinance market. Academics could enrich the discussion of literature on the subject without necessarily having to use only quantitative data, promoting case studies that address profitability (Adem and Dsouza, 2024).

In the social sphere, the issue of transparency in MFIs could be addressed in the literature. The transparency of information can be an object of important academic studies to try to understand how it can affect the performance of MFIs. The transparency and availability of information are especially important so that less enlightened clients can have more visibility of the credit product that will be acquired. Academics could also conduct discussions and formulate indicators on the issue of social and salary benefits for the MFIs employees as a factor of satisfaction, in addition to the issue of policies against moral harassment in the MFIs. MFIs need to keep their staff at a good level of satisfaction. Social commitment needs to start from within the institution.

Some indicators on social outreach could be incorporated into the discussion of literature to broaden it. The "Percentage of customers below the poverty line," for example, is one of these indicators and portrays the depth of social outreach. The literature could also use the indicators "Number of branches" and "Geographic coverage," for example, to portray the breadth of social outreach (Lu and Zhang, 2025). The indicator "Percentage of customers below the poverty line," for example, shows the depth of reach for citizens with family income per person below the floor established by the World Bank, according to Casselman et. Al (2015). The indicators "Number of branches" and "Geographic coverage," for example, show the social reach because, according to Gul et al. (2017), the more branches an MFI has, the greater the probability of it having more customers. Thus, such indicators have potential consequences that could be addressed by the literature.

Customer retention and the ability to increase the number of customers is two issues that are also absent from the literature. Academic researchers could develop studies on the relationship between customer retention and the adoption of strategies to attract new customers, for example. In addition, such researchers could be dedicated to understanding deeply the influence of monitoring microcredit on customer payment punctuality. It should also be said that the issue of accessibility to microfinance services, whether by preventing over-indebtedness or through inclusive services, is an issue that could also be addressed in the literature.

In the environmental context, academics could engage in the discussion around the categorization of loans according to environmental risk and monitor the risks of financed activities, since the lower the environmental risk of the financed activity, the greater the probability that clients will honor the repayment of loans (Rohmana and Wulandari, 2025). In addition, categorization of credits according to environmental risk could create "rankings" of financing according to environmental risk and help MFIs to prioritize credit-granting according to the potentially entailed environmental risk. Regarding the MFIs' ecological footprint, a potential issue to be addressed by the literature is greenhouse gases emissions by MFIs in a more independent way from quantitative data, as these are often strategically restricted or require the realization of environmental audits in MFIs (Grigoryan et al., 2025).

Scholars could also use indicators on incentives for environmentally responsible ventures to portray the MFIs' environmental performance. Due to the importance of green loans, academic researchers could develop an approach to monitoring outstanding green loans, aiming at the viability of these types of loans. It is also worth discussing what types of incentives and services could be offered by MFIs, such as lower interest rates or higher loans for these types of ventures. Table 5 contains a systematization of topics that can be included or indicators that can be contemplated by literature.

Table 5. Systematization of topics to be explored by the literature.

Financial	*Financial management:* **MFIs' financial liquidity.** *Asset quality:* **Financial reserves cover losses on portfolios at risk.** *Profitability:* **Relation between profitability and assets.** *Efficiency and productivity:* **Costs and productivity of credit agents.**
Social	*Transparency:* Information transparency effects on customers. *Employees:* Employee social benefits and anti-harassment policies. *Social outreach:* New indicators of breadth and depth reach. *Clients:* Retention and payment capacity of them. *Social Mission:* Precaution of over-indebtedness and provision of inclusive services.
Environmental	*Environmental risk assessment:* Monitoring environmental risks of loans. *Environmental non-financial services:* Incentives for environmentally responsible activities. *Green microcredit:* Monitoring financial odds *Ecological footprint:* Self-emission of greenhouse gases by MFIs.

Source: Author's elaboration

9. CONCLUSIONS

In this study, 157 MFIs' performance indicators were identified (74 indicators in the financial sphere, 54 in the social area, and 29 in the environmental pillar). This identification was made through the analysis of the 94 articles selected to compose the bibliographic review and 12 methodologies used by the institutions that are dedicated to conducting ratings of MFIs (four for each sphere of sustainability).

Over half of the indicators are addressed simultaneously by the literature and rating agencies (80 out of 157). This suggests that some authors use traditional rating agency indicators to develop their studies. On the other hand, the rating agencies possibly also use indicators developed by literature. Both the literature and the rating agencies address subjects such as well-structured financial planning, social impacts caused by MFIs, and efforts to mitigate environmental risks in financed activities.

Many of the indicators are exclusive to the rating agencies (61 out of 157). This suggests that the evaluation methodologies used by the rating agencies use strategic institutional data, particularly financial data and environmental reports, which many researchers may not have access to. This also suggests that the rating agencies are exploring fields of performance studies that the literature could address more closely, such as financial management, institutional transparency, employee satisfaction, and environmental risk assessment.

Of the universe of indicators studied, few of them are unique to the literature (16 of 157). A considerable portion of these indicators is made up of a set of variables available in open or private databases. These variables help several researchers to elucidate important issues in microfinance, but many other studies could be developed if researchers had access to important indicators or variables that are unavailable due to confidentiality issues or institutional strategy.

Rating agencies' exclusive indicators, in general, reflect microfinance market practices, emphasizing financial factors (such as profitability, risk management, productivity, etc.) combined with the MFIs' social objectives and their contributions to environmental preservation. Meanwhile, the literature is generally more focused on discussions about the importance of the financial services diversity and the accessibility to these services by more vulnerable customers.

It is also worth mentioning that most indicators are focused on financial performance, followed by social performance. Only 29 of the 157 indicators contemplate environmental performance. This suggests the need for future research guided by the discussion or development of new environmental performance indicators of the MFIs. Future research may focus on gaps pointed out by this chapter and discuss potential issues that require more attention. Besides that, rating agencies may be able to address possible topics that were not dealt with yet, so that the MFIs assessment system becomes more comprehensive.

It is necessary to consider a set of indicators that address performance in the social, environmental, and financial dimensions. To accomplish this, it may be useful for researchers in literature and rating agencies to consider the key convergence and divergence factors discussed in this paper and thereby exploit important gaps.

In this sense, the results obtained indicate that the unique financial performance indicators in the literature include the relationship between loans granted and total assets concerning "profitability," consider the variable portfolio at risk concerning "asset quality," and focus on the issue of indebtedness of MFIs when it comes to "financial management." However, for rating agencies, the exclusive financial performance indicators that address the topic of "profitability," do so by comparing it with assets. "Asset quality" is considered from the reserves for financial losses and "financial management" is mainly measured through liquidity indicators of MFIs. In addition, the costs and productivity of credit agents are taken from the "efficiency and productivity" indicators.

Moreover, about social performance indicators, this chapter noted that the literature exclusively shows the importance of offering collective and individual microcredit to "clients." The issue of "social outreach" is mainly addressed through indicators that reflect the demands for services of urban borrowers. Rating agencies have exclusivity in the "transparency" of information to clients, the importance of "employees" benefits and anti-harassment policies, in the expansion of indicators of breadth and depth of "social outreach," in the attention to "clients," their follow-up, and the "social mission" that involves the precaution of over-indebtedness and social inclusion.

About environmental performance indicators, the literature has exclusivity when considering the issue of financing environmentally beneficial activities regarding "green microcredit." It considers relevant to admit indicators that measure the participation of employees in environmental projects as one of the "environmental non-financial services" and institutional culture focused on environmental responsibility, proposing a solid "environmental policy." Rating agencies have exclusivity in monitoring indicators of environmental loan risks in the "environmental risk assessment;" incentives for environmentally responsible activities, as relevant "environmental non-financial services;" measurement of self-emission of greenhouse gases by MFIs, regarding the "ecological footprint," and monitoring the "green microcredit."

The chapter presents a comprehensive analysis of the financial, social, and environmental performance indicators used by microfinance institutions (MFIs), both in academic literature and in rating agency methodologies. The main contribution of the study lies in the systematization and comparison of these indicators from a sustainability perspective, highlighting the degree of convergence and divergence between the two fields. By identifying 157 indicators—of which 80 are common to both the literature and the agencies, 61 are exclusive to the agencies, and only 16 are exclusive to the literature—the chapter reveals a significant asymmetry in the approach to the three pillars of sustainability, with a predominance of the financial dimension.

Among the main convergences, the indicators related to profitability, operational efficiency, social mission, and community engagement stand out. Both the literature and the agencies recognize the importance of financial self-sufficiency and social inclusion as central elements of MFIs' performance. However, the most critical divergences are in environmental coverage and methodological standardization. The environmental dimension remains underdeveloped, with few indicators and low representation in assessment tools. In addition, the lack of a harmonized structure among agencies hinders comparisons and compromises transparency for stakeholders. Literature, in turn, tends to explore qualitative and contextual aspects, while agencies prioritize strategic and operational data, especially financial data.

The implications for research are clear: there is room to deepen the debate on environmental and social indicators, especially those related to transparency, employee well-being, and incentives for environmental responsibility. Literature could benefit from incorporating indicators used exclusively by agencies, expanding its capacity for empirical analysis. For practice, the study suggests that rating agencies could enrich their methodologies by considering variables discussed in the literature, such as the urban impact of clients and institutional culture focused on sustainability. Finally, the limitations of the research include reliance on publicly available data, restricted access to strategic information from agencies, and the need for empirical validation of the proposed indicators. Nevertheless, the chapter provides a solid foundation for future research and improvements in microfinance performance assessment practices.

Despite advances in incorporating environmental, social, and governance (ESG) criteria into microfinance institution (MFI) assessments, rating methodologies still show a strong predominance of the financial dimension. Although institutional rhetoric often highlights a commitment to comprehensive sustainability, in practice, social and environmental indicators are often treated superficially or qualitatively, without the same analytical rigor applied to financial indicators. This asymmetry compromises the ability of assessments to reflect the true impact of MFIs in contexts of social and environmental vulnerability.

Another relevant challenge is the absence of a standardized structure among the different rating agencies. The lack of methodological harmonization makes it difficult to compare institutions and limits transparency for stakeholders, such as impact investors, regulators, and beneficiaries. Without a common basis of indicators and criteria, assessment results can vary significantly, even when applied to institutions with similar profiles. This methodological fragmentation compromises the reliability of ratings and weakens the potential of MFIs as agents of sustainable transformation.

Finally, among the three pillars of sustainability—economic, social, and environmental—environmental performance remains the least developed in the assessment tools currently in use. In contexts where MFIs finance few environmentally focused or “green” productive activities, rating instruments tend to neglect this dimension. Weak environmental coverage not only limits understanding of the ecological impact of operations but also reduces the incentive for MFIs to adopt practices more aligned with the principles of environmental sustainability. Thus, it is urgent to improve assessment methodologies, with greater balance between the three pillars and greater standardization among rating agents.

List of abbreviations

CERISE - Comite d’Echange, de Reflexion et d’Information sur les systemes d’Epargne-credit;

MEPI - Microfinance Environmental Performance Index;

MFI – Microfinance Institution;

PRISMA - Preferred Reporting Items for Systematic Reviews and Meta-Analyses;

SPI - Social Performance Indicators;

10. REFERENCES

Abera, M., Marvadi, C., & Suthar, D. (2025). Digitization strategy and innovation performance of microfinance institutions: Mediating role of innovation capability. *Journal of Accounting & Organizational Change*, *21*(2), 250–277. DOI: 10.1108/JAOC-12-2023-0241

Adem, M., & Dsouza, P. K. (2024). Impact of board characteristics on firm performance: Evidence from Ethiopian microfinance institutions. *Global Business Review*. Advance online publication. DOI: 10.1177/09721509241276957

Afriyie, E. Y. (2022). The impact of custom-made internal risk control systems on bank performance in Ghana. *Forum Scientiae Oeconomia*, *4*, 151–174. DOI: 10.23762/FSO_VOL10_NO4_8

Agathou, N., & Schuite, G. J. (2015). Environmental performance of African microfinance institutions: Using the Green Performance Agenda framework to assess and build the business case for sustainability. *Enterprise Development & Microfinance*, *26*(3), 230–247.

Allet, M. (2014). Why do microfinance institutions go green? An exploratory study. *Journal of Business Ethics*, *122*(3), 405–424.

Amersdorffer, F., Buchenrieder, G., Bokusheva, R., & Wolz, A. (2015). Efficiency in microfinance: Financial and social performance of agricultural credit cooperatives in Bulgaria. *The Journal of the Operational Research Society*, *66*(1), 57–65.

Aria, M., Cuccurullo, C., D'Aniello, L., Misuraca, M., & Spano, M. (2022). Thematic analysis as a new culturomic tool: The social media coverage on COVID-19 pandemic in Italy. *Sustainability*, *14*(6), 3643.

Armendáriz, B., & Morduch, J. (2010). *The economics of microfinance* (2nd ed.). MIT Press.

Ayal, B. A., Tassew, D. T., Alem, Y. T., & Kebede, A. T. (2025). The impact of the Federal Government–Amhara Fano conflict on microfinance and economic outcomes in the Amhara Region, Ethiopia. *Public Organization Review*. Advance online publication. DOI: 10.1007/s11115-025-00863-8

Ayayi, A. G., & James, A. P. (2018). Cost implications of microfinance regulation: Lessons from Ghana. *Journal of Sustainable Finance & Investment*, *8*(3), 259–274.

Basha, S., Elgammal, M. M., & Abuzayed, B. M. (2021). Online peer-to-peer lending: A review of the literature. *Electronic Commerce Research and Applications, 48*, 101069. DOI: 10.1016/j.elerap.2021.101069

Beisland, L. A., Zamore, S., & Mersland, R. (2023). Does it pay to be green? A study of the global microfinance industry. *Nonprofit and Voluntary Sector Quarterly, 52*(3), 631–653. DOI: 10.1177/08997640221110209

Ben Abdelkader, I., & Mansouri, F. (2019). Performance of microfinance institutions in the MENA region: A comparative analysis. *International Journal of Social Economics, 46*(1), 47–65.

Bibi, U., Balli, H. O., Matthews, C. D., & Triple, T. W. L. (2018). New approaches to measure the social performance of microfinance institutions (MFIs). *International Review of Economics & Finance, 53*, 88–97.

Bourlès, R., & Cozarenco, A. (2018). Entrepreneurial motivation and business performance: Evidence from a French microfinance institution. *Small Business Economics, 51*(4), 943–963.

Casselman, R. M., Sama, L. M., & Stefanidis, A. (2015). Differential social performance of religiously-affiliated microfinance institutions (MFIs) in base of pyramid (BoP) markets. *Journal of Business Ethics, 132*(3), 539–552.

Chai, N., Abedin, M. Z., Yang, L., & Shi, B. (2025). Farmers' credit risk evaluation with an explainable hybrid ensemble approach: A closer look in microfinance. *Pacific-Basin Finance Journal, 89*, 102612. DOI: 10.1016/j.pacfin.2024.102612

Chekenya, N. S., & Mundava, S. (2025). CEOs' characteristics and the performance of microfinance institutions in Africa: A multitier model approach. *Cogent Business & Management, 12*(1), 2464224. DOI: 10.1080/23311975.2025.2464224

Chen, M., & Wang, C. (2024). How business model innovation facilitates microcredit in balancing social mission with commercial performance – Evidence from local commercial banks. *Technological Forecasting and Social Change, 202*, 123287. DOI: 10.1016/j.techfore.2024.123287

Chikalipah, S. (2018). Do microsavings stimulate financial performance of microfinance institutions in Sub-Saharan Africa? *Journal of Economic Studies (Glasgow, Scotland), 45*(5), 1072–1087.

D'Espallier, B., Hudon, M., & Szafarz, A. (2017). Aid volatility and social performance in microfinance. *Nonprofit and Voluntary Sector Quarterly, 46*(1), 116–140.

DEH. A. A., & KHOUMA, N. P. (2023). Performance financière des institutions de microfinance au Sénégal et en Côte d'Ivoire: Quels en sont les déterminants? Revue Africaine de Management, 1(9). https://doi.org/DOI: 10.48424/IMIST.PRSM/RAM-V1I9.40402

Diaz-Serrano, L., & Sackey, F. G. (2018). Microfinance and credit rationing: Does the microfinance type matter? *Journal of Sustainable Finance & Investment*, *8*(2), 114–131.

Djoufouet, F. W., & Nzongang, J. (2020). Effets combinés des mécanismes de gouvernance sur la performance des institutions de microfinance au Cameroun. *Journal of Academic Finance*, *11*(1), 22–32. DOI: 10.59051/joaf.v11i1.324

Donou-Adonsou, F. (2025). Financial structure and economic efficiency in Sub-Saharan Africa. *Global Finance Journal*, *67*, 101150. DOI: 10.1016/j.gfj.2025.101150

Elkington, J. (1994). Towards the sustainable corporation: Win-win-win business strategies for sustainable development. *California Management Review*, *36*(2), 90–100. DOI: 10.2307/41165746

Fersi, M., & Boujelbène, M. (2022). Overconfidence and credit risk-taking in microfinance institutions: A cross-regional analysis. *The International Journal of Organizational Analysis*, *30*(6), 1672–1693. DOI: 10.1108/IJOA-11-2020-2510

Freeman, R. E. (2010). *Strategic Management: A Stakeholder Approach* (1st ed.). Cambridge University Press., DOI: 10.1017/CBO9781139192675

Gaganis, C. (2016). Assessing the overall performance of microfinance institutions. International Journal of Banking. *Accounting and Finance*, *7*(1), 52–83.

Golesorkhi, S., Mersland, R., Randøy, T., & Shenkar, O. (2019). The performance impact of culture and formal institutional differences in cross-border alliances: The case of the microfinance industry. *International Business Review*, *28*(1), 104–118.

Grigoryan, A., Khachatryan, K., Hartarska, V., & Mersland, R. (2025). Are all deposit products in the microfinance world created equal? *Emerging Markets Finance & Trade*, *61*(5), 1160–1176. DOI: 10.1080/1540496X.2024.2413172

Gul, F. A., Podder, J., & Shahriar, A. Z. M. (2017). Performance of microfinance institutions: Does government ideology matter? *World Development*, *100*, 1–15.

Hamdani, S., & Ibenrissoul, A. (2017). Sustainable microfinance and global performance proposal for a decision-making support tool. *European Journal of Sustainable Development*, *6*(3), 253–270.

Hermes, N., & Hudon, M. (2018). Determinants of the performance of microfinance institutions: A systematic review. *Journal of Economic Surveys*, *32*(5), 1483–1513.

Hossain, S., Hossain, M. M., & Chong, V. K. (2025). Do client protection principles matter for the economic and social performance of microfinance institutions? *The British Accounting Review*, *57*(4), 101493. DOI: 10.1016/j.bar.2024.101493

Hudon, M., & Allet, M. (2015). Green microfinance: Characteristics of microfinance institutions involved in environmental management. *Journal of Business Ethics*, *126*(3), 395–414.

Hussain, M., Rehman, R. U., Bashir, U., & Faisal, F. (2025). Examining employee well-being and financial performance in microfinance institutions: Insights from cross-country analysis. *Journal of Social and Economic Development*. Advance online publication. DOI: 10.1007/s40847-025-00458-5

Kar, A. K., & Swain, R. B. (2018). Competition, performance and portfolio quality in microfinance markets. *European Journal of Development Research*, *30*(5), 842–870.

Kazemian, S., Rahman, R. A., Mohd-Sanusi, Z., & Adewale, A. A. (2016). Role of market orientation in sustainable performance: The case of a leading microfinance provider. *Humanomics*, *32*(3), 352–375.

Khan, A., Goswami, A., & Choudhury, T. (2025). Technology gaps, social outreach and financial sustainability of South Asian MFIs: Bootstrap DEA meta-frontier approach. *Electronic Commerce Research*, *25*(3), 1577–1606. DOI: 10.1007/s10660-023-09747-9

Kitchenham, B., & Charters, S. (2007). Guidelines for performing systematic literature reviews in software engineering (Technical Report EBSE-2007-01). Keele University and Durham University Joint Report. Retrieved from https://www.cs.auckland.ac.nz/~norsaremah/2007%20Guidelines%20for%20performing%20SLR%20in%20SE%20v2.3.pdf

Ledgerwood, J. (1999). *Microfinance handbook: An institutional and financial perspective*. The World Bank.

Lu, T., & Zhang, Y. (2025). 1 + 1 > 2? Information, humans, and machines. *Information Systems Research*, *36*(1), 394–418. DOI: 10.1287/isre.2023.0305

Marfo, M., Ofei, E. F., Annan, E., Armah, A. A., Adadevoh, L., Evelyn, B. O., & Asante, C. R. (2025). The impact of competitive advantage on the sustainability of microfinance institutions in Ghana: Assessing the moderating role of capacity building. *SN Business & Economics*, *5*(7), 90. DOI: 10.1007/s43546-025-00857-0

Messomo Elle, S. (2021). Caractéristiques des produits de microcrédit et performance financière des institutions de micro finance (IMFs) au Cameroun. *Recherches En Sciences de Gestion, 143*(2), 143–170. DOI: 10.3917/resg.143.0143

Mia, M. A. (2024). Loyalty of rural microfinance borrowers: International evidence. *Bulletin of Economic Research, 76*(1), 67–94. DOI: 10.1111/boer.12415

Mkhitaryan, A. (2022). Critical evaluation of organizational structure and culture impact on the productivity of MFIs within the example of Agroleasing Leasing Credit Company LLC in Armenia. *Review of Applied Socio-Economic Research, 24*(2). Advance online publication. DOI: 10.54609/reaser.v24i2.239

Mohamed, T. S., & Elgammal, M. M. (2023). Are donor funds used effectively? An examination of Islamic and conventional microfinance institutions. *International Journal of Islamic and Middle Eastern Finance and Management, 16*(5), 1009–1029. DOI: 10.1108/IMEFM-11-2021-0462

Moher, D., Shamseer, L., Clarke, M., Ghersi, D., Liberati, A., & Petticrew, M. (2015). Preferred reporting items for systematic review and meta-analysis protocols (PRISMA-P). *Systematic Reviews, 4*(1), 1. PMID: 25554246

Nasrin, S., Rasiah, R., Baskaran, A., & Masud, M. M. (2018). What determines the financial performance of microfinance institutions in Bangladesh? A panel data analysis. *Quality & Quantity, 52*(3), 1409–1422.

Nawaz, A. (2010). Performance of microfinance: The role of subsidies. *Savings and Development, 34*(1), 97–138.

Pattnaik, D., Ray, S., & Hassan, M. K. (2024). Microfinance: A bibliometric exploration of the knowledge landscape. *Heliyon, 10*(10). PMID: 38813228

Peñarreta Quezada, M., & Chavez Alvear, N. (2025). Impacto del capital intelectual en el desempeño financiero de las instituciones microfinancieras de Ecuador. *European Public & Social Innovation Review, 10*, 1–18. DOI: 10.31637/epsir-2025-1588

Piot-Lepetit, I., & Tchakoute Tchuigoua, H. (2022). Ownership and performance of microfinance institutions in Latin America: A pseudo-panel malmquist index approach. *The Journal of the Operational Research Society, 73*(5), 1167–1180. DOI: 10.1080/01605682.2021.1895683

Rohmana, L., & Wulandari, P. (2025). The key determinants of digital repayment performance of ultra-micro entrepreneurs in Indonesia microfinance institution. *Journal of Entrepreneurship and Public Policy, 14*(2), 207–229. DOI: 10.1108/JEPP-04-2024-0050

Sarpong-Danquah, B., Adusei, M., & Magnus Frimpong, J. (2023). Effect of board gender diversity on the financial performance of microfinance institutions: Does judicial efficiency matter? *Annals of Public and Cooperative Economics*, *94*(2), 495–518. DOI: 10.1111/apce.12396

Shettima, U., & Dzolkarnaini, N. (2018). Board characteristics and microfinance institutions' performance: Panel data evidence from Nigeria. *Journal of Accounting in Emerging Economies*, *8*(3), 369–386.

Sierra, J., Muriel-Patino, V., & Rodríguez-López, F. (2024). A comprehensive framework for understanding microfinance performance evaluation methods. *Humanities & Social Sciences Communications*, *11*, 764.

Singh, K. (2024). Social performance, financial risk and financial performance in microfinance institutions. *International Journal of Bank Marketing*, *42*(4), 768–793. DOI: 10.1108/IJBM-01-2023-0005

Siti-Nabiha, A. K., & Siti-Nazariah, A. Z. (2011). Evaluating social performance: A case study of a microfinance institution in Malaysia. *International Journal of Management and Enterprise Development*, *10*(4), 271–290.

Thomas, J. R., & Kumar, J. (2016). Social performance and sustainability of Indian microfinance institutions: An interrogation. *Journal of Sustainable Finance & Investment*, *6*(1), 38–50.

Thrikawala, S., Locke, S., & Reddy, K. (2017). Dynamic endogeneity and corporate governance-performance relationship: Lessons from the microfinance sector. *Journal of Economic Studies (Glasgow, Scotland)*, *44*(5), 727–744.

Timbula, M. A., & Marvadi, C. (2023). Digital transformation: Acceptance and use of technology among microfinance institutions in developing country: An application of UTAUT2 model. *International Journal of Information Technology : an Official Journal of Bharati Vidyapeeth's Institute of Computer Applications and Management*, *15*(8), 4459–4468. DOI: 10.1007/s41870-023-01535-w

Ullah, S., Nobanee, H., Azim, F., & Khiati, M. (2025). Financial foundations for sustainability: How business sophistication, tax policy, and technology shape ESG in Belt and Road Initiative countries. *Global Sustainability*, *8*, e3. DOI: 10.1017/sus.2025.4

Vranovci, S. (2025). Exploring the relationship between client protection practices and sustainable performance in the microfinance sector: A study of Kosovo's microfinance institutions. *WSEAS Transactions on Business and Economics*, *22*, 574–583. DOI: 10.37394/23207.2025.22.51

Wirasedana, I. W. P., Sudarma, M., Andayani, W., & Mulawarman, A. D. (2024). The role of capital in microfinance financial performance and cultural sustainability. *Cogent Business & Management*, *11*(1), 2287770. DOI: 10.1080/23311975.2023.2287770

Zaby, S. (2019). Science mapping of the global knowledge base on microfinance: Influential authors and documents, 1989–2019. *Sustainability*, *11*(14), 1–21.

ADDITIONAL READING

Diab, C. A., & Stubbs, W. (2025). The sustainability of microfinance institutions: How do their financial, social, and environmental indicators align? *Corporate Social Responsibility and Environmental Management*, *32*(5), 1234–1249. DOI: 10.1002/csr.70035

Chapter 4
Integrating Sustainability with Financial Markets:
Risk, Return, and Responsibility

Ananya Pandey
https://orcid.org/0000-0002-2419-6314
Christ University, Bangalore, India

ABSTRACT

This chapter explores the burgeoning field of green finance and its crucial role in aligning financial markets with sustainable development objectives. It examines how incorporating environmental, social, and governance (ESG) factors influences traditional risk and return profiles, presenting both opportunities and challenges for investors and financial institutions. We delve into innovative financial instruments and strategies designed to mobilize capital towards environmentally sound and socially responsible projects. Furthermore, the chapter critically analyzes the evolving concept of fiduciary responsibility in the context of sustainability, arguing for a broader interpretation that encompasses long-term value creation and planetary well-being. By bridging the gap between financial imperatives and sustainability goals, this chapter underscores the transformative potential of integrating responsibility into the core of financial decision-making for a more resilient and equitable future.

INTRODUCTION

As sustainability increasingly informs investment and policy choices, the global financial system is experiencing a considerable change. Traditionally, the focus of financial markets was on profitability and efficiency, with a limited emphasis on risk and return. Nonetheless, the emergence of environmental crises like climate

DOI: 10.4018/979-8-3373-1240-8.ch004

change, biodiversity decline, and resource depletion—coupled with the rise of social inequities—has led to a heightened examination of capital allocation and the duties of financial actors (Sullivan & Mackenzie, 2021). Consequently, sustainability has become a key aspect of financial market analysis. Once regarded as a niche area, sustainable finance has become essential to mainstream investment strategies due to the convergence of stakeholder demand, regulatory requirements, and research demonstrating a connection between financial performance and environmental, social, and governance (ESG) factors (Friede, Busch, & Bassen, 2015).

The interrelated concepts of risk, return, and responsibility—the "three Rs"—are fundamental to this paradigm shift and are transforming how financial decisions are made today. Traditionally, the concepts of risk and return have served as the foundation of financial theory. According to Modern Portfolio Theory (Markowitz, 1952) and the Efficient Market Hypothesis (Fama, 1970), investors should strive to maximize returns for a given level of risk, based on the assumption that markets price assets efficiently and rationally. Nonetheless, the rise of systemic sustainability-related risks—like climate risk, regulatory transitions, social unrest, and reputational threats—has put these assumptions to the test. According to the Network for Greening the Financial System (NGFS) in 2022, these risks not only have an impact on investment outcomes but can also lead to widespread financial instability.

There is a growing trend to redefine the second dimension, return, in relation to long-term value creation and impact, rather than focusing on short-term financial gains. According to Clark, Feiner, and Viehs (2015), recent research has shown that portfolios aligned with ESG principles may yield better performance or exhibit greater resilience in times of market instability. Pension funds and sovereign wealth funds, among other institutional investors, are increasingly incorporating sustainability into their investment frameworks as they acknowledge that ESG factors can act as proxies for effective corporate governance, risk management, and innovation potential. Financial return is now assessed not only by profit margins or share prices, but also by a company's ability to maintain economic performance while tackling societal challenges.

The third pillar, responsibility, embodies the increasing agreement that financial institutions should take a proactive role in reaching wider sustainability objectives. There is a growing expectation for investors to fulfill their fiduciary duty not only by maximizing returns but also by acting in the long-term interests of beneficiaries and society as a whole (Richardson, 2009). This encompasses supporting corporate transparency, endorsing sustainable business practices, and aiding in global initiatives like the United Nations Sustainable Development Goals (SDGs). This shift toward responsible investment behavior is highlighted by the rise of impact investing, ESG integration, and stewardship practices. In this context, responsibility transcends ethical considerations; it is emerging as a fundamental aspect of financial prudence and market resilience.

This chapter seeks to examine how these three foundational concepts—risk, return, and responsibility intersect when sustainability is integrated into financial markets. It starts with establishing a theoretical framework for sustainable finance and examining the ways in which ESG considerations are transforming conventional financial metrics. Subsequently, it examines the characteristics of sustainability-related risks, such as the physical and transitional risks linked to climate change, and explores how these risks are valued and revealed in financial markets. Subsequently, the chapter investigates the empirical connection between sustainability and financial returns, utilizing global case studies and performance analyses. Then, the conversation shifts to the changing understanding of fiduciary duty and the emergence of responsible investing practices in institutional, corporate, and retail contexts. Also examined are regulatory developments, market innovations, and how technology can advance sustainable finance. Finally, the chapter evaluates challenges like greenwashing, data inconsistency, and ethical dilemmas, before proposing future directions for a resilient and equitable financial system. This chapter enhances the understanding of how financial markets can act as catalysts for systemic change by framing sustainability in terms of risk, return, and responsibility. This highlights the need to ensure that capital flows are in accordance with long-term ecological and societal well-being, reinforcing the idea that responsible financial guidance can be a powerful tool for sustainable development.

THEORETICAL FRAMEWORK

Integrating sustainability into financial markets challenges the core theories of finance, necessitating a reassessment of conventional paradigms like the Modern Portfolio Theory (MPT) and the Efficient Market Hypothesis (EMH). Markowitz (1952) introduced MPT, which asserts that investors can build an optimal portfolio that maximizes returns for a given level of risk through diversification. This framework focuses mainly on financial returns and systemic risk, with scant consideration given to extra-financial factors like environmental degradation or social inequality. In a similar vein, the EMH proposed by Fama (1970) indicates that financial markets incorporate all available information completely, which renders it infeasible to achieve returns above the market on a consistent basis.The emergence of sustainable finance has demonstrated that ESG (Environmental, Social, and Governance) information is frequently undervalued or excluded from conventional risk-return assessments, thereby calling into question the assumption of market efficiency.

A paradigm shift has occurred over the last 20 years, acknowledging that sustainability issues can have financial materiality. ESG factors, which were once regarded as non-financial or values-based, are now seen as pertinent to long-term financial performance (Friede, Busch, & Bassen, 2015). Environmental issues like climate change and resource scarcity represent considerable physical and transition risks that have a tangible effect on firm value and asset pricing (TCFD, 2017). Reputation, consumer behavior, and employee retention are influenced by social factors such as labor practices, diversity, and community relations. Governance structures have an impact on transparency, accountability, and decision-making. ESG offers a multidimensional framework that combines traditional financial analysis with sustainability indicators, providing a more comprehensive view of investment risk and opportunity (Sullivan & Mackenzie, 2017). A burgeoning collection of empirical studies indicates that firms demonstrating robust ESG performance frequently show reduced volatility and enhanced long-term returns, though outcomes may differ by region and sector (Clark, Feiner, & Viehs, 2015).

This theoretical transformation is also connected to the ongoing debate between shareholder primacy and stakeholder capitalism. Milton Friedman (1970) advocated for the shareholder model, which is based on neoclassical economics. This model posits that a corporation's main duty is to enhance the value of its shareholders. Broader societal and environmental considerations have historically been marginalized due to this narrow focus on profit maximization. Conversely, the stakeholder model asserts that companies have responsibilities beyond just their shareholders; they must also consider a wider range of constituents, such as employees, customers, suppliers, communities, and the environment (Freeman, 1984). In an economy characterized by globalization and a focus on sustainability, this viewpoint is becoming more pertinent, as corporate actions can have systemic consequences that extend beyond the immediate financial outcomes of the firm.

Changes at the institutional level further emphasize this transition. The Business Roundtable, a major association of U.S. CEOs, redefined the purpose of a corporation in 2019 to promote “an economy that serves all Americans,” placing emphasis on stakeholder interests as well as shareholder returns (Business Roundtable, 2019). This redefinition indicates an increasing awareness among business leaders that creating long-term value is connected to environmental stewardship, social well-being, and ethical governance. In the same vein, investors are adjusting their strategies to be in accordance with stakeholder capitalism. Asset managers like BlackRock have committed to making sustainability a fundamental investment principle, contending that climate risk equates to investment risk (Fink, 2020).

Nevertheless, there are conceptual and practical challenges to incorporating ESG into mainstream finance. According to critics, the absence of standardization and comparability in ESG metrics makes it difficult to evaluate materiality and performance (Boffo & Patalano, 2020). In addition, there are differing opinions on whether ESG integration functions as a means for reducing risk, ethical investment, or real impact. The existence of these ambiguities highlights the necessity of establishing a strong theoretical framework that takes into account the intricacies of sustainable finance while still upholding the fundamental focus on rigor and evidence that characterizes the discipline.

UNDERSTANDING RISK IN SUSTAINABLE FINANCE

To incorporate sustainability into financial decision-making, a fundamental change in the conceptualization, measurement, and management of risk has become necessary. Conventional financial risk metrics—focused on market, credit, liquidity, and operational risks—are becoming increasingly inadequate for capturing the full range of risks linked to environmental, social, and governance (ESG) factors. Sustainability-linked risk metrics have notably emerged to address long-term, systemic, and non-linear threats posed by climate change and other ESG-related challenges (Schoenmaker & Schramade, 2019). Regulatory, reputational, and market pressures are driving the internalization of these risks—often externalized in conventional models—compelling firms and investors to readjust their risk assessment models. Financial risks stemming from climate change are among the most pressing and significant issues on the sustainable finance agenda. They are usually divided into two categories: physical risks and transition risks. Physical risks pertain to the economic expenses and financial damages resulting from severe weather phenomena (like hurricanes, wildfires, and floods) and long-term changes like sea-level rise or modified precipitation patterns (Bolton et al., 2020). These risks can inflict direct harm on assets, disturb supply chains, and lower property values, which in turn affects creditworthiness and asset valuation. On the other hand, transition risks stem from the changes in policy and economics that come with working toward a low-carbon economy. Included are the revaluation of assets with high carbon intensity, the establishment of carbon pricing, tighter environmental regulations, and technological disruptions. With the decarbonization of the global economy, assets and industries that do not align with climate objectives may become stranded, resulting in substantial write-downs (Caldecott et al., 2016). Financial institutions that have exposures to sectors with high emissions must incorporate these transition dynamics into their portfolio strategies.

In addition to climate risks, reputational, regulatory, and litigation risks are becoming increasingly significant in the realm of sustainable finance. A company's ESG practices (or the absence of such practices) can create reputational risk when they do not align with stakeholder expectations. This misalignment can result in consumer backlash, investor divestment, or increased scrutiny from activists. For example, firms identified as being involved in activities that harm the environment or violate human rights may incur market penalties that traditional risk metrics do not immediately capture (Eccles, Ioannou, & Serafeim, 2014). As governments globally implement new disclosure requirements, green taxonomies, and due diligence laws, regulatory risk is also escalating. Regulatory advancements such as the European Union's Sustainable Finance Disclosure Regulation (SFDR) and the proposed climate disclosure rule by the U.S. Securities and Exchange Commission (SEC) exemplify the requirement for a more rigorous integration of ESG factors (EU, 2020; SEC, 2022). Not adhering to these regulations can lead to fines, but it may also diminish investor confidence and access to capital. Another growing worry is litigation risk, particularly for companies that misrepresent their ESG credentials or do not foresee legal liabilities associated with climate-related damages. The rise of climate lawsuits and shareholder activism highlights the growing legal risks that companies encounter in the era of sustainability (Setzer & Higham, 2022). In order to handle these complex risks, companies and investors are adopting standardized risk disclosure frameworks that improve transparency and comparability. One of the most impactful is the Task Force on Climate-related Financial Disclosures (TCFD), which offers guidance on how organizations can disclose climate-related risks and opportunities across governance, strategy, risk management, and metrics and targets (TCFD, 2017). Disclosures aligned with TCFD have become widely adopted across the globe, and several regions, such as the United Kingdom, New Zealand, and Japan, are taking steps to require them by law. To assist in long-term strategic planning, the framework promotes scenario analyses by firms to evaluate their resilience across various climate pathways.

Likewise, the Sustainability Accounting Standards Board (SASB) provides disclosure standards tailored to specific industries that pinpoint financially material ESG issues for investors. The metrics provided by SASB enable a more detailed and decision-useful evaluation of risk, especially when incorporated into corporate reporting and investment analysis (SASB, 2021). It is essential for the establishment of a consistent worldwide standard for sustainability disclosure that these frameworks work together with others, including the Global Reporting Initiative (GRI) and the International Sustainability Standards Board (ISSB). In spite of these advancements, multiple challenges persist. The lack of uniformity and fragmentation of ESG data across jurisdictions impede the reliability and comparability of sustainability-linked risk metrics. Furthermore, there are many uncertainties associated with forward-looking evaluations like scenario analyses, especially when it comes to the speed and extent of climate policy execution or technological advancement. Therefore, to incorporate sustainability into risk management, financial organizations need to improve their data practices and undergo cultural and institutional changes. It is essential that chief risk officers, asset managers, and board directors possess the necessary skills and resources to weave ESG considerations into fundamental decision-making procedures. With the alignment of financial materiality and societal impact, the distinctions separating return, responsibility, and risk have become indistinct. This has bolstered the idea that sustainability is fundamental to long-term value creation and financial stability, rather than being an ancillary concern (UNEP FI, 2021).

RETURN ON SUSTAINABLE INVESTMENT

In both academia and the professional world, discussions have intensified over whether sustainable investments provide financial returns that are competitive with or superior to those of traditional investments. There is a growing body of evidence backing the perspective that investments incorporating Environmental, Social, and Governance (ESG) factors can rival or even exceed the performance of traditional portfolios, especially in the long run. In a thorough meta-analysis conducted by Friede, Busch, and Bassen (2015), which evaluated more than 2,000 empirical studies, it was discovered that most of these studies reported a positive correlation between ESG factors and corporate financial performance. Likewise, recent research has bolstered the idea that sustainable investments provide resilience during periods of market volatility. As an example, during the COVID-19 crisis, ESG-oriented funds showed a reduced downside risk and greater recovery capacity compared to non-ESG funds (Broadstock et al., 2021; Albuquerque et al., 2020). These results call into question the conventional belief that socially responsible investing necessitates sacrificing financial returns.

These results hinge on the notion of financial materiality, which highlights the significance of ESG factors in influencing financial performance. It has been demonstrated that a company's operational efficiency and risk profile can be considerably affected by material ESG issues like carbon emissions, labor practices, and board diversity (Khan, Serafeim, & Yoon, 2016). Financial materiality aids investors in differentiating between "noise" and sustainability metrics that truly pertain to value. . Companies that excel in material ESG aspects often gain advantages such as a bolstered reputation, increased stakeholder trust, and diminished regulatory and litigation risks—factors that can lead to better returns (Giese et al., 2019). This connection has resulted in a greater incorporation of ESG data by mainstream investors, as evidenced by institutions such as BlackRock and Vanguard adopting ESG criteria for reasons beyond ethics, aiming instead to optimize risk-adjusted performance.

Financial instruments like green bonds, sustainability-linked loans, and ESG Exchange-Traded Funds (ETFs) serve as case studies that further illustrate the financial appeal of sustainability-oriented investments. Green bonds, designated for financing projects that benefit the environment, have experienced rapid growth and are linked to lower yields because of their reduced risk profile and high demand from investors (Ehlers & Packer, 2017). As an illustration, the World Bank and the European Investment Bank have both launched green bonds that offer competitive prices while funding projects related to renewable energy and energy efficiency. Sustainability-linked loans connect interest rates to the borrower's sustainability performance, providing incentives for corporate responsibility and financial advantages like lower borrowing costs (Principles for Responsible Investment, 2020). ESG ETFs, like the iShares MSCI USA ESG Select ETF, have seen strong inflows, especially from millennial and institutional investors looking to align with sustainability values while maintaining returns (Morningstar, 2021). These financial instruments demonstrate the increasing demand for offerings that merge fiscal results with environmental and social consequences.

When assessing sustainable investments, it is also crucial to weigh the trade-off between short-term profits and long-term value generation. Historically, traditional financial markets have placed greater importance on quarterly earnings and short-term performance metrics, often compromising long-term sustainability in the process. Nevertheless, ESG investing alters this paradigm by fostering long-term thinking, stewardship, and the preservation of value. According to Eccles and Klimenko (2019), a long-term orientation can foster innovation, enhance operational efficiency, and strengthen stakeholder relationships, all of which contribute to a sustainable competitive advantage. According to Clark, Feiner, and Viehs (2015), companies that engage in strong sustainability practices typically show lower capital costs and a decreased exposure to systemic risks. These factors tend to accumulate positively over time. In addition, investors with long-term perspectives, including pension funds and sovereign wealth funds, are increasingly adopting ESG integration as a means of ensuring their portfolios are prepared for the future. Nevertheless, difficulties persist in precisely measuring the returns on sustainable investments. Investor judgment can be clouded and performance benchmarking hindered by inconsistencies in ESG data, the absence of standardized reporting frameworks, and greenwashing concerns. Even with these limitations, the main trend indicates a convergence of financial and sustainability goals. With the maturation of ESG frameworks and the evolution of data analytics, the connection between responsible investment and risk-adjusted returns is becoming more apparent.

RESPONSIBILITY AND FIDUCIARY DUTY

The interpretation of fiduciary duty has been significantly reshaped by the evolving landscape of financial markets, especially in relation to environmental and social risks. Fiduciary responsibility, which has its roots in the tradition of maximizing shareholder returns, is being examined anew as global markets contend with the long-term risks and opportunities associated with sustainability. The fiduciary duty of asset managers and institutional investors now goes beyond traditional financial performance metrics to include considerations of environmental, social, and governance (ESG) factors. This development is supported by the increasing agreement that ESG risks have financial significance and that ignoring them can lead to a violation of fiduciary duty by not acting in beneficiaries' long-term interests (Sullivan et al., 2015; UNEP FI, 2019). Consequently, courts and regulatory bodies across various jurisdictions—including the European Union, the United States, and Australia—have gradually affirmed the perspective that incorporating sustainability considerations into investment analysis is not just allowable but is mandatory in certain instances (Freshfields Bruckhaus Deringer, 2005; PRI, 2020). Responsible investing signifies a shift in paradigm from strategies that seek short-term profits to investment approaches aimed at generating financial returns alongside positive societal impact. It is usually divided into three interconnected strategies: socially responsible investing (SRI), ESG integration, and impact investing. Investing with social responsibility in mind usually entails using ethical filters—like avoiding investments in tobacco, arms, or fossil fuels—derived from moral or societal values (Renneboog, Ter Horst, & Zhang, 2008). Although it is frequently criticized for being subjective or exclusionary, SRI has established a foundation for more comprehensive strategies.

ESG integration, which is currently the leading approach to responsible investing, involves systematically incorporating ESG factors into financial analysis and investment decisions to mitigate risk and identify opportunities (Friede, Busch, & Bassen, 2015). ESG integration, in contrast to SRI, does not automatically rule out investments; it evaluates the potential impact of ESG issues on a company's performance and resilience. Impact investing, the latest evolution in responsible investment, aims to produce quantifiable social and environmental benefits in addition to financial profits. Impact investing, prevalent in private equity and venture capital, has played a vital role in financing innovations in clean energy, sustainable agriculture, and social entrepreneurship (Jackson & Harji, 2012). Institutional investors, including pension funds, insurance companies, and sovereign wealth funds, are crucial in directing global capital toward sustainability. Institutional investors are in a unique position to affect corporate behavior and market norms because of their size, long-term investment horizons, and fiduciary responsibilities to a wide range of beneficiaries. In recent years, major institutional investors have publicly endorsed

ESG principles, frequently citing their compatibility with long-term value creation and risk management (BlackRock, 2020). As an example, pension funds in nations such as the Netherlands, Sweden, and Canada have established strong ESG frameworks and work actively with portfolio companies to enhance sustainability practices. Shareholder engagement and proxy voting have become essential mechanisms for institutional investors to influence companies to improve transparency, lower carbon emissions, and tackle social issues like labor rights and diversity (Dimson, Karakaş, & Li, 2015). In addition, the rise of collaborative investor initiatives like Climate Action 100+, the UN-backed Principles for Responsible Investment (PRI), and the Net-Zero Asset Owner Alliance illustrates how collective action can enhance the impact of institutional investors and transform corporate accountability. Asset managers, who serve as go-betweens for capital providers and investee companies, play a key role in putting ESG strategies into action within portfolios. There is a growing interpretation of the fiduciary duty of asset managers to encompass the identification and mitigation of sustainability-related risks, especially those associated with climate change. Regulatory frameworks like the EU Sustainable Finance Disclosure Regulation (SFDR) and the proposed ESG disclosure rules from the U.S. Securities and Exchange Commission have solidified expectations for ESG consideration in asset management (European Commission, 2021; SEC, 2022). Moreover, major asset management companies have initiated ESG-themed funds, created their own ESG rating models, and pledged to incorporate sustainability into their investment research and stewardship practices. However, the credibility of these commitments relies on transparency, accountability, and alignment with real-world outcomes—a point emphasized by increasing concerns about greenwashing and inconsistent ESG methodologies (OECD, 2020).

REGULATORY AND POLICY LANDSCAPE

There has been a growing recognition within global regulations and policies of the necessity to incorporate sustainability into financial markets. Major developments in various jurisdictions indicate a transition from voluntary ESG considerations to frameworks that mandate disclosure and compliance. The Sustainable Finance Disclosure Regulation (SFDR) is a key initiative in the European Union. Since March 2021, the SFDR has mandated that asset managers, financial advisers, and institutional investors disclose their integration of sustainability risks into investment decisions, including any potential adverse impacts (European Commission, 2021). The SFDR is in line with the EU's wider Green Taxonomy, which classifies economic activities that are environmentally sustainable to help steer investment towards genuinely green assets and combat greenwashing (European Commission,

2020). This taxonomy, supported by science-based technical screening criteria, is key to aligning investment flows with the EU's climate neutrality objectives outlined in the European Green Deal.

In the U.S., there has been an increase in regulatory momentum, but this occurs within a more fragmented political landscape. The Securities and Exchange Commission (SEC) has put forth proposed ESG disclosure regulations that require publicly traded companies to report on climate-related risks, including greenhouse gas emissions, climate governance structures, and scenario analyses (SEC, 2022). This method aims to bolster transparency and shield investors from significant sustainability risks. These regulatory initiatives demonstrate a growing agreement among financial regulators that climate change presents systemic risks to the stability of financial markets. As an example, central banks and financial supervisory authorities—under the auspices of the Network for Greening the Financial System (NGFS)—have come together to acknowledge the necessity of incorporating climate-related financial risk evaluations into prudential regulation, stress testing, and monetary policy frameworks (NGFS, 2021). Institutions like the Bank of England and the European Central Bank have begun to integrate climate risk into their supervisory expectations and macroprudential policy mandates.

Moreover, authorities are utilizing inducements and obligations to integrate responsible investment practices into the mainstream. Mechanisms like tax incentives for green bonds, sustainability-linked loans, and concessional financing for climate-resilient infrastructure are becoming more prevalent. Mandatory ESG disclosure obligations for pension funds and institutional investors, like those in the UK and Australia, aim to integrate sustainability considerations into fiduciary duty. Stewardship codes that mandate asset managers to engage proactively with investee companies on ESG issues complement these developments. The legal repercussions of overlooking sustainability considerations are increasingly coming to the fore. Various jurisdictions' courts have started to examine whether corporate directors and fiduciaries are meeting their obligations by managing and disclosing ESG risks appropriately. It is worth mentioning that there is a global increase in climate litigation targeting companies and financial institutions, with many cases based on allegations of breach of fiduciary duty, misrepresentation, or failure to consider foreseeable risks (Setzer & Higham, 2022). Legal doctrines are changing to recognize climate risk as a significant factor that should be integrated into investment strategies and corporate governance. Consequently, neglecting to consider sustainability may put entities at risk of both reputational harm and considerable legal liability.

MARKET TRENDS AND INNOVATION

The crossroad of sustainability and financial innovation has sparked a wave of transformative trends in global capital markets. A major development is the emergence of green fintech, which uses digital technologies to advance environmental sustainability in financial offerings. These platforms incorporate sustainability metrics into investment choices, facilitate real-time carbon tracking, and offer consumers and investors clear ESG (Environmental, Social, and Governance) data. For instance, applications like Cooler Future and services like OpenInvest enable investors to tailor their portfolios to climate objectives with customizable ESG filters (Schmitt, 2021). Digital ESG analytics—driven by natural language processing and machine learning—have further improved investors' capability to evaluate non-financial risks and opportunities within complex data sources. These tools are instrumental in bridging the ESG information gap that has historically hindered responsible investing, owing to inconsistent disclosure standards and fragmented data sets (Leitner et al., 2023).

Another important development is the increasing sophistication of carbon markets, which enable the pricing of carbon emissions and motivate companies to lower their carbon footprint. With the expansion of carbon pricing mechanisms, financial products like climate-aligned indices—including the S&P Paris-Aligned Climate Index—are becoming increasingly popular among institutional investors aiming to decarbonize their portfolios (OECD, 2022). These indices favor companies that show credible transition strategies while excluding those that do not align with the goals of the Paris Agreement. At the same time, transition finance has arisen as an essential addition to green finance by aiding carbon-intensive industries—such as steel and aviation—in cutting emissions via technological enhancements and innovation (Climate Bonds Initiative, 2021). Transition finance aims to provide structured support that allows these sectors to fulfill net-zero commitments, rather than completely withdrawing investment from them.

There is also a fast-growing role for big data and artificial intelligence (AI) in sustainable investing. Platforms for ESG analytics powered by AI can analyze enormous amounts of unstructured data—from news articles to satellite images—to reveal concealed environmental threats and governance concerns (Berg et al., 2022). These technologies assist in reducing greenwashing by confirming sustainability claims and providing predictive insights into companies' ESG trajectories. As an example, AI can identify early signs of deforestation, water stress, or labor violations that may not be immediately apparent in formal disclosures. Moreover, the use of machine learning models for creating dynamic ESG scores and simulating future climate scenarios is on the rise, which improves the accuracy of sustainability-aligned risk assessments (Kotsantonis & Serafeim, 2019).

Additionally, private equity (PE) and venture capital (VC) are disproportionately influential in the scaling of sustainable innovations. Private equity firms are progressively incorporating ESG factors into their due diligence processes and portfolio management strategies. This move serves the dual purpose of reducing risks and facilitating long-term value generation through improvements in operational efficiency and brand enhancement (McKinsey & Company, 2022). In the venture capital realm, investments are increasingly directed toward climate tech startups that concentrate on renewable energy, sustainable agriculture, circular economy solutions, and carbon capture technologies. It is noteworthy that in 2022, global venture capital investment in climate tech surpassed $70 billion, with an increasing portion allocated to "deep decarbonization" technologies (PwC, 2023). These developments signify a change in the mindset of investors—from being risk-averse to being impact-oriented—mirroring a broader redefinition of financial performance that encompasses environmental and social value.

CHALLENGES AND LIMITATIONS

Despite the growing momentum toward integrating sustainability into financial markets, several critical challenges and criticisms persist that impede the effective and credible implementation of sustainable finance principles. One of the most pervasive issues is greenwashing, which refers to the practice of misrepresenting or exaggerating the environmental benefits of financial products or corporate behavior. In an environment where sustainability credentials are increasingly tied to financial inflows and market value, companies and asset managers may label activities as "green" or "ESG-compliant" without substantive verification or alignment with actual environmental or social impact (Delmas & Burbano, 2011). This lack of standardization across ESG (Environmental, Social, and Governance) definitions and reporting frameworks further compounds the issue, as inconsistent methodologies and criteria across jurisdictions and institutions make it difficult to compare or verify claims (Berg et al., 2022). The absence of a universally accepted ESG taxonomy creates ambiguity in determining what qualifies as sustainable, leading to market inefficiencies and erosion of investor trust.

Another significant problem lies in the divergence of ESG ratings provided by different agencies. Unlike credit ratings, which tend to converge due to standardized models, ESG scores often vary widely for the same company depending on the provider, due to differences in data inputs, weighting schemes, and methodological transparency (Berg, Kölbel, & Rigobon, 2022). This inconsistency undermines investor confidence and introduces data quality issues, particularly as ESG data remains largely self-reported, unaudited, and fragmented (Eccles, Klimenko, &

Stroehle, 2020). While third-party ESG data providers have proliferated in recent years, the market remains unregulated in many jurisdictions, and there is no consensus on how to reconcile conflicting assessments. This situation not only leads to confusion among stakeholders but also creates potential legal risks as investors act based on potentially misleading or unverifiable ESG ratings.

Furthermore, the challenge of measuring impact remains central to the critique of sustainable investing. While financial performance metrics are relatively straightforward, quantifying environmental and social outcomes is significantly more complex. ESG assessments often rely on proxies or broad indicators that fail to capture the nuanced and long-term impact of investments (Kotsantonis & Serafeim, 2019). The integration of both quantitative and qualitative dimensions in impact measurement presents methodological dilemmas, especially when trying to attribute causality between investments and sustainability outcomes. This raises concerns about the actual effectiveness of ESG investing in driving real-world change, rather than simply aligning portfolios with abstract principles.

In addition to technical issues, ethical dilemmas and unintended consequences pose important critiques of sustainability integration. For instance, divesting from carbon-intensive industries may reduce portfolio emissions on paper but does little to transition those industries toward sustainable practices, possibly exacerbating inequalities or shifting environmental harm elsewhere (Heinkel, Kraus, & Zechner, 2001). Similarly, ESG filters may inadvertently exclude companies in developing countries that lack robust disclosure infrastructure but are critical to achieving global sustainability goals. These dilemmas highlight a potential disconnect between ESG-driven investment strategies and broader systemic change. Furthermore, ethical tensions arise when investors prioritize short-term ESG compliance over long-term societal benefit, leading to questions about whose interests are being served under the guise of responsible investing.

Addressing these challenges requires a multi-pronged approach, including regulatory harmonization, improved ESG data governance, enhanced disclosure standards, and the development of robust impact measurement frameworks. Without these, the credibility of sustainable finance risks being undermined by superficial commitments and misaligned incentives. As sustainable investing continues to shape capital markets, the resolution of these issues will be critical to ensuring that financial flows genuinely contribute to environmental and social transformation rather than simply serving as a marketing tool.

CALL FOR ACTION

As financial markets face growing pressure to address global sustainability challenges, the path forward requires a systemic shift rooted in education, governance, collaboration, and innovation. Integrating sustainability into financial education and corporate governance is foundational to this transformation. Financial education must evolve to equip future professionals with the skills to assess environmental, social, and governance (ESG) risks and opportunities alongside traditional financial metrics. Academic institutions and professional training bodies are increasingly embedding ESG principles into their curricula, recognizing that sustainable finance is no longer a niche but a necessity (Sullivan et al., 2020). This educational shift not only enhances investor literacy but also promotes long-term thinking among asset managers, regulators, and policymakers. Simultaneously, corporate governance structures must adapt to prioritize sustainability in strategic decision-making. Boards of directors are increasingly being held accountable for ESG outcomes, with regulatory regimes in jurisdictions such as the European Union mandating sustainability disclosures and risk assessments under frameworks like the Corporate Sustainability Reporting Directive (European Commission, 2023). Enhanced governance practices that integrate ESG considerations into performance evaluations, risk management, and executive compensation structures are crucial to aligning corporate behavior with global sustainability goals.

Furthermore, public-private partnerships (PPPs) and multilateral development banks (MDBs) play a pivotal role in financing the transition toward sustainable economies. PPPs enable the mobilization of private capital for public goods by de-risking investments through government-backed guarantees, subsidies, and blended finance instruments (World Bank, 2022). These collaborations are essential in sectors with high capital requirements and sustainability impact, such as renewable energy, climate-resilient infrastructure, and sustainable agriculture. MDBs like the World Bank, Asian Development Bank, and the African Development Bank are leveraging their financial capacity and convening power to scale up climate finance, set environmental safeguards, and facilitate knowledge sharing across borders (OECD, 2021). Their role in setting standards and building institutional capacity in developing countries further contributes to inclusive and resilient financial ecosystems.

A sustainable financial future also necessitates a systemic reorientation of financial markets to internalize social and environmental externalities. This entails redefining the purpose of capital markets—from maximizing short-term returns to fostering inclusive, green, and resilient growth. Technological innovations such as green fintech, ESG data analytics, and blockchain for sustainable supply chains can enhance transparency and accountability (Ghosh et al., 2023). Regulatory reforms, including mandatory climate risk disclosures and taxonomies for sustainable economic activities, will provide the infrastructure needed for informed decision-making and the prevention of greenwashing. At the macro level, central banks and financial regulators are incorporating climate-related financial risks into their supervisory frameworks, recognizing the systemic implications of climate change for financial stability (NGFS, 2022). A collective vision, supported by cohesive action from governments, financial institutions, academia, and civil society, is imperative to ensure that financial systems serve both economic and planetary health.

Ultimately, achieving a sustainable financial future depends not only on new tools and policies but on a paradigm shift in values and incentives. The convergence of risk, return, and responsibility offers a compelling framework for embedding sustainability at the core of financial systems. By fostering a culture of stewardship and accountability, the financial sector can become a driving force in the global pursuit of the Sustainable Development Goals and the long-term wellbeing of society.

CONCLUSION

The integration of sustainability into financial markets reflects a transformative shift in how we perceive the relationship between capital, ethics, and long-term value. This chapter has unpacked the dynamic interplay of risk, return, and responsibility—three pillars that increasingly define modern investment and financial decision-making. Key insights reveal that sustainable finance is not merely a moral or ideological stance, but a pragmatic response to material environmental, social, and governance (ESG) factors that impact financial performance and systemic stability. Risk is no longer confined to volatility or default probabilities; it now encompasses climate-related disruptions, regulatory changes, social unrest, and reputational exposures. Returns, traditionally measured in monetary terms, are being reconceptualized to include long-term resilience, stakeholder value, and alignment with the global sustainability agenda. Responsibility, once peripheral to fiduciary duty, is now emerging as a core expectation for institutional investors, asset managers, and corporations, driving transparency, accountability, and impact-driven strategies.

The interconnectedness of risk, return, and responsibility signals a paradigm shift. Ignoring ESG risks can lead to underestimated liabilities and missed opportunities, while integrating sustainability into investment analysis can enhance returns through better risk-adjusted outcomes and long-term resilience. Moreover, responsibility serves as a unifying principle that compels financial actors to consider the broader consequences of their decisions on society and the planet. This triadic framework emphasizes that financial markets are not isolated from the real economy or the natural environment—they are embedded within them and thus must evolve accordingly.

This chapter calls upon scholars to advance interdisciplinary research that bridges finance, law, ethics, and environmental science to refine sustainable finance models. Practitioners must move beyond ESG as a compliance exercise and toward genuine integration that influences capital allocation and corporate behavior. Policymakers are urged to create robust regulatory frameworks that ensure comparability, enforce accountability, and incentivize responsible innovation. As climate risks intensify and global inequalities deepen, the need for a sustainable financial system becomes not only urgent but indispensable. The future of finance lies in its capacity to manage risk prudently, generate value responsibly, and contribute meaningfully to a just and sustainable world.

REFERENCES

Albuquerque, R., Koskinen, Y., Yang, S., & Zhang, C. (2020). Resiliency of environmental and social stocks: An analysis of the exogenous COVID-19 market crash. *The Review of Corporate Finance Studies*, *9*(3), 593–621. DOI: 10.1093/rcfs/cfaa009 PMID: 40504189

Berg, F., Koelbel, J. F., & Rigobon, R. (2022). Aggregate confusion: The divergence of ESG ratings. *Review of Finance*, *26*(6), 1315–1344. DOI: 10.1093/rof/rfac033

BlackRock. (2020). *Sustainability as BlackRock's new standard for investing*. https://www.blackrock.com/corporate/investor-relations/blackrock-client-letter

Boffo, R., & Patalano, R. (2020). *ESG investing: Practices, progress and challenges*. OECD., DOI: 10.1787/67cbbb88-

Bolton, P., Després, M., Pereira da Silva, L. A., Samama, F., & Svartzman, R. (2020). *The green swan: Central banking and financial stability in the age of climate change*. Bank for International Settlements.

Broadstock, D. C., Chan, K., Cheng, L. T. W., & Wang, X. (2021). The role of ESG performance during times of financial crisis: Evidence from COVID-19 in China. *Finance Research Letters*, *38*, 101716. DOI: 10.1016/j.frl.2020.101716 PMID: 32837385

Business Roundtable. (2019). *Statement on the purpose of a corporation*. https://opportunity.businessroundtable.org/ourcommitment/

Caldecott, B., Howarth, N., & McSharry, P. (2016). *Stranded assets in agriculture: Protecting value from environment-related risks*. Smith School of Enterprise and the Environment, University of Oxford.

Clark, G. L., Feiner, A., & Viehs, M. (2015). From the stockholder to the stakeholder: How sustainability can drive financial outperformance. University of Oxford and Arabesque Partners. https://arabesque.com/research/

Climate Bonds Initiative. (2021). *Financing credible transitions: A guide to supporting companies in transition*. https://www.climatebonds.net/resources/reports

Delmas, M. A., & Burbano, V. C. (2011). The drivers of greenwashing. *California Management Review*, *54*(1), 64–87. DOI: 10.1525/cmr.2011.54.1.64

Dimson, E., Karakaş, O., & Li, X. (2015). Active ownership. *Review of Financial Studies*, *28*(12), 3225–3268. DOI: 10.1093/rfs/hhv044

Eccles, R. G., Ioannou, I., & Serafeim, G. (2014). The impact of a corporate culture of sustainability on corporate behavior and performance. *Harvard Business School Working Paper*, 12-035.

Eccles, R. G., & Klimenko, S. (2019). The investor revolution. *Harvard Business Review*, *97*(3), 106–116.

Ehlers, T., & Packer, F. (2017). Green bond finance and certification. *BIS Quarterly Review*, (September), 89–104.

European Commission. (2020). *EU taxonomy for sustainable activities*. https://finance.ec.europa.eu/sustainable-finance/tools-and-standards/eu-taxonomy-sustainable-activities_en

European Commission. (2021). *Sustainable Finance Disclosure Regulation (SFDR)*. https://finance.ec.europa.eu/sustainable-finance/disclosure-and-reporting/sfdr_en

European Commission. (2021). *Sustainable finance: Commission welcomes the adoption of the European Green Bond Standard*. https://ec.europa.eu/info/publications/210507-sustainable-finance-communication_en

European Union. (2020). *Regulation (EU) 2019/2088 on sustainability-related disclosures in the financial services sector (SFDR)*.

Fama, E. F. (1970). Efficient capital markets: A review of theory and empirical work. *The Journal of Finance*, *25*(2), 383–417. DOI: 10.2307/2325486

Fink, L. (2020). *A fundamental reshaping of finance*. BlackRock. https://www.blackrock.com/corporate/investor-relations/larry-fink-ceo-letter

Freeman, R. E. (1984). *Strategic management: A stakeholder approach*. Pitman.

Freshfields Bruckhaus Deringer. (2005). *A legal framework for the integration of environmental, social and governance issues into institutional investment*. UNEP FI.

Friede, G., Busch, T., & Bassen, A. (2015). ESG and financial performance: Aggregated evidence from more than 2000 empirical studies. *Journal of Sustainable Finance & Investment*, *5*(4), 210–233. DOI: 10.1080/20430795.2015.1118917

Friedman, M. (1970, September 13). The social responsibility of business is to increase its profits. *The New York Times Magazine*.

Ghosh, S., Dey, S., & Kumar, S. (2023). Fintech for sustainability: Transformative potential of digital innovation in green finance. *Journal of Sustainable Finance & Investment*, *13*(1), 45–63. DOI: 10.1080/20430795.2022.2107093

Giese, G., Lee, L. E., Melas, D., Nagy, Z., & Nishikawa, L. (2019). Foundations of ESG investing: How ESG affects equity valuation, risk, and performance. *Journal of Portfolio Management*, *45*(5), 69–83.

Heinkel, R., Kraus, A., & Zechner, J. (2001). The effect of green investment on corporate behavior. *Journal of Financial and Quantitative Analysis, 36*(4), 431–449. DOI: 10.2307/2676219

Jackson, E. T., & Harji, K. (2012). *Accelerating impact: Achievements, challenges and what's next in building the impact investing industry*. Rockefeller Foundation.

Khan, M., Serafeim, G., & Yoon, A. (2016). Corporate sustainability: First evidence on materiality. *The Accounting Review, 91*(6), 1697–1724. DOI: 10.2308/accr-51383

Kotsantonis, S., & Serafeim, G. (2019). Four things no one will tell you about ESG data. *Journal of Applied Corporate Finance, 31*(2), 50–58. DOI: 10.1111/jacf.12346

Leitner, J., Reichelstein, S., & Zadek, S. (2023). ESG analytics and the future of sustainable investing. *Finance Research Letters, 54*, 103711. DOI: 10.1016/j.frl.2023.103711

Markowitz, H. (1952). Portfolio selection. *The Journal of Finance*, *7*(1), 77–91. DOI: 10.2307/2975974

McKinsey & Company. (2022). *Creating value with ESG in private equity*. https://www.mckinsey.com/business-functions/sustainability/our-insights/creating-value-with-esg-in-private-equity

Morningstar. (2021). *ESG investing and performance 2021*. https://www.morningstar.com/lp/esg-investing

Network for Greening the Financial System (NGFS). (2021). *Progress report on integrating climate-related and environmental risks into supervision*. https://www.ngfs.net

Network for Greening the Financial System (NGFS). (2022). Climate-related risk assessment practices by financial institutions: A stocktake. https://www.ngfs.net/

OECD. (2020). *ESG investing: Practices, progress and challenges*. https://www.oecd.org/finance/ESG-Investing-Practices-Progress-and-Challenges.pdf

OECD. (2022). *ESG investing and climate transition: Market practices, issues and policy considerations*. https://www.oecd.org/finance/ESG-investing-and-climate-transition.pdf

PRI (Principles for Responsible Investment). (2020). *Fiduciary duty in the 21st century: Final report*. https://www.unpri.org/fiduciary-duty

Principles for Responsible Investment. (2020). *Sustainability-linked loans: Connecting finance to ESG performance*. https://www.unpri.org

PwC. (2023). *The state of climate tech 2023*. https://www.pwc.com/gx/en/services/sustainability/publications/state-of-climate-tech.html

Renneboog, L., Ter Horst, J., & Zhang, C. (2008). Socially responsible investments: Institutional aspects, performance, and investor behavior. *Journal of Banking & Finance*, *32*(9), 1723–1742. DOI: 10.1016/j.jbankfin.2007.12.039

Richardson, B. J. (2009). Keeping ethical investment ethical: Regulatory issues for investing for sustainability. *Journal of Business Ethics*, *87*(4), 555–572. DOI: 10.1007/s10551-008-9958-4

SASB. (2021). *SASB Standards Overview*. Sustainability Accounting Standards Board. https://www.sasb.org

Schmitt, A. (2021). Green fintech: Innovations for sustainable finance. *Journal of Sustainable Finance & Investment*, *11*(2), 245–258. DOI: 10.1080/20430795.2020.1857639

Schoenmaker, D., & Schramade, W. (2019). *Principles of sustainable finance*. Oxford University Press.

SEC. (2022). *Proposed rule: The enhancement and standardization of climate-related disclosures for investors*. U.S. Securities and Exchange Commission. https://www.sec.gov

Securities and Exchange Commission (SEC). (2022). *Proposed rule: Enhancement and standardization of climate-related disclosures for investors*. https://www.sec.gov/news/press-release/2022-46

Setzer, J., & Higham, C. (2022). *Global trends in climate litigation: 2022 snapshot*. Grantham Research Institute on Climate Change and the Environment.

Setzer, J., & Higham, C. (2022). *Global trends in climate litigation: 2022 snapshot*. Grantham Research Institute on Climate Change and the Environment. https://www.lse.ac.uk/granthaminstitute/publication/global-trends-in-climate-litigation-2022-snapshot/

Sullivan, R., & Mackenzie, C. (2017). *Responsible investment: Guide to ESG data providers and relevant trends*. International Finance Corporation.

Sullivan, R., & Mackenzie, C. (2021). *Responsible investment: Guide to ESG data providers and relevant trends*. CFA Institute Research Foundation.

Task Force on Climate-related Financial Disclosures (TCFD). (2017). *Final report: Recommendations of the TCFD*. https://www.fsb-tcfd.org/publications/final-recommendations-report/

UNEP FI. (2019). *Changing course: A comprehensive investor guide to scenario-based methods for climate risk assessment, in response to the TCFD*. https://www.unepfi.org

UNEP FI. (2021). *A new vision of sustainable investing: A holistic approach to ESG integration*. United Nations Environment Programme Finance Initiative.

World Bank. (2022). *Blended finance: Mobilizing private capital for sustainable development*. https://www.worldbank.org/en/topic/financialsector/brief/blended-finance

KEY TERMS AND DEFINITIONS

ESG Criteria (Environmental, Social, and Governance): Think of ESG as a checklist for responsible investing. Instead of only asking, "Will this company make me money?", you also ask: "Is it kind to the environment? Does it treat people fairly? Is it managed honestly?" These three pillars help assess whether a business is doing good while doing well.

Green Bonds: Imagine lending your money to a project that fights climate change — like building wind farms or cleaning polluted rivers — and then getting your money back with interest. That's what green bonds are: a way for investors to fund environmentally friendly projects while earning a return.

Impact Measurement: In sustainable finance, it's not enough to say "we're making a difference" — you have to prove it. Impact measurement is about tracking and showing the real-world effects of an investment, such as how much carbon emissions were reduced or how many communities gained access to clean water.

Risk-Adjusted Return: This is not just about how much you earn but how safely you earn it. A risky investment might promise big returns, but if it could crash tomorrow, is it worth it? Risk-adjusted return compares the reward you get to the risk you take, helping investors make smarter, steadier choices.

Sustainable Investing: This is an approach where investors look beyond just making money — they also care about the long-term health of the planet and society. It means choosing investments that balance profit with positive environmental and social outcomes, so your portfolio grows without costing the Earth.

Chapter 5
Utilizing Green Finance for Sustainable Development:
Pathways, Challenges, and Opportunities

Rishikaysh Marotrao Kaakandikar
https://orcid.org/0000-0003-0349-6788
SaiBalaji International Institute of Management Sciences, India

Shital Sopanrao Newase
https://orcid.org/0009-0000-1536-8201
International Institute of Management and Human Resource Development, India

Manasi Gujrathi
SaiBalaji International Institute of Management Sciences, Pune, India

ABSTRACT

Green finance has emerged as a critical enabler in promoting sustainable development by directing financial flows towards environmentally responsible and climate-friendly initiatives. This paper explores the pathways through which green finance supports economic growth while ensuring environmental protection, such as through green bonds, sustainable loans, and renewable energy investments. It examines key challenges including regulatory inconsistencies, limited market awareness, and risk-return trade-offs that hinder widespread adoption. At the same time, the study highlights significant opportunities, such as policy innovations, technological advancements, and global commitments to climate action, which can accelerate the integration of

DOI: 10.4018/979-8-3373-1240-8.ch005

green finance into mainstream economic planning. By addressing these challenges and leveraging available opportunities, green finance can play a transformative role in achieving long-term sustainability goals and climate resilience.

1 INTRODUCTION TO GREEN FINANCE

Green finance is a rapidly evolving and essential domain that integrates environmental sustainability into the core of financial decision-making. It encompasses the strategic allocation of capital to projects, initiatives, and enterprises that not only yield financial returns but also deliver tangible environmental benefits. These benefits are most commonly associated with efforts to combat climate change, preserve biodiversity, and promote sustainable use of natural resources. Key areas of investment include renewable energy generation (such as solar, wind, and hydro power), energy efficiency upgrades in buildings and industries, sustainable agriculture practices that minimize chemical inputs and preserve soil health, clean transportation systems that reduce greenhouse gas emissions, and pollution control mechanisms that mitigate air and water contamination. Additionally, green finance supports initiatives focused on water conservation, waste management, reforestation, and the development of green technologies.

At its foundation, green finance is driven by a growing global consensus that long-term economic growth and stability must be intrinsically linked to environmental stewardship. Conventional financial models have often neglected environmental externalities, such as carbon emissions, deforestation, and resource depletion, leading to market distortions and long-term ecological risks. This disconnect has contributed to unsustainable development patterns that undermine both environmental health and economic resilience. In contrast, green finance aims to correct these market failures by internalizing environmental costs and incorporating them into the pricing, risk assessment, and structuring of financial products and services.

Through mechanisms such as green bonds, sustainability-linked loans, carbon pricing, and climate risk disclosure frameworks, green finance encourages both public and private sector actors to integrate environmental considerations into investment and policy decisions. It also promotes transparency, accountability, and innovation in financial markets, helping investors align their portfolios with global sustainability goals such as the United Nations Sustainable Development Goals (SDGs) and the Paris Agreement. As such, green finance is not merely a niche market—it is increasingly viewed as a fundamental pillar for achieving a just transition toward a low-carbon, inclusive, and resilient global economy.

Green finance has emerged as a critical catalyst in achieving the global sustainable development agenda, particularly the Sustainable Development Goals (SDGs) and the

Paris Agreement targets (UNEP, 2016). It refers to financial investments flowing into sustainable development projects, environmental products, and policies that encourage the development of a more sustainable economy (Zhang et al., 2019). Green bonds, carbon markets, and climate funds are among the financial instruments designed to channel resources towards environmentally beneficial projects (Flammer, 2021; Tang & Zhang, 2020). Financial institutions, especially development banks, have a pivotal role in mainstreaming sustainability through green lending practices (World Bank, 2019). With growing global awareness, several countries have incorporated green finance into national policies, including China's Green Finance Guidelines and the EU's Sustainable Finance Action Plan (EU, 2018; PBoC, 2016).

1.1 Key Components of Green Finance

1.Green Bonds and Loans:

Green bonds and loans are specialized financial instruments specifically designed to finance projects that deliver environmental benefits. These can include renewable energy installations, energy-efficient buildings, sustainable waste management systems, and clean transportation infrastructure. Green bonds, in particular, have gained significant traction in global capital markets, with issuances growing rapidly across both developed and emerging economies. They function similarly to traditional bonds but come with the added assurance that proceeds will be used for green initiatives, often verified through third-party certification. These instruments not only attract environmentally conscious investors but also help issuers demonstrate their commitment to sustainability.

2.Sustainable Investing (ESG Investing):

Sustainable investing refers to the practice of integrating Environmental, Social, and Governance (ESG) criteria into investment decisions. Rather than focusing solely on financial returns, investors assess companies based on their environmental impact, social responsibility (e.g., labor practices, community relations), and governance standards (e.g., transparency, board diversity). This approach helps mitigate long-term risks and align investment portfolios with ethical and sustainable values. ESG investing has evolved from a niche practice into a mainstream strategy, influencing trillions of dollars in global assets under management and driving corporate behavior toward greater sustainability.

3.Carbon Pricing and Climate Risk Disclosure:

Carbon pricing is an economic tool that assigns a cost to emitting carbon dioxide, typically through mechanisms like carbon taxes or cap-and-trade systems. By placing a financial penalty on greenhouse gas emissions, carbon pricing incentivizes businesses to reduce their carbon footprint and invest in cleaner alternatives. Alongside this, climate risk disclosure involves the transparent reporting of climate-related financial risks by corporations. Frameworks like the Task Force on Climate-related Financial Disclosures (TCFD) encourage organizations to disclose how climate risks impact their operations and finances. These practices increase accountability and enable investors to make more informed decisions by understanding the climate-related risks embedded in their investments.

4.Public-Private Partnerships (PPPs):

Public-private partnerships are collaborative arrangements where government bodies, multilateral development banks, and private sector entities jointly fund and implement large-scale green projects. These partnerships leverage the strengths of both sectors—public institutions provide policy support, regulatory frameworks, and initial capital, while private players bring in innovation, technology, and efficient project execution. PPPs are particularly effective in financing green infrastructure, such as smart cities, renewable energy grids, sustainable transportation networks, and climate-resilient urban planning. By sharing risks and returns, PPPs help overcome funding gaps and accelerate the transition to a more sustainable economy. Despite these strides, green finance implementation faces multiple challenges. One significant hurdle is the lack of standardised definitions and frameworks, leading to confusion and risks of greenwashing (OECD, 2020). Moreover, emerging economies often encounter limited access to green financing due to weak institutional frameworks and financial infrastructure (Ghosh, 2020). Data gaps and inconsistent ESG disclosures further obstruct informed investment decisions (Friede et al., 2015). Risk aversion by private investors and unclear regulatory incentives also deter large-scale capital mobilization (Campiglio et al., 2018). Additionally, limited financial literacy and public awareness about green finance options hinder broader participation (Taghizadeh-Hesary & Yoshino, 2020).

1.2 Importance of Green Finance

Green finance plays a critical role in transitioning to a low-carbon economy. Mobilizing financial resources toward sustainable development helps mitigate climate risks, foster innovation in green technologies, and create green jobs. Moreover, it contributes to achieving global frameworks such as the Paris Agreement, which aims to limit global warming, and the United Nations Sustainable Development

Goals (SDGs), particularly Goal 13 on climate action and Goal 7 on affordable and clean energy.

Global Trends and Challenges: Governments, financial institutions, and regulators worldwide increasingly recognize the importance of green finance. Major economies like the European Union, China, and India are implementing policies encouraging green financing, such as tax incentives, green taxonomy standards, and mandatory ESG disclosures.However, challenges remain. These include:

- There is a lack of standardized definitions and frameworks for what constitutes a "green" activity.
- Limited awareness and capacity in emerging markets.
- The perceived trade-off between financial returns and environmental impact.

Nonetheless, the opportunities are substantial. Green finance enables capital flows into renewable energy, sustainable agriculture, water sanitation, and climate-resilient infrastructure, contributing directly to SDGs (United Nations, 2020). Innovative tools such as sustainability-linked loans, ESG indexes, and blended finance structures attract both public and private sector interest (Inderst et al., 2012). Technology also plays a critical role, with fintech and blockchain applications enhancing transparency and traceability in green investments (Li et al., 2021). Moreover, the financial sector is witnessing increasing pressure from investors demanding alignment with climate goals and social impact (Clark et al., 2015). Green finance not only mitigates climate risks but also creates jobs, boosts economic resilience, and fosters inclusive development (Carney, 2015).

1.3 Definition of Green Finance:

Zadek and Flynn (2013): "Green finance is often used interchangeably with green investment. However, green finance is a broader lens that includes more than investments, as defined by Bloomberg New Energy Finance and others. Most importantly, it includes operational costs of green investments that are not included under the definition of green investment. It would consist of significant project preparation and land acquisition costs, which can pose distinct financing challenges. (Flynn, 2013)

Pricewaterhouse Coopers Consultants (PWC) (2013): "For the banking sector, green finance is defined as financial products and services, under the consideration of environmental factors throughout the lending decision making, ex-post monitoring and risk management processes, provided to promote environmentally responsible investments and stimulate low-carbon technologies, projects, industries and businesses." ((PWC), 2013)

1.4 Scope of green finance:

The scope of green finance is broad and includes a variety of sectors, instruments, stakeholders, and policy measures. It extends beyond funding environmental projects to transforming how the financial system assesses risk, return, and impact.

Green finance supports projects in:

- Renewable energy (solar, wind, hydro)
- Energy efficiency
- Sustainable transport
- Climate-smart agriculture
- Waste management
- Water resource management
- Pollution control
- Ecosystem restoration

Financial Instruments

- Green Bonds: Fund green projects.
- Green Loans: Finance green projects.
- Sustainability-linked Loans/Bonds: Tied to environmental performance.
- Green Funds/Indices: Invest in eco-friendly companies.
- Climate Risk Insurance: Mitigate climate-related financial risks.

Stakeholders

- Governments: Set regulations and incentives.
- Financial Institutions: Integrate ESG factors.
- Corporates: Issue green bonds and transition to sustainable practices.
- Development Banks: Provide concessional finance.
- Rating Agencies: Certify green credentials.

Regulatory and Policy Frameworks

- National green finance strategies
- Green taxonomies (e.g., EU Taxonomy)
- Climate risk disclosure frameworks (e.g., TCFD)

1.5 Evolution and significance in the global context:

Evolution of Green Finance

The concept of green finance has evolved over the past few decades, gaining traction as the environmental impact of economic activities became more evident. Its development can be traced through several key phases:

1. Early Foundations (1970s–1990s):
    - Environmental concerns began to be recognized in financial and policy discussions, particularly following the 1972 UN Conference on the Human Environment.
    - Environmental economics and cost-benefit analysis emerged, but finance remained detached from ecological concerns.
2. Emergence of Sustainable Finance (1990s–2000s):
    - The 1992 Earth Summit (Rio de Janeiro) and the formation of Agenda 21 spurred interest in sustainable development.
    - Financial institutions began incorporating environmental, social, and governance (ESG) criteria, laying the groundwork for sustainable and green finance.
    - The rise of socially responsible investing (SRI) introduced the idea that investments could align with ethical and environmental values.
3. Rise of Green Finance (2010s–present):
    - The 2015 Paris Agreement marked a turning point, emphasizing the need for climate finance to meet global climate goals.
    - The launch of the Green Bond Principles by the International Capital Market Association (ICMA) and the growth of green bond markets accelerated the formalization of green finance.
    - Institutions such as the World Bank, Asian Development Bank (ADB), and private financial actors expanded their green finance portfolios.
    - Global regulatory efforts, such as the EU Green Taxonomy and frameworks like TCFD (Task Force on Climate-related Financial Disclosures), became mainstream.

1.6 Significance in the Global Context

Green finance plays a pivotal role in addressing one of the most pressing challenges of our time: climate change. Its global significance can be understood through the following dimensions:

Table 1. Significance in the Global Context

Key Area	Description
1. Mobilizing Capital for Climate Action	Green finance exceeds $600 billion annually, but $4-6 trillion is needed to meet 2050 net-zero targets.
2. Supporting SDGs	Contributes to SDGs: • SDG 7: Affordable energy • SDG 11: Sustainable cities • SDG 13: Climate action.
3. Financial System Resilience	Enhances financial stability by integrating ESG and climate risks, mitigating fossil fuel-related risks.
4. Innovation & Green Technologies	Promotes clean tech like solar panels, EVs, and green hydrogen, driving economic growth.
5. Global Cooperation	Supports initiatives like the Green Climate Fund and cross-border green bonds, encouraging global collaboration.

2. LITERATURE REVIEW

Introduction to Green Finance

The concept of green finance has emerged as a pivotal mechanism for aligning financial systems with environmental sustainability objectives. According to Zhang and Zhang (2021), green finance encompasses financial investments directed toward projects that yield environmental benefits, including renewable energy, energy efficiency, pollution prevention, and sustainable land use. The United Nations Environment Programme (UNEP, 2016) defines green finance as a subset of sustainable finance aimed at supporting the transition to a low-carbon, climate-resilient economy. Over the past decade, its importance has grown in light of the Paris Agreement (2015) and the United Nations Sustainable Development Goals (SDGs), particularly Goal 13 (Climate Action) and Goal 7 (Affordable and Clean Energy).

Pathways of Green Finance

Several pathways have been identified in the literature for utilizing green finance to achieve sustainable development:

- **Green Bonds:** First introduced by the European Investment Bank in 2007, green bonds have become a major instrument for funding environmentally beneficial projects (Flammer, 2021). They provide capital for renewable energy, sustainable transport, and water management systems.
- **Green Loans and Credit Lines:** Banks and multilateral financial institutions have developed dedicated green credit facilities to finance low-carbon technologies (OECD, 2020).
- **Sustainable Investment Funds:** Institutional investors increasingly integrate Environmental, Social, and Governance (ESG) criteria into investment

decisions (Friede, Busch & Bassen, 2015), enabling capital allocation toward sustainable business practices.

- **Public–Private Partnerships (PPPs):** PPP models in green infrastructure allow governments and private investors to share risks and benefits, accelerating large-scale sustainable projects (World Bank, 2019).

The Role of Green Finance in Sustainable Development

The linkage between green finance and sustainable development is well established. Green finance supports **climate mitigation, adaptation projects, biodiversity conservation**, and **resource efficiency**, which contribute directly to multiple SDGs (Banga, 2019). Empirical studies in emerging economies have shown that green finance can promote economic growth while reducing environmental degradation, provided that regulatory frameworks are robust (Wang et al., 2022). Furthermore, green financial flows enhance technological innovation, which is a key driver for sustainable industrial development (Porter & van der Linde, 1995).

Challenges in Implementing Green Finance

Despite its potential, literature identifies several barriers:

- **Lack of Standardized Taxonomies:** There is no globally uniform definition of what constitutes a "green" project, leading to risks of greenwashing (EU Technical Expert Group on Sustainable Finance, 2020).
- **High Transaction Costs:** Green bonds and climate-friendly loans often involve higher monitoring and certification costs, discouraging small-scale issuers (Kidney et al., 2017).
- **Limited Investor Awareness:** Many investors remain hesitant to prioritize environmental returns over short-term financial gains (Broadstock et al., 2021).
- **Policy and Regulatory Gaps:** Weak enforcement of environmental regulations and inadequate incentives hinder the scaling up of green finance in developing economies (Bhattacharya & Kojima, 2012).

Opportunities in the Green Finance Landscape

The transition to a sustainable economy opens significant opportunities:

- **Technological Innovations:** Advancements in renewable energy, energy storage, and green hydrogen provide new avenues for investment (IRENA, 2022).
- **Blended Finance Mechanisms:** Combining concessional public finance with private capital reduces investment risk and mobilizes large-scale funding (OECD, 2021).

- **Digital Finance for Green Goals:** Fintech tools such as blockchain-based carbon trading and AI-driven ESG analytics can improve transparency and efficiency (Chen & Volz, 2022).
- **Global Cooperation:** International climate finance commitments, such as the $100 billion annual pledge under the Paris Agreement, can be leveraged for capacity building in least developed countries (LDCs) (UNFCCC, 2021).

Research Gaps

Existing literature often focuses on developed nations, while the unique barriers and potential of green finance in developing and emerging economies remain under-explored. Furthermore, longitudinal empirical studies are scarce in measuring the direct impact of green finance instruments on specific SDGs. There is also a need for more interdisciplinary research integrating economics, environmental science, and technology perspectives.

The literature underscores that green finance is a vital enabler for sustainable development, offering structured pathways through innovative financial instruments and policy support. However, achieving its full potential requires overcoming challenges related to regulation, awareness, and access to finance. Addressing these gaps can accelerate the global shift toward a climate-resilient and socially inclusive economy.

2.1 Role in achieving Sustainable Development Goals (SDGs):

The UN's 2030 Agenda for Sustainable Development includes 17 SDGs, requiring $5–7 trillion annually, with a large portion needed in developing countries. Green finance has emerged to bridge the funding gap, directing investments into sustainable and climate-friendly projects across energy, infrastructure, health, agriculture, and urban development sectors.

2.2 Direct Alignment of Green Finance with SDGs:

1. SDG 7: Affordable and Clean Energy
2. Green finance expands access to renewable energy, especially in remote areas, via green bonds and concessional loans.
3. Example: The World Bank's Scaling Solar initiative in Africa.
4. SDG 9: Industry, Innovation, and Infrastructure
5. Supports sustainable industrialization with energy-efficient tech, green infrastructure, and electric mobility.
6. Example: Green bonds in China for eco-industrial parks.
7. SDG 11: Sustainable Cities and Communities

8. Finances eco-friendly housing, mass transit, and climate-resilient infrastructure for growing urban areas.
9. Example: The European Investment Bank's Smart Sustainable Cities framework.
10. SDG 12: Responsible Consumption and Production
11. Encourages circular economy models, waste reduction, and eco-conscious supply chains.
12. Example: Impact investment funds supporting biodegradable packaging startups.
13. SDG 13: Climate Action
14. Mobilizes capital for climate mitigation and adaptation projects, like carbon reduction and climate-smart infrastructure.
15. Example: The Green Climate Fund supports vulnerable countries' climate projects.
16. SDG 15: Life on Land
17. Supports biodiversity, reforestation, and land restoration through instruments like conservation bonds.
18. Example: The Seychelles' blue bond for marine ecosystem protection.

Direct Alignment of Green Finance with SDGs

Table 2. Direct Alignment of Green Finance with SDGs

Indirect Contribution to SDGs	Description
SDG 1 & 10: No Poverty and Reduced Inequalities	Green finance creates green jobs and boosts inclusive growth, reducing vulnerability in developing communities.
SDG 3: Good Health and Well-Being	Reduces pollution and promotes clean air/water, improving public health (e.g., electric transport reduces respiratory diseases).
SDG 8: Decent Work and Economic Growth	Green sectors like renewable energy and sustainable agriculture create significant employment opportunities.

Green Finance Mechanisms:

Table 3. Green Finance Mechanisms:

Mechanism	Description
Green Bonds and Loans	Raise funds for environmental projects.
Sustainability-Linked Instruments	Links returns to ESG performance.
Green Investment Funds	Channels private capital into sustainable projects.
Blended Finance	Combines public and private finance to de-risk investments in emerging markets.
Carbon Pricing and Emissions Trading	Incentivizes carbon footprint reduction.

2.3 Challenges in Leveraging Green Finance for the SDGs

Here's a shortened version of the content:
Barriers to Green Finance:

- **Lack of Harmonized Standards**: Differing definitions lead to confusion and greenwashing.
- **Access Barriers**: SMEs and low-income countries struggle to access green capital.
- **Risk Perception**: Investors consider green projects high-risk, especially in emerging markets.
- **Data and Transparency Gaps**: Lack of reliable ESG and climate data undermines confidence.

3 PATHWAYS FOR UTILIZING GREEN FINANCE

3.1 Policy and Regulatory Frameworks

- Develop National Green Finance Strategies (e.g., EU Green Deal).
- Implement Green Taxonomies to define "green" activities.
- Enforce ESG Disclosure Standards (e.g., TCFD, ISSB).

3.2 Mobilizing Private Sector Investments

- Green Bonds and Loans for specific green projects.
- Blended Finance Models to share risk with private investors.
- Sustainability-Linked Financing tied to ESG performance.

3.3 Greening Financial Institutions and Portfolios

- ESG Integration in lending and investment.
- Divest from high-carbon assets.
- Offer green banking products like green mortgages and EV loans.

3.4 Developing Green Financial Markets

- Establish Green Stock Indices and ETFs for sustainable investments.
- Use Credit Enhancement Mechanisms for green projects.
- Support Green Venture Capital and Impact Investing.

3.5 International Cooperation and Climate Finance

- Global Climate Funds (e.g., Green Climate Fund) for low-income countries.
- Facilitate Cross-Border Green Bonds.
- Promote Knowledge Sharing and Capacity Building.

3.6 Technology-Enabled Green Finance

- Use Blockchain for Green Bond Issuance.
- Leverage AI and Big Data for ESG risk assessments.
- Utilize Fintech platforms for Micro Green Loans.

3.7 Empowering Local Communities and SMEs

- Microfinance for clean energy access.
- Community-Based Green Funds for local conservation projects.
- Capacity building to help SMEs access green finance.

4 GREEN BONDS AND CLIMATE BONDS

4.1 Definition

Green Bonds are fixed-income instruments used to fund climate and environmental projects. Their proceeds are dedicated to green initiatives like renewable energy and sustainable infrastructure.

Climate Bonds are a subset of green bonds focused specifically on combating climate change. They are issued under stricter standards set by the Climate Bonds Initiative (CBI) to align with global climate goals.

4.2 Growth of the Green Bond Market

Since the European Investment Bank issued its first green bond in 2007, the market has expanded rapidly. From 2021 to 2023 alone, cumulative issuances surpassed $1 trillion. Major issuers include sovereigns (e.g., France, Germany), development banks (e.g., World Bank), and corporations (e.g., Apple, Tesla), with Europe, China, and the U.S. as leading markets. An emerging trend is sovereign green bonds from developing nations such as Nigeria, Chile, and India.

4.3 Benefits and Challenges

Green and climate bonds finance projects that reduce emissions promote efficiency, and support adaptation. They attract ESG-focused investors, often offering a "freemium" or pricing advantage. However, risks like greenwashing and inconsistent standards can undermine credibility.

4.4 Key Standards and Guidelines

- Green Bond Principles (ICMA): Voluntary guidelines for using proceeds, project evaluation, and reporting.
- Climate Bonds Standard (CBI): A science-based taxonomy and certification scheme.
- EU Green Bond Standard: A proposed regulatory framework to harmonize criteria and enhance trust.

4.5 Notable Green Bond Examples

- France: Issued €7 billion in sovereign green bonds for renewables and biodiversity protection, setting a global precedent.
- Apple Inc.: Raised $2.2 billion to fund energy-efficient data centers and clean energy, influencing the tech sector.

4.6 Green Banking and Sustainable Lending

Green banking integrates ESG into operations, financing eco-friendly initiatives and adopting energy-efficient branches and digital banking practices. Sustainable lending supports projects with positive environmental or social impacts, such as:

- Green Loans: Favorable terms for eco-projects.
- Sustainability-Linked Loans: Rates tied to ESG performance.
- Impact Investing: Financing with measurable environmental or social outcomes.

5 TRENDS IN SUSTAINABLE FINANCE

Sustainable finance is experiencing a transformative surge as climate change, environmental degradation, and social equity concerns take center stage in global economic planning. Several significant trends are shaping the evolution of this field, indicating a systemic shift in how capital is mobilized, allocated, and managed with sustainability in mind.

1. Rising Demand Driven by Climate Concerns and Regulatory Mandates

The escalating urgency of the climate crisis has led to heightened awareness among investors, governments, and corporations about the environmental and social impacts of financial decisions. As a result, demand for green financial instruments has surged. Regulatory frameworks such as the European Union's Sustainable Finance Disclosure Regulation (EU SFDR) and the Task Force on Climate-related Financial Disclosures (TCFD) are now requiring financial market participants to disclose how sustainability risks are integrated into their investment processes.

These regulations enhance transparency and accountability, pushing financial institutions to consider not only financial performance but also the broader environmental and social consequences of their actions. The pressure from regulators, stakeholders, and civil society has accelerated the adoption of sustainable finance practices across sectors.

Policymakers, regulators, and financial institutions must collaborate to scale up green finance. Governments can introduce tax incentives, risk guarantees, and regulatory mandates to attract private capital (IMF, 2021). Clear taxonomies and impact measurement frameworks will reduce ambiguities and improve market integrity (EU, 2020). Capacity building initiatives and public-private partnerships are essential in developing countries to strengthen local financial systems and project pipelines (Ameli et al., 2021). Multilateral organizations like the UNDP and GCF can also bridge financing gaps and offer technical assistance (UNDP, 2019; GCF, 2021). Institutional reforms and cross-sectoral coordination can enable a more inclusive, resilient, and sustainable financial ecosystem (Banga, 2019).

2. Integration of ESG Risk into Credit Assessments

Traditional credit assessments are evolving to incorporate Environmental, Social, and Governance (ESG) risks alongside financial metrics. Banks and credit rating agencies are now factoring in how environmental risks—such as carbon emissions, climate vulnerability, and resource depletion—can impact a borrower's financial health and long-term viability.

This shift reflects a broader recognition that ESG-related risks can lead to financial losses if not adequately managed. For example, a company operating in a water-scarce region or with poor labor practices may face operational disruptions or reputational damage, affecting its creditworthiness. Integrating ESG risk into lending decisions promotes more responsible corporate behavior and helps safeguard financial institutions against future liabilities.

3. Strategic Partnerships with Development Finance Institutions (DFIs)

Commercial banks and private investors are increasingly partnering with Development Finance Institutions (DFIs) to scale up green investments, particularly in emerging markets where access to capital for sustainable projects is limited. DFIs, such as the World Bank's International Finance Corporation (IFC) or the Asian Development Bank (ADB), provide technical assistance, de-risking mechanisms, and blended finance structures to make green projects more attractive to private capital.

These collaborations enable the financing of critical infrastructure in sectors like clean energy, water sanitation, sustainable agriculture, and climate-resilient urban planning. DFIs play a catalytic role by mobilizing private investments, setting standards for project sustainability, and fostering innovation in financial products.

4. Mainstreaming of Green Funds and ESG-Linked Portfolios

What was once a niche investment strategy has now entered the mainstream. Green funds—mutual funds or exchange-traded funds (ETFs) that invest in environmentally responsible companies—and ESG-linked portfolios are increasingly popular among both institutional and retail investors. These portfolios are designed to align with sustainability values while still aiming for competitive returns.

Fund managers are launching sustainability-themed products, including low-carbon indexes, clean energy funds, and ESG-screened equity portfolios. Asset owners, including pension funds and sovereign wealth funds, are reallocating capital toward these vehicles to meet both ethical objectives and long-term performance goals. The increased flow of capital into ESG-linked investments is also encouraging companies to improve their sustainability practices to attract funding.

Together, these trends reflect a paradigm shift in global finance, where sustainability is no longer a peripheral concern but a core determinant of financial performance, risk management, and market relevance. As regulatory expectations intensify and climate risks become more material, sustainable finance will continue to evolve, driving innovation and resilience in the financial ecosystem.

5.1 Institutional Leadership and Impact

Institutional leadership is central to the growth and success of green finance. Leading financial institutions—such as DBS Bank, BNP Paribas, Industrial and Commercial Bank of China (ICBC), and Standard Chartered—are playing transformative roles in mainstreaming sustainability into global financial systems. These banks are not only responding to market and regulatory demands but also proactively setting benchmarks, issuing innovative financial instruments, and influencing sustainable finance policy agendas worldwide.

1. Issuance of Green Bonds and Sustainability-Linked Instruments

Banks like BNP Paribas and ICBC have emerged as top issuers and underwriters of green bonds, social bonds, and sustainability-linked bonds. These instruments are used to raise funds specifically for projects that deliver environmental or social benefits, such as renewable energy development, clean transportation, sustainable water management, and energy-efficient infrastructure.

DBS Bank, for example, has launched green bonds to support solar energy, green buildings, and energy transition projects across Asia.

BNP Paribas has been a pioneer in structuring sustainability-linked loans (SLLs), which offer lower interest rates to borrowers upon meeting predefined ESG performance targets.

This strategic move not only expands access to green capital but also encourages corporate clients to improve their sustainability performance.

2. Adoption of Sustainable Lending Frameworks

Major institutions are embedding sustainability into their credit policies and lending frameworks. By doing so, they evaluate loan proposals based not just on financial metrics, but also on environmental and social implications.

Standard Chartered has introduced a Green and Sustainable Product Framework aligned with global standards like the Green Bond Principles and Sustainability Linked Loan Principles. This framework ensures that loans and investments meet rigorous environmental criteria.

ICBC, as the largest bank in China, is supporting the nation's carbon neutrality targets by financing clean energy, green transportation, and low-carbon industries.

These frameworks help ensure that lending decisions support long-term environmental goals and that financial resources are channeled toward climate-resilient and low-impact activities.

3. ESG Risk Assessment and Integration

Institutions are increasingly recognizing that environmental, social, and governance (ESG) risks pose material financial risks. As such, banks are developing sophisticated ESG risk assessment tools to integrate sustainability into risk management.

For instance, BNP Paribas uses advanced ESG scoring models to evaluate clients and projects, influencing not only credit decisions but also the terms and pricing of financial products.

DBS Bank integrates ESG criteria into its overall risk governance framework, ensuring that projects with high environmental risks are subjected to enhanced due diligence or are excluded from financing.

By integrating ESG risk assessments, banks can reduce exposure to stranded assets, reputational damage, and regulatory penalties.

4. Development of Green Investment Products

Banks are also innovating in retail and institutional investment spaces by offering green investment products, such as ESG-focused mutual funds, climate impact portfolios, and green wealth management solutions.

Standard Chartered provides ESG advisory and sustainable investment solutions to its high-net-worth and institutional clients.

DBS Bank has launched retail green deposits, where customer savings are deployed into climate-aligned projects, allowing individuals to contribute to environmental goals through everyday banking.

These products democratize access to green finance and increase awareness among consumers and investors.

5. Policy Influence and Global Collaboration

Major financial institutions are engaging with policymakers, regulators, and global alliances to shape the sustainable finance agenda. By participating in networks such as the UN Principles for Responsible Banking, the Net-Zero Banking Alliance, and the Green Investment Principles for the Belt and Road Initiative, banks influence standard-setting and promote global convergence in green finance practices.

For example:

BNP Paribas is an active member of the Task Force on Climate-related Financial Disclosures (TCFD) and advocates for mandatory climate-related financial disclosures.

Standard Chartered collaborates with global bodies to advance taxonomies and frameworks that guide what constitutes green and sustainable economic activities.

5.2 Green Investment and Impact Investing

Green investment funds target eco-sectors like clean energy and sustainable agriculture. These include green bond funds, ETFs, and private equity. Impact investing seeks dual goals: financial returns and measurable environmental or social outcomes. Key players include Calvert Impact Capital, Blue Orchard, and Acumen Fund, which fund projects from clean energy to affordable housing and microfinance.

5.3 Differences Between Green Investment Funds and Impact Investing

Table 4. Differences Between Green Investment Funds and Impact Investing

Aspect	Green Investment Funds	Impact Investing
Primary Focus	Environmental sustainability (e.g., renewable energy, green tech)	Both environmental and social outcomes (e.g., poverty, health, climate)
Investment Scope	Focus on environmental projects and companies	Broader, addressing social and environmental issues simultaneously
Return Expectations	Generally financial returns with environmental impact	Financial returns alongside social/ environmental impact
Impact Measurement	Focus on environmental metrics (e.g., carbon emissions)	Social and environmental metrics (e.g., people served, carbon reduction)
Risk Profile	Can be similar to traditional financial markets, but focused on green sectors	Varies widely — can involve higher risks but focuses on intentional change

5.4 Benefits and Challenges of Green and Impact Investing

Green investing offers diversification, environmental impact, and competitive returns but faces challenges like limited project availability and greenwashing risks. Impact investing targets social and environmental issues (e.g., poverty, climate change) while generating financial returns. It supports long-term change but struggles with impact measurement and can involve higher risk or lower returns.

5.4.1 Rise of ESG Investing

ESG investing focuses on companies' environmental, social, and governance practices. It's gaining popularity due to increased climate awareness and evidence that ESG-strong firms often perform better and face fewer risks. Strategies include exclusion (e.g., avoiding fossil fuels) and positive screening (selecting top ESG performers). However, inconsistent standards and greenwashing remain concerns.

5.4.2 Public-Private Partnerships (PPPs)

PPPs enable collaboration between governments and private firms to fund and operate sustainable infrastructure. They combine public support with private-sector innovation and financing. Key benefits include access to capital and advanced technology. Examples include India's solar initiatives, Bogotá's green transit, and the Netherlands' flood resilience projects. Challenges include complex coordination, shifting policies, and public resistance.

6 COLLABORATION MODELS

Collaboration in green projects often includes joint ventures, co-financing, and government-backed incentives. Through shared investment and expertise, these models support renewable energy, EV infrastructure, climate-resilient systems, and sustainable urban development.

Table 5. Collaborative model

Collaboration Model	Description	Examples	Key Benefits
Public-Private Partnerships (PPPs)	Collaboration between government and private sector for infrastructure projects.	- Wind and solar power projects. - Green infrastructure (e.g., EV charging stations, smart grids).	- Risk sharing - Long-term contracts - Financing flexibility
Integrated Project Financing Models	Combining multiple financial instruments and stakeholders to fund large-scale projects.	- **Green Bonds**: Funding renewable energy projects. - **Climate Investment Funds (CIF)**.	- Blended finance - Attracts private investment - De-risking projects
Joint Ventures (JVs)	Two or more companies combine resources to develop renewable energy projects.	- **Offshore Wind Farms**: Siemens Gamesa & Orsted. - **Solar Projects**: First Solar with local developers.	- Expertise sharing - Shared financial risk
Collaborative Research and Development (R&D)	Joint efforts in developing innovative renewable energy technologies.	- **International Solar Alliance (ISA)**: Cost-reduction in solar tech. - Tesla & Panasonic's battery storage R&D.	- Accelerates innovation - Reduces costs
Community-Based Renewable Energy Projects	Local communities own and operate renewable energy assets, ensuring local participation.	- Community Wind Projects: Denmark, Germany. - Solar Microgrids: Africa.	- Local ownership - Capacity building - Increased social acceptance

continued on following page

Table 5. Continued

Collaboration Model	Description	Examples	Key Benefits
Multilateral Development Bank (MDB) Collaboration	MDBs provide financing and technical support for renewable energy projects.	- Clean Technology Fund (CTF): Renewable projects in low-income countries. - Africa Renewable Energy Initiative (AREI).	- Reduces financing risk - Technical support - Attracts private sector investments
Co-Development and Licensing Agreements	Companies collaborate on co-developing or licensing renewable energy technologies.	- **Offshore Wind Licensing**: Siemens Gamesa & GE. - **Battery Licensing**: CATL & Tesla.	- Intellectual property sharing - Market access - Technology transfer

7 CARBON MARKETS AND EMISSIONS TRADING SCHEMES

7.1 Definition: Systems Where Carbon Emissions Are Bought And Sold To Incentivize Emission Reductions

- **Components:**
- Carbon Credits: Represent the right to emit 1 ton of CO_2.
- Cap-and-Trade: Total emissions are capped, and allowances are traded.
- Carbon Offsetting: Companies invest in projects like reforestation to offset emissions.

7.2 Emissions Trading Schemes (ETS)

- Definition: A specific type of carbon market where governments cap emissions and companies trade allowances.
- Process:

1. Cap Setting: The government sets an emissions cap for sectors.
2. Allowance Allocation: Companies are given or auctioned allowances (1 ton CO_2 per allowance).
3. Trading: Companies buy/sell allowances to meet their targets.
4. Monitoring & Reporting: Companies report emissions, which are verified independently.
5. Banking & Borrowing: Unused allowances can be saved or borrowed.

7.3 Types of Carbon Markets

- Compliance Markets (Mandatory Carbon Markets):
- Governed by laws or international agreements (e.g., Kyoto Protocol, Paris Agreement).
- Examples:
- EU ETS: Largest carbon market, covering power plants and industries in the EU.
- California Cap-and-Trade: Covers industries like power generation, manufacturing, and transportation.

7.4 Voluntary Carbon Markets:

- Businesses or individuals voluntarily purchase carbon credits to offset emissions.
- Examples:
- Verified Carbon Standard (VCS): Certifies carbon offset projects.
- Gold Standard: Certifies high-quality, sustainable carbon offset projects.

8 GLOBAL TRENDS & ADOPTION

- Expansion of Carbon Pricing:
- Over 60 carbon pricing initiatives globally, covering 22% of global emissions.
- Examples:
- China's National Carbon Market: Largest by volume, initially covering power generation.
- South Korea's ETS: Launched in 2015 as part of Paris Agreement goals.

Integration of Carbon Markets:

- Example: EU ETS and Swiss ETS linking in 2020 to allow cross-border trading.

9 SUCCESS STORIES

9.1 EU ETS

- Reduced emissions by 35% since 2005.

- Introduced Market Stability Reserve (MSR) to stabilize carbon prices.

9.2 California Cap-and-Trade

- Reduced GHG emissions by 15% below 2005 levels by 2020.
- Raised billions in revenue and reinvested in clean energy projects.

9.3 Carbon Pricing in British Columbia

- Introduced a carbon tax in 2008, reducing emissions by 5-15%.
- Revenue is used to reduce income taxes and contribute to economic growth.

10 CHALLENGES AND CRITICISMS

- Market Volatility:
- Carbon prices fluctuate due to political or economic factors, complicating long-term planning.

Over-allocation of Credits:

- Too many allowances can reduce the carbon price and undermine the system.

Equity Issues:

- Concerns that carbon markets may negatively impact low-income communities or developing nations.

Lack of Global Coordination:

- There is no universal carbon market; fragmentation limits emissions reduction potential and increases complexity.

11 MECHANISMS FOR CARBON CREDIT FINANCING

11.1.1 Carbon Credit Creation and Certification

- Project Development & Validation:

- Projects (e.g., renewable energy, reforestation) are developed to reduce emissions.
- Third-party validation ensures the project's emissions reduction potential.

Monitoring & Verification:

- Ongoing monitoring and third-party verification ensure the reductions are real and additional.

Certification:

- Verified projects receive carbon credits (1 ton of CO_2 reduction per credit).
- Examples of certification standards are VCS, Gold Standard, and CDM.

11.1.2 Carbon Credit Financing Models

- Project-Based Financing:
- Funds raised for specific projects, with returns from carbon credit sales.

Carbon Credit Purchase Agreements (CPA):

- Long-term contracts where buyers commit to purchasing carbon credits.

Blended Finance:

- Public and private capital are combined to de-risk projects, especially in developing countries.

Carbon Credit-backed Securities:

- Financial instruments are based on the value of carbon credits.

Green and Impact Investment Funds:

- Investment vehicles focused on financing environmental projects generating carbon credits.

11.1.3 Trading and Sale of Carbon Credits

- Carbon Credit Exchanges:

- Platforms (e.g., EU ETS) where credits are bought and sold, providing transparency and liquidity.

Over-the-Counter (OTC) Trading:

- Direct transactions between buyers and sellers offer more flexibility.

11.2 Challenges and Opportunities

- Challenges:
- Regulatory complexity, price volatility, ensuring additionality and permanence of credits.

Opportunities:

- Scaling up clean technologies, enhancing corporate sustainability, and supporting local communities through co-benefits.

12 TECHNOLOGICAL INNOVATIONS ENABLING GREEN FINANCE

12.1 Blockchain Technology

- Applications:
- **Carbon Credit Trading**: Ensures transparency and traceability in carbon credit markets.
- **Sustainable Supply Chain**: Tracks and verifies the sustainability of products.
- **Smart Contracts**: Automates issuance of green bonds, reducing administrative costs.

Example: IBM Blockchain for Carbon Credits.

12.2 Artificial Intelligence (AI) and Machine Learning

- Applications:
- **Green Investment Screening**: AI analyzes data to identify green investment opportunities.
- **Risk Assessment**: AI models assess climate-related risks for green projects.

- **Green Credit Scoring**: AI helps assign sustainability scores for creditworthiness.

  Example: BlackRock uses AI tools for ESG analysis.

12.3 Digital Platforms and Green Fintech Solutions

- Applications:
- **Crowdfunding for Green Projects**: Allows small-scale investors to fund sustainable projects.
- **Green Bond Platforms**: Facilitates the issuance and tracking of green bonds.
- **Sustainable Investing Apps**: Provides users with easy access to sustainable investment options.

  Example: Trine for solar energy projects.

12.4 Internet of Things (IoT) and Smart Infrastructure

- Applications:
- **Energy Efficiency Monitoring**: IoT sensors track energy use, reducing inefficiencies.
- **Smart Grids for Renewable Energy**: Optimizes energy distribution and reduces waste.

  Example: Siemens' smart buildings use IoT for energy optimization.

12.5 Big Data and Analytics

- Applications:
- **Climate Risk Analytics**: Analyzes climate data to assess investment risks.
- **Impact Measurement & Reporting**: Measures and reports the effectiveness of green projects.

  Example: S&P Global's Climate Risk Analytics.

12.6 Virtual Reality (VR) and Augmented Reality (AR)

- Applications:
- **Virtual Tours of Green Projects**: Provides immersive experiences of sustainable investments.

- **Environmental Impact Simulations**: Visualizes the long-term benefits of green projects.

Example: Green Building Council using AR for virtual tours.

12.7 AI in Green Data Modeling and Forecasting

- Applications:
- **Predictive Modeling for Renewable Energy**: AI predicts energy production for renewable projects.
- **Forecasting Carbon Markets**: AI forecasts trends in carbon pricing and market conditions.

Example: Google DeepMind predicting wind farm energy output.

These innovations make green finance more efficient, transparent, and scalable, allowing for greater sustainability and better investment decisions

13 CHALLENGES IN PROMOTING GREEN FINANCE

Here's the information organized into a **table** for better clarity:

Table 6. Challenges in Promoting Green Finance

Challenge	Impact	Solutions
1. Lack of Standardization and Clear Definitions	- Confusion in evaluating green investments. - Risk of greenwashing.	- Green Bond Principles (GBP) and Climate Bonds Standard. - Regional and international cooperation for harmonized definitions.
2. Greenwashing	- Investor skepticism and reduced capital flow into green projects. - Regulatory scrutiny.	- Enhanced transparency via rigorous reporting and third-party verification. - Stronger regulation and penalties for misleading claims.
3. Insufficient Knowledge and Expertise	- Financial institutions hesitant to invest due to complexity. - Misallocation of capital, underfunding impactful projects.	- Capacity building and training in ESG metrics and environmental risk assessments. - Collaboration with environmental experts and project developers.
4. High Initial Costs of Green Projects	- Difficulty securing initial funding, especially in developing regions. - Investor reluctance due to long payback periods.	- Blended finance models combining public and private capital. - Government incentives (subsidies, green bonds).

continued on following page

Table 6. Continued

Challenge	Impact	Solutions
5. Regulatory and Policy Uncertainty	- Market volatility and investment delays. - Unpredictable returns on green investments.	- Stable regulatory frameworks and long-term policy commitments. - International cooperation to align climate-related policies.
6. Limited Access to Green Finance in Developing Countries	- Capital flow imbalance between developed and developing countries. - Missed opportunities for sustainable projects in low-income regions.	- Capacity building and technical assistance. - Green investment funds and mechanisms like the Green Climate Fund (GCF).
7. Risk and Return Perception	- Risk aversion from investors, limiting green finance flows. - Lower investment in green projects.	- Risk mitigation instruments (guarantees, insurance). - Standardized valuation metrics for financial and environmental returns.

13.1 Greenwashing Risks

Greenwashing occurs when companies, financial institutions, or investment products mislead stakeholders about their environmental benefits to attract eco-conscious consumers and investors. This practice undermines the credibility of the green finance sector and can significantly distort market behaviour and investment decisions.

Key Risks and Impacts:

1. Erosion of Trust
2. Greenwashing leads to investor and consumer scepticism, reducing confidence in green investments and discouraging genuine participation. As a result, sustainable projects may struggle to attract funding, hindering overall progress.
3. Market Distortion
4. False claims about sustainability misallocate resources toward low-impact initiatives, creating a misleading picture of environmental progress and reducing the efficiency of green finance in achieving real change.
5. Regulatory Backlash
6. Increased cases of greenwashing have triggered tighter regulations and enforcement actions. These can raise compliance costs and limit access to the market, particularly for smaller firms unable to meet stringent standards.
7. Reputational Damage
8. When greenwashing is exposed, companies risk losing credibility, damaging their brand value, and facing public and media backlash. Financial institutions may lose clients and face lawsuits.
9. Weakening of ESG Criteria

10. Greenwashing undermines the reliability of ESG ratings by allowing companies with weak sustainability credentials to appear compliant, thus reducing the impact of ESG investing.
11. Financial Losses
12. Investors may face losses from underperforming "green" investments and may pursue legal action if misled. Misrepresented projects often fail to deliver expected returns.

Common Greenwashing Examples:

- **Misleading Claims**: A company markets products as "eco-friendly" due to minor packaging changes while continuing harmful production methods.
- **Superficial Green Bonds**: Bonds fund projects with minimal sustainability impact, such as buildings with basic efficiency measures but no significant carbon reduction.
- **ESG Funds with Hidden Risks**: Funds claiming sustainability may still invest in polluting industries under the pretext of "transitioning."

Combating Greenwashing:

- **Transparency and Disclosure**: Adopting global frameworks like the Task Force on Climate-related Financial Disclosures (TCFD) ensures accountability.
- **Third-Party Verification**: Independent bodies (e.g., Climate Bonds Initiative) help validate sustainability claims.

13.2 Limited Access to Green Finance in Developing Economies

Developing economies, particularly Small and Medium-sized Enterprises (SMEs), face numerous barriers when trying to access green finance. These barriers limit their ability to invest in sustainable practices and technologies. The primary challenges include high capital costs, lack of expertise, regulatory complexities, and limited access to green financial instruments. Let's explore these challenges in detail, followed by solutions that could help overcome them:

Challenges:

High Capital Costs:

Issue: Developing economies often face high upfront costs for adopting green technologies or sustainable practices. These costs can be prohibitive for SMEs that have limited access to capital and are already struggling with financing day-to-day operations.

Effect: This results in a reluctance to invest in energy-efficient infrastructure, renewable energy, or other sustainable solutions that would otherwise be beneficial in the long term.

Lack of Expertise:

Issue: Many SMEs in developing countries lack the technical know-how to assess and implement green technologies or understand how green finance works.

Effect: This knowledge gap results in missed opportunities for securing green finance, as these businesses might not be aware of available programs or the benefits of adopting sustainable practices.

Regulatory Complexities:

Issue: Developing economies often have weak or complex regulatory frameworks for green finance. Even when green finance options exist, the process to access these funds can be overly complicated and bureaucratic.

Effect: SMEs and other stakeholders may be deterred from applying for green finance due to confusion, excessive paperwork, or cumbersome compliance requirements, making it harder to access sustainable investment opportunities.

Limited Access to Green Financial Instruments:

Issue: Green bonds, sustainable loans, and other green financial instruments are still in their nascent stages in many developing economies. There is often a lack of financial products that cater specifically to the needs of green projects.

Effect: This creates a barrier for businesses looking to invest in sustainability. With limited access to tailored green finance, SMEs are forced to rely on traditional financing mechanisms, which may not be suitable for green projects.

Solutions:

Simplified Regulations and Better Green Finance Policies:

Solution: Governments need to create a clear, transparent, and simplified regulatory environment that encourages investment in green technologies. This involves streamlining the application process, reducing bureaucracy, and creating clear guidelines for green projects.

Impact: Simplified regulations would make it easier for SMEs to apply for green finance. Clear policies can also help build confidence in both investors and SMEs, fostering a more favorable environment for green investments.

Capacity-Building Programs:

Solution: Governments and international organizations should offer capacity-building programs to educate SMEs and local businesses on green finance, sustainable technologies, and how to apply for green funding. These programs could include training workshops, online resources, or partnerships with local institutions to raise awareness.

Impact: By increasing the knowledge and capabilities of SMEs, these programs would empower businesses to make informed decisions and increase the number of successful applications for green finance. A well-trained workforce and entrepreneur community would also promote innovation in sustainability.

International Climate Fund Access:

Solution: Developing economies can tap into international climate finance initiatives, such as the Green Climate Fund (GCF) or Global Environment Facility (GEF), to access funding and technical assistance. These funds can help reduce the financial burden of green projects and facilitate the transition to a green economy.

Impact: Access to international climate funds can alleviate financial barriers by providing subsidies, low-interest loans, or grants to support green projects. This external support can help overcome the high capital costs faced by SMEs in developing countries.

Government Incentives and Risk Mitigation Tools:

Solution: Governments can implement incentives such as tax breaks, subsidies, and grants for businesses adopting green technologies. In addition, risk mitigation tools like loan guarantees or insurance can be introduced to reduce the perceived financial risks associated with green investments.

Impact: These incentives would make green projects more financially viable by reducing the upfront costs and lowering the risks for investors. For SMEs, these tools could offer much-needed financial security, making it easier for them to adopt sustainable practices. Additionally, such measures could stimulate private sector investment in green projects, creating a more sustainable and resilient economy.

14 OPPORTUNITIES

Green finance can drive renewable energy growth, job creation, innovation in clean tech, and long-term sustainable economic development in developing regions.

Table 7. Green finance Opportunities

Opportunity	Description	Example
Investment in Renewable Energy	Funding for renewable energy projects like solar, wind, hydro, and geothermal to reduce fossil fuel dependence.	Reduced costs of solar and wind energy, government incentives driving investment.
Sustainable Infrastructure Development	Financing eco-friendly infrastructure like green buildings, sustainable transport, and water systems.	Green bonds funding energy-efficient buildings and smart cities.
Green Bonds Market Growth	Growth in green bonds offering fixed returns while financing green projects like renewable energy and sustainable agriculture.	Global green bond issuance exceeded $250 billion in 2020.
Sustainable Agriculture and Food Systems	Financing for projects promoting sustainable farming practices, organic farming, and climate-resilient food systems.	Financing regenerative agriculture that improves soil health and reduces chemical inputs.
Impact Investing and ESG Funds	Directing capital towards companies and projects that prioritize environmental, social, and governance (ESG) factors.	ESG funds growing in popularity as investors seek socially responsible investments.
Climate Adaptation and Resilience Projects	Investments in projects that help communities adapt to climate change through resilience projects like flood protection and disaster preparedness.	Coastal flood protection systems funded by green finance.
Circular Economy Investments	Funding projects that reduce waste, recycle materials, and promote sustainable product life-cycle management.	E-waste recycling and sustainable packaging attracting green finance investments.
Green Banking and Financing Innovations	Financial institutions offering green loans, sustainable mortgages, and eco-friendly investment products.	Special interest rates for energy-efficient home upgrades or green business practices.
Technology and Innovation in Green Finance	Leveraging technology like blockchain and AI to track carbon credits, monitor environmental performance, and optimize investments.	Blockchain-based carbon credit trading platforms and AI-driven tools for energy consumption optimization.
Job Creation in Green Sectors	Green finance supporting job creation in renewable energy, clean tech, sustainable agriculture, and energy efficiency sectors.	Growth in solar and wind energy industries creating manufacturing, installation, and R&D jobs.

Green finance drives innovation in renewable energy and clean technologies while fostering economic growth through green job creation and diversification. Funding sustainable projects accelerates the transition to a low-carbon economy, supports technological advancement, and promotes resilient, inclusive development across sectors like energy, transport, and infrastructure.

Enhancing Financial Market Stability

Green finance strengthens financial market stability by integrating climate and environmental risks into economic decisions. It helps manage long-term risks, reduces exposure to stranded assets, promotes transparency through ESG disclosures, and aligns investments with sustainable policy goals—fostering a more resilient financial system.

14.1 Role of green finance in de-risking portfolios

Green finance plays a vital role in reducing financial risk and enhancing the resilience of investment portfolios through the following ways:

1. Mitigating Climate and Environmental Risks
2. By directing capital toward sustainable sectors, green finance helps investors avoid industries vulnerable to climate regulation, resource scarcity, and extreme weather events.
3. Avoiding Stranded Assets
4. Investments in carbon-intensive industries risk becoming obsolete due to stricter environmental policies. Green finance encourages a shift to future-ready assets more likely to retain value.
5. Improved Risk Assessment
6. ESG integration enables investors to identify long-term ecological, social, and governance risks that traditional financial models may overlook.

14.2 Strengthening Global Climate Action and Policy Alignment

Table 8. Strengthening Global Climate Action and Policy Alignment

Aspect	Role of Green Finance
Mobilizing Climate Finance	Channels capital into low-carbon and climate-resilient projects supporting the Paris Agreement.
Policy Alignment and Compliance	Helps align financial activities with climate policies, regulations, and carbon targets.
Supporting NDC Implementation	Funds national climate action plans (NDCs), including clean energy and sustainable transport.
International Cooperation	Enables collaboration among countries, development banks, and institutions for global action.
Public-Private Partnerships (PPPs	Promotes joint financing of green infrastructure and technologies between governments and investors.
Accelerating SDGs	Contributes directly to SDGs like clean energy (SDG 7), climate action (SDG 13), and more.

15 SUCCESSFUL GREEN FINANCE MODELS FROM EUROPE, ASIA, AND AFRICA

Green finance has become a vital tool for promoting sustainable development across regions. Europe, Asia, and Africa have each implemented unique and impactful models that illustrate how green finance can accelerate environmental goals, attract investment, and promote economic resilience. Green finance represents a strategic lever to address environmental degradation, climate change, and social inequality in tandem. By identifying pathways and addressing systemic barriers, stakeholders can unlock its full potential (Sachs et al., 2019). Accelerating green finance requires harmonized efforts across global, national, and local levels, underpinned by political will, innovation, and public trust (Kreibiehl et al., 2022). As global sustainability transitions unfold, green finance must be positioned not as an alternative but as the new norm in financial decision-making.

15.1 Europe

1. The European Union Green Bond Standard (EU GBS)

The EU Green Bond Standard is a voluntary framework to enhance transparency, accountability, and credibility in green bond issuance. Funds are directed toward renewable energy, clean transport, and sustainable infrastructure projects.

Success: The EU GBS has made the EU a global leader in green bond issuance, influencing global financial markets and encouraging the replication of similar frameworks worldwide.

15.2 Nordic Countries (Sweden, Denmark, Finland, Norway)

Nordic countries are at the forefront of green finance, integrating sustainability into national financial systems through responsible investment policies and green public procurement. Sweden, for instance, has issued sovereign green bonds to fund climate-smart investments.

Success: These nations aim for carbon neutrality by 2050. Their robust green finance ecosystems attract domestic and international investment, fueling clean technology and renewable energy initiatives.

15.3 Asia

1. China's Green Credit and Green Bond Initiatives

China's Green Credit Guidelines incentivize banks to fund green projects, while green bonds are promoted to finance sustainable infrastructure. Government-backed standards ensure that funded projects meet environmental goals.

Success: China is now one of the world's largest green bond issuers, using proceeds to support energy efficiency, pollution control, and green transportation.

2. India's National Action Plan on Climate Change (NAPCC)

India's NAPCC integrates climate strategies into national development. Green bonds, subsidies, and government-backed guarantees fund renewable energy and climate-resilient infrastructure.

Success: India has financed major solar and wind projects through green bonds, helping meet its target of 500 GW of non-fossil fuel capacity by 2030.

3. Japan's Expanding Green Bond Market

Japan's Ministry of the Environment has established guidelines for green bond issuance, ensuring transparency and proper fund utilization. Projects supported include renewable energy, disaster resilience, and clean transportation.

Success: Japan's clear framework has attracted institutional investors and helped fund large-scale projects that reduce emissions and promote sustainability.

15.4 Africa

1. South Africa's Green Bond Market

South Africa pioneered green bonds in Africa, focusing on energy efficiency, water infrastructure, and sustainable transport. The Johannesburg Stock Exchange supports green listings aligned with global standards.

Success: Green bonds have financed critical infrastructure and attracted local and international investors to sustainable projects.

2. Kenya's Renewable Energy Investments

Kenya has heavily invested in wind, solar, and geothermal energy. The government utilizes public-private partnerships and green finance tools to fund large-scale projects.

Success: Projects like the Lake Turkana Wind Power Project have made Kenya a continental leader in renewable energy, enhancing energy access and reducing emissions.

3. Morocco's Solar Energy Financing

Morocco has mobilized green finance to develop large-scale solar projects like the Noor Ouarzazate Solar Complex. Funding comes from multilateral institutions and green bonds.

Success: Morocco is now a leader in solar energy in Africa, demonstrating how strategic green finance can transform national energy landscapes.

Key Takeaways

- **Clear Standards:** Transparent guidelines like the EU GBS foster investor trust.
- **Policy Alignment:** National strategies (e.g., China's green credit or India's NAPCC) ensure green finance supports climate goals.
- **Public-Private Collaboration:** Partnerships in Africa and Asia accelerate green infrastructure funding and innovation.

These models show that tailored green finance strategies can unlock capital, drive innovation, and support climate goals globally.

16 POLICY RECOMMENDATIONS AND STRATEGIC ROADMAP

A clear regulatory framework is crucial to accelerate green finance, starting with a standardized taxonomy to reduce greenwashing and enhance investor confidence. Incentivizing green investments through tax benefits and subsidies can draw in private sector participation and stimulate the development of clean technologies. Introducing carbon pricing and sustainable lending guidelines aligns market activity with environmental goals.

16.1 Unified Green Finance Taxonomy

Developing a unified taxonomy establishes clear definitions of sustainable activities, such as renewable energy or energy efficiency. It must align with global goals (e.g., the Paris Agreement), be adaptable to regional needs, and be regularly updated. A transparent taxonomy improves investor trust, ensures accountability, prevents greenwashing, and attracts more capital. Examples include the EU Green Taxonomy and China's Green Bond Catalogue.

16.2 Public-Private Sector Collaboration

Adequate green finance depends on strong public-private partnerships (PPPs). Governments should offer enabling policies—such as green bonds and risk-sharing tools—while businesses align strategies with sustainability targets. Blended finance can de-risk investments, and public leadership in long-term planning ensures consistency and innovation.

16.3 Capacity Building and Awareness

Capacity building through education and training helps stakeholders—from banks to SMEs—adopt green finance practices. Public campaigns and industry engagement spread awareness while sharing best practices and offering regulatory guidance to support widespread adoption and sustainable behaviour.

16.4 Sustainability in Risk Assessment

Integrating ESG and climate-related factors into financial risk assessments strengthens resilience. This includes scenario analysis, climate modelling, and assessing long-term risks such as stranded assets. Doing so enables better decision-making and attracts environmentally conscious investments.

16.5 Innovation through Incentives

Governments and institutions can accelerate green innovation by providing grants, tax breaks, and subsidies for R&D in renewable energy, sustainable agriculture, and energy-efficient technologies. Supporting pilot projects and collaborations with academia and industry drives impactful solutions.

16.6 Transparency and Accountability

Transparent reporting using global standards (e.g., TCFD, GRI) is vital to tracking the impact of green finance. Independent audits and standardized disclosures prevent greenwashing, ensure effective fund use, and increase investor confidence. Regulatory enforcement plays a critical role.

16.7 Conclusion

Green finance plays a pivotal role in addressing pressing environmental challenges while simultaneously fostering sustainable economic growth. It refers to financial investments that support sustainable development projects and initiatives aimed at reducing carbon emissions, conserving natural resources, and promoting environmental stewardship. By embedding sustainability into financial systems, governments, institutions, and businesses can redirect capital flows toward low-carbon, climate-resilient activities, creating a powerful mechanism to combat climate change.

The integration of green finance helps countries align their economic strategies with global environmental commitments such as the Paris Agreement and the United Nations Sustainable Development Goals (SDGs). It ensures that climate risks are considered in financial decision-making, encouraging transparency and long-term planning in both public and private sectors.

Moreover, green finance generates a wide range of economic benefits. It spurs innovation in clean technologies and sustainable infrastructure, paving the way for new markets and business models. The transition to a green economy also fosters job creation, especially in sectors like renewable energy, sustainable agriculture, waste management, and eco-friendly construction. Additionally, by investing in climate-resilient systems, countries can enhance their economic resilience against natural disasters and environmental disruptions, thereby reducing future costs associated with climate-related damages.

In essence, green finance is not just a tool for environmental preservation—it is a strategic approach to secure long-term economic prosperity, social equity, and planetary health. It empowers economies to grow responsibly while safeguarding the needs of future generations.

16.8 Summary of Pathways, Challenges, And Future Outlook

Here's a table summarizing the pathways, challenges, and future outlook of green finance:

Table 9. pathways, challenges, and future outlook of green finance

Category	Details
Pathways	1. **Green Financial Instruments**: Green bonds, sustainable loans, and ESG investments. 2. **Public-Private Partnerships (PPPs)**: Collaborative funding for sustainable infrastructure. 3. **Integration of ESG in Investment**: Incorporating ESG factors into financial strategies. 4. **Incentives and Grants**: Government support for green technology innovation. 5. **Carbon Markets and Emissions Trading**: Mechanisms to promote climate-related accountability. 6. **Strengthening Regulation and Standards**: Development of green taxonomies and reporting standards (e.g., TCFD, EU Taxonomy).
Challenges	1. **Lack of Standardization**: Difficulty in assessing green investments without clear definitions. 2. **Awareness and Capacity Gaps**: Limited knowledge, particularly in emerging markets. 3. **Greenwashing**: Misrepresentation of sustainability credentials. 4. **High Upfront Costs and Financial Risks**: Perception of high risks and initial investment costs. 5. **Measurement and Reporting Issues**: Challenges in tracking and verifying the impact of green finance.
Future Outlook	1. **Growing Market Demand**: Increased demand for sustainable investments as climate risks rise. 2. **Technological Advancements**: Innovation in renewable energy and sustainable technologies. 3. **Stronger Regulatory Support**: Anticipated tightening of regulations and clearer standards. 4. **Global Cooperation**: Enhanced international efforts for scaling up green finance. 5. **Increased Transparency**: Improved transparency in green finance practices, fostering trust and investment.

This table highlights the key pathways that drive green finance, the challenges that need to be addressed, and the outlook for the future of green finance.

REFERENCES

Ameli, N., Drummond, P., Bisaro, A., Grubb, M., & Chenet, H. (2021). Climate finance and disclosure for institutional investors: Why transparency is not enough. *Climate Policy*, *21*(4), 495–512.

Banga, J. (2019). The green bond market: A potential source of climate finance for developing countries. *Journal of Sustainable Finance & Investment*, *9*(1), 17–32.

Banga, J. (2019). The green bond market: A potential source of climate finance for developing countries. *Journal of Sustainable Finance & Investment*, *9*(1), 17–32. DOI: 10.1080/20430795.2018.1498617

Bhattacharya, A., & Kojima, S. (2012). Power sector investment risk and renewable energy: A Japanese case study using portfolio risk optimization method. *Energy Policy*, *40*, 69–80. DOI: 10.1016/j.enpol.2010.06.044

Broadstock, D. C., Chan, K., Cheng, L. T. W., & Wang, X. (2021). The role of ESG performance during times of financial crisis: Evidence from COVID-19 in China. *Finance Research Letters*, *38*, 101716. DOI: 10.1016/j.frl.2020.101716 PMID: 32837385

Campiglio, E., Dafermos, Y., Monnin, P., Ryan-Collins, J., Schotten, G., & Tanaka, M. (2018). Climate change challenges for central banks and financial regulators. *Nature Climate Change*, *8*(6), 462–468.

Carney, M. (2015). *Breaking the tragedy of the horizon—climate change and financial stability*. Speech at Lloyd's of London.

Chen, Y., & Volz, U. (2022). Green finance and fintech: Emerging issues and prospects. *Journal of Sustainable Finance & Investment*, *12*(2), 329–347. DOI: 10.1080/20430795.2020.1802815

. Clark, G. L., Feiner, A., & Viehs, M. (2015). From the stockholder to the stakeholder: How sustainability can drive financial outperformance. *Oxford University Research Report*.

EU. (2018). *EU Action Plan on Sustainable Finance*. European Commission.

EU. (2020). *EU Taxonomy Regulation*. Official Journal of the European Union.

EU Technical Expert Group on Sustainable Finance. (2020). *Taxonomy: Final report of the Technical Expert Group on Sustainable Finance*. European Commission. https://ec.europa.eu/info/publications/sustainable-finance-technical-expert-group_en

Flammer, C. (2021). Corporate green bonds. *Journal of Financial Economics, 142*(2), 499–516.

Flammer, C. (2021). Corporate green bonds. *Journal of Financial Economics, 142*(2), 499–516. DOI: 10.1016/j.jfineco.2021.01.010

Friede, G., Busch, T., & Bassen, A. (2015). ESG and financial performance: Aggregated evidence from more than 2000 empirical studies. *Journal of Sustainable Finance & Investment*, *5*(4), 210–233.

Friede, G., Busch, T., & Bassen, A. (2015). ESG and financial performance: Aggregated evidence from more than 2000 empirical studies. *Journal of Sustainable Finance & Investment*, *5*(4), 210–233. DOI: 10.1080/20430795.2015.1118917

GCF. (2021). *Green Climate Fund Annual Results Report*. Retrieved from https://www.greenclimate.fund/

Ghosh, S. (2020). *Financing green recovery in developing Asia*. Asian Development Bank Institute.

IMF. (2021). *Mobilizing Private Climate Financing in Emerging Market and Developing Economies*. International Monetary Fund.

Inderst, G., Kaminker, C., & Stewart, F. (2012). Defining and measuring green investments. *OECD Working Papers on Finance, Insurance and Private Pensions*, No. 24.

International Renewable Energy Agency. (2022). *World energy transitions outlook 2022*. IRENA. https://www.irena.org/publications

Kidney, S., Oliver, P., Sonerud, B., & Sullivan, R. (2017). *Unlocking green finance for developing countries*. Climate Bonds Initiative. https://www.climatebonds.net

Kreibiehl, S., Battiston, S., & Downing, L.. (2022). *Climate Finance – IPCC Working Group III Sixth Assessment Report*. IPCC.

Li, J., Xu, L., & Li, X. (2021). Fintech, ESG and sustainable finance: A literature review. *Sustainability*, *13*(15), 8448.

OECD. (2020). *Developing Sustainable Finance Definitions and Taxonomies*. OECD Publishing.

Organisation for Economic Co-operation and Development. (2020). *Developing sustainable finance definitions and taxonomies*. OECD Publishing., DOI: 10.1787/134a2dbe-

Organisation for Economic Co-operation and Development. (2021). *Blended finance in the least developed countries 2020*. OECD Publishing., DOI: 10.1787/57620d04-

PBoC. (2016). *Guidelines for Establishing the Green Financial System*. People's Bank of China.

Porter, M. E., & van der Linde, C. (1995). Toward a new conception of the environment-competitiveness relationship. *The Journal of Economic Perspectives, 9*(4), 97–118. DOI: 10.1257/jep.9.4.97

Sachs, J. D., Woo, W. T., Yoshino, N., & Taghizadeh-Hesary, F. (2019). *Handbook of Green Finance: Energy Security and Sustainable Development*. Springer.

Taghizadeh-Hesary, F., & Yoshino, N. (2020). The way to induce private participation in green finance and investment. *Finance Research Letters, 31*, 100828.

UNEP. (2016). *Definitions and concepts: Background note for the G20 Green Finance Study Group*. United Nations Environment Programme.

United Nations Environment Programme. (2016). *Green finance for developing countries: Needs, concerns and innovations*. UNEP. https://wedocs.unep.org

United Nations Framework Convention on Climate Change. (2021). *Introduction to climate finance*. UNFCCC. https://unfccc.int/topics/climate-finance

Wang, Y., Zhi, Q., Zhang, H., & Wei, Y. (2022). Can green finance promote sustainable economic growth? Evidence from China. *Journal of Cleaner Production, 339*, 130652. DOI: 10.1016/j.jclepro.2022.130652

World Bank. (2019). *Public-private partnerships for sustainable development*. World Bank Group. https://ppp.worldbank.org

Zadek, S., & Flynn, C. (2013). South-originating green finance: Exploring the potential. United Nations Environment Programme & Geneva International Finance Dialogues. https://www.unepfi.org/fileadmin/documents/south-originating_green_finance.pdf

Zhang, D., & Zhang, Z. (2021). Green finance in China: Emerging trends and policy implications. *Sustainability, 13*(2), 769. DOI: 10.3390/su13020769

Chapter 6
Green Orientation Strategies:
An Imperative for Enhancing SME Sustainability in Digital Age

Shweta Jaiswal
https://orcid.org/0000-0002-7849-3461
CMP Degree College, University of Allahabad, India

Nishtha Agrawal
https://orcid.org/0009-0008-4902-1175
CMP Degree College, University of Allahabad, India

Shafqat Ali
https://orcid.org/0009-0007-4912-779X
CMP Degree College, University of Allahabad, India

ABSTRACT

Green orientation as a strategic tool in achieving sustainability in SMEs has turned out to be an imperative and conscious shift towards business processes that strive to be environment friendly. The study attempts to explore the green orientation tools, challenges and the possible outcomes when employed as a strategy in SMEs. The study gives an idea about some of the main elements and factors that would ease the achievement of sustainability through green orientation in SMEs and the factors that could hinder or act as a barrier in achieving the sustainability through the employment of green orientation. The study investigates the probable challenges exclusively faced by the small and medium enterprises and businesses like financial restraints, lack of expertise and lack of the desire to adapt to changes in the con-

DOI: 10.4018/979-8-3373-1240-8.ch006

cerned corporate culture. The study also gave the recommendation for SMEs who are interested in implementation of green orientation as a strategy in achieving and ensuring the long-term sustainability of their businesses.

1. INTRODUCTION

Green orientation is seen as a strategic approach towards sustainability by many small and medium-sized enterprises (SMEs) in this digital era. The main driver of this shift is the understanding of which green innovations are not only good for protecting the environment but also for improving economic results (Ruggieri et al., 2016). Green product innovation has the highest impact on economic as well as environmental terms, pointing to green innovations as core competencies of SMEs that address sustainability performance (Muangmee et al., 2021) Moreover, incorporating green entrepreneurial orientation in the model may help better leverage external knowledge and resources to contribute towards a holistic view of sustainability encompassing economic, environmental, and social dimensions (Vrontis et al., 2022). Studies also reveal a positive relationship between the level of green innovation activity and business sustainability in SME´s, strengthening the claim that green innovation plays an important role in promoting sustainable economic development (Khan et al., 2024). This finding illuminates the degree to which adopting sustainability has been a priority over recent years, and especially necessary with COVID-19 restrictions, as established businesses pivot towards more sustainable methods (Gomes et al., 2024). The COVID pandemic makes more sense now for SMEs to carry out green practices as a response strategy driven by the current situation at hand, but it also highlights the need for an environmental consciousness drought in everyday operations (Ishaq et al., 2024).

This approach enhances customer engagement and reduces environmental footprints, thus fostering a competitive edge. Social media marketing also plays a crucial role in communicating green initiatives, thereby improving green. marketing performance (Aftab et al., 2024). The achievements of small- and medium-sized enterprises (SME) are largely dependent on the contributions of managers and employees. These individuals play a crucial role in determining the success or failure of a company, particularly given the constraints faced by SMEs such as limited resources, capital, and technology (Sohu et al., 2024). However, as long as they have a high and unique commitment compared with competitors, we would expect to see that the company will become successful, and business independence will be achieved by the presence of indicators for success in term of financial and non-financial performance (Tazhibekova & Shametova, 2024). Demonstrating a commitment to environmental sustainability will appeal to pro-environmental consumers who are seeking unique and distinct products that differ from those that use synthetic colours and printing, even though the price may be higher (Omar et al., 2024). Despite the advancements in the digital era, it is crucial to enhance efforts towards promoting eco-friendly creativity and business independence (X. Zhang et al., 2024). This can be achieved by leveraging green IT empowerment, which aims to improve performance and competitive advantage (Rehman et al., 2024).

Technological advancements in this scenario help to harness limited resources effectively and productively while providing a competitive edge for remote control operations (El-Kassar & Singh, 2019). The way technology and sustainability interact with one another is immeasurably complex and varied. Innovation is the key variable among the factors that drive the shape of an institution and resource allocation around these innovative practices (Suchek & Franco, 2024a);Zameer et al., 2024).

2. GREEN ORIENTATION

Green orientation has generated a great deal of curiosity in how operations are fostered by businesses especially when pursuing environmental sustainability goals (Aftab et al., 2024). Designed as a strategic imperative for an organization, it involves incorporating environmental considerations alike marketing, human resource development etc., into the overall business strategies undertaken. Based on research, SMEs take an important position in terms of sustainable practices and sustainably innovative activities may present three modes to adopt. (Sohu et al., 2024). The SME orientation is particularly significant in that it may enable digital technologies to contribute to both economic sustainability and social value (Sabihaini et al., 2024). Results of the research have revealed a significant moderating role played by entrepreneurial orientation in linking social and economic value creation to performance outcomes for SMEs (Vrontis et al., 2022).

The most basic pillar of green orientation is Green Entrepreneur Orientation (GEO) which implies identification and exploitation in environmental opportunities proactively (Ruggieri et al., 2016). GEO is a powerful determinant of GIP and EP within firms. For example, factors influencing the discrepancy among countries such as green absorptive capacity and environmental cooperation have a significant impact on GEO which emphasizes that collaboration has an important role in sustainable practices (Oxborrow & Brindley, 2013). This is in accordance that SMEs can exploit their flexibility and creativity to implement green practices where environmental harms are reduced while at the same time benefiting its competitive position. (Suki et al., 2023).

3. NEXUS OF GREEN ORIENTATION VIA SUSTAINABILITY IN SMEs

The nexus, on promoting friendly practices within small and medium sized businesses is gaining importance for improving both environmental impact and financial sustainability (Siegel et al., 2024). Green Entrepreneurial Orientation (GEO) positively impacts environmental performance in SMEs, with Corporate Social Responsibility (CSR) and Green Innovation (GI) mediating this relationship, enhancing sustainability practices. the paper focuses on entrepreneurial orientation's impact on SME profitability, not specifically on green orientation or sustainability (Suchek & Franco, 2024).

The integration of information systems (Green IS) is another important factor that helps small and medium enterprises (SMEs) in their sustainability efforts. Studies show that adopting Green IS measures like pollution prevention and product stewardship can greatly improve a companys social performance.(Jalil et al., 2025) These initiatives not boost operational efficiency but also align SMEs objectives with wider sustainability targets to ensure their long-term success, in a competitive business environment. In addition to that point the incorporation of technologies and focusing on regional markets has proven to be a key factor in predicting innovation success for small and medium sized enterprises (SMEs) highlighting the importance of align with local market needs and sustainable methods. Another essential element is the adoption of information systems (Green IS) which plays a crucial role in assisting SMEs towards sustainability goals.(*Digital Literacy, Digital Intelligence and Small and Medium Enterprises' (SMEs) Sustainability: The Mediating Role of Digital Technology Usage - Masud Ibrahim, Elizabeth Wetania Aduah, 2025*, n.d.) Studies show that implementing Green IS practices such, as pollution control and product stewardship can greatly improve outcomes by enhancing environmental and social performance (Brezavšček et al., 2019). These methods not help improve how smoothly things run but also make sure that small to medium sized businesses are working toward larger sustainability goals to stay competitive in the long run (Tai et al., 2024).

4. GREEN STRATEGIES IN SMEs

Green marketing tools are the strategies and techniques that companies use to sell products or services that they consider environmentally friendly. Such tools leverage data, analytics, and digital communication to promote and implement sustainability initiatives (Karuppiah et al., 2020). Energy Management Software (EMS) is a digital application that helps manage, analyze, and control energy consumption agreements across an organization. Utilizing machine learning and advanced analytics, the EMS Platform delivers actionable insights on energy utilization to businesses, assisting in managing costs while upgrading performance in order to reach higher standards of sustainability.(*Dynamic Capabilities and Green Strategy in Green Entrepreneurship and Circular Economy: A Study - Mondal - Business Strategy and the Environment - Wiley Online Library*, 2025) Energy usage in buildings or industrial facilities is tracked by solutions such as the Energy Star Portfolio Manager, Enel X, and Honeywell Forge to identify inefficiencies and optimize energy consumption (Nuryakin & Maryati, 2022a).

Sustainable supply chain platforms are digital tools and systems that help organizations to monitor their supply chain and improve their environmental, social, and economic impacts. They allow insight, transparency, and control in their supply chains for sustainable practices. IBM Food Trust and Provenance are examples of traceability solutions that use blockchains and other technologies.(*Exploring the Impact of Green Entrepreneurial Orientation on Sustainable Performance: Insights from CSR, Policy and Innovation | Management Decision | Emerald Publishing*, 2024) They trace the origin and journey of products to ensure sustainable sources and ethical practices while Supply Chain Optimization Software includes SAP Ariba and Eco Vadis which helps businesses manage their supply chains sustainably with focusing on actively reducing waste, energy use, and emissions. (Ghazilla et al., 2015)

The carbon footprint calculator is a tool created and used to measure or estimate the total, direct, and indirect greenhouse gas emissions caused by an organization's product (Madrid-Guijarro & Duréndez, 2024). Carbon calculators enable the calculation of carbon footprints and offer a holistic approach that enables people, businesses, or organizations to estimate their impact on climate change using activity data to determine areas where reductions are possible and develop strategies for emission reduction (Fernandez-Lores et al., 2022) There are many individual and corporate online tools for calculating the carbon footprint. For individuals, the WWF Carbon Footprint Calculator or My Climate is useful for estimating their personal carbon footprint based on choices relevant to food and housing. In turn, the Salesforce Sustainability Cloud, Sphera, and Persefoni are examples of corporate carbon accounting platforms for calculating, tracking, and reporting carbon emissions aligned with sustainability aspirations and sometimes regulatory requirements (Ardyan et al., 2017).

Project management software with sustainability features wraps traditional project management tools to support your current and future efforts for sustainable work (Rizos et al., 2016) More usefully, this enables organizations to manage projects in a way that decreases impact on the environment while supporting social responsibility and contributing at a macro level towards sustainability goals. Tools like Asana and

Trello also work for this by tracking sustainability initiatives, goals, and projects along the lines of going green(Liu et al., 2022).

Digital communication tools are software applications and platforms created to support diverse forms of communication between people and groups using a digital approach (Musa & Chinniah, 2016). As a result, individuals and organizations can exchange information, cooperate to develop projects, and keep in touch no matter where they are situated. For example, platforms such as Slack and Microsoft Teams can render the setting that will enable remote work, thus reducing the need to travel and produce related emissions.(Shandilya et al., 2024)

Internet of Things (IoT) sensors are devices that collect data from the physical environment and send this data via the Internet or over other networks to be processed, analyzed, and used for various applications (Fechtelpeter et al., 2017). They are pivotal to the Internet of Things (IoT) ecosystem, allowing devices to "sense" their environment and proactively react in real time. Real-time data from devices that monitor energy use, water consumption or environmental conditions help optimize the resources and reduce waste (Rozman Cafuta, 2015).

Virtual collaboration tools are software and platforms that are used to enable the collaboration of teams regardless of their physical location; they help to improve virtual teamwork and work together more efficiently (Purwandani & Michaud, 2021) .These tools simplify communication, project management, document sharing, and collaboration in the digital space. Tools such as Zoom or Google Meet can minimize physical meetings, and thus reduce travel-related emissions.

5. DRIVERS TO ENHANCE THE EMPLOYMENT OF GREEN STRATEGIES IN SMEs

The contribution of small and medium-sized enterprises (SMEs) are critical to support sustainability by allowing ecological friendly protocols to be adopted widely. Specifically, there are several important reasons for small and medium-sized enterprises (SMEs) to adopt ecological sustainability.

- **The regulation on SMEs of more stringent nature**: The environmental requirements for emissions, waste management and resource utilization are strict types while those small and medium-sized enterprises (SME) should strictly obey the provisions of law and administrative regulations that are related to mandatory.(*Integrating Sustainability in Small Scale Industries: From Environmental Degradation to Cleaner Practices: Environmental Claims Journal*) It is compulsory to ensure that these laws are stuck with, for all protecting reasons so as not to find a good pace punishment.

- **Revenue incentives and subsidies:** Governments commonly offer tax breaks or revenue incentives to help encourage the adoption of environmentally sound technology or practices, which in turn encourages SMEs (small- and medium-sized enterprises) to apply certain forms of sustainability into their business operations.(Joeliaty, 2024)
- **Market Demand and Consumer Preferences:** Observations suggest there is an increasing demand for environmentally sustainable products and services in the market. The eco-friendly solutions used by SMEs make the products and services more competitive in relation to an environmentally-oriented public. Even among the smallest and medium enterprises (SMEs), environmental rules are often forced upon them as the biggest players in their business areas have made regulation a precondition to suppliers on general terms, putting SMEs doing anything but environmentally good behaviours out of business rapidly (Asad et al., 2024).
- **Cost savings and optimisation analysis:** Eco practices such as saving on energy, water usage or waste management can lead to substantial cost reduction. The same goes for small to mid-market businesses, this is generally their number one motivation
- **Conservation of energy:** With the use of renewable sources of energy and energy-efficient machinery, a lot of cost-related expenses will be saved by SMEs. This can enhance the appeal of green ventures.
- **Exploitation of New Markets and Potential Markets Opportunities:** Acquiring green certification opens up new ways for SMEs to penetrate new markets, especially within overseas markets where sustainability is a significant issue and green credentials are at the front end of anyone's procurement list Dimensions of opportunity: Such a reputation would attract potential cooperation and collaborations with other organizations claiming to be environmentally friendly. This would have the effect of enhancing the competitive capabilities of SMEs (Yousaf, 2021).
- **Advancements in technology:** clean technologies at the cutting edge of development are necessary for small and medium-sized firms (SMEs) to implement environmentally friendly solutions at relatively cheaper costs, such as renewable energy solutions, energy-efficient machinery, and sustainable materials.(Alshebami, 2023).

6. FOCUSING COMPETITIVENESS THROUGH GREEN ORIENTATION IN SMEs

Small and medium-sized enterprises (SMEs) are becoming more aware of sustainability in the current business environment, evolving at a warp speed. As environmental awareness comes to the forefront, incorporating green orientation into business strategies has become a powerful method for sustaining competitiveness (Mady et al., 2023). By complying with sustainable practices in their way of doing business, SMEs can differentiate themselves from their competitors, lower costs, and meet the demand for eco-friendly products or services. The most direct and quickest ROI for green orientation is decreased cost. The implementation of energy-efficient practices can lead to a substantial decrease in operational expenditures (Suwandi & Badrianto, 2023). In this sense, SMEs can save bills by deploying energy-saving technologies along with the optimal use of resources which means that less waste results in higher profit margins. Moreover, sustainable resource management supports recycling and reuse of material to help save money and protect the environment. Like any other company, in a crowded marketplace, it is essential to set yourself apart, and standing out through green orientation is an avenue for differentiation (Toryanto & Indriani, 2022). In particular, consumers today are smarter and mindful of their carbon footprint, so they turn more towards products or services that fit their values. By offering green alternatives, SMEs can enter niche markets and build a loyal customer base that values sustainability (Nuryakin & Maryati, 2022b). Further, a solid commitment to sustainability can improve brand reputation and make businesses more appealing to consumers, potential partners, and investors. With governments worldwide tightening environmental regulations, businesses have to stay a step ahead of compliance and avoid penalties (Siegel et al., 2024) Sustainability-minded SMEs are typically able to comply with these requirements, minimizing the chances of being fined and experiencing operational disruption. Moreover, Governments and organizations have special incentives such as grants or tax breaks to encourage businesses that are willing to adopt more green practices, which means that additional aid could go to bundles of companies that will be the first movers in their sustainability efforts (Jansson et al., 2017).

Sustainability is the key driver of innovation, and companies that embrace green orientation are frequently found in ambassadors for new product development, process re-engineering, and packaging innovation. This focus on sustainability and innovation not only unlocks new business opportunities but also makes the company more flexible within a changing market.(Nuryakin & Maryati, 2022) Small- and medium-sized enterprises (SMEs) that integrate sustainability within their core business practices are in a stronger position to adapt themselves to changing consumer preferences and market conditions be they regulatory, thereby leading them to ensure long-term survival. Transparency in green practices contributes to trust, which is a staple of successful businesses (J. A. Zhang & Walton, 2017) It provides customers with confidence that a company is serious about sustainability, helping to develop significant customer loyalty This, in turn, can lead to better customer retention and word-of-mouth promotion, two irreplaceable assets for the growth of a business.(Jeyadevi J, 2023) Moreover, customers driven by sustainability often have a higher level of brand engagement, leading to increased sales opportunities. Growth is the blood of any organization, with financial resources a key support for growth, and green orientation enables access to additional sprouts for adding new branches (Muangmee et al., 2021b) Green financing solutions, such as low-interest loans or investment funds specifically targeting sustainable initiatives or enterprises, and even earmarked platforms on crowdfunding have been introduced by some financial institutions to create a new asset class that rewards those committed to being green and circularly healthy organizations (Siegel et al., 2019) These instruments will help green-oriented SMEs have a first-mover advantage in the competition for business expansion, innovation, and sustainability measures. Green orientation is not just a trend, but in an eco-friendly world, it becomes necessary for SMEs to comply with their strategy (Kosasih et al., 2023a). With sustainability in mind, economic development is, of course, the worthiest pursuit; it will help SMEs be more cost-effective, provide consumers with an attractive market product, and increase long-term survival (Cerchione et al., 2018). The global drive towards sustainability shows no sign of slowing, and with ever-shifting consumer expectations leading to strengthened environmental standards, SMEs who get ahead will be more likely to thrive in a sustainable business ecosystem. The future of business is green, and those who can capitalize on this shift will emerge as victors in a sustainable, affluent world (Klewitz & Hansen, 2014).

7. ACHIEVING SUSTAINABILITY BY LEVERAGING GREEN ORIENTATION IN SMEs

Sustainability has become vitally important to small and medium enterprises (SMEs) in this digital era, even more than ever before, in business operations. As environmental laws and the public desire for green practices continues to grow, SMEs need a new gameplan that includes sustainability or runs the risk of falling behind (Zhan et al., 2018). One of the most suitable policies is green orientation, which includes numerous pro-environmental practices and strategies that reduce business environmental degradation. Green orientation could also appeal to small or medium enterprises (SMEs) in manufacturing industries because they represent an enormous share of global resource use and pollution loadings generated by their operations

(Khana et al., 2020). The existing research provides a significant contribution that SMEs, by going for green orientation strategies, can improve not only their environmental performance but also help in exploiting new business possibilities that are now playing up and coming areas of eco-industry and clean-tech markets (R. K. Singh et al., 2022). SMEs that invest in sustainability are also poised to benefit from a broader societal shift that demands eco-friendly products and services, turning these small businesses into providers of green goods and services. The adoption of green orientation can also reinforce the internal competencies and capacities necessary for sound environmental management (Sajan et al., 2017). The implementation of green human resource management practices (e.g., green recruitment, training and development, and performance appraisal) can be considered the core competencies that SMEs use to connect skills and expertise to meet environmental opportunities. Providing employees with knowledge and the means to take action in these areas can help build a spirit of environmental stewardship within the organization, turning it into an army of sustainability champions (Dey et al., 2020).

Real world scenarios/ case studies:

Case study 1 — ZANDERiot: IoT energy monitoring for a distributed SME network (industry deployment)

What happened: The Zander Group (a wholesale with many branches) and digital partner Codestryke deployed an IoT energy monitoring solution (ZANDERiot) to collect meter-level data across outlets, push it to the cloud, and provide dashboards and alerts for store managers. The solution focused on low-effort installation and actionable insights (kWh by device/area, anomaly detection).

Environmental impact & lessons:

- Rapid transparency: previously hidden consumption profiles became visible to managers — enabling simple fixes (schedule HVAC, reduce overnight loads).
- Measurable savings: pilot branches reported electricity cost reductions and faster detection of faulty equipment.
- DSN tie-ins: sharing anonymized branch dashboards and tips across their internal network helped replicate wins quickly.

Why this maps to GIoT+DSN: simple, energy-efficient IoT sensors + cloud analytics generated data that was then turned into shared knowledge across branches (an internal DSN), amplifying environmental gains.

Case study 2 — IoT-based sustainable energy solutions for SMEs (academic pilot + forecasting)

What happened: An academic/industry study developed IoT data collection across multiple SMEs (energy meters, IoT gateways) and combined it with LSTM forecasting to predict short-term energy demand and enable scheduling/optimization interventions. The paper documents the data pipeline, preprocessing, forecasting model and potential savings.

Environmental impact & lessons:

- Forecasting + control reduces peak consumption and improves load scheduling (less grid stress, lower bills).
- Edge preprocessing reduced data transmission needs (green design).
- Reproducible method: the study demonstrates a replicable pipeline SMEs or intermediaries (ESCOs) can apply at low marginal cost.

Why relevant to the framework: combines green sensor design, ML forecasting and the organizational step of translating forecasts into actions (which can be accelerated by DSN — e.g., peer forums where SMEs share successful scheduling rules).

Case study 3 — SMEnergy / Energy footprint management for SMEs (EU project & toolkit)

What happened: EU-backed projects and toolkits (e.g., SMEnergy / SME energy footprint initiatives) created practical guides, measurement templates and low-cost toolchains for SMEs to map and manage their energy footprint. They emphasize simple IoT deployments, training, and shared resources.

Environmental impact & lessons:

- Policy + program support lowers adoption barriers (training, templates, co-funding).
- Community effect: SMEs in the same sector that shared dashboards and practices improved faster than isolated firms.
- Replicable assets: toolkits and templates reduced design time for new SME pilots.

Role of DSN: these programs often embed peer groups, online portals and local meetings (digital + physical) that function as DSN to spread best practices and coordinate action.

Case study 4 — Social-media / digital networking driving sustainability adoption (empirical studies)

What the literature shows: Multiple empirical studies find social media/digital platform adoption correlates with better sustainability outcomes in SMEs — by improving stakeholder engagement, enabling access to green markets, and facilitating learning and reputation building. Studies from developing and emerging economies (e.g., Ghana, Pakistan) show DSN usage helps SMEs translate digital strategy into environmental performance gains.

Practical examples & mechanisms:

- SMEs publish energy/waste KPIs to customers on social channels → customers reward greener firms → motivates management to optimize.
- Industry WhatsApp/Facebook groups exchange low-cost IoT tips (which sensors to buy, how to configure timers).
- Crowdsourced troubleshooting: when an SME posts an anomaly screenshot, peers or vendors propose fixes — accelerating remedies.

This empirical backing supports treating DSN explicitly as a mediator in the GIoT adoption framework.

Case study 5 — Illustrative applied case: Indian textile SME uses GIoT + DSN (design/applied example)

(Explicitly labelled as an applied/illustrative case — not a pre-existing published case.)

Scenario: A 60-employee textile dyeing SME in Uttar Pradesh installs low-cost IoT sensors on boiler, compressor, and main electrical panel; deploys edge gateways to aggregate and compress data; and connects dashboards to an industry WhatsApp group and a local textile cluster portal.

Sequence & outcomes (expected/grounded in literature):

1. **Install & baseline** — sensors + cloud = baseline energy and water map in 2 weeks.
2. **Quick wins** — schedule boilers to avoid idle heat (reduce natural gas use), fix leaky steam trap detected via pressure anomalies → ~8–12% energy savings in first 3 months (realistic given similar pilots).
3. **DSN leverage** — SME posts anonymized dashboard and the corrective action in the textile cluster portal; three neighboring units replicate the fix within weeks, scaling aggregate reductions.
4. **Finance & scaling** — cluster negotiates bulk purchase of variable-speed drives (VSDs) with an equipment vendor via the DSN, lowering unit cost and speeding uptake.
5. **Sustainability branding** — SME publishes monthly KPI snapshots to customers on LinkedIn and local procurement networks, improving tender success for green buyers.

Why this is credible: It mirrors documented mechanisms in the literature (IoT→insights→action) and the documented role of DSN in spreading practices among SMEs and improving sustainability.

8. BARRIERS FACED DURING THE IMPLEMENTATION OF GREEN STRATEGIES IN SMEs

An increasing number of small and medium-sized enterprises (SMEs) are realizing the need to use green strategies to minimize their environmental footprint, ensure sustainability, and achieve competitive advantage (Raharjo, 2019). Nevertheless, as awareness of becoming green has spread more among SMEs than before, these businesses are fraught with hindrances to sustainable implementation. Accessibility to finance has been identified as one of the primary barriers facing small- and medium-sized enterprises (SMEs) when it comes to adopting good sustainability practices (Isensee et al., 2020). For instance, many green technologies or eco-materials require significant upfront investment. With less access to capital, since SMEs are smaller and have a more limited credit history, it is risky for the formal financial system to lend money because they represent potential losses. Green strategies also involve understanding sustainability practices, regulatory requirements, and practical implications for business operations (Cherrafi et al., 2017). The problem is that SMEs do not always have the skills in-house to manage these complexities and may be too expensive or prohibitive cost-wise for them to hire consultants or provide their own staff with the necessary training (Caldera et al., 2017). Regulation of environmental sustainability is complex and inconsistent across countries. These regulations can be difficult to follow, and SMEs, in particular those working internationally across different jurisdictions, may find it difficult to comply. Meeting the red tape compliance of certifications and permits is a bureaucratic weakness, at its best (Thanki & Thakkar, 2020).

Many small and medium enterprises (SMEs) operate under suppliers with global reach, or in limited and non-optimized supply chains that lack sustainability optimization. This operational inefficiency can inhibit SMEs from moving towards greener practices (Yadav & Gahlot, 2022). In such cases, if key suppliers are not mapping with green raw materials or when the logistics partner is against carbon-neutral options for transportation, it limits the possibility that these small medium enterprises comply with their sustainability goals. While an increasing number of people are choosing green products or services, not all customers are willing to pay eco-friendly purchases at a higher price (J. Singh et al., 2020). SMEs can struggle to meet environmental standards while remaining price competitive, and may be reluctant to invest in sustainability measures if they are not convinced of the ROI and better accept green products. The implementation of green technology can involve significant changes such as replacing existing processes, equipment, or systems for SMEs (Kovilage, 2021). Many businesses, particularly in the traditional industries, find it difficult to adopt newer (and greener) technologies. The type of technologies that will meet both the scale and custom requirements of an SME may be unavailable, or there could be existing infrastructure limitations to implement new systems (Kosasih et al., 2023).

In SMEs, change management is a heavy hang for shoulder efforts. Green strategies require a cultural change, and the very nature of an organization can resist it, especially when management or even customers have become comfortable with business as usual. To penetrate this resistance, communication and leadership commitment are required, along with the reconfiguration of business priorities (Hallam & Contreras, 2016) Financial pressures and the immediacy of returns usually lead SMEs to operate in the short term. By contrast, green strategies have more intangible and long-term results, such as cost savings on energy efficiency initiatives, a better brand reputation when compared to other market entrants or established competitors in the share of voice that environmental groups play out within social media, for example, and overall compliance with increasingly stricter regulatory requirements (Bhattacharya et al., 2019). For SMEs, the challenge is to determine how to juggle the immediate costs and disturbances of adopting green strategies with potential long-term benefits that may not be realized for many years. It is difficult for SMEs to measure the impact of green strategies and report on their sustainability performance. Unlike large players with digital technology, SMEs cannot afford elaborate tracking and reporting systems (Garza-Reyes, 2015) This drawback makes it difficult to evaluate the effectiveness of green strategies, obtain stakeholder commitment, and communicate their achievements to customers and investors. However, with the necessary financial and non-financial support in place, such as finance, knowledge, or technology transfer, SMEs can surmount these hurdles and adopt a more sustainable business model (Chugani et al., 2017). A key part of this will involve governments, bodies, and larger enterprises aiding SMEs on their path, providing grants, demonstrations, and integration opportunities If the world is serious in accelerating progress towards sustainability, then it will rely heavily on SMEs, which can help diversify growth and greening (Afum et al., 2021).

9. EMERGING FUTURE TRENDS IN GREEN ORIENTATION SUSTAINABILITY IN SMEs

The tendency toward green orientation and sustainability in small and medium-sized enterprises within the digital era is an increasingly digitalized trend. As SMEs struggle to ensure sustainability, both challenges and opportunities are inherited in digital technologies and innovations.(*The Long Path to Achieving Green Economy Performance for Micro Small Medium Enterprise | Journal of Innovation and Entrepreneurship*, 2024) The purpose of the current synthesis is to discuss critical factors affecting SMEs' propensity to adopt green practices with regard to such an option as digitalization as a key facilitator of sustainable innovation The process of digital transformation plays a crucial role for SMEs in terms of promoting their sustainability. In this context, 'transformation readiness' as a construct can be associated with readiness of SMEs to digital transformation, which is closely and significantly influenced by sustainability. More importantly, the integration of 'people', 'processes', and 'technology' elements can not only ease the transition to digital platforms but also boost the sustainability of the enterprises (Citraresmi et al., 2023). Today's COVID-19 crisis has contributed to styling the digitization of small and middle enterprises overall. Particularly, the need for digital payments and digital solutions has emerged in light of managing and sustaining production. (Bai et al., 2021) . Small and medium-sized enterprises (SMEs) can benefit from changes in market demands and regulations by incorporating technology (Xiumei et al., 2023).

Environmental regulations are significant in driving sustainable innovation among SMEs. The integration of sustainability into core strategies is one of the best solutions for SME that pursue higher operational efficiency while attempting to reduce waste and spoilage. The impact under consideration is caused by the digitalization concept, as SMEs use technologies to introduce and maintain sustainability in their operations and delivery mechanisms for products or services. With the help of modern technologies, owners and managers of these firms can follow and manage their resource use as precisely as possible.

10. CONCLUSION

In summary, incorporating green orientation as a strategy framework for SMEs in the digital era not only contributes to environmental factors, but also increases the economic performance and sustainability of firms. Green orientation is a framework that can help SMEs build the capability to participate effectively in contemporary business realities and opportunities, including rapidly changing trends of sustainability in a sustainable market practice-induced digital era. Organizational behavioural preparedness, in terms of green entrepreneurial and market orientations, which is integrated with world best practices for human resource management, can foster environmental performance and economic viability. Apart from providing a competitive advantage to SMEs, the targeted use of green practices is in line with broader social environmental objectives. This means that SMEs can use digital technologies to improve their environmental performance and resource efficiency and reduce waste. This type of technology can not only help you make decisions based on data, but it will also help in communicating effectively and more clearly green initiatives to stakeholders, which would enable the corporation to develop a brand reputation with even higher competitiveness within the market. As new digital innovation progresses, SMEs that adopt a green mindset will stay in a better shape to face sustainability pain points and be prepared for what is shaping up as an unprecedented time moving forward into the Green Economy.

11. POLICY IMPLICATIONS

The policy implications of such strategies are significant, as they require shifts in regulatory frameworks, market incentives, and industry standards. Policymakers may need to create incentives for businesses to adopt green practices, such as tax breaks, subsidies, or grants for green technologies. Additionally, regulations may be necessary to enforce sustainability standards, like carbon emissions limits or waste reduction targets. Moreover, green orientation strategies can influence trade policies, encourage eco-friendly imports and exports, while promoting transparency in environmental impact reporting. In the financial sector, policies that support green financing can boost investments in renewable energy and other sustainable industries, thereby contributing to long-term environmental goals. On a global scale, governments may need to collaborate on environmental agreements and standards, ensuring that countries work together to reduce greenhouse gas emissions and promote green technology transfer. Trade policies might evolve to include environmental clauses, favoring eco-friendly goods and services.

Overall, the shift toward green orientation strategies has broad implications, impacting everything from public health and energy policy to economic growth and international relations. These changes challenge policymakers to balance economic development with the urgency of addressing climate change and environmental degradation.

12. REFERENCES

Aftab, J., Veneziani, M., Sarwar, H., & Abid, N. (2024). Do green practices drive business excellence in SMEs? Investigating how green entrepreneurial orientation improves firm's performance. *Total Quality Management & Business Excellence, 35*(5–6), 529–558. DOI: 10.1080/14783363.2024.2315442

Afum, E., Zhang, R., Agyabeng-Mensah, Y., & Sun, Z. (2021). Sustainability excellence: The interactions of lean production, internal green practices and green product innovation. *International Journal of Lean Six Sigma, 12*(6), 1089–1114.

Alshebami, A. S. (2023). Green innovation, self-efficacy, entrepreneurial orientation and economic performance: Interactions among Saudi small enterprises. *Sustainability, 15*(3), 1961.

Ardyan, E., Nurtantiono, A., Istiyanto, B., & Rahmawan, G. (2017). Green innovation capability as driver of sustainable competitive advantages and smes marketing performance. *Technology, 8*(8), 1114–1122.

Asad, M., Aledeinat, M., Majali, T., Almajali, D. A., & Shrafat, F. D. (2024). Mediating role of green innovation and moderating role of resource acquisition with firm age between green entrepreneurial orientation and performance of entrepreneurial firms. *Cogent Business & Management, 11*(1), 2291850. DOI: 10.1080/23311975.2023.2291850

Bai, C., Quayson, M., & Sarkis, J. (2021). COVID-19 pandemic digitization lessons for sustainable development of micro-and small- enterprises. *Sustainable Production and Consumption, 27*. Advance online publication. DOI: 10.1016/j.spc.2021.04.035 PMID: 34722843

Bhattacharya, A., Nand, A., & Castka, P. (2019). Lean-green integration and its impact on sustainability performance: A critical review. *Journal of Cleaner Production, 236*, 117697.

Caldera, H. T. S., Desha, C., & Dawes, L. (2017). Exploring the role of lean thinking in sustainable business practice: A systematic literature review. *Journal of Cleaner Production, 167*, 1546–1565.

Cerchione, R., Centobelli, P., & Shabani, A. (2018). Sustainability orientation, supply chain integration, and SMEs performance: A causal analysis. *Benchmarking, 25*(9), 3679–3701.

Cherrafi, A., Elfezazi, S., Govindan, K., Garza-Reyes, J. A., Benhida, K., & Mokhlis, A. (2017). A framework for the integration of Green and Lean Six Sigma for superior sustainability performance. *International Journal of Production Research*, *55*(15), 4481–4515. DOI: 10.1080/00207543.2016.1266406

Chugani, N., Kumar, V., Garza-Reyes, J. A., Rocha-Lona, L., & Upadhyay, A. (2017). Investigating the green impact of Lean, Six Sigma and Lean Six Sigma: A systematic literature review. *International Journal of Lean Six Sigma*, *8*(1), 7–32.

Citraresmi, A. D. P., Rucitra, A. L., Amalia, F., & Mustaniroh, S. A. (2023). Effect of sustainability readiness on digital transformation adoption in SMEs. *Advances in Food Science. Sustainable Agriculture and Agroindustrial Engineering*, *6*(4). Advance online publication. DOI: 10.21776/ub.afssaae.2023.006.04.2

Dey, P. K., Malesios, C., De, D., Chowdhury, S., & Abdelaziz, F. B. (2020). The Impact of Lean Management Practices and Sustainably-Oriented Innovation on Sustainability Performance of Small and Medium-Sized Enterprises: Empirical Evidence from the UK. *British Journal of Management*, *31*(1), 141–161. DOI: 10.1111/1467-8551.12388

Digital literacy, digital intelligence and small and medium enterprises' (SMEs) sustainability: The mediating role of digital technology usage—Masud Ibrahim, Elizabeth Wetania Aduah, 2025. (n.d.). Retrieved August 11, 2025, from https://journals.sagepub.com/doi/abs/10.1177/02666669251335001

Dynamic Capabilities and Green Strategy in Green Entrepreneurship and Circular Economy: A Study—Mondal—Business Strategy and the Environment—Wiley Online Library. (n.d.). Retrieved August 11, 2025, from https://onlinelibrary.wiley.com/doi/abs/10.1002/bse.70030

El-Kassar, A.-N., & Singh, S. K. (2019). Green innovation and organizational performance: The influence of big data and the moderating role of management commitment and HR practices. *Technological Forecasting and Social Change*, *144*, 483–498. DOI: 10.1016/j.techfore.2017.12.016

Exploring the impact of green entrepreneurial orientation on sustainable performance: Insights from CSR, policy and innovation | Management Decision | Emerald Publishing. (n.d.). Retrieved August 11, 2025, from https://www.emerald.com/md/article-abstract/62/12/3946/1228791/Exploring-the-impact-of-green-entrepreneurial?redirectedFrom=fulltext

Fechtelpeter, C., Kuehn, A., Dumitrescu, R., & Ebbesmeyer, P. (2017). Integrated technology transfer concept for fostering innovation in SMEs. *26th Int. Assoc. Manag. Technol. Conf. IAMOT*, 1028–1048. https://www.researchgate.net/profile/Christian-Fechtelpeter/publication/344427721_Integrated_Technology_Transfer_Concept_For_Fostering_Innovation_In_SMEs/links/5f8e9679458515b7cf8dd629/Integrated-Technology-Transfer-Concept-For-Fostering-Innovation-In-SMEs.pdf

Fernandez-Lores, S., Crespo-Tejero, N., & Fernández-Hernández, R. (2022). Driving traffic to the museum: The role of the digital communication tools. *Technological Forecasting and Social Change*, *174*, 121273.

Garza-Reyes, J. A. (2015). Lean and green–a systematic review of the state of the art literature. *Journal of Cleaner Production*, *102*, 18–29.

Ghazilla, R. A. R., Sakundarini, N., Abdul-Rashid, S. H., Ayub, N. S., Olugu, E. U., & Musa, S. N. (2015). Drivers and barriers analysis for green manufacturing practices in Malaysian SMEs: A preliminary findings. *Procedia CIRP*, *26*, 658–663.

Gomes, S., Pinho, M., & Lopes, J. M. (2024). From environmental sustainability practices to green innovations: Evidence from small and medium-sized manufacturing companies. *Corporate Social Responsibility and Environmental Management*, *31*(3), 1677–1687. DOI: 10.1002/csr.2657

Hallam, C., & Contreras, C. (2016). Integrating lean and green management. *Management Decision*, *54*(9), 2157–2187.

Integrating Sustainability in Small Scale Industries: From Environmental Degradation to Cleaner Practices: Environmental Claims Journal: Vol 0, No 0. (n.d.). Retrieved August 11, 2025, from https://www.tandfonline.com/doi/abs/10.1080/10406026.2025.2506658

Isensee, C., Teuteberg, F., Griese, K.-M., & Topi, C. (2020). The relationship between organizational culture, sustainability, and digitalization in SMEs: A systematic review. *Journal of Cleaner Production*, *275*, 122944.

Ishaq, M. I., Sarwar, H., Aftab, J., Franzoni, S., & Raza, A. (2024). Accomplishing sustainable performance through leaders' competencies, green entrepreneurial orientation, and innovation in an emerging economy: Moderating role of institutional support. *Business Strategy and the Environment*, *33*(2), 1515–1532. DOI: 10.1002/bse.3557

Jalil, M. F., Marikan, D. A. B. A., & Jais, M. bin, Ayupp, K., & Shukri, M. H. bin M. (2025). A Green Internet of Things (GIoT) Adoption Framework to Enhance Environmental Performance of SMEs Through the Digital Social Networking. *Business Strategy & Development*, *8*(3), e70179. DOI: 10.1002/bsd2.70179

Jansson, J., Nilsson, J., Modig, F., & Hed Vall, G. (2017). Commitment to Sustainability in Small and Medium-Sized Enterprises: The Influence of Strategic Orientations and Management Values. *Business Strategy and the Environment*, *26*(1), 69–83. DOI: 10.1002/bse.1901

Jeyadevi J, C. (2023). *SUSTAINABLE DEVELOPMENTS THROUGH MSMEs: A PATHWAY TO SELF-RELIANT INDIA SUSTAINABLE DEVELOPMENTS THROUGH MSMEs: A PATHWAY TO SELF-RELIANT INDIA*.

Joeliaty, J. (2024). Green Growth and Beyond: The Influence of Environmental Practices, Financial Management, Market Access, and Digital Integration on the Resilience and Sustainability Business Practices of MSMEs in Indonesia. *International Journal of Business, Law, and Education*, *5*(1), 1. Advance online publication. DOI: 10.56442/ijble.v5i1.446

Karuppiah, K., Sankaranarayanan, B., Ali, S. M., Chowdhury, P., & Paul, S. K. (2020). An integrated approach to modeling the barriers in implementing green manufacturing practices in SMEs. *Journal of Cleaner Production*, *265*, 121737.

Khan, F., Din, A. U., Jehangir, M., Farooq, S. H., & Riviezzo, A. (2024). The nexus of technology orientation and green innovation performance: The potential mediating role of innovation capability. *The Journal of High Technology Management Research*, *35*(2), 100509.

Khana, M. P., Talibb, N. A., & Kowangc, T. O. (2020). The development of a sustainability framework via lean green six sigma practices in SMEs based upon RBV theory. *Development*, *12*(5), 135–156.

Klewitz, J., & Hansen, E. G. (2014). Sustainability-oriented innovation of SMEs: A systematic review. *Journal of Cleaner Production*, *65*, 57–75.

Kosasih, W., Pujawan, I. N., & Karningsih, P. D. (2023a). Integrated Lean-Green Practices and Supply Chain Sustainability for Manufacturing SMEs: A Systematic Literature Review and Research Agenda. *Sustainability*, *15*(16), 12192.

Kosasih, W., Pujawan, I. N., & Karningsih, P. D. (2023b). Integrated Lean-Green Practices and Supply Chain Sustainability for Manufacturing SMEs: A Systematic Literature Review and Research Agenda. *Sustainability*, *15*(16), 12192.

Kovilage, M. P. (2021). Influence of lean–green practices on organizational sustainable performance. *Journal of Asian Business and Economic Studies*, *28*(2), 121–142.

Liu, H., Yao, P., Latif, S., Aslam, S., & Iqbal, N. (2022). Impact of Green financing, FinTech, and financial inclusion on energy efficiency. *Environmental Science and Pollution Research International*, *29*(13), 18955–18966. DOI: 10.1007/s11356-021-16949-x PMID: 34705207

Madrid-Guijarro, A., & Duréndez, A. (2024). Sustainable development barriers and pressures in SMEs: The mediating effect of management commitment to environmental practices. *Business Strategy and the Environment*, *33*(2), 949–967. DOI: 10.1002/bse.3537

Mady, K., Battour, M., Aboelmaged, M., & Abdelkareem, R. S. (2023). Linking internal environmental capabilities to sustainable competitive advantage in manufacturing SMEs: The mediating role of eco-innovation. *Journal of Cleaner Production*, *417*, 137928. DOI: 10.1016/j.jclepro.2023.137928

Muangmee, C., Dacko-Pikiewicz, Z., Meekaewkunchorn, N., Kassakorn, N., & Khalid, B. (2021a). Green entrepreneurial orientation and green innovation in small and medium-sized enterprises (SMEs). *Social Sciences*, *10*(4), 136.

Muangmee, C., Dacko-Pikiewicz, Z., Meekaewkunchorn, N., Kassakorn, N., & Khalid, B. (2021b). Green entrepreneurial orientation and green innovation in small and medium-sized enterprises (SMEs). *Social Sciences*, *10*(4), 136.

Musa, H., & Chinniah, M. (2016). Malaysian SMEs development: Future and challenges on going green. *Procedia: Social and Behavioral Sciences*, *224*, 254–262.

Nuryakin, N., & Maryati, T. (2022a). Do green innovation and green competitive advantage mediate the effect of green marketing orientation on SMEs' green marketing performance? *Cogent Business & Management*, *9*(1), 2065948. DOI: 10.1080/23311975.2022.2065948

Nuryakin, N., & Maryati, T. (2022b). Do green innovation and green competitive advantage mediate the effect of green marketing orientation on SMEs' green marketing performance? *Cogent Business & Management*, *9*(1), 2065948. DOI: 10.1080/23311975.2022.2065948

Nuryakin, N., & Maryati, T. (2022c). Do green innovation and green competitive advantage mediate the effect of green marketing orientation on SMEs' green marketing performance? *Cogent Business & Management*, *9*(1), 2065948. DOI: 10.1080/23311975.2022.2065948

Omar, A., Al-shari, A., Shah, S. H. A., Erkol Bayram, G., Zameer Rahman, E., & Valeri, M. (2024). Green manufacturing practices and SMEs' sustainable performance: A moderated mediation mechanisms of green innovation and managerial discretion. *European Business Review*, *36*(4), 588–609.

Purwandani, J. A., & Michaud, G. (2021). What are the drivers and barriers for green business practice adoption for SMEs? *Environment Systems & Decisions*, *41*(4), 577–593. DOI: 10.1007/s10669-021-09821-3 PMID: 34155474

Raharjo, K. (2019). The role of green management in creating sustainability performance on the small and medium enterprises. *Management of Environmental Quality*, *30*(3), 557–577.

Rehman, R. U., Ahmad, M. I., Belas, J., Battisti, E., & Santoro, G. (2024). Green learning orientation and corporate environmental performance: The mediation role of green knowledge acquisition-management and the moderating role of CEO-gender. *Journal of Knowledge Management*. https://www.emerald.com/insight/content/doi/10.1108/JKM-08-2023-0752/full/html

Rizos, V., Behrens, A., Van der Gaast, W., Hofman, E., Ioannou, A., Kafyeke, T., Flamos, A., Rinaldi, R., Papadelis, S., & Hirschnitz-Garbers, M. (2016). Implementation of circular economy business models by small and medium-sized enterprises (SMEs): Barriers and enablers. *Sustainability*, *8*(11), 1212.

Rozman Cafuta, M. (2015). Open space evaluation methodology and three dimensional evaluation model as a base for sustainable development tracking. *Sustainability*, *7*(10), 13690–13712.

Ruggieri, A., Braccini, A. M., Poponi, S., & Mosconi, E. M. (2016). A meta-model of inter-organisational cooperation for the transition to a circular economy. *Sustainability*, *8*(11), 1153.

Sajan, M. P., Shalij, P. R., & Ramesh, A. (2017). Lean manufacturing practices in Indian manufacturing SMEs and their effect on sustainability performance. *Journal of Manufacturing Technology Management*, *28*(6), 772–793.

Shandilya, S. K., Datta, A., Kartik, Y., & Nagar, A. (2024). Navigating the Regulatory Landscape. In S. K. Shandilya, A. Datta, Y. Kartik, & A. Nagar, *Digital Resilience: Navigating Disruption and Safeguarding Data Privacy* (pp. 127–240). Springer Nature Switzerland. https://doi.org/DOI: 10.1007/978-3-031-53290-0_3

Siegel, R., Antony, J., Garza-Reyes, J. A., Cherrafi, A., & Lameijer, B. (2019). Integrated green lean approach and sustainability for SMEs: From literature review to a conceptual framework. *Journal of Cleaner Production*, *240*, 118205.

Siegel, R., Antony, J., Govindan, K., Garza-Reyes, J. A., Lameijer, B., & Samadhiya, A. (2024a). A framework for the systematic implementation of Green-Lean and sustainability in SMEs. *Production Planning and Control, 35*(1), 71–89. DOI: 10.1080/09537287.2022.2052200

Siegel, R., Antony, J., Govindan, K., Garza-Reyes, J. A., Lameijer, B., & Samadhiya, A. (2024b). A framework for the systematic implementation of Green-Lean and sustainability in SMEs. *Production Planning and Control, 35*(1), 71–89. DOI: 10.1080/09537287.2022.2052200

Singh, J., Singh, H., & Kumar, A. (2020). Impact of lean practices on organizational sustainability through green supply chain management–an empirical investigation. *International Journal of Lean Six Sigma, 11*(6), 1035–1068.

Singh, R. K., Kumar Mangla, S., Bhatia, M. S., & Luthra, S. (2022). Integration of green and lean practices for sustainable business management. *Business Strategy and the Environment, 31*(1), 353–370. DOI: 10.1002/bse.2897

Sohu, J. M., Hongyun, T., Junejo, I., Akhtar, S., Ejaz, F., Dunay, A., & Hossain, M. B. (2024). Driving sustainable competitiveness: Unveiling the nexus of green intellectual capital and environmental regulations on greening SME performance. *Frontiers in Environmental Science, 12*, 1348994.

Suchek, N., & Franco, M. (2024a). Inter-organisational Cooperation Oriented Towards Sustainability Involving SMEs: A Systematic Literature Review. *Journal of the Knowledge Economy, 15*(1), 1952–1972. DOI: 10.1007/s13132-023-01196-x PMID: 40478941

Suchek, N., & Franco, M. (2024b). Inter-organisational Cooperation Oriented Towards Sustainability Involving SMEs: A Systematic Literature Review. *Journal of the Knowledge Economy, 15*(1), 1952–1972. DOI: 10.1007/s13132-023-01196-x PMID: 40478941

Suwandi, S., & Badrianto, Y. (2023). The Role of Competitive Strategy and Green Supply Chain Management in MSME Performance. *Jurnal Multidisiplin Madani, 3*(10), 10. Advance online publication. DOI: 10.55927/mudima.v3i10.6512

Tazhibekova, K., & Shametova, A. (2024). Ecological Initiatives and Their Influence on the Competitiveness and Sustainability of Companies: "Green" Strategies of SMEs. *Journal of the Knowledge Economy*. Advance online publication. DOI: 10.1007/s13132-024-02062-0

Thanki, S., & Thakkar, J. J. (2020). An investigation on lean–green performance of Indian manufacturing SMEs. *International Journal of Productivity and Performance Management, 69*(3), 489–517.

The long path to achieving green economy performance for micro small medium enterprise | Journal of Innovation and Entrepreneurship. (n.d.). Retrieved August 11, 2025, from https://link.springer.com/article/10.1186/s13731-022-00209-4

Toryanto, C. J. K., & Indriani, F. (2022). Green Marketing Orientation Towards Competitive Advantage and Marketing Performance of Non-Food SMEs in Java. [IJSRM]. *International Journal of Scientific Research and Management, 10*(02), 02. Advance online publication. DOI: 10.18535/ijsrm/v10i2.em06

Vrontis, D., Chaudhuri, R., & Chatterjee, S. (2022). Adoption of Digital Technologies by SMEs for Sustainability and Value Creation: Moderating Role of Entrepreneurial Orientation. *Sustainability, 14*(13), 13. Advance online publication. DOI: 10.3390/su14137949

Xiumei, X., Ruolan, J., Shahzad, U., & Xiao, F. (2023). Sustainable Innovation in Small and Medium-Sized Enterprises: Environmental Regulations and Digitalization as Catalyst. *The Journal of Environment &Amp. Development, 32*(4). Advance online publication. DOI: 10.1177/10704965231211585

Yadav, V., & Gahlot, P. (2022). Green Lean Six Sigma sustainability-oriented framework for small and medium enterprises. *International Journal of Quality & Reliability Management, 39*(7), 1787–1807. DOI: 10.1108/IJQRM-08-2021-0297

Yousaf, Z. (2021). Go for green: Green innovation through green dynamic capabilities: accessing the mediating role of green practices and green value co-creation. *Environmental Science and Pollution Research International, 28*(39), 54863–54875. DOI: 10.1007/s11356-021-14343-1 PMID: 34018115

Zameer, H., Yasmeen, H., Wang, Y., & Saeed, M. R. (2024). Sustainability-oriented corporate strategy: Green image and innovation capabilities. *Management Decision*. https://www.emerald.com/insight/content/doi/10.1108/MD-08-2023-1407/full/html

Zhan, Y., Tan, K. H., Ji, G., & Tseng, M.-L. (2018). Sustainable Chinese manufacturing competitiveness in the 21st century: Green and lean practices, pressure and performance. *International Journal of Computer Integrated Manufacturing, 31*(6), 523–536. DOI: 10.1080/0951192X.2016.1268721

Zhang, J. A., & Walton, S. (2017). Eco-innovation and business performance: The moderating effects of environmental orientation and resource commitment in green-oriented SME s. *R & D Management, 47*(5). Advance online publication. DOI: 10.1111/radm.12241

Zhang, X., Wang, W., Teng, X., & Yang, L. (2024). Navigating Competitive Intensity: The Role of Digital Orientation in SMEs' Green Innovations. *Journal of the Knowledge Economy*. Advance online publication. DOI: 10.1007/s13132-024-02110-9

Chapter 7
The Contribution of the Equator Principles to Sustainable Finance

Syrine Ben Romdhane
https://orcid.org/0000-0001-6644-8252
Ecole Supérieure des Sciences Economiques et Commerciales de Tunis, University of Tunis, Tunisia

ABSTRACT

The purpose of this chapter is to show how firms can theoretically be both profitable and socially responsible by examining the main motivations (economic and ethical) for adopting Equator Principles. A study, by theme and by principle, of the main contributions of version IV of the Equator Principles compared to version III, makes it possible. This chapter presents a literature review of the main studies examining the degree of integration of sustainability issues in the governance systems of banks. Through this theoretical as well as empirical literature review, this study attempts to assess the relevance of Equator Principles as a tool for implementing Corporate Social Responsibility in the banking sector and to clarify the stakes of an evolution towards a socially and environmentally responsible project financing policy. There are many questions surrounding the actual impacts of Equator Principles and whether they can produce the desired results. The answers to these questions allow for truly informed decisions to be made. However, providing an answer is a rather complex task and such an evaluation would be well beyond the scope of this research.

DOI: 10.4018/979-8-3373-1240-8.ch007

INTRODUCTION

As the financial sector faces mounting pressure to align with global sustainability objectives, the question of how finance can support environmental protection has become central. This evolution has led to the emergence of new frameworks and standards aimed at reconciling profitability with responsibility (Wang et al., 2019).

With the introduction of the Equator Principles (EPs) in 2003, the relationship between finance and the environment has gained increasing prominence. Financial activities are progressively shifting toward environmentally responsible practices. As public awareness of corporate externalities grows, the traditional paradigm of shareholder value maximization is evolving to incorporate the expectations of a broader range of stakeholders, including society and the natural environment (Aras et al., 2018). At the same time, "green" technologies and other environmentally sound investments with strong financial potential have begun to attract significant investor interest (Liu et al., 2022). The mounting global awareness of environmental degradation and climate risks has prompted a growing interest among policymakers and academics in integrating sustainability principles into financial systems, giving rise to the expanding field of green finance (Tao et al., 2022).

Several studies have underscored the central role of the banking sector -an essential intermediary within the economic system (Mnasri & Ben Romdhane, 2024; Xu et al., 2023; Contreras et al., 2019; Duan, 2021; Jeucken & Bouma, 1999; Batae et al., 2021)- in advancing sustainability objectives (Power & Tandja-M, 2024; Jeucken, 2004; Plihon, 2010; De Perthuis, 2003). Morin (2006) highlights that project finance has become a strategic issue in an era where competitive pressures increasingly revolve around socially responsible behavior. According to Sarfraz et al. (2018), the adoption of the EPs not only helps manage environmental risks but also enhances the profitability of the banking sector.

Building on these observations, this chapter offers a comprehensive review of the literature addressing the integration of sustainability considerations into the governance systems of banks. The aim is to evaluate the relevance of the EPs as a mechanism for implementing Corporate Social Responsibility (CSR) in the banking industry and to shed light on how they promote the transition toward socially and environmentally responsible project finance. Accordingly, this study seeks to answer the following question: *To what extent do the Equator Principles, particularly in their latest 2019 version, foster tangible corporate governance commitments to strengthen banks' CSR strategies?*

The chapter is organized as follows. The first section reviews key theoretical foundations related to CSR and its implications for the banking sector, focusing on three major frameworks: the Resource Dependence Theory (Pfeffer & Salancik, 1978), the Trust Theory in Banking (Williamson, 1993), and the Legitimacy Theory (Suchman,

1995). The second section examines the relevance of the Equator Principles (EP 4, 2019) as an operational tool for implementing CSR within banks. The final section provides both theoretical and empirical insights into the contribution of the EPs to sustainable finance, followed by concluding remarks and policy recommendations.

1. THE CSR CONCEPT AND ITS IMPLICATIONS IN THE BANKING SECTOR: A REVIEW OF THE THEORETICAL LITERATURE

CSR is defined as the voluntary integration by firms of social and environmental concerns into their business activities and their relations with stakeholders (European Commission, 2004, 2014a, 2014b, 2014c). It is a principle widely spread in the social body especially under the acception of sustainable development (Domergue, 2018). This concept is based on the mutual dependence between the firm and society. With the emergence of non-governmental organizations (NGOs), CSR was born in France in the 1980s with the creation of tools to identify the level of corporate responsibility. It gained prominence about 20 years ago with the creation of the law on New Economic Regulations (NRE). The objectives of this law are to improve transparency in economic relations and the inclusion of sustainable development within firms.

According to Gond and Igalens (2008), CSR can be perceived as an instrument for regulating relations between society and the firm, or as the result of a power relationship between stakeholders and the firm. It can also be considered in relation to its cultural environment, to which it must adapt, or finally it can be the result of a negotiation between the firm and society concerning values and social problems. According to Maignan and Ralston (2002), CSR reflects a multidimensional interaction between the firm and its key constituencies -including stakeholders, government, the natural environment, ethical norms, and the pursuit of sustainable competitive advantage. In this perspective, CSR constitutes not only a moral or regulatory obligation but also a strategic opportunity for corporate decision-makers to enhance organizational efficiency, reduce costs, and strengthen the firm's reputation as a responsible corporate citizen (Normann & Ramirez, 1993). Beyond these typical characteristics, CSR allows firms to achieve a positive image and reputation among its customers (Gholami, 2011).

The CSR concept and its implications have been the subject of ongoing debate and several studies over the past fifty years, particularly in management literature. The principle of sustainable development, launched in the late 1990s, has also been extensively researched. Recently, banks around the world have begun to adopt social disclosure practices to demonstrate their adherence to CSR and sustainable development principles, by publishing annual CSR reports and even social balance sheets. Social reporting is a document dedicated to stating a firm's CSR vision and reporting on its social performance. This report represents a label rewarding the best reports, which is a plus for the image and reputation of the bank (Thiétart, 2007). In their annual reports on CSR, banks specify the components of their governance. By governance, we mean all the mechanisms that circumscribe the freedom of decision in business (Pasquero, 2005): the organization of shareholders' meetings, the composition and functioning of the board of directors, namely the accounts committee, the internal control committee, or the audit committee, the appointments committee, the remuneration committee (Reynaud & Walas, 2015). According to Ablender (2011), the extensive literature on the topic of CSR in banks leads to a recent reflection on the ambiguity of CSR between a political perspective, describing it as a commitment of the firm to the environment and the firm's economic activities, and on the other hand, a technical perspective, which is based on ethics in the decision-making process and the corresponding managerial practices. The objective of this section is therefore to present a review of the theoretical literature studying CSR as a source of value in the banking industry.

1.1 CSR and the Resource-Based View of Pfeffer and Salancik (1978)

Resource dependence theory (RDT) was first introduced in the 1970s in a publication entitled "*External Control of Organizations: A Resource Dependence Perspective.*" This theory, founded by Pfeffer and Salancik in 1978, makes the organization dependent on the actors in its environment and asserts that its sustainability depends on its ability to manage the demands of different groups, especially those whose resources and support are critical to its survival (Pfeffer & Salancik, 1978, cited in Capron & Quairel-Lanoizelée, 2007). Through this theory, Pfeffer and Salancik (1978) postulate that organizations seek to reduce uncertainty related to the environment. An organization's vulnerability to its environment is dependent on its ability to obtain the resources it needs. In this framework, the actions and results of the firm are judged to be "acceptable" and its performance is assessed according to the internal criteria of efficiency or profitability.

An organization's vulnerability stems from its dependence on external resources and the fact that access to these resources is largely governed by its surrounding environment. When the groups or actors that control these critical resources decide to withdraw their support, the organization's survival may be jeopardized. Such resources extend beyond financial capital to include human capital, particularly in terms of the firm's attractiveness to potential recruits, as well as customer relationships. For instance, firms may face consumer boycotts or the loss of key clients if they fail to comply with the environmental, social, or ethical standards expected by their stakeholders.

While RDT sheds light on the phenomena of power distribution within the organization and on the political games between the latter and its external partners (Arrègle, 2006), and while it highlights the search for power maximization in the management of relationships of mutual dependence, it is nevertheless criticized, on the one hand, for the excessive emphasis it places on political phenomena at the expense of managerial rationality and the vagueness of a certain number of notions, such as that of "strategic contingency" (Weick, 1995), and on the other hand, for the fact that it considers that the environment is not an objective reality over which managers have no power.

1.2 CSR and the Theory of Trust in Banking (Williamson, 1993)

The subprime crisis in the United States in July 2007 made the relationship between banks and their stakeholders much more complex. The role of banks, which consists in making exchanges more fluid, is now misunderstood by the public, if not questioned (Domergue, 2018). The management of the banking sector crisis highlighted several contradictory points between the image that banks wish to convey and the actual perception of these institutions (Mercanti-Guérin, 2011). It is as if banks wanted to avoid their own societal responsibility. Banks must then take actions to restore trust (Barbot, 2010). Williamson (1993) considers trusting behavior because of an agent's evaluation of the incentives of other agents to behave honorably. According to him, trust is not a personal and moral attribute, but rather that of a social, legal and economic context. Hosmer (1995) defines trust as "the anticipation by a person, group, or firm of ethically justifiable behavior, i.e., morally correct decisions and actions based on ethical analytical principles, on the part of the other person, group, or firm in a joint endeavor or economic exchange." This new need for trust therefore accelerated the significance of CSR development in the banking sector. Banks will work on their ethics regarding their choice of financing, investment or on management to improve their reputation, as the impact on reputation is a central factor in the adoption of voluntary codes for a sector where trust is essential (Sethi, 2002; Florini, 2003; Dam, 2008).

A study by Mercanti-Guérin (2011) shows that the theoretical and managerial implications involve the importance of different forms of trust (institutional, interpersonal, relational), the power of image and the attitude towards money. The results show that the crisis appears to depend on the level of trust between the brand and its consumer before the crisis occurs, and that the level of reputation of the brand is a determining factor in the success or failure of crisis management. For their part, and based on the halo effect, Christiansen and Vendelo (2003) have demonstrated that a good relationship between the consumer and the brand before the crisis facilitates the acceptance by the consumer of new information about the brand and increases confidence in the crisis management.

1.3 The Politics of Sustainable Development and the Legitimacy Theory (Suchman, 1995)

If the idea of sustainable development seems to be accepted by society in general, it is appropriate to ask why and how banks apply this principle in their strategy and discourse (Pupion, 2013). The explanations are perhaps to be found in the quest for social legitimacy, which guarantees the survival of the organization to a large extent.

Developed in a highly heterogeneous way based on the fundamental work of Parsons (1960), the concept of organizational legitimacy has been approached in several ways in management science (Suchman, 1995). Legitimacy is defined by Suchman (1995) as "a generalized perception or assumption that the actions of an entity are desirable, proper or appropriate within some socially constructed system of norms, values, and beliefs". These differences oppose two major trends: the strategic trend (Oliver, 1991; Suchman, 1995; Buisson, 2008) and the social acceptability trend. The former sees legitimacy as a manipulable resource and is concerned with aspects of power and control over resources, as well as with forms of environmental influence, while the latter emphasizes the importance of obtaining legitimacy "in order to demonstrate social merit and mobilize resources" (Oliver, 1991). According to Buisson (2008), legitimacy results from a constant and contextualized process of legitimization, the interactive aspects of which are formalized in Suchman's (1995) definition.

According to the legitimacy theory, CSR communication can be understood as a tool for legitimization among stakeholders. Beyond the conflicts between institutional and strategic approaches to legitimacy, this approach is interested in the link between CSR and the legitimacy of organizations through an interactive approach to legitimacy, which can be found in the work of Suchman (1995). Based on his analysis of the different approaches to legitimacy, Suchman presents a typology of legitimization strategies based on the pragmatic, normative and cognitive dynamics that coexist in most real environments. In other words, according to this author, managers must legitimize their policies with stakeholders, firstly from a pragmatic point of view, by meeting their expectations, through a behavior that creates stakeholder support for the values constructed and conveyed by the organization, through a process that consists in influencing stakeholders by involving them in the definition of the strategy (Ramonjy, 1997). Suchman thus goes beyond the analysis and structuring of the literature on legitimacy, adding to Scott's (1979) regulatory dimension the dimension of conformity to the expectations and interests of the collective audience.

Secondly, from a moral point of view, they give meaning to their strategy and make it consistent with the values of the actors and of society. Like Scott's (1979) normative dimension, this strategy refers to the integration of societal norms and values into activities, which are essential to social life and are induced by the social system. It marks the organization's effort to translate its commitments and its consideration of the interests and values of its collective audience directly into its activities. Finally, from a cognitive point of view, it provides a representation of its policy that allows stakeholders to understand it, by conducting a policy of communication and justification of the strategy to the different stakeholders. However, Pupion (2013) points out that the accountability relationship may be different depending on the nature and characteristics of the stakeholders (public authorities, supervisory authorities, professional bodies, customers, suppliers, employees, etc.).

2. CONTRIBUTIONS OF VERSION IV OF THE EQUATOR PRINCIPLES: STUDY BY THEME AND PRINCIPLE

The elaboration of EPs is recognition of the social responsibility of the banking sector and of the role that financiers can play in promoting responsible environmental management and social development. The purpose of the EPs is to serve as a common base and reference for the implementation, by each signatory financial institution, of its own policies, procedures and internal standards in the social and environmental field of project financing.

2.1 Study by Theme

The first version of the Equator Principles (EP 1), which came into being in June 2003, covered the following ten banks: ABN Amro, Barclays, Citigroup, Credit Lyonnais, Credit Suisse, Hypo, Rabobank, Royal Bank of Scotland, West LB and Westpac Banking Corp. These financial institutions are in line with the requirement that projects meet the same international standards, namely the International Finance Corporation's social and environmental sustainability performance standards and its sector-specific environmental, health and safety guidelines. According to Weber and Acheta (2014), the 2006 revision (EP 2) was perhaps retrospective in the sense that the EPs had been operational for three years. They view this first revision as a response to a "first test" of implementation. According to Plihon and Rigot (2022), these Principles for Responsible Investment, launched in 2006, aim to encourage professional investors to integrate environmental, social and governance considerations into their investment decisions and shareholding practices. This has led to a more diversified range of financial products and services, such as green bonds[1] and green and sustainable bank loans[2], socially responsible investment (SRI) funds that implement screening strategies[3], and shareholder engagement, which refers to the influence exercised by investors on company management (via proxy votes, shareholder resolutions or dialogue through investor networks).

The second revision of 2012 (EP 3) is broader and more demanding than the former ones, it included project-based loans and bridge loans (**Table 1**). These are short-term financing modes intended to reduce the financing activities of unsustainable social and environmental projects. This was a kind of appeasement to civil society, including Bank Track, which had argued for the need to respect human rights and climate change.

From a social point of view, the EP version II considered two major sub-categories: due diligence regarding social risks and free, prior and informed consultation. With the advent of EP 3, the focus is on an emerging and contemporary issue, that of human rights; human beings are still at the center of socio-environmental policies for project financing. The third version of the EPs emphasized the need for increased due diligence and focused on climate change issues. With this revision, Equator Principles Financial Institutions (EPFI) members agreed to share social and environmental information with other mandated financial institutions. Changes have also been made regarding the designated countries. These are countries considered to have strong environmental and social governance, legislative frameworks, and robust institutions capable of protecting their people and the natural environment (The EPs, 2013). These countries have become high-income OECD countries.

Although the successive iterations of the EPs have been designed to enhance sustainability within the financial sector, an open question persists as to whether these frameworks effectively achieve their intended objectives and drive substantive changes in the operational practices of the financial institutions that adopt them. The fourth version of the EPs (EP 4), the financial sector benchmark that EPFIs use to assess and manage the environmental and social risks associated with international project finance, came into effect in 2020. EPFIs are committed to financing only those projects that meet the applicable requirements of EP 4, recognizing the growing importance of considering climate change, human rights, and consultation with indigenous peoples[4] at the project assessment stage.

2.2. Study by Principle

The 2013 revision of the EPs establishes a comprehensive framework for assessing, managing, and monitoring the environmental and social risks associated with project finance. Designed as a voluntary yet globally recognized benchmark, the EPs aim to harmonize financial institutions' due diligence practices with the IFC

Performance Standards and the World Bank's Environmental, Health, and Safety Guidelines, particularly for projects located in non-OECD or lower-income economies.

The framework begins with the categorization of projects according to the magnitude and sensitivity of their potential impacts, classified as A (high risk), B (medium risk), or C (low risk)[5]. Once categorized, project sponsors are required to undertake a comprehensive environmental and social assessment, the adequacy of which must satisfy the EPFIs. This assessment forms the basis for the development of an environmental and social management system and a corresponding action plan, specifying mitigation, monitoring, and remediation measures proportionate to the identified risks.

In addition, the EPs emphasize stakeholder engagement as an essential dimension of responsible project governance. For high- and medium-risk projects, proponents are expected to consult affected communities in a transparent and culturally sensitive manner, ensuring informed participation and access to a formal grievance mechanism throughout the project's life cycle.

To strengthen accountability, the EP framework mandates independent review and monitoring, typically conducted by external experts who assess compliance with environmental and social requirements. These obligations are further reinforced through contractual covenants with borrowers and host-country authorities, including commitments to periodic reporting and, where relevant, project decommissioning.

Finally, the principles underline the importance of transparency and disclosure: EPFIs must report publicly on their implementation progress and performance outcomes, thereby contributing to the broader legitimacy and credibility of sustainable finance practices within the global banking sector.

Table 2 illustrates the changes by principle in Version IV of the EPs compared to Version III. The following is a summary of the main contributions of Version IV of the EPs. The effects that are predicted make climate change a global issue as well as a moral issue, with significant implications for demographics, global equality, and even security. The Paris climate agreement (2015) marks a turning point by enacting the need to consider climate change in financial activities to promote low-carbon development. The idea is to incentivize banks and investors to finance sustainable projects by creating a reliable signal about the green quality of projects (Plihon & Rigot, 2022).

The EPs have undergone progressive revisions since their introduction in 2003, reflecting both the expansion of their scope and the strengthening of sustainability-related requirements. The initiative began with only ten participating financial institutions under EP 1, grew to forty under EP 2, seventy-eight under EP 3, and reached around 136 institutions under EP 4. Initially, the EPs were confined to lending activities. The 2006 revision extended their reach to project finance advisory services. EP 3 (2013) incorporated project-related corporate loans and bridge financing, while EP 4 (2019) further included project-related refinancing and acquisition finance, thereby broadening the coverage of financial instruments subject to environmental and social due diligence. The early framework required no standardized reporting. EP 2 introduced basic disclosure, such as the number of screened and closed transactions. EP 3 went further by specifying the need to disclose data on project category, sector, region, and whether independent reviews had been undertaken. Under EP 4, disclosure obligations became considerably more stringent: project names for project finance (with client consent), public online summaries of Environmental and Social Impact Assessments (ESIAs), and detailed information on human rights and climate-related risks must be provided. Moreover, projects emitting over 100,000 tonnes of CO_2-equivalent annually are now required to publicly report operational greenhouse gas (GHG) emissions. EPFIs are also encouraged to share non-confidential biodiversity data with the Global Biodiversity Information Facility (GBIF) and other databases.

The sustainability dimension of the EPs has evolved substantially. EP 1 mainly emphasized environmental risk assessment, with limited attention to social or climate aspects. EP 2 integrated social risk analysis and the principle of free, prior, and informed consultation. EP 3 aligned due diligence more closely with the World Bank and IFC Performance Standards, incorporating climate change considerations and introducing human rights into risk management. EP 4 consolidates this evolution by explicitly referring to the UN Guiding Principles on Business and Human Rights (UNGPs) and the Protect, Respect, and Remedy Framework. It also introduces a climate risk assessment requirement, the depth of which must reflect the type and severity of project-specific risks.

Initially informal, the process of sharing environmental and social information among co-financiers became progressively formalized. By EP 4, such exchanges must respect corporate confidentiality, privacy laws, and national regulations, and are restricted to ensuring consistent application of the Principles across financial institutions.

As for country designation, early versions equated assessments in high-income OECD countries to IFC standards. EP 3 introduced the distinction between designated and non-designated countries: in non-designated contexts, projects are evaluated against IFC performance standards and World Bank environmental, health, and safety guidelines, while in designated countries, compliance with domestic environmental and social legislation remains the benchmark. EP 2 and subsequent versions introduced a glossary to harmonize terminology used in loan documentation, enhancing clarity and standardization across financial agreements.

The EPs apply to specific financial products that exceed defined monetary thresholds. Under EP 4, the threshold for project-related corporate loans has been reduced from a total aggregate loan amount of US$100 million to US$50 million.

Consequently, both the total aggregate loan amount and the EPFI's individual commitment must now meet or exceed the US$50 million threshold. EP 4 also expands the scope of application to include project-related refinancing and acquisition financing, provided that certain conditions are met: the original project must have been financed in accordance with the EP framework, no material changes in project scale or scope must have occurred, and the project must remain incomplete at the time the new facility or loan agreement is executed. Conversely, export financing in the form of supplier credit has been explicitly excluded from the definition of project-related corporate loans. Furthermore, the scope of EP 4 has been broadened to encompass all Category A and, where relevant, Category B loans extended to national, regional, or local governments, their departments, and agencies, as well as loans financing the expansion or upgrade of existing projects.

The preamble to the Draft EP 4 states that financial institutions will fulfill their responsibility to respect human rights in accordance with the United Nations Guiding Principles on Business and Human Rights (UNGPs) by conducting human rights due diligence and human rights impact assessments of proposed projects, including lower risk projects that do not require a full impact assessment.

The 2020 revision of the Equator Principles (EP 4) introduced significant clarifications regarding human rights due diligence. Principle 2 reinforces the integration of human rights considerations within environmental and social assessment processes by explicitly requiring that potential adverse impacts on human rights be examined for all projects -irrespective of their risk classification or the type of assessment undertaken. This marks a clear alignment with the UN Guiding Principles on Business and Human Rights (UNGPs), which now serve as a formalized framework for identifying, managing, and mitigating project-related human rights risks.

In this context, Principle 10 extends transparency obligations for Category A projects and, when applicable, Category B projects -excluding refinancing or acquisition transactions- by mandating the inclusion of human rights risk analyses within Environmental and Social Impact Assessments (ESIAs). These assessments must be made publicly accessible, thereby enhancing accountability and disclosure practices in project finance.

Under Principle 3, the provisions applicable to projects located in designated countries remain substantively unchanged from previous iterations. Environmental and social assessments must continue to comply with domestic legal frameworks, regulatory procedures, and permitting requirements. However, EPFIs are now encouraged to undertake an additional level of scrutiny: they must determine whether specific project risks warrant the application of one or more IFC Performance Standards as supplementary benchmarks. Where such standards are relevant, EPFIs retain discretion to conduct further due diligence in order to address the identified risk dimensions more comprehensively.

Principle 5, dealing with stakeholder engagement, reiterates the centrality of meaningful consultation with affected communities, particularly Indigenous peoples, and explicitly operationalizes the principle of Free, Prior, and Informed Consent (FPIC) in accordance with IFC Performance Standard 7 (PS7). The revised framework introduces an independent verification mechanism: an environmental and social consultant must assess whether engagement processes meet both host-country regulatory expectations and IFC PS7 criteria. In instances where the adequacy of FPIC is uncertain, EPFIs, supported by the independent consultant's findings, may determine whether the deviation is justified or whether corrective measures should be implemented to ensure compliance with international standards.

Finally, Principle 10 also encourages EPFIs to promote the voluntary disclosure of non-commercially sensitive biodiversity data through recognized platforms such as the Global Biodiversity Information Facility (GBIF) or other relevant databases. This addition reflects a broader commitment within EP 4 to align project finance with open-data principles and global environmental governance objectives, thereby reinforcing transparency and scientific collaboration in biodiversity conservation.

Table 1. Modifications of EP versions I, II, III and IV

Themes	EP Version I (2003)	EP Version II (2006)	EP Version III (2013)	EP Version IV (2019)
Number of signatory institutions	10	40	78	136 (current)
Scope of application	Applied solely to lending operations.	Extended to project finance advisory services.	Covered project finance, advisory mandates, project-related corporate loans, and bridge loans.	Further broadened to include project-related refinancing and acquisition finance.
Reporting and disclosure	No reporting format required.	Basic reporting on the number of screened and closed transactions.	Disclosure of closed projects by category, sector, region, and indication of independent review.	Public online summary of ESIA including climate and human rights risks. Mandatory disclosure of annual GHG emissions above 100,000 tCO_2e and non-sensitive biodiversity data to GBIF and similar databases.

continued on following page

Table 1. Continued

Themes	EP Version I (2003)	EP Version II (2006)	EP Version III (2013)	EP Version IV (2019)
Alignment with IFC standards and sustainability focus	Emphasis on environmental assessment only; social risks and climate issues not explicitly addressed.	Inclusion of social due diligence and free, prior, and informed consultation.	Integration of climate change within due diligence and stronger alignment with World Bank and IFC guidelines; incorporation of human rights considerations.	Reinforcement of social and human rights due diligence, explicit reference to UNGPs, and requirement to assess physical climate risks proportional to project type and severity.
Information sharing among financial institutions	Informal exchanges of environmental and social information.	Formalized cooperation among co-financiers on environmental and social matters.	Shared information respecting company privacy and applicable regulations.	Structured sharing mechanism ensuring consistent EP application, subject to confidentiality and legal compliance.
Country designation criteria	Assessment in high-income OECD countries considered equivalent to IFC standards.	Similar equivalence applied.	Introduction of "designated" countries list—high-income OECD jurisdictions deemed equivalent.	Distinction maintained: designated countries assessed under domestic laws; non-designated countries evaluated against IFC Performance Standards and World Bank EHS Guidelines.
Glossary of key terms	Not included.	Glossary added to clarify loan documentation terminology.	Glossary maintained and refined.	Continuation of standardized glossary for consistency in loan documentation.

Source: Author's contributions with reference to the article of Weber, O. & Acheta, E. (2014). The Equator Principles: Ten Teenage Years of Implementation and a Search for Outcome (24). Waterloo, ON: CIGI.

3. THE CONTRIBUTION OF THE EQUATOR PRINCIPLES TO SUSTAINABLE FINANCE: A REVIEW OF THEORETICAL AND EMPIRICAL LITERATURE

The EP adoption agenda emerged in response to great pressure from governments, stakeholders, and some environmental activists (Aboutorabifard, 2016). Starting with the need to identify, assess, and manage environmental and social risks in large infrastructure projects, these principles aim to prevent negative impacts on ecosystems, communities, and climate, and provide a process for lenders to focus on environmental and social responsibility related to large industrial and social projects (Bratu & Jacquin, 2007).

The purpose of this section is to present a review of the empirical literature on the impact of EPs on the sustainability of banks.

3.1 Green Credit and EPs: Credit Risk Mitigation

The global concept of "green credit" is largely informed by the EPs, which represent the first internationally recognized framework to incorporate environmental protection as a central criterion within corporate finance decision-making. These principles obligate financial institutions to account for the environmental and social consequences of project financing alongside conventional credit risk assessments. In addition, they encourage banks to allocate financial resources to projects that promote energy efficiency, reduce emissions, and contribute to environmental stability.

The EPs further emphasize a collaborative engagement between signatory financial institutions and their clients, encompassing environmental and social impact assessments, the implementation of social management systems and action plans, stakeholder engagement, grievance mechanisms, independent reviews, and ongoing monitoring and reporting (Macve & Chen, 2010). This collaborative framework serves to mitigate information asymmetries between lenders and borrowers, reduce opportunities for corruption, and address risks associated with incomplete contractual arrangements.Finally, by adhering to transnational socio-environmental and human rights standards, as well as the laws and regulations of both home and host countries, the EPs help mitigate various other types of risks, such as political and legal risks, by ensuring that legal permissions and clearances are obtained from the relevant authorities. In essence, financial institutions that are signatories to the EPs are strongly motivated to carefully identify, assess, and manage investment risks to ensure loan repayment. By improving the identification and management of both economic (financial) and non-economic (non-financial) risks, the EPs contribute to making projects safer investments and loans. Taken together, these insights highlight the multifaceted role of the Equator Principles in promoting sustainable finance. By integrating environmental and social considerations into project appraisal and financing decisions, the EPs not only facilitate the adoption of green credit practices but also contribute to effective management of climate change risks (Watchman, 2006). Simultaneously, adherence to the EPs can reinforce a financial institution's commitment to CSR, shaping lending behavior and influencing borrower risk perceptions. Empirical evidence further suggests that EP adoption may enhance bank liquidity and financial stability, as compliance with these principles encourages robust risk assessment, transparency, and stakeholder engagement. Collectively, this body of research underscores the potential of the EPs to align financial performance with environmental sustainability, while fostering trust and resilience in the banking sector.

According to Power and Tandja-M (2024), financial institutions that choose to follow the Equator Principles commit to overseeing the environmental and social (ESG) implications of the projects they support. Their study examines how these obligations affect corporate borrowers, while also exploring whether there are advantages such as more favorable lending conditions. Drawing on comprehensive global loan datasets, their findings indicate that companies engaging with environmentally responsible banks benefit in various ways, including reduced loan spreads. The authors suggest that working with such "green banks" enables firms to signal their dedication to ESG standards and supports them in mitigating post-financing ESG-related risks.

Viewed through the framework of the EPs, Xu et al. (2023) explore whether green loans steer corporate innovation toward environmentally friendly technologies. The results show that, within pollution-intensive industries, firms receiving green loans exhibit a higher proportion of environmental patents relative to total patents compared to those in less polluting sectors. Furthermore, the authors highlight the influential governance roles played by analysts' scrutiny and gender diversity on corporate boards in encouraging companies with green loans to shift toward sustainable practices. The results carry important implications for the banking sector. The central government's green credit policy lacks detailed technical specifications and operational guidelines, leaving banks without a standardized approach to its implementation. In contrast, the EPs apply life-cycle assessment mechanisms in granting green loans, offering process-oriented tools for identifying, evaluating, and categorizing corporate environmental risks. They also set out technical and performance benchmarks across industries for managing environmental and social risks. By creating targeted action plans for identified risk areas, polluting firms can advance their green technology adoption and accelerate the long-term sustainability transition of high-emission industries.

As a result, green and sustainable lending has become more popular, and banks are under increasing pressure to reduce lending to fossil fuel companies and address environmental threats. Thus, banks with different environmental strategies may treat borrowers differently and change the debt-pollution relationship (Flammer, 2021). Socially responsible investing and lending incorporate the non-financial and ethical dimensions of a client's performance and operational policies (Scholtens, 2009). Within this framework, banks are expected to undertake activities such as screening credit applicants, monitoring ongoing credit performance, evaluating associated risks, and reporting on lending practices. Goss and Roberts (2011) observe that banks tend to impose less favorable loan conditions on clients perceived as higher risk from a CSR perspective. Moreover, consistent with agency theory, CSR-related expenditures by lower-quality borrowers may be interpreted as overinvestment, resulting in financial penalties in the form of extended loan maturities and elevated debt costs.

These practices are designed to increase the interest of companies in undertaking environmentally friendly projects. Some studies have highlighted the significant effects of green credits on business success given that the EPs require banks to increase the amount of loans to be disbursed, reduce the interest on those loans, as well as lengthen the repayment period (Cullen, 2018). In total, green banks and creditors can help reduce pollution from their borrowers. While green loans still represent a small fraction of total loans, green finance has the potential to reap environmental benefits (Tang & Zhou, 2020).

Table 2. Versions III and IV of the Equator Principles: Modifications by principle

Principle	EP 3	EP 4
Principle 1: Review and Categorization	EPFIs are required to assess project-associated risks and categorize projects as Category A, B, or C.	EPFIs conduct an internal environmental and social review, categorizing projects based on potential environmental and social risks, including human rights, climate change, and biodiversity considerations.
Principle 2: Environmental and Social Impact Assessment	An Environmental and Social Impact Assessment (ESIA) is mandatory for all Category A and B projects.	Category A projects, and where applicable Category B, require a Climate Change Risk Assessment, tailored to project type and risk magnitude, as part of the ESIA.
Principle 3: Application of Environmental and Social Standards	Compliance with host country laws is required for projects in designated countries; for non-designated countries, compliance with IFC standards and World Bank EHS Guidelines is required.	Due diligence evaluates compliance for all Category A and B projects. Non-designated countries: IFC Performance Standards and World Bank EHS Guidelines. Designated countries: host country laws, regulations, and permits.
Principle 4: Environmental and Social Management System (ESMS) and Action Plan	Clients must develop an ESMS and Environmental and Social Management Plan (ESMP) to address ESIA findings.	Clients are required to develop and/ or maintain an ESMS to address issues identified during the assessment process, including measures to comply with applicable standards.
Principle 5: Stakeholder Engagement	Clients must implement ongoing, structured stakeholder engagement with affected communities and other stakeholders.	An independent consultant evaluates consultation processes, particularly with indigenous peoples, in line with host country laws and IFC PS7 requirements.
Principle 6: Grievance Mechanisms	For Category A (and, where appropriate, Category B) projects, clients must establish grievance mechanisms within the ESMS.	No change.
Principle 7: Independent Review	Independent Environmental and Social Consultants review ESIA, ESMP, ESMS, and stakeholder engagement documentation for Category A and B projects.	No change. For Category B projects, prior due diligence by multilateral/bilateral institutions or OECD export credit agencies may suffice.

continued on following page

Table 2. Continued

Principle	EP 3	EP 4
Principle 8: Covenants	Clients covenant in financing documentation to comply with host country environmental and social laws and the EPs; periodic reporting and decommissioning plans are required.	No change. EPFIs ensure existing environmental and social obligations continue in new financial documentation.
Principle 9: Independent Monitoring and Review	EPFIs require independent monitoring of ESMS compliance, via external experts or independent consultants, throughout the project lifecycle.	No change. Multilateral or bilateral controls by OECD member institutions may be considered.
Principle 10: Reporting and Transparency	EP 3 specifies public reporting requirements for environmental and social data, including ESIA, ESMP, and GHG emissions; annual EP activity reporting by EPFIs is required.	Clients must report annually on ESIA summaries including human rights and climate change risks. Projects emitting >100,000 tCO_2e/year must disclose operational GHG emissions. EPFIs encourage disclosure of biodiversity data to GBIF and relevant databases.

Source: Author's contributions based on the site (www.equator-principles.com).

3.2 Climate Risk Consistency and Integration

According to Rani (2025), "Sustainability and ecosystem services are key to ensuring healthy ecosystems in the long run, and involve ensuring that natural resources are used in a way that meets current needs while preserving the ability of future generations to meet their own needs." Sustainability and profit should not be viewed as separate concepts, as sustainable and feasible policies ensure that factors critical to long-term profitability are taken into account. Wilbanks and Fernandez (2014) highlight that climate change presents risks to goals such as poverty reduction and economic prosperity. Therefore, societies must figure out how to manage these risks and determine acceptable levels of risk, without compromising their core values. Risk management and the assessment of different types of risks depend on how societies define what consequences are considered acceptable, tolerable, or intolerable. According to Li and Gallagher (2022), governments, investors, and communities are becoming more proactive in addressing climate risks. For example, the Task Force on Climate-related Financial Disclosures (TCFD) was established in 2015 to improve and expand climate-related financial reporting. Similarly, the Network for Greening the Financial System, created in 2017, aims to promote the exchange of best practices on climate risk management among central banks and regulators. The latest version of the Equator Principles (EP 4) mandates a climate change risk assessment for projects and advocates for climate infrastructure. By understanding the baseline of climate risks associated with global assets, policymakers and organizations can better develop climate-related policies or guidelines. The assessment of greenhouse gas emissions has gained increasing importance with this new version of the EPs.

Climate change risk is generally conceptualized as comprising two interrelated dimensions: physical risk and transition risk. Physical risk encompasses the potential loss in the value of financial assets resulting from the increasing frequency and severity of extreme weather events, as well as from more gradual, long-term climatic shifts. Transition risk, by contrast, relates to the capacity of a project or organization to adjust to the structural transformations required for a low-carbon economy (Macci et al., 2022). The integration of climate risk assessment and management into project evaluation, particularly through adherence to the Eps, can enhance access to capital by strengthening investor and lender confidence in the project's resilience and sustainability performance (TCFD, 2021).

Sheehama (2021) analyzes the impact of transition risks under EP4, particularly the "transition to an ethical, low-carbon economy," and examines whether this new addition will support or hinder oil and gas project financing in Africa, amid the ongoing energy transition. The author challenges the assumptions underlying the policy design. Sheehama concludes that considering project finance in Africa could meet the continent's energy needs while compelling governments to address climate change by establishing processes, policies, and systems to manage these risks. Furthermore, the broad formulation of transition risks and implementation standards in EP4 allows for flexibility, enabling the principles to be tailored to various regimes that positively contribute to these areas. This approach ensures the consideration of ethical transitions and promotes coordination and consistency across different policy sectors.

3.3 Brief Review of the Empirical Literature on the Impact of the Equator Principles

A substantial body of research has examined the strengths and limitations of the EPs (Mnasri & Ben Romdhane, 2024; Amalric, 2005; Conley & Williams, 2011; Eisenbach et al., 2014; Hardenbrook, 2007; Scholtens & Lammertjan, 2007; Wright & Rwabizambuga, 2006; Lawrence & Thomas, 2004). Yet, research directly assessing their influence on banks' performance and sustainability remains scarce. Some findings even present conflicting conclusions, and EP implementation continues to pose challenges for EPFIs. Although the EPs are designed to guide the financial sector toward greater sustainability, it is still uncertain whether they fully achieve this goal or lead to tangible changes in the practices of the institutions that adopt them (Mnasri & Ben Romdhane, 2024). The findings of these studies remain mixed.

Scholtens and Lammertjan (2007) reported that the adoption of the EPs exerted a positive influence on the CSR ratings of EPFIs. However, they did not detect any significant improvement in shareholder value following the announcement of EP adoption -an outcome likely attributable to the relatively limited role of project finance within the broader operational scope of EPFIs. In a similar vein, Chih et al. (2010) found no statistically significant relationship between EP adoption and the financial performance of EPFIs. Nonetheless, their analysis revealed that in more competitive banking environments, institutions adhering to this voluntary code of conduct tend to exhibit stronger commitments to environmental and social responsibility, presumably as a means of enhancing their competitive positioning under such market conditions.

Weber and Feltmate (2016) analyzed the reports published by EP signatories and noted that EPs were primarily adopted to improve the reputation and risk management of signatories. They conclude that EPs have not made significant contributions to both project sustainability and the financial system. Previous research also indicated that EP adoption was primarily used to signal responsible conduct and found no significant improvement in financial performance between adopters and non-adopters, except for environmental impact. Ben Emukufia and Aduloju (2020) surveyed 124 managers from the top ten depository banks in Nigeria to study the level of awareness and adoption of EPs. Their results show that although banking stakeholders in Nigeria are aware of EPs, there is a low level of adoption. These authors point out that the difficulties in measuring the benefits of EP adoption and the lack of enforcement of sanctions for non-compliance limit the number of financial institutions adhering to these principles in Nigeria. According to the authors, the EP code, in its current form, appears to lack the power to compel members to implement the principles and the authority to monitor compliance (Aboutorabifard, 2016), hence its low appeal to many institutions. Batae et al. (2021) challenge the assumptions of agency theory, which suggests that environmental spending and emissions reduction initiatives directly impact shareholder wealth. They argue that operational efficiency in many environmental aspects of the banking business has not yet been fully reflected, implying that the financial benefits of such initiatives may not be immediately apparent.

Conversely, several studies have demonstrated that the adoption of the EPs yields positive effects on economic development and is positively correlated with bank liquidity and overall financial performance. Empirical evidence suggests that financial institutions adhering to ethical and environmental codes of conduct tend to disclose more comprehensive sustainability information compared to non-signatory institutions. Assuming that disclosure practices reflect underlying business behavior, such findings imply that EP membership exerts a favorable influence on the sustainability orientation of member institutions. For instance, Chen et al. (2022) examined the impact of EP adoption on the liquidity position of banks engaged in project finance over the period 2003-2010. Their results indicate that EPFIs maintain higher levels of liquidity relative to non-EPFIs. This outcome is attributed to the increased risks and compliance costs inherent in EP adoption, as well as to more robust internal regulatory mechanisms. Furthermore, the authors recommend that banks intending to adopt the EPs should strengthen their liquidity buffers in anticipation of these requirements. They also argue that regulatory authorities should incentivize non-EPFIs to adhere to the EPs or comparable sustainability frameworks as a means of reinforcing financial stability and promoting green banking practices.

To analyze the impact of EPs on its signatories, Weber and Acheta (2016) conducted interviews with EPFI representatives. The questions addressed the benefits and risks of EPs for EPFIs, their impact on evaluation procedures, and the sustainability of projects. The results of the interviews suggest that EPs are beneficial to the reputation of signatories. EPFIs take environmental and societal issues into consideration when financing projects, thereby ensuring their social license to operate. In addition, EPs help assess a project's environmental and societal risks in a more standardized and transparent way.

In a recent study, Macci et al. (2022) examined the applicability of the EPs from the standpoint of an Engineering, Procurement, and Construction (EPC) contractor. Their analysis highlights how EPC contractors can adopt a proactive approach to ensure and demonstrate project compliance with the EPs, particularly in relation to greenhouse gas (GHG) emissions accounting. The authors proposed a methodological framework for quantifying GHG emissions, assessing climate-related risks, and evaluating the economic implications of alternative project options. This framework is characterized by its adaptability, allowing for the integration of various technological alternatives and consideration of the specific contextual conditions of different geographical regions. It operates on multiple levels: first, it illustrates that EPC contractors are capable of delivering projects consistent with the environmental and social standards defined by the EPs; second, it enables contractors to provide clients with a portfolio of technological solutions, thereby facilitating the selection of the most environmentally sustainable options.

While a few studies have reported a positive link between the adoption of the EPs and improvements in banks' financial and operational outcomes, the evidence remains insufficient to draw firm conclusions. Further research -both theoretical and empirical- supported by more extensive data is necessary. Future studies could also explore the effectiveness of the latest EP provisions in evaluating and managing climate change risks associated with projects. Nonetheless, developing reliable metrics and standards to assess banks' environmental and climate performance remains a significant challenge in this field.

CONCLUSION AND RECOMMENDATIONS

Owing to the extensive scope and interpretative flexibility of EP 4, the revised provisions addressing climate-related risks are unlikely to constrain the financing of oil and gas projects, particularly within the African context. The revision primarily aims to incentivize governments and policymakers to adopt a more proactive and strategic approach to climate governance, while simultaneously acknowledging the structural challenges associated with ensuring universal energy access. In this regard, African economies are expected not only to continue the exploration and development of oil and gas resources but also to progressively integrate sustainability considerations, promote energy diversification as an adaptive response to climate change, and pursue a phased transition towards low-carbon energy systems.

Thus, policymakers and regulators are increasingly aware of the importance of adopting these principles. Their role is important because they have the power to change and control the dynamics and landscape of finance and rapidly address the challenges of climate change. Indeed, financial institutions, as the main players in green finance, should promote EPs, fully consider environmental risks in their financial activities, cultivate a green financial culture, and cooperate with relevant government departments to support the development of green and low-carbon industries. EPs represent, therefore, a form of self-regulation that financial institutions can adopt in response to environmental and societal concerns about their lending activities in financing projects (Contreras et al., 2019). The long-term success of EPs depends on the likelihood that financial institutions will adopt them[6] but also on the mechanisms that ensure their implementation.

One of the strengths of EPs is the integration of compliance commitments (Principle 8). This Principle assumes that if a client fails to meet its environmental and social commitments, EPFI will explore corrective measures with the latter to provide support in bringing the project back into compliance. In addition, if the client fails to do so within an agreed-upon period, EPFI has the right to pursue any necessary remedies.

Despite the relevance of these mechanisms for analyzing the effectiveness of EPs, Coulee and Motte-Baumvol (2018) show that the analysis of their practice testifies to their negligible impact. These authors argue that the lack of enforcement is due to some fundamental shortcomings of the text, related to the informal and unenforceable nature of monitoring and sanctioning[7].

In addition, there are many questions surrounding the actual impacts of EPs and whether they can produce the desired results (Mnasri & Ben Romdhane, 2024). The answers to these questions allow for truly informed decisions to be made. Dikau and Volz (2020) notes that their impact must be assessed in terms of effectiveness, efficiency, and equity, both from a financial perspective and a sustainability perspective. However, providing an answer to this question is a rather complex task and such an evaluation would be well beyond the scope of this research. As a result, there is little empirical evidence from which to draw lessons. This is clearly an area where additional research is needed to assist policy makers.

Overall, this study contributes to the growing body of literature on sustainable finance by emphasizing the Equator Principles as a central instrument for embedding environmental and social responsibility within the financial sector. Beyond their role as a voluntary standard, the EPs reflect the evolving governance dynamics between financial institutions, regulatory authorities, and global sustainability agendas. Strengthening their effectiveness requires not only enhanced monitoring and enforcement mechanisms but also greater integration with national regulatory frameworks and international climate commitments. Future research should thus explore how the EPs interact with other sustainable finance instruments, such as green bonds, ESG disclosure frameworks, and climate-related risk assessments, and assess their combined impact on the alignment of financial systems with the objectives of the Paris Agreement and the UN Sustainable Development Goals (SDGs).

REFERENCES

Ablender, M. S. (2011). Corporate social responsibility as subsidiary co-responsibility: A macroeconomic perspective. *Journal of Business Ethics, 99*, 115–128.

Aboutorabifard, H. (2016). Equator Principles and Climate Change Issues: Examining the EPs' Climate Change Policies and Analyzing the Likely Effectiveness of these Policies. UWSpace. http://hdl.handle.net/10012/10361

Amalric, F. (2005). The Equator Principles : A Step Towards Sustainability? *CCRS Working Paper Series Working Paper No. 01 / 05*

Aras, G., Tezcan, N., & Kutlu Furtuna, O. (2018). Multidimensional comprehensive corporate sustainability performance evaluation model: Evidence from an emerging market banking sector. *Journal of Cleaner Production, 185*, 600–609. DOI: 10.1016/j.jclepro.2018.01.175

Arrègle, J. L. (2006). "Resource Based" analysis and identification of strategic assets. *French Management Journal, 160*, 241–259.

Barbot, G. (2010). The social utility of the bank in question. Some reflections for the post-crisis period. *Life & Economic Sciences, 3-4* (185-186).

Batae, O. M., Dragomir, V., & Ionescu-Feleaga, L. (2021). The Relationship between Environmental, Social, and Financial Performance in the Banking Sector: A European Study. [January.]. *Journal of Cleaner Production, 290*, 125791.

Ben Emukufia, A. O., & Aduloju, S. A. (2020). Adoption of Voluntary Global Governance Initiatives: Equator Principles and Banks In Nigeria. Facta Universitatis, Series: Economics and Organization, 249-260.https://doi.org/DOI: 10.22190/FUEO200416016O

Bratu, D., & Jacquin, M. P. (2007). Communicating around CSR and sustainable development: The case of the savings bank. *CEREN Notebook, 21*, 52–63.

Buisson, M. L. (2008). Legitimacy and management sciences: State of play and perspectives. *Humanism and Business, 289*, 29–57.

Capron, M., & Quairel-Lanoizelée, F. (2007). *Corporate social responsability.* Repères Collection.

Chen, S., Wang, K., & Liu, H. (2022). The Impact of the Equator Principle on Carbon Financial Markets: A Case Study Based on China's Green Credit Data. SSRN *Electronic Journal.* https://doi.org/DOI: 10.2139/ssrn.4113787

Chih, H.-L., Chih, H.-H., & Chen, T.-Y. (2010). On the Déterminants of Corporate Social Responsibility: International Evidence on the Financial Industry. *Journal of Business Ethics*, *93*, 115–135.

Christiansen, J. K., & Vendelo, M. T. (2003). The Role of Reputation Building in International R&D Project Collaboration. *Corporate Reputation Review*, *5*, 304–329.

Conley, J. M., & Williams, C. A. (2011). Global banks as global sustainability regulators?: The equator principles. *Law & Policy*, *33*(4), 542–575. DOI: 10.1111/j.1467-9930.2011.00348.x

Contreras, G., Jaap, W. B., & Kleimeier, S. (2019). Self-regulation in sustainable finance: The adoption of the Equator Principles. *World Development, Elsevier*, *122*(C), 306–324.

Coulee, F. & Motte-Baumvol, J. (2018). Rapport de recherche sur l'effectivité des codes de gouvernance d'entreprise, de l'intérêt du droit international pour apprécier l'opportunité d'une réforme législative en France. HAL Science Ouverte. hal-04527939, version 1.

Cullen, J. (2018, August). After "HLEG": EU Banks, Climate Change Abatement and the Precautionary Principle. *Cambridge Yearbook of European Legal Studies*, *20*, 61–87. DOI: 10.1017/cel.2018.7

Dam, L. (2008). *Corporate social responsibility and financial markets*. Doctoral Thesis, Rijksuniversiteit Groningen, PrintPartners Ipskamp, Nederland.

De Perthuis, C. (2003). La génération future a-t-elle un avenir? Développement durable et mondialisation, Paris: Belin.

Dikau, S., & Volz, U. (2020). Central Bank Mandates, Sustainability Objectives and the Promotion of Green Finance. Working Papers 232, Department of Economics, SOAS University of London, UK.

Domergue, F. (2018). CSR in the banking sector, a tool for regaining confidence in times of crisis? https://hal.archives-ouvertes.fr

Duan, K. (2021, August). Green into Gold: The Sustainable Development of Commercial Banks from the Perspective of the Equator Principles. *International Journal of Theoretical and Applied Mathematics.*, *7*(4), 57–67.

Eisenbach, S., Schiereck, D., Trillig, J., & von Flotow, P. (2014). Sustainable project finance, the adoption of the equator principles and shareholder value effects. *Business Strategy and the Environment*, *23*(6), 375–394. DOI: 10.1002/bse.1789

European Commission. (2004). Recommendation on remuneration of directors in listed companies (2004/913/EC). Working Document. Brussels: European Commission. www.ec.europa.eu

European Commission. (2014b). European Commission proposes to strengthen shareholder engagement and introduce a 'say on pay' for Europe's largest companies." Press Release (April 9). Brussels: European Commission. www.ec.europa.eu

European Commission. (2014c). EU Audit Directive and Regulation." Factsheet. Brussels: European Commission. www.ec.europa.eu

European Commission (2014a). Directive of the European Parliament and of the Council: Amending Directive 2007/36/EC." Proposal. Brussels: European Commission.

Flammer, C. (2021). Corporate green bonds. *Journal of Financial Economics*, *142*(2), 499–516. DOI: 10.1016/j.jfineco.2021.01.010

Florini, A. (2003). Business and Global Governance: The Growing Role of Corporate Codes of Conduct. *The Brookings Review*, *21*(2), 4–8.

Gholami, S. (2011). Value creation model through corporate social responsibility (CSR). *International Journal of Business and Management*, *6*(9), 148–154.

Gond, J. P., & Igalens, J. (2008). Corporate social responsibility. Collection: What do I know? Publisher: Presses Universitaires de France, 128 pages.

Goss, A., & Roberts, G. S. (2011). The impact of corporate social responsibility on the cost of bank loans. *Journal of Banking & Finance*, *35*(7), 1794–1810. DOI: 10.1016/j.jbankfin.2010.12.002

Hardenbrook, A. (2007). The Equator Principles : The Private Financial Sector's Attempt at Environmental Responsibility. *Vanderbilt Journal of Transnational Law*, *40*(1), 197–232.

Hosmer, L. T. (1995). Trust: The Connecting Link between Organizational Theory and Philosophical Ethics. *Academy of Management Review*, *20*, 379–403.

Jeucken, M. (2004). Sustainability in Finance. Banking on the planet. Delft, The Netherlands: Eburon.

Jeucken, M., & Bouma, J. J. (1999). The Changing Environment of Banks. *Greener Management International*, *27*, 21–35.

Lawrence, R. F., & Thomas, W. L. (2004). The Equator Principles and Project Finance: Sustainability in Practice? *Natural Resources and Environment*, *19*(2), 20–26.

Li, X., & Gallagher, K. P. (2022). Assessing the climate change exposure of foreign direct investment. *Nature Communications*, *13*(1), 1–9. DOI: 10.1038/s41467-022-28975-5 PMID: 35304443

Liu, L., Li, Z., Fu, X., Liu, X., Li, Z., & Zheng, W. (2022). Impact of power on uneven development: Evaluating built-up area changes in Chengdu based on NPP-VIIRS images (2015–2019). *Landscape*, *11*(4), 489.

Macci, I., Joli, L., Franzoni, G., Rigolio, M., Frassoldati, A., & Micheli, G. J. L. (2022). On the Impact of the Equator Principles Compliance: Supporting the Decision Making in Projects. *Chemical Engineering Transactions*, *91*(May), 7–12. DOI: 10.3303/CET2291002

Macve, R., & Chen, X. (2010). The "equator principles": A success for voluntary codes? *Accounting, Auditing & Accountability Journal*, *23*(7), 890–919. DOI: 10.1108/09513571011080171

Maignan, I., & Ralston, D.-A. (2002). Corporate social responsibility in Europe and the U.S.: Insights from businesses' self-representations. *Journal of International Business Studies*, *33*(3), 497–514.

Mercanti-Guérin, M. (2011). Crisis in the banking sector and portrait of the ideal bank: A study conducted among young consumers. *The Journal of Management Sciences*, *3-4*(249-250), 57–64.

Mnasri, K. & Ben Romdhane, S. (2024). Towards an Environmental Finance Framework: The Contribution of the Equator Principles. *Bankers, Markets, Investors*, Focus On, 179, December 2024.

Morin, M. (2006). *Banking and sustainable development. From communication to action*. L'Harmattan.

Normann, R., & Ramirez, R. (1993). From value chain to value constellation: Designing interactive strategy. *Harvard Business Review*, *71*, 65–75. PMID: 10127040

Oliver, C. (1991). Strategic Responses to Institutional Processes. *Academy of Management Review*, *16*(1), 145–179.

Parsons, T. (1960). Structure and Process in Modern Societies. *American Journal of Sociology*, 66(5), 344 pages.

Pasquero, J. (2005). Corporate social responsibility as an object of management science: A historical look. In B.-Turcotte M.F. and Salmon A., Corporate social and environment responsibility, *Presses of Québec University*.

Pfeffer, J., & Salancik, G. (1978). *The External Control of Organizations: A Resource Dependence Perspective*. Harper & Row.

Plihon, D. (2010). Global Regulation in the Aftermath of the Subprime Crisis. In CRIFO P., Ponssard J-P. *Corporate social responsibility: from compliance to opportunity*, Editions of the Ecole Polytechnique, 17-26.

Plihon, D., & Rigot, S. (2022). Public financial intermediaries and climate change. Presses de Sciences Po. *Revue économique*, *73*, 243–266.

Power, G. J., & Tandja-M, D. C. (2024). Does it pay to be Green? The impact of equator principles on project loans. *European Journal of Finance*, *31*(5), 616–646. DOI: 10.1080/1351847X.2024.2419568

Principles, E. (2006). *The Equator Principles. A Financial Industry Benchmark for Determining, Assessing and Managing Social & Environmental Risk in Project Financing,* Equator Principles Financial Institutions, Washington, DC. Retrieved from: http://www.equator-principles.com/documents/Equator_Principles.pdf

Principles, E. (2011). *Summary Response by Equator Principles Association to the Equator Principles Strategic Review Report*, Equator Principles Financial Institutions, Washington, DC. Retrieved from http://www.equator-principles.com/resources/ep _association_summary_response_ strategic_review.pdf

Principles, E. (2013a). *The Equator Principles Association Governance Rules.* Equator Principles Financial Institutions, Washington, DC. Retrieved from http:// www.equator principles.com/resources/ep_governance_rules_december_2013.pdf

Principles, E. (2013b). *The Equator Principles III.* Equator Principles Financial Institutions, Washington, DC. Retrieved from http://www.equatorprinciples. com/ index.php/ep3/ep3

Principles, E. (2014). *The Equator Principles Implementation Note*. Equator Principles Financial Institutions, Washington, DC. Retrieved from http://www.equator -principles.com/ resources/equator_principles_implementation_note_july_2014.pdf

Pupion, P. C. (2013). Sustainable development-CSR: A quest for legitimacy of European banks. Association for Research and Publications in Management. *Gestion, 2000*(30), 39–59.

Ramonjy, D. (1997). Contribution to the study of organizational legitimacy: Comparative study of the legitimacy strategies of two fair trade organizations in France. Free Communication presented at the 75th ACFAS congress.

Rani, J. (2025). Cultural and social norms supporting sustainability. In IGI Global eBooks, 43-78. https://doi.org/DOI: 10.4018/979-8-3373-1280-4.ch003

Reynaud, E., & Walas, A. (2015). Discourse on CSR in the process of legitimizing the bank. *French Management Review*, *41*(248), 187–209.

Sarfraz, M., Qun, W., Hui, L., & Abdullah, M. I. (2018). Environmental risk management strategies and the moderating role of corporate social responsibility in project financing decisions. *Sustainability (Switzerland)*, *10*(8). Advance online publication. DOI: 10.3390/su10082771

Scholtens, B. (2009). Corporate social responsibility in the international banking industry. *Journal of Business Ethics*, *86*(2), 159–175. DOI: 10.1007/s10551-008-9841-x

Scholtens, B., & Lammertjan, D. (2007). Banking on the Equator. Are Banks that Adopted the Equator Principles Different from Non-Adopters? *World Development*, *35*(8), 1307–1328. DOI: 10.1016/j.worlddev.2006.10.013

Scott, J. (1979). *The Moral Economy of the Peasant*. Yale University Press.

Sethi, S. P. (2002). Standards for corporate conduct in the international arena: Challenges and opportunities for multinational corporations. *Business and Society Review*, *107*, 20–40.

Sheehama, A. P. G. (2021). Equator Principles 4-Revised Climate Change Risk: What Does This Mean For Project Financing in Africa Amidst The Ongoing Energy Transition? *Journal of Sustainable Development Law and Policy*, *12*(1), 72–91. DOI: 10.4314/jsdlp.v12i1.4

Suchman, M. C. (1995). Managing Legitimacy: Strategic and Institutional Approaches. *Academy of Management Review*, *20*(3), 571–610.

Tang, Y., & Zhou, Y. (2020). Performance evaluation and application of banking industry based on equator principles. *E3S Web of Conferences*, *214*(December 2007), 1-5. https://doi.org/DOI: 10.1051/e3sconf/202021402055

Tao, H., Zhuang, S., Xue, R., Cao, W., Tian, J., & Shan, Y. (2022). Environmental Finance: An Interdisciplinary Review. *Technological Forecasting and Social Change*, *179*, 121639. DOI: 10.1016/j.techfore.2022.121639

Thiétart, R.-A. (2007). Introduction. In *Management Research Method*. Dunod.

Wang, E., Liu, X., Wu, J., & Cai, D. (2019). Green Credit, Debt Maturity, and Corporate Investment-Evidence from China. *Sustainability (Switzerland)*, *11*(3), 1–19. DOI: 10.3390/su11030583

Watchman, P. (2006). Banks, business, and human rights. *Butterworths Journal of International Banking and Financial Law*, *2*, 47–50.

Weber, O. (2014). The financial sector's impact on sustainable development. *Journal of Sustainable Finance & Investment*, *4*(1), 1–8.

Weber, O., & Acheta, E. (2014). *The Equator Principles: Ten Teenage Years of Implementation and a Search for Outcome (24)*. CIGI.

Weber, O., & Acheta, E. (2016). The Equator Principles: Do They Make Banks More Sustainable? Working Paper, Unep Inquiry, February.

Weber, O., & Feltmate, B. (2016). *Sustainable Banking: Managing the Social and Environmental Impact of Financial Institutions*. Business & Sustainability Series G- Reference, Information and Interdisciplinary Subjects Series.

Weick, K. E. (1995). *Sensemaking in organizations*. Sage Publications.

Wilbanks, T. J., & Fernandez, S. J. (2014). Climate Change and Infrastructure, Urban Systems, and Vulnerabilities: Technical Report for the U.S. *Department of Energy in Support of the National Climate Assessment*, 1–92. https://doi.org/.DOI: 10.5822/978-1-61091-556-4

Williamson, O. (1993). Opportunism and Its Critics. *Managerial and Decision Economics*, *14*, 97–107.

Wright, C., & Rwabizambuga, A. (2006). Institutional Pressures, Corporate Reputation, and Voluntary Codes of Conduct: An Examination of the Equator Principles. *Business and Society Review*, *111*(1), 89–117.

Xu, J., Xu, J., Zeng, S., & Cui, J. (2023), Green Finance and Corporate Green Innovation: Evidence from the Equator Principles. Available at *SSRN*: https://ssrn.com/abstract=4405067 or

ENDNOTES

1 Debt securities issued by governments, public and private banks, companies or local authorities to finance activities or projects that are sustainable.

2 Through green bank loans, firms are encouraged to change their business strategy towards green practices to benefit from less stringent financing conditions.

3 Socially Responsible Investment (SRI) practices generally rely on three principal portfolio management approaches. First, the best-in-class strategy involves selecting firms that demonstrate superior performance on environmental, social, and governance (ESG) criteria, as assessed by internal evaluation frameworks or by specialized external rating agencies and sustainability indices. Second, the exclusionary or negative screening strategy entails removing from investment portfolios companies operating in, or significantly exposed to, controversial industries such as arms manufacturing, tobacco, or fossil fuels. Finally, the thematic investment approach focuses on channeling capital toward sectors directly contributing to sustainable development goals, including renewable energy, clean technologies, or environmental innovation.

4 Indigenous peoples have a historical connection to a specific territory that predates colonization and maintain a deep relationship with their lands. They continue to preserve, at least in part, unique social, economic, and political systems. They have their own languages, cultures, beliefs, and knowledge systems. They are dedicated to preserving and nurturing their distinct identities and institutions, and they represent a non-dominant group within society.

5 Source: Equator Principles Association (2013).

6 Following a relational approach, Contreras et al. (2019) show that the adoption of the Equator Principles is more likely when there is pressure from banks that have already adopted the principles. This pressure is the result of collaboration between banks through, for example, syndicated loans. However, for pressure and susceptibility to lead to future widespread adoption of EPs, there must be enough existing adopters in the market.

7 Coulee and Motte-Baumvol (2018) studied the latest annual reports prepared by the four French EFPIs (Crédit Agricole, BNP Paribas, Natixis, and Société Générale). These authors stipulate that these reports do not provide information about the "appropriate remedies" these institutions implemented with respect to defaulting customers. Nor do the reports include a list of corrective measures to help clients bring their projects back into compliance, nor is there any mention of the implementation of grievance mechanisms. The annual reports - and the websites of these institutions - also lack the specific institutional "practice" with respect to the EPs.

Chapter 8
Leveraging Green Finance for Sustainable Development:
An Empirical Analysis of Economic Growth and Environmental Sustainability of Asian OECD Economies

Pragti Dixit
https://orcid.org/0009-0002-4034-4572
Chandigarh University, India

Mukul Bhatnagar
https://orcid.org/0000-0002-7773-5641
Graphic Era University, India

Rajinder Kaur
https://orcid.org/0000-0002-7049-0434
Chandigarh University, India

Nikhil Varghese
Christ University, India

Vibhuti Jain
https://orcid.org/0009-0009-8602-6116
Graphic Era University, India

DOI: 10.4018/979-8-3373-1240-8.ch008

ABSTRACT

Present study investigates the impact of Green Finance and CO2 emissions on GDP per capita of four Asian OECD economies controlling for Expenditure on Education, and Foreign Direct Investment using panel data for the time-period 2015 to 2023, applying pooled OLS, Fixed Effects, and Random Effects Models, and ultimately selecting the Fixed Effects Model based on robust statistical tests (Hausman and Breusch-Pagan LM), revealing that Green Finance significantly enhances GDP per capita, Expenditure on Education unexpectedly hinders it in the short term, and both CO2 emissions and Foreign Direct Investment lack statistically significant effects within countries, thereby underscoring the importance of internal structural factors and advocating for tailored, sustainability-driven, and context-sensitive economic growth strategies.

INTRODUCTION

Against intensifying climate change, environmental degradation, and the urgent global pursuit of sustainable development, the integration of green finance—through investments in renewable energy, clean technologies, and environmentally responsible practices—has come forth as a strategic cornerstone to simultaneously drive economic growth and environmental sustainability, making it crucial to empirically examine how such financial mechanisms and associated factors like education, foreign direct investment, and carbon emissions influence national GDP trajectories and ecological outcomes within a dynamic, country-specific context (Gurbanov & Suleymanli, 2022; K.-C. Zhang et al., 2024).

The emergence of green finance represents a transformative shift in global financial systems, driven by the growing recognition that aligning capital flows with environmental sustainability—through mechanisms like green bonds, sustainable investments (Volz et al., 2015), and climate-focused funding—can effectively mobilize resources toward low-carbon infrastructure, renewable energy, and climate resilience initiatives, thereby positioning green finance as a critical enabler of long-term economic prosperity and ecological balance in response to mounting environmental and climate challenges (Lu et al., 2022).

The relevance of green finance to economic growth lies in its capacity to simultaneously foster sustainable development by channeling investments into green technologies, renewable energy, and climate-resilient infrastructure (Khan et al., 2023), which not only stimulate job creation, innovation, and productivity but also enhance energy security, reduce long-term environmental risks, and contribute to achieving broader economic goals, making it a vital component for countries striving to achieve both economic prosperity and environmental sustainability in an era of climate change (Lau et al., 2025).

Green finance is crucial for improving environmental sustainability as it directs financial resources towards projects that diminish carbon emissions, elevate the use of renewable energy, and strengthen eco-friendly technologies, thereby supporting the transition to a low-carbon economy, mitigating environmental degradation, and enabling countries to meet global climate goals, while simultaneously fostering long-term ecological balance (Afanasiev & Belenchuk, 2021).

Green finance is highly relevant to OECD economies as it offers a strategic pathway to transition towards low-carbon, resource-efficient economies by attracting investment into sustainable infrastructure, renewable energy, and clean technologies, thus helping these countries achieve their ambitious climate targets, enhance their competitive advantage in green industries, stimulate job creation in green sectors, and ensure long-term economic resilience while addressing environmental challenges and fulfilling their commitments under international climate agreements like the Paris Agreement (Safi et al., 2024).

The policy and institutional contexts of Japan, Korea, Israel, and Turkey present a fascinating array of approaches to green finance, each shaped by the specific economic and environmental challenges these nations face. Japan, as a global leader in technological innovation, has integrated green finance into its national agenda through extensive governmental support, including the Green Growth Strategy and the establishment of a comprehensive regulatory framework for green bonds and sustainable investments, alongside active participation in international climate accords. In contrast, Korea has positioned itself at the forefront of green finance within Asia by embedding environmental sustainability into its industrial policies, particularly through its Green New Deal, which emphasizes the expansion of green infrastructure, renewable energy, and low-carbon technologies, supported by both fiscal incentives and stringent environmental regulations. Israel, with its high-tech-driven economy, has tailored green finance to promote innovation in renewable energy and environmental technologies, supported by government-led initiatives such as the Green Investment Fund and a regulatory environment that encourages private sector participation in sustainable ventures. Turkey, facing the dual challenges of rapid industrialization and environmental degradation, has focused its green finance efforts on state-led investments in renewable energy, particularly through its Renewable Energy Resource Zones initiative, and a nascent green bond market. It has also gradually improved its institutional frameworks to better integrate sustainability into its economic and financial policies. Despite their common membership in the OECD, these four nations exhibit diverse strategies in addressing green finance, reflecting the intricate relationship between domestic policy environments, institutional capacity, and national priorities in achieving sustainable development.

Despite the growing global emphasis on green finance, there exists a notable dearth of literature specifically examining its impact on Asian OECD economies, as bulk of existing studies predominantly focus on Western economies, leaving questions unanswered on how green finance mechanisms interact with the unique economic (Ali et al., 2024; Zheng et al., 2023), political, and environmental contexts of Asian OECD countries, and how these nations can leverage green finance to balance economic growth with environmental sustainability in the face of rapid industrialization and urbanization.

In light of this the present study aims to evaluate the effect of Green Finance and CO_2 emissions on GDP per capita of Asian OECD economies controlling for Expenditure on Education and FDI.

RELEVANCE TO GLOBAL SUSTAINABILITY AGENDAS (SDGS AND PARIS AGREEMENT): EXTENDED INTERPRETATION

The empirical configuration—wherein green finance (lnGREF) exhibits a positive within-country elasticity with GDP per capita under the preferred fixed-effects specification, while the marginal contributions of CO_2 emissions (lnCO2), FDI, and short-horizon education outlays (EDU) are attenuated or negative—aligns teleologically with the UN 2030 Agenda and the Paris Agreement's reorientation of capital toward climate-consistent growth. Substantively, the lnGREF→lnGDP linkage is consonant with SDG 8 (productivity and decent work) and SDG 9 (industry, innovation, and infrastructure), with ancillary propulsion of SDG 7 via the R&D and systems-upgrade channel (target 7.a) and SDG 13 by reallocating financing to low-emission assets; in effect, it operationalizes Article 2.1(c) by demonstrating that income expansion can be underwritten by taxonomy-concordant investment rather than emissions-intensive accumulation. The divergence between pooled/RE correlations (where legacy carbon- and investment-heavy structures track income) and FE estimates (where incremental emissions fail to raise GDP once time-invariant heterogeneity is purged) intimates a decoupling trajectory—relative, if not incipiently absolute—consistent with NDC-aligned transition pathways (Altaf et al., 2025). The insignificance or sign reversal on FDI underscores the primacy of *quality* over *quantity*: without disclosure discipline, credible taxonomies, and risk-pricing scaffolds, cross-border inflows need not advance SDG 13 or Article 2.1(c); conversely, blended-finance architectures, transition-finance guidance, and sovereign/DFI de-risking can canalize private capital into grid modernization, industrial electrification, and storage, thereby lowering system costs and amplifying growth multipliers. The short-run negative association on EDU should be read as an intertemporal artifact—gestation lags in human-capital accumulation—rather than a repudiation of SDG 4, with dynamic specifications (longer lags, persistence controls) expected to restore a positive productivity nexus compatible with SDG 8.2. Policywise, the results rationalize a programmatic package: mission-oriented green R&D and network investments (SDGs 7, 9); mainstreaming climate-risk and taxonomy screening in public budgets and state-anchored intermediaries to satisfy Article 2.1(c); calibrated recourse to Article 6 cooperation to compress marginal abatement costs while safeguarding integrity (SDG 13); and just-transition instruments that internalize labor reallocation and distributional equity (SDG 8.5). Taken together, the evidence suggests that when institutions integrate sustainability into the financial calculus, economies can increase income while bending the emissions curve, translating global compacts into actionable, investable national pathways (Li, 2024).

LITERATURE REVIEW

The evolution of green finance as a catalytic tool in achieving sustainable development has garnered significant intellectual and policy traction in the context of Asian OECD economies. Within this ambit, scholars have progressively interrogated the multifaceted intersections of environmental sustainability and macroeconomic dynamics, delineating green finance not merely as a funding modality but as a transformative paradigm within the broader developmental architecture (Miao et al., 2025). The theoretical edifice underpinning green finance orbits around the integration of environmental externalities and the reconfiguration of capital flows toward ecologically benign and resource-efficient sectors, hence inducing a structural metamorphosis in conventional economic trajectories (Krinichansky & Rubtsov, 2022).

Initial discourses on sustainable growth pivoted on the dichotomy between economic expansion and environmental degradation, positing an inevitable trade-off scenario (Kukreti et al., 2024a; Sehajpal & Sidhu, 2024). However, with the ascendancy of the green finance doctrine, this bifurcation has been increasingly challenged (Saha et al., 2022). Contemporary analytical frameworks increasingly underscore the synergistic potential of green fiscal instruments—green bonds, climate funds, environmental risk-weighted assets, and sustainability-linked loans—in reconciling growth imperatives with environmental constraints (Klasen & Vassard, 2023). These instruments are engineered to align private sector profitability with public ecological objectives, thereby reorienting market incentives through regulatory nudges and risk mitigation mechanisms (Tufail et al., 2024).

Asian OECD nations, due to their heterogeneous developmental stages and variegated institutional architectures, exhibit disparate trajectories of green finance integration. Nations such as Japan and South Korea, with mature financial ecosystems and robust regulatory scaffolding, have instituted sophisticated green taxonomies and stringent environmental disclosure regimes. Their central banks and financial regulators are progressively embedding climate-related financial risks within monetary policy and prudential supervisory frameworks, thus mainstreaming sustainability into macro-financial governance (Varchenko et al., 2024). Contrastingly, economies at the nascent stage of green financial institutionalization encounter systemic bottlenecks such as information asymmetry, underdeveloped ESG benchmarks, and constrained market depth.

The empirical landscape within the literature presents a nuanced and at times, ambivalent narrative regarding the efficacy of green finance in engendering economic growth. Certain econometric inquiries reveal a positive elasticity between green financial flows and GDP expansion, mediated through enhanced green technology adoption, energy efficiency gains, and employment multipliers in clean energy sectors (Huang et al., 2023; Wu, 2023). These studies accentuate the catalytic role of financial innovation and green entrepreneurial ecosystems in bolstering productivity while curbing carbon intensity. Other strands of inquiry, however, signal potential crowding-out effects where an overemphasis on green instruments could inadvertently divert capital from other critical but less sustainable sectors, thereby impeding short-term output maximization.

Environmental sustainability, in the analytical purview of green finance, is often operationalized through metrics such as carbon footprint reduction, renewable energy capacity augmentation, and ecological footprint minimization. In this context, the literature identifies institutional quality, regulatory coherence, and fiscal transparency as critical intervening variables that modulate the green finance–sustainability nexus (Li, 2024; Umar & Safi, 2023). Where governance regimes are characterized by opacity, policy discontinuities, or weak enforcement, the allocative efficiency of green finance instruments is significantly attenuated, undermining their potential to precipitate substantive environmental dividends.

Additionally, transnational financial flows and cross-border investment dynamics have been scrutinized for their role in either reinforcing or diluting national green agendas. The globalization of green capital markets has enabled the mobilization of climate finance at an unprecedented scale (Voronova et al., 2023). Nevertheless, this process is fraught with challenges related to currency volatility, sovereign risk perceptions, and institutional misalignment between donor and recipient jurisdictions. The literature also critiques the performative nature of green financial commitments in the absence of enforceable accountability frameworks and independent impact verification protocols, which can render such flows superficial or even counterproductive in long-term sustainability metrics (Zhu et al., 2024).

An emerging body of scholarship interrogates the endogenous evolution of green finance within endogenous growth theory. Here, the recursive link between environmental policy stringency and green technological innovation assumes centrality. Green finance, by channelling resources into R&D-intensive sectors and de-risking pioneering clean technologies, is hypothesized to engender a virtuous cycle of innovation-led growth (Tiwari et al., 2024). This endogenous feedback loop, however, is contingent upon the absorptive capacity of domestic economies—particularly the presence of skilled human capital, digital infrastructure, and intellectual property protection—that can capitalize on green investments and translate them into scalable, market-ready solutions (Bakhsh et al., 2024).

Furthermore, financial inclusion and democratization of access to green capital emerge as vital themes in the discourse. The literature articulates concern that green finance, if predominantly targeted at large-scale industrial actors or limited to urban financial centres, may exacerbate socio-economic inequities and exclude marginalized communities from sustainability transitions (Gu et al., 2023). Therefore, frameworks that facilitate micro-green finance, community-driven renewable energy cooperatives, and bottom-up ESG investment models are posited as corrective strategies to promote inclusive sustainability (Khalfaoui et al., 2024).

Interdisciplinary engagements within the literature also delve into the epistemological contours of green finance, critiquing the definitional ambiguities and inconsistent standards that plague its operationalization (Can & Can, 2025). The proliferation of diverse ESG metrics, greenwashing allegations, and the absence of universally accepted performance benchmarks are cited as impediments to the integrity and scalability of green finance. The ontological debate on what constitutes 'green' within differing socio-cultural and political contexts further complicates empirical generalizations and policy harmonization across jurisdictions (Zhong et al., 2024).

In sum, the extant literature traverses a complex terrain of theoretical constructs, empirical findings, and normative prescriptions, indicating that green finance is neither a panacea nor a peripheral phenomenon in the quest for sustainable development (Y. Wang & Taghizadeh-Hesary, 2023). Rather, it constitutes an evolving institutional domain whose effectiveness is intrinsically tied to contextual variables such as political will, market maturity, regulatory evolution, and societal awareness (Kukreti et al., 2024b, 2024c). For Asian OECD economies, the challenge and opportunity lie in institutionalizing green finance through a context-sensitive, innovation-driven, and inclusivity-oriented strategy that harmonizes economic aspirations with environmental imperatives (Y. Zhang, 2022).

The evolution of green finance, as a transformative force within global financial systems, assumes particular relevance within the distinct economic and institutional contexts of Asian OECD economies, such as Japan, Korea, Israel, and Turkey (Li, 2024). These nations, each marked by their unique historical trajectories, economic structures, and political landscapes, have pioneered a variety of green financial instruments and policy frameworks tailored to their specific developmental needs and environmental imperatives. Japan, with its advanced technological infrastructure and regulatory sophistication, has adopted a multifaceted approach to green finance, integrating stringent ecological regulations with innovative financing mechanisms such as green bonds and sustainable infrastructure investments, thereby ensuring its leadership in the transition to a low-carbon economy. Similarly, Korea, leveraging its robust industrial base, has systematically embedded environmental sustainability into its financial sector by fostering green technology investments and establishing comprehensive green taxonomies, creating a synergy between economic growth and ecological responsibility. Israel, with its burgeoning tech-driven economy, has focused on integrating green finance within its innovation ecosystem, driving investments towards renewable energy and sustainable technologies (Zhong et al., 2024). At the same time, Turkey, grappling with the dual challenges of rapid industrialization and climate change, has adopted a progressively nuanced approach to green finance by emphasizing state-led investments in renewable energy, clean technologies, and sustainable urban development. Each of these countries has approached green finance with a distinctive blend of policy interventions, market-driven solutions, and international collaboration; yet, their individual strategies underscore the broader challenges and opportunities within the Asian OECD group in leveraging green finance for sustainable growth (Umar & Safi, 2023). This divergence in national approaches reflects a critical need for context-sensitive frameworks that reconcile environmental goals with economic growth trajectories, highlighting the varying roles that policy innovation, financial regulation, and market dynamics play in the green transition (T. Wang et al., 2023). The nuanced differences between these countries' green finance initiatives not only underscore the varied institutional and infrastructural capacities at play but also illuminate the broader, more complex landscape in which green finance interacts with national economies, thus providing a more granular understanding of its effectiveness and potential in different geopolitical and economic contexts.

Policy and Institutional Context in Asian OECD Economies

Across the Asian OECD cohort, green-finance policy and institutions are heterogeneous yet convergent in intent: Japan embeds decarbonization into core market plumbing through an expansive "green transformation" agenda that couples transition-finance guidance, robust climate-risk disclosure expectations, and an active sovereign and corporate green/transition-bond pipeline, leveraging deep capital markets, powerful industrial ministries, and municipal utilities to crowd in private investment across hydrogen, grid modernization, and electrification; Korea aligns green finance with industrial policy via a long-running emissions-trading scheme, a government-led taxonomy and disclosure roadmap, and public financial intermediaries that de-risk clean-tech deployment, thereby channeling bank credit and bond issuance toward low-carbon assets even in hard-to-abate sectors; Israel's innovation-centric architecture uses targeted regulation, public guarantees, and sovereign issuance to seed renewable-energy and storage projects while mobilizing venture and infrastructure funds, with the central bank and market regulator pushing climate-risk management and ESG reporting across lenders and listed firms; and Türkiye links sustainable finance to competitiveness and energy security through a Green Deal action plan, large-scale renewable auctions, a sovereign sustainable-finance framework, and preparatory work for emissions trading, complemented by supervisory guidance that mainstreams ESG risk practices in banks and corporates (Xu & Cai, 2024a). These distinct mixes of mandates, disclosure regimes, public balance-sheet support, and market-development tools generate different investment pipelines and adjustment speeds, helping explain cross-country variation in the estimated effects of green finance, emissions, education outlays, and FDI on GDP per capita within the empirical results (Khan et al., 2023).

DATA SOURCES AND METHODOLOGY

The study aims to analyse the effect of Green Finance and CO_2 emissions on GDP per capita of Asian OECD economies (Israel, Japan, Korea, Turkiye) for the time-period 2015 to 2023. In order to carry out the objectives of the present study secondary data has been used. The study examines the impact of Green Finance and CO_2 emissions (independent variables) on GDP per capita (dependent variable), controlling for Expenditure on Education and Foreign Direct Investment. Data pertaining to GDP per capita [GDP per capita (constant 2015 US$)][1], Expenditure on Education [Government Expenditure on Education, Total (% of GDP)][2] and Foreign Direct Investment [Foreign direct investment, net inflows (% of GDP)][3] has been extracted from the World Development Indicators (WDI) database of World Bank and data on CO_2 emissions [CO2 emissions (metric tons per capita)][4] has been taken from Sustainable Development Goals (SDGs) database of World Bank. Data on Green Finance [Environment Related Government R&D budget in US dollars, PPP converted, Millions at 2020 constant prices][5] was extracted from OECD statistics. Log transformation of GDP per capita, Green Finance and CO_2 emissions was undertaken before conducting panel data analysis using pooled OLS, Fixed Effect Model (FEM) and Random Effects Model (REM) based on robust statistical tests (Hausman and Breusch-Pagan LM). Table 1 provides the category, notation and sources of the variables used in the present study and Table 2 indicates summary statistics for each variable.

Table 1. Notation and Sources of Variables

Variable	Category	Notation	Source
Log of GDP per capita	Dependent	lnGDP	WDI Database
Log of Green Finance	Independent	lnGREF	OECD Statistics
Log of CO_2 emissions	Independent	$lnCO_2$	SDGs Database
Expenditure on Education	Control	EDU	WDI Database
Foreign Direct Investment	Control	FDI	WDI Database

Figure 1. Conceptual Model

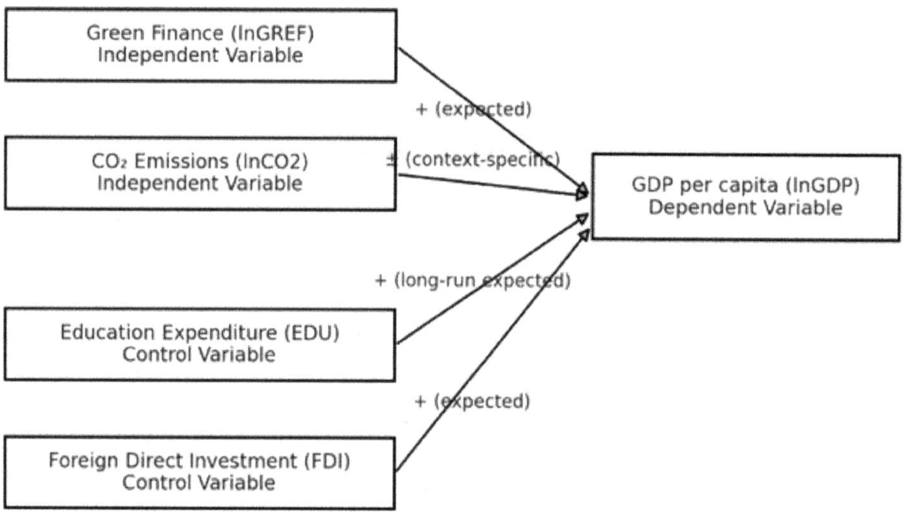

Conceptually, in Figure 1, lnGDP = f(lnGREF, $lnCO_2$, EDU, FDI)—with green finance (lnGREF) expected to be positive, CO_2 context-dependent (±), and EDU/FDI as controls shaping capacity; empirically (FE), more lnGREF↑ → lnGDP↑, while CO_2/FDI ≈ neutral, and EDU shows short-run negative (lagged returns).

Table 2. Summary Statistics (2000-2023)

Variable Name	Observations	Mean	Standard Deviation	Minimum Value	Maximum Value
lnGDP	36	10.21	0.47	9.31	10.67
lnGREF	36	9.53	1.27	7.60	11.45
lnCO2	36	2.04	0.33	1.50	2.50
EDU	36	4.48	1.17	2.61	6.53
FDI	36	1.82	1.56	0.12	5.73

RESULTS AND DISCUSSION

Table 3. Pooled OLS Results

Variable	Coefficient	Standard Error	z- statistic	p-value	95% Confidence Interval
lnGREF	0.205	0.094	2.180	0.029**	[0.020, 0.389]
lnCO2	0.960	0.203	4.720	0.000***	[0.561, 1.359]
EDU	0.022	0.087	0.250	0.801	[-0.149, 0.193]
FDI	0.278	0.061	4.550	0.000***	[0.159, 0.398]
_cons	5.696	0.966	5.900	0.000***	[3.803, 7.589]

Note: Dependent Variable: lnGDP.
*** implies significant at 0.01 level.
** implies significant at 0.05 level.
Source: Authors' own calculations.

The Pooled OLS regression results exhibited in Table 3 reveal that, controlling for other variables, a 1% increase in lnGREF is linked to a statistically significant 0.205% increase in GDP, indicating a positive impact of green energy on economic growth at the 5% significance level; lnCO2 exhibit a strong and highly significant positive relationship with GDP, where a 1% increase in emissions corresponds to a 0.96% rise in GDP, implying that economic activities associated with emissions still contribute substantially to growth; FDI also plays a crucial and statistically significant role, as a 1-unit escalation in FDI leads to a 0.278% increase in GDP, underscoring the importance of capital inflows for economic performance; however, EDU appears to have no meaningful direct effect on GDP in this model, with a very small coefficient (0.022), an insignificant z-statistic (0.250), and a high p-value (0.801), suggesting that, at least in the short run or in this sample, educational investment does not directly translate into measurable economic output, while the positive and significant constant term (5.696) represents the baseline level of GDP when all explanatory variables are held at zero.

Table 4. Summary Statistics of Pooled OLS

Statistic	No. of Obs.	No. of Groups	Within R^2	Between R^2	Overall R^2	Wald $chi^2(4)$	Prob > chi^2
Value	36	4	0.0085	0.8834	0.7232	80.98	0.000***

Note: Dependent Variable: lnGDP.
*** implies significant at 0.01 level.
Source: Authors' own calculations.

The summary statistics of the Pooled OLS model shown in Table 4 indicate that with 36 observations across 4 groups, the model explains 72.32% of the overall variation in lnGDP (Overall R-square = 0.7232), with a particularly strong explanatory power between groups (Between R-square = 0.8834) but very low explanatory power within groups (Within R-square = 0.0085), and the model as a whole is highly statistically significant as indicated by the Wald chi-square test statistic of 80.98 and a p-value of 0.000, confirming that the joint impact of the independent variables on GDP is not due to chance at the 1% level.

Table 5. Results of REM

Variable	Coef.	Std. Err.	z- statistic	p-value	95% Confidence Interval
lnGREF	0.205	0.094	2.180	0.029**	[0.020, 0.389]
lnCO2	0.960	0.203	4.720	0.000***	[0.561, 1.359]
EDU	0.022	0.087	0.250	0.801	[-0.149, 0.193]
FDI	0.278	0.061	4.550	0.000***	[0.159, 0.398]
_cons	5.696	0.966	5.900	0.000***	[3.803, 7.589]

Note: Dependent Variable: lnGDP.
*** implies significant at 0.01 level.
** implies significant at 0.05 level.
Source: Authors' own calculations.

The REM results shown in Table 5 indicate that, after accounting for both within- and between-entity variations, lnGREF has a statistically significant and positive effect on GDP at the 5% level, with a 1% increase in lnGREF leading to a 0.205% increase in GDP; lnCO2 and FDI both have strong, highly significant positive effects on GDP at the 1% level—suggesting that economic activity linked to emissions and foreign investment substantially drive growth—while EDU shows a small, statistically insignificant effect, implying no measurable direct impact on GDP within the model, and the constant term (5.696) is large and significant, reflecting the baseline GDP level when explanatory variables are held at zero.

Table 6. Summary Statistics of REM

Statistic	No. of Obs.	No. of groups	R^2 within	R^2 between	R^2 overall	Wald $chi^2(4)$	Prob > chi^2	rho
Value	36	4	0.0085	0.8834	0.7232	80.98	0.000***	0

Note: Dependent Variable: lnGDP.
*** implies significant at 0.01 level.
Source: Authors' own calculations.

The summary statistics for the REM given in Table 6 reveal that with 36 observations across 4 groups, the model explains 72.32% of the overall variation in GDP (R-square overall = 0.7232) and shows very strong explanatory power between groups (R-square between = 0.8834), although it explains very little variation within groups (R-square within = 0.0085), while the model is highly statistically significant overall (Wald chi2(4) = 80.98, p = 0.000), and the rho value of 0 suggests no proportion of the variance in the error term is due to individual-specific effects, implying minimal unobserved heterogeneity across entities in this case.

Table 7. Results of Breusch and Pagan Lagrangian

Test	Value
Null Hypothesis	Var(u) = 0
$chibar^2(01)$	0.000
Prob > $chibar^2$	1.000

Note: Dependent Variable: lnGDP.
Source: Authors' own calculations.

Table 8. Summary Statistics of Breusch and Pagan Lagrangian

Component	Variance	Standard Deviation
lnGDP	0.219	0.467
e (Residual)	0.003	0.056
u (RE)	0.000	0.000

Note: Dependent Variable: lnGDP.
Source: Authors' own calculations.

The results of the Breusch and Pagan Lagrangian Multiplier (LM) Test for Random Effects (Tables 7 and 8) show that the null hypothesis of zero variance across entities (Var(u) = 0) cannot be rejected (chibar2 = 0.000, p = 1.000), indicating that the variance due to unobserved individual-specific effects is statistically zero (u = 0.000), and therefore, a pooled OLS model is more appropriate than the random effects model for this dataset, as there is no significant gain in using REM over OLS due to the absence of meaningful random variation across groups.

Table 9. Results of FEM

Variable	Coefficient	Standard Error	t- statistic	p- value	95% Confidence Interval
lnGREF	0.106	0.048	2.220	0.035**	[0.008, 0.205]
lnCO2	-0.236	0.187	-1.260	0.217	[-0.620, 0.147]
EDU	-0.080	0.030	-2.680	0.012**	[-0.142, -0.019]
FDI	-0.022	0.019	-1.160	0.256	[-0.062, 0.017]
_cons	10.082	0.763	13.220	0.000***	[8.520, 11.645]

Note: Dependent Variable: lnGDP.
*** implies significant at 0.01 level.
** implies significant at 0.05 level.
Source: Authors' own calculations.

The FEM results given in Table 9 indicate that, after accounting for time-invariant group-specific effects, lnGREF has a positive and statistically significant effect on GDP at the 5% level, with a 1% increase in lnGREF associated with a 0.106% rise in GDP; in contrast, lnCO_2 have a negative but statistically insignificant effect, EDU shows a statistically significant negative impact—suggesting that in the short term or within-country variations, increased education investment may be linked with lower GDP likely due to time lags or structural inefficiencies—and FDI also has a small, negative, and statistically insignificant relationship with GDP, while the large and highly significant constant (10.082) reflects strong baseline GDP levels across the sample.

Table 10. Summary Statistics of FEM

Statistic	No. of observations	No. of groups	R^2 within	R^2 between	R^2 overall	F (4,28)	Prob > F	rho	F test that all u_i=0	Prob > F (u_i=0)
Value	36	4	0.365	0.139	0.123	4.020	0.011	0.993	219.030	0.000***

Note: Dependent Variable: lnGDP.
*** implies significant at 0.01 level.
Source: Authors' own calculations.

The summary statistics for the FEM shown in Table 10 reveal that with 36 observations across 4 groups, the model explains 36.5% of the variation in GDP within groups (R-square within = 0.365), but much less variation between groups (R-square between = 0.139) and overall (R-square overall = 0.123), with the model being statistically significant as a whole (F(4,28) = 4.020, p = 0.011), the high intra-group correlation (rho = 0.993) indicating strong entity-specific effects, and the highly significant F-test for individual effects (F = 219.030, p = 0.000) confirming the presence of fixed effects and justifying the use of the FEM over a pooled OLS model.

Table 11. Coefficient Comparison (Hausman Test)

Variable	Fixed Effects (b)	Random Effects (B)	Difference (b-B)	S.E. (sqrt(diag(V_b-V_B)))
lnGREF	0.1062927	0.2049353	-0.0986426	-
lnCO2	-0.2362043	0.9600516	-1.196256	-
EDU	-0.0804142	0.0220039	-0.102418	-
FDI	-0.0224543	0.2784095	-0.3008638	-

Note: Dependent Variable: lnGDP.
Source: Authors' own calculations.

Table 12. Results of Hausman Test

Statistic	Value
Chi2(4)	265.45
Prob > chi2	0.000***

Note: V_b-V_B is not positive definite.
Dependent Variable: lnGDP.
Source: Authors' own calculations.

The results from the Hausman Test (Tables 11 and 12) show a highly significant chi-square statistic (Chi2(4) = 265.45, p = 0.000), indicating that the differences between the FE and RE coefficients are systematic and statistically significant, and since the null hypothesis that the random effects model is appropriate is rejected, the FEM is preferred over REM for analyzing the relationship between the explanatory variables and lnGDP—despite V_b - V_B not being positive definite, which often occurs with large coefficient differences or multicollinearity, the strong significance supports FEM as the consistent estimator.

Taken together, Tables 1–12 provide a coherent arc from construct definition to estimator choice and substantive inference: Table 1 formalizes the analytical schema—lnGDP as the dependent variable, lnGREF and lnCO2 as core regressors, EDU and

FDI as controls—while Table 2 orients the reader to sample size (36 country-years, four countries), dispersion, and plausible ranges, indicating adequate between-country variation (e.g., lnGDP and lnGREF) alongside tighter within-country movement for others; the baseline pooled OLS in Table 3 shows economically and statistically meaningful elasticities for lnGREF (≈0.205) and lnCO2 (≈0.96) and a positive FDI effect (≈0.278) with EDU insignificant, a pattern consistent with cross-sectional differences in green-finance depth, carbon intensity, and capital inflows, and the global fit diagnostics in Table 4 (overall $R^2 \approx 0.72$; strong between-R^2) confirm that much of the explained variation is cross-country rather than within-country; REM results in Table 5 mirror pooled OLS—further signaling dominance of between-effects—while Table 6 reiterates high model significance and a rho of zero, anticipating the Breusch–Pagan LM outcome in Tables 7–8 (Var(u)=0), which rules out gains from random effects relative to pooled OLS; by contrast, the FEM in Table 9 reframes the narrative around within-country dynamics, with lnGREF remaining positive and significant (≈0.106) but lnCO2 turning negative and insignificant and EDU becoming significantly negative, implying that incremental changes inside countries over time need not mimic cross-sectional associations (e.g., emissions growth does not systematically raise income once country fixed traits are purged); Table 10 corroborates the salience of fixed effects (very high rho; decisive F-test rejecting u_i=0) and, in combination with the Hausman contrast in Tables 11–12 (χ^2 strongly significant), establishes FEM as the consistent, preferred estimator over REM (and effectively over pooled OLS given the fixed-effects F-test), thereby justifying interpretation that privileges within-country policy and investment shifts—especially green-finance mobilization—over static cross-sectional correlations when explaining movements in GDP per capita across the Asian OECD sample.

ROBUSTNESS AND SENSITIVITY ANALYSES

To assess the stability of the main results, we outline a multi-pronged robustness strategy tailored to the short panel (T=9; 2015–2023) and small country set (N=4). First, we re-estimate the baseline with richer fixed effects and inference corrections: (i) country and year fixed effects (two-way FE); (ii) clustered standard errors at the country level; (iii) Driscoll–Kraay standard errors to guard against heteroskedasticity, autocorrelation, and cross-sectional dependence; and (iv) correlated random effects à la Mundlak to probe time-invariant heterogeneity. Second, we introduce dynamic structure and timing: (v) a lagged dependent variable in a difference GMM or system GMM setup as a check against persistence and potential endogeneity; (vi) distributed lags for key regressors—lnGREF (t−1, t−2) to reflect policy-to-investment gestation, lnCO2 (t−1) for emissions intensity adjustments, FDI (t−1) for investment realization lags, and a longer lag window for EDU (e.g., t−2 to t−3) to reflect delayed human-capital payoffs—subject to degrees-of-freedom constraints. Third, we address specification and measurement: (vii) alternative functional forms (levels, standardized z-scores) and logarithmic re-scalings; (viii) alternative proxies where available—e.g., green bonds/certified green loans per capita for green finance; CO_2 intensity (CO_2/GDP) or total CO_2 for emissions; real education outlays per capita or secondary/tertiary enrollment rates for education; FDI stocks or green-sector FDI shares for external capital. Fourth, we examine influence and sample sensitivity: (ix) leave-one-country-out (LOCO) and leave-one-year-out (LOYO) estimations; (x) leverage and influence diagnostics (Cook's distance, DFBetas) with 1–5% winsorization of regressors; and (xi) split-sample analyses (Japan/Korea vs. Israel/Türkiye; pre-2019 vs. 2019–2023) to distinguish structural from cyclical effects. Fifth, we run diagnostic checks: (xii) multicollinearity (VIFs), (xiii) residual serial correlation and panel cross-section dependence tests, and (xiv) panel unit-root considerations with caution given small T. Collectively, these exercises are designed to verify sign consistency, effect-size stability, and inference robustness without asserting causal identification; any deviations from the baseline are discussed alongside plausible mechanisms (policy timing, measurement breadth of "green finance," or country-specific shocks).

CASE BOX: POLICY-TO-PRACTICE ILLUSTRATIONS

Japan (transition finance and grid modernization). Japan's transition-finance guidance has catalyzed capital toward hard-to-abate sectors and grid upgrades that accommodate variable renewables. In practice, programmatic issuances and bank syndications channel resources to hydrogen pilots, industrial electrification, and transmission reinforcement. In the context of our model, such initiatives map to higher lnGREF with plausible medium-run links to lnGDP via productivity and resilience, while the near-term lnCO2 response may be muted if legacy assets remain online during transition (Lu et al., 2022).

Türkiye (renewable auctions and investment mobilization). Large-scale renewable tenders (e.g., utility-scale solar and wind zones) have standardized procurement, reduced offtake risk, and attracted domestic–foreign consortia. Financing structures typically blend commercial loans with concessional or guarantee features, lowering the cost of capital and crowding in private investment. Within our framework, these mechanisms can affect FDI (via project equity and supply-chain entry), raise lnGREF where public R&D or de-risking is recorded, and, over time, support lnGDP through capacity expansion and import-substitution of fuels, with the emissions pathway depending on coal-to-renewable displacement speed (Xu & Cai, 2024b).

IMPLICATIONS

The detailed implication of this study, based on the preferred FEM, is that while Green Finance (lnGREF) has a statistically significant and positive impact on economic growth within countries over time—suggesting that sustainability-oriented energy policies can contribute to GDP (lnGDP) expansion—Expenditure on Education (EDU) surprisingly shows a statistically significant negative relationship, potentially reflecting short-term costs or inefficiencies in educational systems that delay economic returns, and CO_2 emissions (lnCO2) as well as Foreign Direct Investment (FDI) show statistically insignificant and negative effects, indicating that the economic benefits commonly associated with emissions-intensive industrial activity and external capital inflows may not uniformly materialize within countries after accounting for fixed, unobserved heterogeneity, thereby emphasizing the importance of domestic structural factors and long-term planning in shaping the effectiveness of growth-oriented policies.

MAJOR CHALLENGES IN GREEN FINANCE: INTEGRITY RISKS, STANDARDIZATION DEFICITS, AND INSTITUTIONAL FRICTIONS

Green finance across the Asian OECD milieu is mediated by a dense web of frictions that dampen the translation of nominal "green" capital into real decarbonization and productivity gains. Greenwashing persists where use-of-proceeds taxonomies are plastic, KPI architectures are permissive, and post-issuance verification is episodic—inviting adverse selection, moral hazard, and impact inflation (Ali et al., 2024). Standardization deficits—non-isomorphic taxonomies, heterogeneous disclosure baselines, and fragmented assurance practices—impair cross-jurisdictional comparability, elevate diligence costs, and thin secondary-market liquidity. Institutional bottlenecks—permitting sclerosis, grid inflexibilities, project-preparation deficits, and shallow local-currency depth—inflate hurdle rates and elongate gestation, particularly under currency-mismatch and sovereign-risk premia (Y. Zhang, 2022). Intermediation constraints arise when public balance-sheet de-risking is subscale or slow, and when private lenders lack climate-risk analytics to price transition trajectories, thereby rationing credit to first-of-a-kind assets. These frictions jointly rationalize the empirical pattern whereby lnGREF retains a within-country growth elasticity while incremental $lnCO_2$ and undifferentiated FDI do not: it is alignment and institutional complementarity, not gross volume, that determines real-economy traction (Huang et al., 2023).

GROWTH–SUSTAINABILITY TENSION: THEORETICAL AND POLICY SYNTHESIS

The divergence between cross-sectional correlations (pooled/RE) and within-country estimates (FE) is emblematic of the growth–environment trade-off's dynamic nature. Cross-sectionally, higher income co-moves with legacy carbon- and investment-intensive endowments; within countries over time, incremental emissions do not reliably raise income once time-invariant heterogeneity is purged—consistent with directed technical change, Porter-type productivity effects, and decoupling dynamics. Reconciling growth with sustainability thus requires policy sequencing and co-deployment: (i) credible transition pathways and carbon constraints that reprice externalities (Huang et al., 2023); (ii) enabling networks—transmission, storage, digital orchestration—so green capex scales with high capacity factors (Y. Zhang, 2022); (iii) patient public co-finance (guarantees, first-loss, local-currency windows) to collapse risk premia (Han & Gao, 2024); and (iv) just-transition apparatus to internalize labor reallocation and distributional equity (Gu et al., 2023). Under such meso-institutional conditions, green capital becomes a productivity-enhancing general-purpose investment, not a compliance surcharge.

COUNTRY-BY-COUNTRY OBSTACLES AND OPPORTUNITIES

Japan. *Endowments:* deep capital markets, sophisticated disclosure regime, high municipal/utility agency. *Binding constraints:* aging grid segments, hard-to-abate industrial clusters, coordination failures in retrofits. *Opportunity frontier:* transition finance for electrification/hydrogen, grid digitalization and flexibility assets, high-multipliers in efficiency revamps (Wu, 2023).

Korea. *Endowments:* economy-wide emissions management, dense manufacturing ecosystems. *Binding constraints:* sectoral capex cliffs (steel, petrochemicals, shipping) and sequencing of abatement technologies. *Opportunity frontier:* battery and renewable supply chains, scale electrification with performance-linked credit channels via public–private intermediaries (Habib et al., 2025).

Israel. *Endowments:* innovation-dense ecosystem, active VC/infrastructure intermediation. *Binding constraints:* grid flexibility, land and permitting frictions, small domestic offtake limiting utility-scale economies. *Opportunity frontier:* distributed solar/storage, digital demand response, water–energy efficiency, exportable climate tech with deep linkages (Alvi et al., 2025).

Türkiye. *Endowments:* large renewable resource base, auction platforms, industrial depth. *Binding constraints:* FX/macro volatility, elevated risk premia, subscale de-risking and local-currency tenor. *Opportunity frontier:* guarantee/first-loss stacks, local-currency green lending, supply-chain localization for equipment, accelerated grid reinforcement to absorb build-out (Shi & Nisar, 2025).

INTEGRATING EMERGING TRENDS: FINTECH, INCLUSION, AND DATA INFRASTRUCTURE AS CORE MECHANICS

Digitalization—such as tokenized/programmable bonds, on-chain MRV, and IoT-enabled asset telemetry—can reduce verification costs, mitigate greenwashing, and enhance price discovery. Convergent ESG regimes and interoperable taxonomies attenuate classification risk and lubricate cross-border flows. Climate-risk supervision (scenario analytics, capital planning) renders transition risks bank-priceable, reallocating credit toward low-emission assets (R. Wang et al., 2024). Financial inclusion—green MSME credit, pay-as-you-go solar, efficiency loans—broadens diffusion and accelerates household/SME adoption, yet remains under-captured by public R&D proxies; augmenting metrics with green-loan/bond volumes and taxonomy-aligned credit shares would better map the lnGREF→lnGDP transmission channel. Regionally, embedding these trends into supervisory practice and market design should steepen the productivity gradient of green investment while damping emissions reliance (Jin et al., 2023).

INTERPRETING UNEXPECTED FINDINGS: EDUCATION AND FDI IN CONTEXT

The negative EDU coefficient in FE likely reflects intertemporal and compositional artifacts: education outlays have long gestations, are procyclical in composition, and—measured as a GDP share—can rise in downturns (denominator effect). Skill–task mismatch and administrative absorptive capacity further mediate payoffs. Methodologically, longer lags, alternative proxies (STEM/technical enrollment, apprenticeship intensity), and interaction terms (EDU × digital/grid readiness) are warranted. The weak/negative FDI finding underscores quality over quantity: enclave-type or carbon-intensive inflows can crowd out domestic investment and entrench high-emission lock-ins; conversely, taxonomy-aligned, supply-chain-integrating FDI with MRV obligations and local capability building should flip the sign. Designs that condition incentives on green alignment and domestic linkages will tilt FDI from scale to structural transformation.

POLICY AND PRACTICE: PRIORITY ACTIONS

1. **Institutionalize integrity:** codify precise taxonomies, standardized KPIs, and independent, continuous impact assurance to neutralize greenwashing and compress diligence spreads.
2. **Scale de-risking at system nodes:** enlarge guarantees, first-loss tranches, and local-currency facilities to neutralize FX/sovereign premia and unlock private balance sheets.
3. **Prioritize enabling capital:** fast-track transmission, storage, and permitting reforms; treat flexibility as a prerequisite, not an adjunct.
4. **Green FDI by design:** tie incentives to taxonomy alignment, verifiable decarbonization milestones, and supply-chain localization; embed just-transition and skills covenants.
5. **Upgrade measurement:** complement public R&D with granular green-credit/bond flows, sectoral capex, and alignment ratios to better proxy the effective lnGREF stock.
6. **Shorten human-capital lags:** couple EDU with sector-specific training, dual-education models, and firm-linked apprenticeships; evaluate with distributed lags and threshold tests.
7. **Digitize supervision and markets:** integrate climate analytics into underwriting and stress testing; deploy programmable instruments and open data to enhance allocative efficiency.
8. **Embed adaptive learning:** mandate post-issuance impact audits and periodic taxonomy recalibration to iterate toward higher allocative efficiency.

REGIONAL AND INSTITUTIONAL TRENDS: LINKING QUANTITATIVE RESULTS TO IMPLEMENTATION REALITY

The fixed-effects results—where green finance (lnGREF) associates positively with income growth while incremental CO_2 emissions, FDI, and short-horizon education outlays do not systematically raise GDP—are most intelligible when read through regional and institutional lenses that condition how "green" capital is originated, intermediated, and absorbed (Mitra & Guseva, 2021). In the Northeast Asian pair (Japan, Korea), dense policy "stacks" (taxonomy/guidance, disclosure, carbon constraints, public co-finance) and deep manufacturing bases create high absorptive capacity for transition spending; green R&D and grid/industry upgrades translate into productivity and resilience rather than purely additive emissions, consistent with a positive lnGREF→lnGDP elasticity and a muted within-country role for $\ln CO_2$ once legacy structure is differenced out (Chow & Fung, 2025). By contrast, in smaller, innovation-centric Israel and policy-transitioning Türkiye, the growth payoffs from green finance hinge more acutely on pipeline formation (bankable projects), currency/sovereign risk management, and procurement/permits; where these frictions bite, extra inflows (including FDI) need not lift near-term output unless they are taxonomy-aligned, hedged, and timed to grid and supply-chain readiness—helping explain the weak or negative within-country coefficients on FDI and the short-run EDU headwind (gestation lags in human capital). Across the four systems, several convergent implementation challenges emerge: (i) sequencing—carbon-pricing/ETS, disclosure, and taxonomy must precede or accompany large-scale issuance so that capital is not stranded or greenwashed (Nenavath, 2025); (ii) infrastructure complementarity—grid flexibility, storage, and permitting discipline are prerequisites for R&D and project finance to spill over into GDP (Dellis, 2024); (iii) intermediation architecture—public banks, guarantee schemes, and blended-finance vehicles are critical to derisk first-of-a-kind assets and crowd in private balance sheets; (iv) FX and macro stability—in more volatile settings, currency risk can erase investment multipliers unless hedging and concessional layers are present (Beljić et al., 2023); (v) industrial policy fit—heavy-industry incumbency favors transition instruments (retrofit, electrification, hydrogen) in Japan/Korea, while build-out instruments (auctions/PPAs, distributed solar, storage) dominate in Israel/Türkiye (Barrell & Nahhas, 2022); and (vi) capability and timing—skills pipelines and administrative capacity determine whether education spending is a near-term drag or a medium-run engine. The upshot is that the positive within-country payoff to lnGREF observed in the panel is not merely a funding effect but an institutional-complementarities effect: where standards, carbon constraints, procurement, and public de-risking move in concert, green finance is converted into productivity and income with limited incremental emissions; where these complements are thin, inflows and policy announcements alone do not translate into growth within the sample window (Raza et al., 2021). This regional–institutional framing thus provides a practical narrative bridge from the statistical output to the on-the-ground mechanics of implementing green finance in heterogeneous economic systems.

COMPARATIVE POLICY AND INSTITUTIONAL CONTEXT: JAPAN, KOREA, ISRAEL, AND TURKIYE

Across the Asian OECD group, the regulatory architectures, market intermediation channels, and instrument menus for green finance are heterogeneous in design but convergent in purpose, shaping distinct pathways through which sustainability capital reaches the real economy. Japan's mature disclosure regime and deep capital markets encourage large-scale transition and use-of-proceeds issuance alongside bank-based project finance, enabling rapid scaling of low-carbon infrastructure and industrial decarbonization. Korea couples economy-wide emissions management and sectoral guidance with a state-steered taxonomy and phased ESG reporting, aligning bank credit, corporate bonds, and public financial intermediaries toward clean technologies in heavy industry and power. Israel's innovation-centric ecosystem mobilizes venture capital, infrastructure funds, and utility-scale procurement to diffuse renewable and storage solutions, while supervisory nudges on climate-risk management push lenders and listed firms to internalize environmental externalities. Turkiye, operating at the nexus of export competitiveness and energy security, utilizes large-scale renewable energy procurement, sovereign and corporate sustainable finance frameworks, and incremental supervisory guidance to attract private capital and reduce financing costs for green assets. These policy–institutional contrasts—spanning mandate design, disclosure depth, public balance-sheet support, and market-development tools—create different investment pipelines, cost-of-capital profiles, and adjustment speeds, offering a coherent explanation for cross-country variation in the estimated effects of green finance (lnGREF), emissions (lnCO2), education outlays (EDU), and FDI on lnGDP within the panel as per Table 13.

Table 13. Comparative Snapshot

Country	Regulatory environment (orientation)	Green-finance infrastructure (intermediaries/markets)	Policy instruments (illustrative)	Source
Japan	Strong disclosure and transition-finance guidance; coordination among economic and energy ministries	Deep bond market, active bank project finance, municipal/utility participation	Transition/green bonds, de-risking facilities, technology demonstration/R&D support	(Ogbeifun & Shobande, 2020)
Korea	Economy-wide emissions management with sectoral targeting; taxonomy and phased ESG reporting	Public financial institutions co-invest with banks and markets	Emissions constraints, green-loan programs, targeted guarantees/incentives for clean tech	(Tsamadias et al., 2019)
Israel	Innovation-led supervision emphasizing climate-risk practices	VC and infrastructure funds; IPP/utility procurement channels	Renewable auctions/PPAs, storage support, SME green-credit lines	(Gholipour & Al-Mulali, 2014)
Turkiye	Gradual integration of sustainability into financial oversight aligned with trade/energy policy	Expanding corporate/sovereign sustainable-finance frameworks; auction platforms	Large-scale renewable tenders, concessional/guarantee schemes, emerging market-based tools	(Mitra & Guseva, 2021)

INSTITUTIONAL PATTERNS, REGIONAL CHALLENGES, AND FORWARD-LOOKING REFLECTIONS

Cross-country differences in the estimated effects—positive within-country elasticity of green finance (lnGREF) with lnGDP alongside muted or negative within-country associations for CO_2 (lnCO2), FDI, and short-horizon education outlays (EDU)—are plausibly driven by institutional "stacks" that shape how capital is originated, intermediated, and absorbed. In systems with dense policy architectures (clear taxonomy/guidance, credible disclosure, carbon constraints, public co-finance) and deep industrial bases (typical of Japan/Korea), green funds translate into productivity upgrades and resilience rather than incremental emissions, whereas in systems where project pipelines, FX stability, and permitting discipline are still consolidating (more salient in Israel/Türkiye), inflows and spending can face gestation lags or misalignment with grid and supply-chain readiness—dampening near-term growth payoffs and obscuring the EDU channel within short panels. The table below distills recurring patterns, the mechanisms through which they operate, and their expected imprint on the fixed-effects coefficients observed in this study (Table 14).

Table 14. Reflections

Institutional pattern / regional challenge	Mechanism for transmission to real economy	Expected FE imprint	Source
Coherent "policy stack" (taxonomy + disclosure + carbon constraint + public de-risking)	Reduces information and policy risk; crowds in private balance sheets; accelerates project NPV	**lnGREF→lnGDP:** ↑; **lnCO2:** ~ / ↓ (decoupling)	(Ahmad et al., 2020)
Project-pipeline quality (bankable renewables/efficiency, credible PPAs, permitting)	Converts allocated finance into shovel-ready assets; minimizes delays	**lnGREF→lnGDP:** ↑; weakens need for emissions-led growth **(lnCO2: ↓/~)**	(Ghosh & Wang, 2010)
Grid readiness & storage	Raises capacity factor of renewables; unlocks productivity spillovers	**lnGREF→lnGDP:** ↑; **lnCO2: ↓ over time**	(Boubacar, 2016)
Public intermediation (DFIs, guarantees, blended finance)	De-risks first-of-a-kind/ transition assets; lowers cost of capital	**lnGREF→lnGDP:** ↑; **FDI: sign depends on green share**	(Mitra & Guseva, 2021)
Macroeconomic & FX volatility	Elevates hurdle rates; truncates investment cycles; amplifies dollar debt risk	**lnGREF→lnGDP:** ~ / ↓; **FDI:** ~ / ↓ (unless hedged)	(Chow & Fung, 2025)

continued on following page

Table 14. Continued

Institutional pattern / regional challenge	**Mechanism for transmission to real economy**	**Expected FE imprint**	**Source**
Industrial structure (heavy-industry incumbency vs. greenfield build-out)	Determines mix of retrofits vs. new assets; affects timing of emissions reductions	**lnGREF→lnGDP: ↑; lnCO2: ~ initially, ↓ with transition**	(Nenavath, 2025)
Human-capital and administrative capacity	Governs absorption of R&D, execution speed, and O&M productivity	**EDU: short-run ↓ / neutral**; medium-run ↑ with lags	(Dellis, 2024)
FDI quality & alignment (taxonomy-concordant vs. carbon-intensive)	Drives technology transfer and supply-chain deepening vs. lock-in	**FDI: ↑ if green-aligned; ~ / ↓ if misaligned**	(Beljić et al., 2023)

FORWARD-LOOKING REFLECTIONS

1. **Tighten alignment instruments.** Move from high-level principles to binding taxonomies, sectoral transition pathways, and procurement rules that hard-wire Article 2.1(c)-style alignment; this should increase the probability that marginal green finance raises lnGDP without raising $lnCO_2$.
2. **Scale de-risking where FX and sovereign risk bind.** Expand guarantee windows, local-currency facilities, and blended-finance layers to improve bankability in Israel/Türkiye-type contexts; expect stronger FDI/lnGREF growth elasticities once currency risk is hedged.
3. **Prioritize grid and storage as "enabling capital."** Treat transmission, flexibility, and storage as preconditions; this improves the conversion rate of green R&D and project finance into measured output.
4. **Make FDI *green by design*.** Condition incentives on taxonomy alignment, supply-chain localization, and MRV standards; this should shift the FDI coefficient toward positive territory in within-country estimates.
5. **Bridge human-capital lags.** Pair EDU outlays with targeted apprenticeships, just-transition programs, and firm-linked training to shorten gestation; over a longer window, the EDU coefficient should invert to positive.
6. **Institutionalize learning loops.** Mandate post-issuance impact reporting, ex-post cost-of-capital audits, and adaptive updates to taxonomies; these feedbacks raise allocative efficiency and stabilize the lnGREF→lnGDP channel.

EMERGING TRENDS AND FUTURE DIRECTIONS IN GREEN FINANCE (ASIAN OECD PERSPECTIVE)

Across Japan, Korea, Israel, and Türkiye, green finance is accelerating along several frontier vectors that will shape pipeline quality, cost of capital, and data integrity over the next cycle: (1) Digital and tokenized green bonds that embed on-chain use-of-proceeds tracking, real-time coupon features, and retail access, tightening the link between issuance, MRV, and investor confidence (Barrell & Nahhas, 2022); (2) Convergence of ESG rules and taxonomies—including transition-finance guidance and clearer KPI standards for sustainability-linked instruments—reducing classification risk and facilitating cross-border capital flows (Raza et al., 2021); (3) Climate-risk disclosure and prudential supervision moving from voluntary alignment toward mandatory ISSB/TCFD-style reporting, double-materiality assessments, and climate scenario analysis in bank stress tests (Ogbeifun & Shobande, 2020); (4) Carbon-market and transition instruments—expanding ETS coverage, higher integrity in crediting, and the use of carbon contracts-for-difference—to de-risk hard-to-abate investments (Tsamadias et al., 2019); (5) Blended-finance platforms that scale guarantees, first-loss tranches, and local-currency facilities, especially salient where FX volatility or sovereign risk elevates hurdle rates (Gholipour & Al-Mulali, 2014); (6) Grid and flexibility investment (transmission, storage, demand response) recognized as "enabling capital," improving the conversion rate of green R&D and project finance into measured output (Ahmad et al., 2025); (7) Nature-related finance (TNFD-aligned disclosure, water and biodiversity metrics) broadening the asset universe and integrating physical-risk management (Yoon & Ko, 2025); and (8) Supply-chain decarbonization and just transition, with Scope-3 targets, procurement standards, and labor-reskilling programs tightening the growth–emissions trade-off and improving social acceptability (Ketchoua et al., 2024). These trajectories collectively strengthen the institutional complements that our empirical results identify as pivotal for translating green finance into productivity and income gains without commensurate emissions growth.

STUDY LIMITATIONS

This analysis is constrained by a short panel (2015–2023) and a narrow cross-section (n = 4), which limits statistical power, attenuates within-country variation, and heightens sensitivity to country-specific shocks; the use of environment-related government R&D (PPP, 2020 prices) as the sole proxy for "green finance" may not capture private green credit, sustainable loans, or bond issuance, introducing measurement error and comparability issues; log-linear specifications estimated with pooled OLS, FEM, and REM assume stable elasticities and may be affected by endogeneity (reverse causality between growth and finance/emissions), omitted variables (e.g., energy prices, trade intensity, policy shocks), cross-sectional dependence, and dynamic persistence that a static model cannot absorb; while robust tests inform model choice, the small T undermines panel unit-root/cointegration diagnostics and reduces the reliability of asymptotic inferences; finally, external validity is circumscribed—the results generalize to Asian OECD economies with similar institutional structures, not to the broader OECD or emerging markets—and the counterintuitive negative EDU coefficient in FEM should be interpreted as short-run, within-entity association potentially driven by lags or reallocation effects rather than a structural causal impact. Future work could reinforce credibility via alternative green-finance proxies (e.g., green bonds/loans volumes), dynamic panels or IV/GMM to address endogeneity, Driscoll–Kraay or PCSE to handle dependence, and non-linear/threshold tests to detect regime effects.

CONCLUSION

In conclusion, the study—employing a panel data approach and ultimately favoring the FEM based on the results of the Hausman test and Breusch-Pagan LM test—demonstrates that Green Finance has a statistically significant and positive influence on GDP per capita, suggesting that transitioning towards greener energy sources can stimulate economic growth within countries over time, whereas EDU, contrary to conventional expectations, exhibits a statistically significant negative relationship with GDP per capita in the short run, possibly due to delayed economic returns on educational investment or inefficiencies in educational spending; lnCO2 and FDI show negative and statistically insignificant effects in FEM, contrasting with their positive and significant roles in the pooled OLS and REM, thereby highlighting the critical role of unobserved, time-invariant country-specific factors in shaping these relationships and ultimately emphasizing that sustainable economic policies must be context-specific, strategically designed, and attentive to both the structural realities and long-term impacts of key development indicators.

REFERENCES

Afanasiev, M. P., & Belenchuk, A. A. (2021). Towards to the first green federal budget of Russia: Basis and elaboration. *Voprosy Ekonomiki, 11*, 71–88. DOI: 10.32609/0042-8736-2021-11-71-88

Ahmad, M., Khattak, S. I., Khan, A., & Rahman, Z. U. (2020). Innovation, foreign direct investment (FDI), and the energy–pollution–growth nexus in OECD region: A simultaneous equation modeling approach. *Environmental and Ecological Statistics, 27*(2), 203–232. DOI: 10.1007/s10651-020-00442-8

Ahmad, M., Khattak, S. I., Khan, A., & Rahman, Z. U. (2025). Correction to: Innovation, foreign direct investment (FDI), and the energy–pollution–growth nexus in OECD region: a simultaneous equation modeling approach (Environmental and Ecological Statistics, (2020), 27, 2, (203-232),). *Environmental and Ecological Statistics, 32*(1), 383–384. https://doi.org/DOI: 10.1007/s10651-020-00442-8

Ali, M., Seraj, M., Turuc, F., Tursoy, T., & Uktamov, K. F. (2024). Green finance investment and climate change mitigation in OECD-15 European countries: RALS and QARDL evidence. *Environment, Development and Sustainability, 26*(11), 27409–27429. DOI: 10.1007/s10668-023-03765-1

Altaf, A., Anwar, M. A., Shahzad, U., & Bilan, Y. (2025). Exploring the nexus among green finance, renewable energy and environmental sustainability: Evidence from OECD economies. *Renewable Energy, 244*. Advance online publication. DOI: 10.1016/j.renene.2025.122589

Alvi, S., Ahmad, I., Naeem Nawaz, S. M., Connell, W., Anser, M. K., & Ul Hassan, M. (2025). The role of green finance, energy transition, and digitalization in OECD greenhouse gas emissions. *Journal of Cleaner Production, 518*. Advance online publication. DOI: 10.1016/j.jclepro.2025.145865

Bakhsh, S., Alam, M. S., & Zhang, W. (2024). Green finance and Sustainable Development Goals: Is there a role for geopolitical uncertainty? *Economic Change and Restructuring, 57*(4). Advance online publication. DOI: 10.1007/s10644-024-09719-5

Barrell, R. J., & Nahhas, A. (2022). Regional integration and bilateral FDI stocks in the OECD. *International Journal of Finance & Economics, 27*(3), 3032–3050. DOI: 10.1002/ijfe.2311

Beljić, M., Glavaški, O., Beker Pucar, E., Stojkov, S., & Pejčić, J. (2023). Asymmetric Effects of Tax Competition on FDI vs. Budget Balance in European OECD Economies: Heterogeneous Panel Approach †. *Risks, 11*(12). Advance online publication. DOI: 10.3390/risks11120219

Boubacar, I. (2016). Spatial determinants of U.S. FDI and exports in OECD countries. *Economic Systems*, *40*(1), 135–144. DOI: 10.1016/j.ecosys.2015.04.005

Can, U., & Can, Z. G. (2025). *Financing or taxation? Assessing the effectiveness of carbon emissions reduction programs*. Borsa Istanbul Review., DOI: 10.1016/j.bir.2025.03.005

Chow, W. W., & Fung, M. K. (2025). Relative ESG positions among OECD countries in the presence of international competition for FDI inflow: A gravity model perspective. *Research in International Business and Finance*, *76*. Advance online publication. DOI: 10.1016/j.ribaf.2025.102851

Dellis, K. (2024). Financial distance and FDI flows: Evidence from OECD economies. *World Economy*, *47*(6), 2536–2573. DOI: 10.1111/twec.13552

Gholipour, H. F., & Al-Mulali, U. (2014). The interaction between tourism and FDI in real estate in OECD countries. *Current Issues in Tourism*, *17*(2), 105–113. DOI: 10.1080/13683500.2012.733359

Ghosh, M., & Wang, W. (2010). Does FDI accelerate economic growth? the OECD experience based on panel data estimates for the period 1980-2004. *Global Economy Journal*, *9*(4). Advance online publication. DOI: 10.2202/1524-5861.1496

Gu, X., Alamri, A. M., Ahmad, M., Alsagr, N., Zhong, X., & Wu, T. (2023). Natural resources extraction and green finance: Dutch disease and COP27 targets for OECD countries. *Resources Policy*, *81*. Advance online publication. DOI: 10.1016/j.resourpol.2023.103404

Gurbanov, S., & Suleymanli, F. (2022). Analytical Assessment of Green Digital Finance Progress in the Republic of Georgia. *Economics, Law, and Institutions in Asia Pacific*, 205 – 222. https://doi.org/DOI: 10.1007/978-981-19-2662-4_10

Habib, Y., Abd Rahman, N. R., Hashmi, S. H., & Ali, M. (2025). Green finance and environmental decentralization drive OECD low carbon transitions. *Scientific Reports*, *15*(1). Advance online publication. DOI: 10.1038/s41598-025-11967-y PMID: 40750618

Han, J., & Gao, H. (2024). Green finance, social inclusion, and sustainable economic growth in OECD member countries. *Humanities & Social Sciences Communications*, *11*(1). Advance online publication. DOI: 10.1057/s41599-024-02662-w

Huang, L., Cao, Y., & Zhu, Y. (2023). Is there any recovery power for economic growth from green finance? Evidence from OECD member countries. *Economic Change and Restructuring*, *56*(6), 3909–3926. DOI: 10.1007/s10644-022-09458-5

Jin, C., Lv, Z., Li, Z., & Sun, K. (2023). Green finance, renewable energy and carbon neutrality in OECD countries. *Renewable Energy, 211*, 279–284. DOI: 10.1016/j.renene.2023.04.105

Ketchoua, G. S., Arogundade, S. T., & Biyase, M. (2024). Revaluating the Sustainable Development Thesis: exploring the moderating influence of Technological Innovation on the impact of Foreign Direct Investment (FDI) on Green Growth in the OECD Countries. *Discover Sustainability, 5*(1). https://doi.org/DOI: 10.1007/s43621-024-00433-w

Khalfaoui, H., Guenichi, H., Nabli, M. A., Belghouthi, H., & Guesmi, M. (2024). Threshold effects of credit risk on renewable energy consumption and green financial policies nexus: Evidence from OECD countries. *Environment, Development and Sustainability*. Advance online publication. DOI: 10.1007/s10668-024-05625-y

Khan, M. N., & Omar, A. Bin, Azizan, N. A., & Abidin, S. Z. (2023). The Role of Green Finance and Green Technology in Improving Environmental Performance Across OECD Economies: An in-depth Investigation Using Advanced Quantile Modeling. *Cuadernos de Economía (Santiago, Chile), 46*(132), 157–169. DOI: 10.32826/cude.v46i132.1215

Klasen, A., & Vassard, J. (2023). The new OECD arrangement on export credits: Breakthrough or bad compromise? *Global Policy, 14*(5), 958–961. DOI: 10.1111/1758-5899.13255

Krinichansky, K. V., & Rubtsov, B. B. (2022). Financial Sector Regulation on the Agenda of Economic Policy Reforms [Регулирование финансового сектора в повестке реформ экономической политики]. *Finance: Theory and Practice, 26*(5), 6–21. DOI: 10.26794/2587-5671-2022-26-5-6-21

Kukreti, M., Sehajpal, S., Tiwari, R., & Sood, K. (2024a). Driving global health and sustainable development goals with smart technology. In *Driving Global Health and Sustainable Development Goals With Smart Technology*. IGI Global., DOI: 10.4018/979-8-3373-0240-9

Kukreti, M., Sehajpal, S., Tiwari, R., & Sood, K. (2024b). Introduction. In *Driving Global Health and Sustainable Development Goals With Smart Technology*. IGI Global.

Kukreti, M., Sehajpal, S., Tiwari, R., & Sood, K. (2024c). Preface. In *Driving Global Health and Sustainable Development Goals With Smart Technology*. IGI Global.

Lau, C. K., Padhan, H., Kumar Das, A., Tiwari, A. K., Gozgor, G., & Jain, P. (2025). The role of green bonds on industrial sustainability for achieving carbon neutrality: Evidence from the artificial neural network method. *Research in International Business and Finance, 73*. Advance online publication. DOI: 10.1016/j.ribaf.2024.102659

Li, D. (2024). Green finance, fossil fuel efficiency, and sustainable development in OECD. *Resources Policy, 98*. Advance online publication. DOI: 10.1016/j.resourpol.2024.105306

Lu, L., Zheng, H., Chen, M., & Najam, H. (2022). Tackling carbon intensity with green finance in the covid-19-era: recommendations for OECD economies. *Climate Change Economics (Singapore), 13*(3). Advance online publication. DOI: 10.1142/S2010007822400140

Miao, Y., Tian, Y., Cao, J., & Yu, X. (2025). Green finance and privatization of green projects in the fossil fuels industry. *Resources Policy, 103*. Advance online publication. DOI: 10.1016/j.resourpol.2025.105547

Mitra, R., & Guseva, M. E. (2021). Does Population Ageing Reduce FDI Inflows in OECD Countries? Evidence from Bayesian Panel VAR Estimates. In *Contributions to Management Science*. https://doi.org/DOI: 10.1007/978-3-030-60354-0_6

Nenavath, S. (2025). Analysing FDI inflow effects on CO2 emissions: A comparative study of OECD and BRICS nations with PHH and PHE models. *International Journal of Energy Sector Management, 19*(1), 80–100. DOI: 10.1108/IJESM-02-2024-0006

Ogbeifun, L., & Shobande, O. A. (2020). Causality Analysis of Disaggregated FDI Inflows on Sectorial Growth in OECD Area. *Studia Universitatis Vasile Goldis Arad. Economics Series, 30*(4), 92–110. DOI: 10.2478/sues-2020-0026

Raza, S. A., Shah, N., & Arif, I. (2021). Relationship Between FDI and Economic Growth in the Presence of Good Governance System: Evidence from OECD Countries. *Global Business Review, 22*(6), 1471–1489. DOI: 10.1177/0972150919833484

Safi, A., Kchouri, B., Elgammal, W., Nicolas, M. K., & Umar, M. (2024). Bridging the green gap: Do green finance and digital transformation influence sustainable development? *Energy Economics, 134*. Advance online publication. DOI: 10.1016/j.eneco.2024.107566

Saha, T., Sinha, A., & Abbas, S. (2022). Green financing of eco-innovations: Is the gender inclusivity taken care of? *Economic Research-Ekonomska Istrazivanja, 35*(1), 5514–5535. DOI: 10.1080/1331677X.2022.2029715

Sehajpal, S., & Sidhu, N. K. (2024). Neuroscience, nursing, and financial innovation: A synergistic approach to optimized patient care and economic well-being. In *Neuromarketing's Role in Sustainable Finance*. IGI Global., DOI: 10.4018/979-8-3693-9117-4.ch008

Shi, S., & Nisar, A. (2025). The Effects of Circular Economy, Green Finance and ICT Developments on Resource Productivity aimed Ecological Sustainability: Evidence from OECD Countries Using a CS-ARDL Approach; Wpływ gospodarki o obiegu zamkniętym, zielonych finansów i rozwoju technologii ICT na produktywność zasobów ukierunkowaną na ekologiczną zrównoważoność: dowody z krajów OECD stosujących podejście CS-ARDL. *Problemy Ekorozwoju*, *20*(2), 223–245. DOI: 10.35784/preko.7059

Tiwari, S., Cheong, C. W. H., See Mey, L., & Saji, T. G. (2024). Does fintech really matter for energy, economy and environment? From the lenses of SDG-7, SDG-8, SDG-13, COP27 and COP28. *Resources Policy*, *98*. Advance online publication. DOI: 10.1016/j.resourpol.2024.105318

Tsamadias, C. P., Pegkas, P., Mamatzakis, E. C., & Staikouras, C. K. (2019). Does R&D, human capital and FDI matter for TFP in OECD countries? *Economics of Innovation and New Technology*, *28*(4), 386–406. DOI: 10.1080/10438599.2018.1502394

Tufail, M., Song, L., & Khan, Z. (2024). Green finance and green growth nexus: Evaluating the role of globalization and human capital. *Journal of Applied Econometrics*, *27*(1). Advance online publication. DOI: 10.1080/15140326.2024.2309437

Umar, M., & Safi, A. (2023). Do green finance and innovation matter for environmental protection? A case of OECD economies. *Energy Economics*, *119*. Advance online publication. DOI: 10.1016/j.eneco.2023.106560

Varchenko, O., Varchenko, O., Drahan, O., Tkachenko, K., Rybak, N., & Zubchenko, V. (2024). «Green Finance» in the post-war reconstruction of Ukraine: organizational and financial aspects. *Financial and Credit Activity: Problems of Theory and Practice*, *3*(56), 75–85. DOI: 10.55643/fcaptp.3.56.2024.4403

Volz, U., Böhnke, J., Eidt, V., Knierim, L., Richert, K., & Roeber, G.-M. (2015). Financing the green transformation: How to make green finance work in Indonesia. In *Financing the Green Transformation: How to Make Green Finance Work in Indonesia*. Palgrave Macmillan. https://doi.org/DOI: 10.1007/978-1-137-48612-7

Voronova, E., Simonova, M., & Yarnykh, E. (2023). "Green" Investments in Renewable Energy in the Context of Innovative Development and Digitalization. In *Digital International Relations*. Springer Nature. https://doi.org/DOI: 10.1007/978-981-99-3467-6_14

Wang, R., Destek, M. A., Weimei, C., Albahooth, B., & Khan, Z. A. (2024). Drivers of Sustainable Green Finance: Country's Level Risk and Trade Perspective for OECD Countries. *Journal of Environment & Development*, *33*(1), 125–148. DOI: 10.1177/10704965231217046

Wang, T., Umar, M., Li, M., & Shan, S. (2023). Green finance and clean taxes are the ways to curb carbon emissions: An OECD experience. *Energy Economics*, *124*. Advance online publication. DOI: 10.1016/j.eneco.2023.106842

Wang, Y., & Taghizadeh-Hesary, F. (2023). Green bonds markets and renewable energy development: Policy integration for achieving carbon neutrality. *Energy Economics*, *123*. Advance online publication. DOI: 10.1016/j.eneco.2023.106725

Wu, H. (2023). Evaluating the role of renewable energy investment resources and green finance on the economic performance: Evidence from OECD economies. *Resources Policy*, *80*. Advance online publication. DOI: 10.1016/j.resourpol.2022.103149

Xu, Y., & Cai, Y. (2024a). Is green finance a motivator for energy transformation investments in the OECD? *Economic Change and Restructuring*, *57*(3). Advance online publication. DOI: 10.1007/s10644-024-09705-x

Xu, Y., & Cai, Y. (2024b). RETRACTED ARTICLE: Is green finance a motivator for energy transformation investments in the OECD? (Economic Change and Restructuring, (2024), 57, 3, (120),). *Economic Change and Restructuring*, *57*(6). https://doi.org/DOI: 10.1007/s10644-024-09705-x

Yoon, S., & Ko, J. (2025). The effect of FDI regulatory barriers: Evidence from OECD countries. *Applied Economics Letters*, *32*(10), 1484–1497. DOI: 10.1080/13504851.2024.2308558

Zhang, K.-C., Safi, A., Kchouri, B., Banerjee, A., & Wang, L. (2024). The three greens: Innovation, finance, and taxes—Performance analysis and future implications. *Journal of Innovation and Knowledge*, *9*(4). Advance online publication. DOI: 10.1016/j.jik.2024.100627

Zhang, Y. (2022). How Economic Performance of OECD economies influences through Green Finance and Renewable Energy Investment Resources? *Resources Policy*, *79*. Advance online publication. DOI: 10.1016/j.resourpol.2022.102925

Zheng, M., Feng, G.-F., & Chang, C.-P. (2023). Is green finance capable of promoting renewable energy technology? Empirical investigation for 64 economies worldwide. *Oeconomia Copernicana*, *14*(2), 483–510. DOI: 10.24136/oc.2023.013

Zhong, M., Umar, M., Mirza, N., & Safi, A. (2024). Mineral resource Optimization: The Nexus of sustainability, digital transformation, and green finance in OECD economies. *Resources Policy*, *90*. Advance online publication. DOI: 10.1016/j.resourpol.2024.104829

Zhu, H., Chen, M., & Zhao, S. (2024). Natural resource rent, green finance, and CO2 emissions from the industrial sector. *Resources Policy*, *98*. Advance online publication.

ENDNOTES

1 According to World Development Indicators Database of World Bank, "GDP per capita is gross domestic product divided by midyear population. GDP is the sum of gross value added by all resident producers in the economy plus any product taxes and minus any subsidies not included in the value of the products. It is calculated without making deductions for depreciation of fabricated assets or for depletion and degradation of natural resources. Data are in constant 2015 U.S. dollars."

2 According to World Development Indicators Database of World Bank, "General government expenditure on education (current, capital, and transfers) is expressed as a percentage of GDP. It includes expenditure funded by transfers from international sources to government. General government usually refers to local, regional and central governments."

3 According to World Development Indicators Database of World Bank, "Foreign direct investment are the net inflows of investment to acquire a lasting management interest (10 percent or more of voting stock) in an enterprise operating in an economy other than that of the investor. It is the sum of equity capital, reinvestment of earnings, other long-term capital, and short-term capital as shown in the balance of payments. This series shows net inflows (new investment inflows less disinvestment) in the reporting economy from foreign investors, and is divided by GDP."

4 According to Sustainable Development Goals Database of World Bank, "Carbon dioxide emissions are those stemming from the burning of fossil fuels and the manufacture of cement. They include carbon dioxide produced during consumption of solid, liquid, and gas fuels and gas flaring."

5 According to OECD Statistics, “Environment Related Government R&D budget includes Government budget allocations for R&D (GBARD) by socio-economic objective (SEO), using the NABS 2007 classification.”

Chapter 9
Fostering Sustainable Finance Through Green Initiatives by the Reserve Bank of India

Neetu Ahmed
https://orcid.org/0000-0002-6776-7295
GD Goenka University, India

Gurleen Kaur
https://orcid.org/0000-0003-0960-7119
Sri Guru Gobind Singh College of Commerce, New Delhi, India

ABSTRACT

Climate change leads to extreme weather conditions, which produce economic disruption, financial instability, and sector risk. Financial institutions stand to face greater losses should they neglect the risks. Network for Greening the Financial System (NGFS), established in 2017, advocates for sustainable finance. Central banks greenlight green investment and environmental management of risk. Green finance drives capital into green energy and climate-friendly projects and connects growth and climate objectives. India's net-zero by 2070 will need 2.5% of GDP invested every year by 2030. The Reserve Bank of India (RBI) facilitates green finance with policies, refinancing, and green bonds. Green finance needs to be strengthened for a low-carbon, resilient economy, with central banks taking the lead.

DOI: 10.4018/979-8-3373-1240-8.ch009

1. INTRODUCTION

Green finance or green investment is a pivotal instrument that support different type of financial activities required for the transition towards low-carbon, sustainable economy while addressing global challenges we face and furthering global sustainable development goals. Green finance is the raising of capital for investment that delivers environmental and climate goals. It included a variety of different financial instruments, policies and tools to provide funding for environmentally friendly development activities aiming at environmental investments like renewable energy projects, improving energy efficiency in the world; sustainable infrastructure; measures to adapt climate change (Benedict, 2012).

Green finance is vital in dealing with immediate environmental problems like climate change, pollution, resource depletion and loss of biodiversity simultaneously providing a framework and factors for increased social equity resilience. With the globe's concerted efforts to transition into an economy that is low-carbon or carbon neutral, green finance offers a pathway through which investors, financial institutions, governments and businesses can make their financial activities work in line with plans for sustainable development. By embedding environmental, social and governance (ESG) factors in investment decisions, green finance mitigates environmental risks and creates chances for innovation, jobs and shared growth (Liu & Xiong 2022; Zhang et al., 2021).

In 2015, the Paris Agreement was signed by 178 parties. The aim of this agreement is to collectively tackle adverse changes in our global climate, and limit overall warming to 1.5 degrees Celsius. According to World Energy Transitions Outlook 2023 (IRENA, 2023) meeting this target will require a cumulative sum of USD 150 trillion by 2050. As green finance channel funding into environmental friendly enterprises and projects that are less resource consuming sectors as well as giving a better return on investment (ROI) for investor to invest in renewable energy sectors. On the other hand, should the financial crisis take those returns away from such endeavours, stability in a country's financial situation is an essential condition for this kind of behaviour to deliver greener results.

In India itself, the fact that climate change needs to be addressed urgently and sustainable development has begun to gain some visibility. It seems obvious that this vast nation, a rising population and an ever-enlarging need is going to have transition its fuel resources into clean & sustainable. These goals have also created new sources of finance for greener economies, as the government is trying to be more and more dependent on renewable energy. India has undergone an pronounced transformation in its concepts of sustainability and stewardship of nature in recent years. One very visible development over the years has since been the repositioning of green finance within a wider and deep-integration with economic system as we know it in response to current global climate changes challenges. One of the key positive factors underpinning possible rapid scaling up and development in renewable energy is green finance, which invests financial capital towards projects that are sustainable and environmentally friendly.

In India, a crucial aspect of green finance is the alignment of sustainability and financial returns. Once upon a time, many of us assumed that this kind investment might jeopardize return rates. The rapidly evolving terrain of green finance, however, is overturning this understanding. Investors now know that ecologically sensitive businesses, particularly in such sectors as renewable energy, not only keep the earth from getting dirtier but also yield tidy profits. Incentives, subsidies, green bonds and regulatory frameworks can give a shot in the arm to investment in projects that are environmentally sustainable.

For green finance in India, as indicated above, the waves are opening up many opportunities for both investors and enterprises. Financial instruments of various kinds, including green bonds and environmental investment funds, are making their appearance. Recently REC Ltd released Green bonds of 5 years, 5.25 years and 10 years maturity under its US$ 10 billion Global Medium Term Notes Programme (Anand, 2024). And so, a number of mechanisms are providing a funding channel for investments which promote renewable energy sources generation, energy efficiency and such like ecological projects.

India has committed itself to renewable energy, setting ambitious targets for 2030 that would see 500 GW of renewable energy capacity completed. Over the past few years, solar and wind energy projects have taken off in India, funded through both domestic equity as well as international capital. The Indian Government is building a favorable financing environment for green projects. Initiatives like making domestic manufacturing the focus of PLI (production-linked incentive) schemes underscore their commitment to provide financial support for sustainable project and eco-friendly development. Additionally, policy measures and regulatory frameworks are being designed to attract investment into renewable energy sector in order to build a lively green finance ecosystem.

Green finance, as it is similar to traditional finance in its major function characteristic, the growth of Green Finance may offer a space for economic expansion. Spending on green innovation can boost economic growth, create jobs and improve competitiveness. The International Finance Corporation (IFC) through its Climate Business Department makes investments in creative green technologies and startups that are designed to encourage durable power, sustainable farming and adjustment of climate change solutions within the fields that are observed to be upcoming industries globally operating in these markets around (IFC, 2021).

The world needs a growth path for what is still, in purchasing power parity terms, its third-largest economy. So this goes well with our vision to become carbon neutral by 2070 i.e. a natural immunity in fight against climate change. This is where green finance has the power to help nudge our economy in that direction. One that comes with a caveat in this case-the financial markets are much calmer and crisis-free. The rise of green finance in India holds great promise. However, challenges still confront green finance's development in India, such as project risks and uncertainties in policy. In addition, the lack of standard green finance indicators also presents obstacles to this industry developing further. Nonetheless, getting the sector to move forward is not an impossible task. The emergence of green finance in India reflects an overall international trend in environmental investment and sustainable development.

Further to the aforementioned context, the present chapter aims to outline the significance of green finance by defining its objectives and examining diverse financial instruments it encompasses. Following this, it delves into green initiatives taken by central banks worldwide with special reference to India, while scrutinizing the associated challenges. Finally, it explores future imperatives of green finance and advocates certain policy suggestions for governments, central banks and policymakers before concluding the chapter.

1.1 Role of Green Financing

The role of green financing is multi-faceted and crucial to future environmental sustainability. Even more vital, it is a bridge work for necessary transitions towards low-carbon and climate-resilient economies. In contrast to the conventional finance, green finance considers both environmental considerations and economic gains, thus making financial flows coherent with sustainability goals. The escalating climate change concerns, rising resource scarcity, and obligations under global agreements such as the Paris Accord have heightened the importance of green finance across various sectors. Here are a few facets of its role:

1.1.1 Major capital mobilization: Green Financing invests capital in those projects or initiatives that have the least negative impact on the environment. By providing financing arrangements to develop sustainable energy, continuing public transportation, sustainable agriculture. In addition, multilateral agencies such as the World Bank, Asian Development Bank (ADB), and Green Climate Fund have a critical function in facilitating capital flows into emerging economies, where financial resources generally restrict sustainability transitions. Essentially, green finance builds a connection between international capital markets and local sustainability requirements, speeding up the deployment of clean technologies. For example, by issuing green bonds the Indian Renewable Energy Development Agency (IREDA) financed the Bhadla Solar Park in Rajasthan, which is among the world's largest solar parks (IREDA, 2021).

1.1.2 Encourage Innovation And Energy Efficiency: By promoting green financing, technologies are stimulated that inspire new levels of efficiency (both in terms of reducing environmental footprints and resource productivity) processes as well as business models. It creates an environment where firms have incentives to invest in renewable energy, green infrastructure and sustainable technologies making the development and deployment of clean and efficient solutions inevitable. Green financing allows you to invest in energy-efficient technologies and practices for industries, buildings, transportation. This will not only allow the country to reduce its energy intensity and greenhouse gas emission levels, but also ensure economic competitiveness (IEA, 2021).

1.1.3 Mitigating Environmental Risks: Based on green financing, much of the risk flowing from climate change, pollution, species loss and loss of natural resources can be avoided. It also reduces investment risk through environmental, social, governance (ESG) criteria, cutting the chance that assets will become stranded due to regulation or that companies will incur reputational risks. Green financing helps India by supporting climate-resilient agriculture like water projects and mitigation of natural disasters. By investing in climate adaptation, India can reduce vulnerability to the Projects: The Tata Steel Jamshedpur Plant now also has energy-saving measures, funded by green loans and government incentives (Tata Steel, 2021).

1.1.4 Creating Economic Opportunities: Using green financing will stimulate economic growth and job creation in the green sectors. It can be used to promote innovation, competition and durability of any economy through its support for such areas as renewable energy expansion, sustainable agriculture, eco-tourism and other ways of living in nature (UNDP, 2020; UNEP, 2021). The shift towards a low-carbon economy needs new skill sets, thus generating employment opportunities in the development of technology, installation, and maintenance of green infrastructure. Small and medium-sized enterprises (SMEs) involved in environmentally friendly products and services are also supported by affordable green credit, enhancing inclusive economic growth. Through opening new markets and business models, green finance makes economies more resilient and competitive in the long run on an international level.

1.1.5 Enhancing Corporate Responsibility: By helping companies stand by green financing, it promotes corporate responsibility and accountability. Integrating ESG issues in investment analysis and engagement encourages companies to improve their environmental performance as well as increase their social responsibility. Green financing requires robust monitoring, reporting, and verification of environmental outcomes, thereby promoting accountability. Organizations that embrace such practices strengthen stakeholder trust, improve brand reputation, and gain competitive advantages. Additionally, by aligning with sustainability principles, businesses demonstrate leadership in corporate social responsibility (CSR), reinforcing their commitment to ethical and environmentally conscious operations.

1.1.6 Fostering Resilience and Adaptation: Green financing contributes to both climate resilience and adaptation. By financing infrastructure investments, rehabilitation of ecosystems, community resilience measures, it both helps keep regions secure against disaster but also in the long run benefits climate change preparedness (UNEP, 2018).

Climate change threatens economies and societies with systemic risk, prompting resilience and adaptation measures. Green financing facilitates the investment in adaptive assets like flood-resilient housing, climate-resilient agriculture, and resilient energy infrastructure that keeps communities safe from extreme weather and resource drought. By directing money into adaptive capacity-building projects, green finance minimizes vulnerability, prevents economic loss, and improves social welfare. This forward-thinking way ensures that economies will be strong regardless of the uncertainties brought by climate and protect the most vulnerable sectors.

1.1.7 Aligning with Sustainable Development Goals: Green financing aligns with the objectives of the United Nations Sustainable Development Goals (SDGs) by addressing such environmental problems such as air and water pollution, waste and biodiversity loss. It is consistent with a sustainable economic growth framework based on inclusivity. Moreover, it contributes to the realization of global sustainability goals through channels supportive of those aims (UNDP, 2020).

1.1.8 Sustainable Infrastructure Development: Green finance supports sustainable infrastructure construction, covering rail networks, environmental buildings and waste management facilities. With sustainable infrastructure India gains increased resource efficiency, greater urban resilience and expanded opportunities. This development supports the nation's efforts to maintain its current rate of robust economic growth (ADB, 2018). Green finance encourages investment in renewable energy sources such as solar power, wind farms, and hydroelectric projects. This will enable the country to reduce its reliance on fossil fuels and cut greenhouse gas emissions into the bargain. India has set ambitious goals for the creation of renewable energy generating capacity, and green finance serves as an important tool in raising the finance needed to reach these targets (BNEF, 2020).

1.1.9 Social implications and community development: Financial innovation and financial development have a profound effect on many aspects of human society. The success of Financial Inclusion and the consequent poverty reduction is the most successful example which defines this relationship. As a very special kind of financial product, green finance also enhances the development of society. The year after year, this will generate a higher return on investment than before: earnings of this size entirely can be devote to future earnings itself rather than local.

Green finance is an all-encompassing weapon, yet specific measures are never universal. Green financing brings environmental considerations into the realm of decision-making for financial products, sure enough leading to some remarkable outcomes. Through green financing mechanisms, India can achieve its environmental objectives and economic targets while helping to fight climate change at a global level–in pursuit of the Sustainable Development Goals.

1.2 Objectives of Green Financing

The aim of green financing is to direct fund flows to environmentally sustainable projects and programs which will facilitate a low-carbon, resilient economy. The following are some of the key objectives of green financing:

1.2.1 Environmental Sustainability: Green financing seeks to address environmental problems such as climate change pollution, loss of biodiversity and depletion of resources by directing investment toward energy renewable (not naturally occurring), energy efficient and sustainable infrastructure projects (for instance building hydropower station or electrified rail network), clean transportation systems, ecosystem conservation activities and so forth.

By directing capital towards eco-friendly projects, green finance encourages businesses and governments to adopt practices that do not harm the environment, thus ensuring the long-term health of the planet. Green financing contributes to United Nations SDG goals by addressing a triple bottom-line problem social environmental and economic challenges which comprises of poverty alleviation, gender equality, clean energy access and enhancing competitiveness.

1.2.2 Climate Mitigation And Adaptation: According to IEA (2020), green finance intends to mitigate emissions of greenhouse gases and improve climate resilience among other things by supporting investment in renewable energy deployment; constructing smaller energy-emission buildings that are more efficient relative to their predecessors; building farm operations whose design enhance climate, food security and disaster resilience; Medium- and long-term solutions to the problem of disasters, such as upgrading road or bridge networks so they are impervious to flooding Natural disasters preparedness.

By financing climate-resilient infrastructure and innovative technologies, green finance reduces the risks associated with extreme weather events and ensures sustainable economic growth in the face of environmental challenges.

1.2.3 Resource Efficiency: Green finance conforms to the principle of resource efficiency and circular economy through its projects and processes making up as little waste as possible while utilizing resources to maximum for minimizing their environmental burden at all stages from production to consumption. It emphasizes recycling and reuse and reduce environmental footprint across industries and supply chains.

1.2.4 Risk Reduction: Green finance also seeks to inject environmental risk management into financial processes. Finance tends to ignore climate risk, which has far-reaching economic consequences. Green finance by incorporating environmental risk evaluation into financial choice minimizes the susceptibility of financial systems to environmental disturbances. Through the integration of environmental, social and governance (ESG) factors in investment decision-making, green finance strives to mitigate environmental threats such as those posed by climate change, regulatory complexity and evolving consumer preferences.

1.2.5 Market Transformation: Green financing contributes to market transformation by incentivizing innovation, technology development, and adoption of sustainable business practices across sectors, thereby creating new market opportunities, stimulating economic growth, and enhancing competitiveness. It encourages upgrades in practices, and new technologies and business models to come onto the market in vices such as energy efficiency.

Green finance also promotes entrepreneurship and start-ups that focus on sustainability-driven business models. By lowering financial barriers and sharing risks, it stimulates creative solutions that might otherwise struggle to gain traction in traditional markets. This fosters a culture of continuous innovation aligned with environmental goals.

1.2.6 Investor Demand: Green finance has grown in existence as socially responsible and environmentally sustainable investment in response to growing demand from investors, who are now increasingly taking into account environmental, social and governance (ESG) in their investment strategies and seeking to align their portfolios with sustainability objectives. Green finance encourages the development of sustainable public transport systems that pollute less and make better use of resources, including subway lines, bus rapid transit (BRT), cycling lanes, etc.. Examples like the Kochi Metro Rail in Kerala have received funding from green bonds and loans to finance its construction and expansion (KMRL, 2021).

1.2.7 Driving Innovation and Technological Advancements: Green Financing promotes innovation, development of new technology in clean energy; sustainable agriculture, green building design etc. Investments in green R&D spur technological change, enhance economic adaptive capacities and green business claims.

Overall, green financing aims to harness the power of finance for investments which benefit environmental sustainability and climate resilience; resource efficiency and sustainable development, while ensuring that present needs are met without compromising future generations.

2. INSTRUMENTS OF GREEN FINANCING

Green finance includes many types of financial products and services divided into investment, banking, and insurance. The main financial products that constitute green finance are debt and equity. These tools provide investors, financial institutions and private companies a way to deploy their capital into activities that are climate-friendly. New financial tools such as green bonds carbon market instruments and new financial institutions like the Green Banks and Green Funds have been set up to cater to this growing demand. The key instruments of green financing are:

2.1 Green Bonds: Debt securities that are issued to raise money for projects and activities with environmental benefits, including but not limited to renewable energy, energy efficiency and sustainable infrastructure as well as those that support climate change mitigation or adaptation efforts. The proceeds raised through green bonds come with specific use of funds and they are usually externally certified for transparency and accountability purposes. Central banks are buying green bonds as part of their asset-purchase or quantitative-easing programs to underpin environmentally sustainable investment. Central banks have, for one, been buying green bonds in order to support the development of a liquid and vibrant market (BIS, 2020), which should provide an incentive for issuers looking to finance new investments.

2.2 Green Loans: Green loans act as financing mechanisms to provide clean energy projects and investments finance. Banks, development financial institutions or other reputable lenders may offer these loans and they are used to finance green projects like renewable energy, building retrofitting (like those done in Singapore), sustainable transportation and other environment friendly initiatives. Green loans may have more beneficial terms, including lower interest rates or extended repayment periods to encourage green investment. The Suzlon Wind Farm in Tamil Nadu is an example of the benefits provided to projects by a green loan offered through banks and financial institutions for establishing wind turbine setup along with related infrastructure (Kumar & Majid, 2020).

2.3 Green Mortgages: Green mortgages are a type of mortgage that encourages the purchase or renovation of homes to be more energy efficient. These mortgages may offer incentives in the form of discounted interest rates, and can help borrowers buy or improve energy-efficient homes (or implement upgrades) that include renewable energy systems with low-down payment requirements.

2.4 Green Equity Investments: In the green equity investments we are acquiring stakes in companies or projects that offer improvements to environmental sustainability For example, investors may buy shares in green listed companies operating on renewable energy, clean farms and wind parks - as well as the safe transportation system.

2.5 Green Funds: Green funds, often called sustainable investment or environmental funds, buy stakes in a range of environmentally-friendly assets by raising capital from multiple investors. These funds invest in green bonds equities (Companies that score better on ESG metrics), renewable energy or sustainable infrastructure, offering investors diversification while mitigating risk side-by-side supporting green initiatives.

2.6 Carbon Finance: The buying and selling of carbon credits or offsets to pay for reducing emissions. To offset their carbon footprint or for regulatory and corporate sustainability targets, companies can pay to invest in emissions reduction projects via mechanisms like carbon trading schemes as well as markets based on voluntary action pursuing offsets.

2.7 Green Insurance: Green insurance covers green risks and environmental liabilities of green projects. Some of the products in the category are pollution liability insurance, renewable energy project insurance, and climate-risk-based insurance policies. These products ensure companies are safeguarded against financial losses as a result of natural catastrophes, environmental accidents, or non-compliance with environmental regulations, thus increasing investor confidence in green projects.

In this way green financing instruments contribute to shift capital flows from unsustainable projects and policies, in order to move us closer towards the goal of an environmentally sustainable economy /pro-environmental initiatives which need mobilization, support by these financial solutions are currently being pressed over.

3. GREEN FINANCING STRATEGIES FOR DEVELOPED & DEVELOPING ECONOMIES

Green financing needs are determined by differences in economic contexts, institutional capabilities, policy frameworks and investment priorities between developing and developed nations. But there are some key differences in how green financing is on offer for each of the two. Here's a break down with real-world examples:

3.1 Economic Conditions and Investment Requirements

Green financing can be a challenge for developing countries which frequently struggle to secure affordable funding, given their limited fiscal resources, infrastructure deficits and conflicting development imperatives. At the national level, green financing primarily addresses fundamental infrastructure demands, spurs investments in clean energy access and enhances climate resilience. For instance, in

India green financing is applied to projects such as the National Solar Mission that strives to add up their solar capacity 100 GW by the year of 2022 (MNRE, 2000).

Mature financial market and more developed capital base of the rich countries provide a variety of flexible green financing tools. In these countries, the vast majority of green financing is for clean technologies, raising energy efficiency levels, reinforcing sustainable urban infrastructure and facilities upgrading to mitigate climate risks. For instance in the European Union, Green Bonds are issued by the European Investment Bank (EIB) to finance projects aligned with EU climate goals indicated under the Green Bond Framework Document (EIB, 2021).

3.2 Policy and Regulatory Landscapes

In turn, developing countries often do not have the powerful regulatory systems and incentives necessary to attract green investment. Policy intervention such as feed-in tariffs, tax incentives, subsidies and regulatory mandates will incentivise private sector participation in green projects. In Brazil, government provides tax incentives and concessional financing to stimulate renewable energy projects (MME, 2021).

To a certain extent, developed countries have regulatory frameworks and policy instruments for green financing such as renewable energy targets, emission trading scheme or standards of financial supervision about the dimensions of sustainable finance. Green financing in these nations benefits from supportive policy environments that encourage sustainable investment and innovation. In the United Kingdom, for instance, a Green Finance Strategy outlines government intentions to channel private sector investments into clean growth and climate objectives (HM Treasury, 2019).

3.3 Institutional Capacities and Market Development

Green financing in developing countries may be hindered by a lack of institutional capacities, technical expertise and market infrastructure. In short, building local know-how through capacity-building efforts and training trainers, transferring knowledge in all financial sectors as needed (banking/ non-banking/ pension system providers) internationally collaborating on regulatory frameworks constructing sustainable finance ecosystems continue to be a significant component. One example is that the Green Climate Fund (GCF) supports capacity-building and readiness activities in developing countries to access climate finance for high impact green projects (GCF, 2021).

For the developed world, we have financial institutions using market systems and regulation to invest in green financing. These markets have mature financial systems, demand from investors for sustainable investments and well established frameworks around green bond issuance, impact investing, environmental risk management. In Japan, this year saw the publication of Green Bond Guidelines which establish a framework for green bond certification and disclosure environmental impact information (JGBL, 2017).

Green Finance and Developing Economies

Green finance is now a priority development strategy for emerging economies as central banks act as the key enablers to build sustainable financial architectures. These initiatives appear increasingly in policy frameworks and markets such as green bond markets and other climate-aligned financial instruments aimed at addressing systemic environmental risks with a view to maintaining economic and financial stability. Nevertheless, institutional challenges—like data fragmentation, capacity constraints and inconsistent regulation—are still holding the pace back, so cross-border co-ordination and standards are going to assist the cause (SEACEN 2024).

In countries such as India, the Reserve Bank of India (RBI) has also played an active role in broadening green financial horizons by operationalising a dedicated framework for green deposits and easing sovereign access towards foreign investment through Sovereign Green Bonds – indicative of a regulatory ecosystem that is increasingly aligning itself towards sustainable development efforts (SEACEN, 2024, p. 13). Among the SEACEN member central bank, the central bank of Malaysia has mainstreamed Islamic finance into its sustainability agenda with an initial issuance of Green Sukuk that will be used to fund infrastructure and energy projects that are in line with Shariah principles. Additionally, the People's Bank of China has operationalized green finance by developing specific re-lending facilities that provide subsidized loans to banks for investment in environmentally-friendly projects aligning their monetary policy instruments with environmental sustainability goals.

In summary, the nature of green finance differs across countries in both developed and developing countries due to differences in economic conditions, policy frameworks and institutional capacities. Developing nations are mostly concerned with basic infrastructure requirements and investment for renewable energy deployment, whereas the top spot is taken by advanced technologies, attachment rate enhancements in energy efficiency as well significant innovations on sustainable finance from developed countries. It is important that we work together between countries, international organizations and the private sector so as to bridge this green financing gap in our way towards global sustainability.

4. HOW THE ROLE OF CENTRAL BANKS CAN CONTRIBUTE TOWARDS GREEN FINANCING?

Central banks are also crucial in fostering green financing as they introduce a series of policies, guidelines and initiatives which help to funnel investment into environmentally sustainable ventures across economies. Here's an overview of the role of central banks in green financing:

4.1 Green Bonds Purchases

Purchasing green bonds by central banks in relation to the implementation of traditional monetary policy operations, as a contribution from such investments that are environmentally sustainable. Central banks underpin the green bond market, their purchase of which also sends liquidity into this same circulatory system and also fulfils its role in sustaining certain projects with a positive environmental connotation. The People's Bank of China (PBOC) includes these green bonds in open market operations to fund eco-friendly projects and foster onshore sustainable bond investment markets. PBOC buys green bonds to provide ecological protection, support renewable energy development and safeguard sustainable infrastructure investment (PBOC, 2019) a big move to foster sustainable finance tsunami in the Eurozone, The European Central Bank (ECB) has officially opened its gates for green bonds under its asset buying program. ECB is designed to help boost green investment, reduce the CO2 intensity and achieve a strong economic contribution (ECB, 2021).

4.2 Development of Green Finance Guidelines

An accompanying green banking with a combined blueprint of recommendations made by central banks to help financial institutions incorporate environmental care in their lending and investment operations. Central banks apply the guidelines and principles to encourage green finance best practice, such as promoting sustainable lending policy development with targeted guidance, and promote awareness of various Green Financial Products/Services (PBOC, 2020). Guidelines for green finance driven by the Central Bank of Brazil (BCB) guides to greener financial practices, support Brazilian investments in sustainability. These stimuli contemplate green finance eligibility criteria, mandatory disclosure requirements and encouragement of financial institutions to invest in sustainability projects (PBOC, 2020).

The Bank of England proposed green finance guidelines to promote Britain's sustainable funding and help direct capital flows towards domestic green investments. Guidelines laid out by the BoE covers green finance standards, disclosure requirements and incentives in order to direct financial industry investment into Green projects (BoE, 2020).

In the UK, this is done through a Green Finance Strategy which details how the government will align private sector financial flows with clean growth and climate objectives. It lists a range of government policy actions, regulatory reforms and market interventions to facilitate green finance and sustainable investment (HM Treasury, 2019).

4.3 Climate-related Stress Testing

Central banks carry out climate-related stress tests to determine the ability of financial entities to cope with further risks and hence, test for their compliance against international standards on Addressing Climate Change. Central banks promote increasing openness of climate risks to unlock its management and disclosure by associating them with the incorporation into stress testing frameworks. Introduce disclosers as well as reporting standards for financial institutions by central banks to ensure transparency, accountability and comparability of climate-related information. They are disclosing frameworks and regulatory requirements that top or central banks develop to give financial institutions and investors better information on the climate risks affecting their balance sheet (TCFD, 2017).

The Central Bank of Kenya (CBK) carries out the stress tests to evaluate banks exposure based on different climate risks such as changes in weather patterns for agriculture and food security, changes in energy demand due rise in temperature (CBK, 2021). They have even entered in climate-related stress tests to look at the exposure by banks and as a check on financial stability implications. For instance, The Bank of Canada (BoC) stress tests assess how banks are affected by climate risks such as the impacts of adverse weather events; transition risks and physical outcomes from a changing world (BoC, 2021).

4.4 Capacity Building and Technical Support

The central bankscentral banks offer capacity-building & technical assistance to the financial institutions, regulators and policy makers to help them become familiar with green finance concepts; promulgate sustainable finance frameworks; strengthen their regulatory & supervisory capabilities. This was encapsulated in the various capacity building workshops on green finance concepts and sustainable finance practices among financial institutions, facilitated by the Central Bank of Nigeria (CBN). CBN interventions on capacity building are anchored on the training of bankers, regulators as well policymakers in Green Finance principles and risk assessment models coupled with sustainability reporting (CBN, 2020).

In the US, capacity building programmes and workshops are conducted to introduce green finance concepts in practice among financial institutions by Federal Reserve System (FRS) authorities. FRS implements trainings regarding green finance principles, risk assessment methodologies and sustainability reporting to build up the capacities of bankers, regulators and policy makers (FRS, 2020).

4.5 Research and Data Provision

Central Banks conducts research and analysis on environmental trends including: environmental trends, climate change risk analysis, green finance developments. They further our knowledge of how environmental degradation and climate change affects the economy, leading to more robust policy decisions around markets.

In so doing, central banks have a vital role to play in supporting green financing, sustainable development goals and climate resilience at the national level.

5. CHALLENGES OF GREEN FINANCING

5.1 Low Awareness and Capacity: Few investors, financial institutions, or businesses are familiar with green financing principles, products and opportunities. Therefore, it hampers the functionality of green finance practices and capital outflow to environment friendly projects (Agrawal et al., 2023). The GCF furthers its commitment to work with developing countries by offering them support on capacity-building in areas including understanding green finance concepts, strengthening institutional capacities and accessing climate funds for projects (GCF, 2021).

5.2 Data availability and quality: The Reliable data need to be available with regard the impact on nature of green projects. It increases transparency to the investor about how their investments are doing with regards to sustainability goals. It enables better risk assessment by providing data on the long-term viability and resilience of green projects.

5.3 Transaction Risk: Many industries will need to change the way they do business in order for a low-carbon economy transition, and this can affect their investor's portfolios. Customers can also have a shift in their demands and, technological development might not be following the demand for green finance. At the same time, this may lead to a negative effect upon investor portfolios. These risks are often difficult to evaluate and price, particularly for new or innovative green investments.

5.4 Market Fragmentation and Standardization: The green finance market is fragmented with a variety of standards, definitions, frameworks for what constitutes as Green investments. This lack of aligned standards and certification mechanisms has the potential to be confusing, inconsistent or non-credible for both investors and issuers. The Climate Bonds Initiative (CBI) has created the Climate Bonds Standard to serve as a certification scheme for green bonds so that investors have an understandable and robust way of identifying where they are putting their money and give opportunity for evaluating their investments.

5.6 Financial Viability and ROI: Most green projects will encounter obstacles in proving their financial viability, generating a strong return on investment - especially for emerging markets or those with high upfront costs followed by long periods of returns.

The development of climate central banks for low and middle income countries is much more difficult due to their narrow mandates, relatively less developed financial systems and incomplete data and methods. Such banks often lack clear sustainability mandates in their governing frameworks, leaving the legal and operational implementation of climate tools complex. Further, the absence of mature climate-risk models and forward-looking analytics mean that they struggle to diagnose environmental threats in a timely fashion, let alone to suggest how best deal with them. In turn, this can undermine the effectiveness of green interventions by limiting their reach and penetration while also undermining the coherence and legitimacy of central-bank-led climate action through the absence of macroprudential integration and alignment with broader industrial and fiscal policies. The international financial agencies and global communities need to step forward to overcome these obstacles for a more unified and greener global future.

6. CENTRAL BANKS AND CURRENT STRATEGIES TOWARDS GREEN FINANCING

Purpose Central Banks are expected to construct a regulatory framework as part of their mandate to promote the durability and financial returns on green finance actions. As the general vocabulary has it, interest rates and inflation walk together hand in hand - we all know central bank monetary policy stance results either into increased cost of capital or lowering inflation. Lower interest rates can be an incentive for more investors to participate in sustainable finance. To have a green sustainable growth centred economy, It is the job of Central Banks to manage the volatile interplay between monetary policy, economic landscape and shadowy Green finance market.

On the regulatory side, a new sustainable finance regime has been established under the European Union's Sustainable Finance Action Plan via measures like the EU Taxonomy Regulation and Sustainable Finance Disclosure Regulations to foster green investments as well as increase transparency in this regard (European Commission, 2021).

The regulator and operational framework based central banking theories shall also be revisited as at times such regulatory or operations are conflicting which might dilute even possibly discourage green financial practices. Latest Global Central Bank Green Finance Initiatives (Table 6.1) below outlines the most current green finance approaches across various developed and developing economies adopted by central banks worldwide.

Table 1. Initiatives Taken by Central banks for promoting green financing

S.No	*Economy*	*Central Bank*	*Year*	*Name of the Green initiative*	*Objective*
1	Europe	The European Central Bank	2016	Corporate Sector Purchase Programme (CSPP)	Through the CSPP, the ECB provided liquidity to the corporate bond market, incentivized issuers to fund green projects, and contributed to the development of green finance markets in the Eurozone (European Central Bank, 2016).
2	England	The Bank of England (BoE)	2021	Climate Biennial Exploratory Scenario (CBES)	CBES simulated various climate scenarios and integrated them into stress testing frameworks. The CBES findings will inform future policy actions to enhance the resilience of the financial system to climate change (Babk of England, 2021).
3	United States	Federal Reserve System (FRS)	2021	supervisory guidance on climate risk management	The guidance outlined expectations for banks' governance, risk management, and disclosure practices regarding climate risks to improve transparency and disclosure of climate-related financial information (Federal Reserve System, 2021).
4	Canada	Bank of Canada	2021	climate-related stress testing	To understand climate risks, inform risk management practices, and support policy development to strengthen the resilience of the financial system to climate change (Bank . of Canada, 2021.
5	China	People's Bank of China	2016	Green Finance Guidelines	The guidelines provide principles, standards, and recommendations for financial institutions to integrate environmental considerations into their lending and investment activities (People's Bank of China, 2016).

continued on following page

Table 1. Continued

S.No	*Economy*	*Central Bank*	*Year*	*Name of the Green initiative*	*Objective*
6	India	Reserve Bank of India	2020	Sustainable Finance Framework	The framework outlines principles and best practices for integrating sustainability considerations into credit risk assessment, loan pricing, and portfolio management (Reserve Bank of India, 2020).
7	Indonesia	Bank Indonesia	2019	Sustainable Finance Roadmap	The roadmap provides guidance and incentives for banks to integrate environmental, social, and governance (ESG) considerations into their lending and investment activities (Bank of Indonesia, 2019).
8	South Africa	South African Reserve Bank	2020	Climate Risk Prudential Practice Guide	The guide provides methodologies, tools, and recommendations for banks to incorporate climate risk considerations into their risk management frameworks, stress testing exercises, and disclosure practices (South African Reserve Bank, 2020).

Source: Compiled by the Authors

Therefore, through asset purchase programs, stress testing exercises, and collaboration with stakeholders, central banks play a crucial role in mainstreaming climate risk management and green financing practices in the financial sector.

7. GREEN FINANCING INITIATIVES AND ALLIED REGULATORY FRAMEWORKS BY THE RBI

RBI advises banks to help fund initiatives like green energy, sustainable infrastructure and disclose their environmental risks. The RBI has promoted sustainable finance to support India's SDGs, improve financial stability and address climate risk (Reserve Bank of India, 2020). The key Initiatives of RBI in the field of Green Finance are:

7.1 Introduction of Green Bonds

In 2015, RBI issued guidelines on green bonds for financing projects related to non-conventional energy sources. These guidelines will serve as the main reference to support issuers in mobilising funds through green bonds and ensure appropriate transparency, credibility, and integrity of information. The guidelines issued by the RBI provide a set of eligible categories for green projects, disclosures and tracking requirements applicable to green bond issuances.

The Indian railway company IRFC (Indian Railway Finance Corporation) in 2017 issued India's first green bond for Rs.1,000 crore ~USD143 million The bond was meant to raise funds for Indian railways that would be used in building renewable energy projects such as solar and wind power installations to help lower the carbon footprint of rail travel by an eco-sensitive India (Economic Times, 2017). ReNew Power also sold India's first US dollar green bond of $475 million in 2018. The funds raised from the bond issuance were used towards funding renewable energy projects such as wind and solar power installations thereby promoting India's transition to clean sources of energy (Reuters, 2018).

7.2 Inclusion of Renewable Energy Projects in Priority Sector Lending

The RBI has included financing for renewable energy projects under the priority sector lending framework but banks should furnish certificates issued by professional certifying agencies prescribed to assess and validate environmental impact due from greenhouse gas emissions. The move is directed towards encouraging banks to lend their capital for renewable energy projects, thus ensuring that the Indian climate depends less on carbon and moves closer to a low-carbon economy.

The State Bank of India (SBI) in 2018, announced that it would provide financing for completed grid-connected solar projects aggregating to a capacity of at least 15 GW under the priority sector lending framework. In November 2018, SBI tied up with the Indian government's Solar Energy Corporation of India (SECI) to provide loans for bankable solar projects and contribute towards meeting the country's set renewable energy targets (Business Standard, 2018). In 2019, the Indian renewable energy company Azure Power had also raised debt from State Bank of India (SBI) under priority sector lending guidelines to construct a 200 MW solar power project in Rajasthan. The SBI provided funding for the project as part of its commitment to fund renewable energy projects using PLS framework (Economic Times, 2019).

7.3 Guidelines on ESG Risk Management for Banks, Financial Institutions

The RBI issued Guidelines for Banks and Financial Institutions on Environmental, Social & Governance (ESG) Risk Management in 2021. The guidelines established principles on the integration of ESG factors in risk management and described best practices, disclosure requirements for financial institutions implementing environmentally sustainable financing solutions. Banks and financial institutions can identify, manage environmental risks (including climate-related ones), promote sustainable finance by embedding ESG considerations in their operations (RBI, 2021).

It is the initiatives taken by RBI towards greening of financing, aiding renewable energy projects and mainstreaming media driven green finance in banking domain for building sustainable country like India. RBI plays an important role in mainstreaming green finance and promoting sustainable development through policy measures, regulatory guidelines and market interventions.

7.4 Framework for financing sustainable development goals (SDGs)

To promote banks and financial institutions to realign their lending and investment activities with United Nations' Sustainable Development Goals (SDGs), the RBI came out with a framework for SDG financing in 2018. This framework gives recommendations for the inclusion of SDG contextualized criteria within credit assessment, project appraisal and investment decision-making processes. To add in, the RBI aims to support India's endeavours towards realizing the SDGs and aligning its financing with these global goals as it addresses critical sustainability issues which could be achieved by promoting SDG-aligned financing (RBI, 2021).

7.5 National Strategy for Green Banking

In order to push the banks towards adopting sustainable banking practices and catalyze their role as environmental steward, RBI built up a National Strategy for Green Banking in coordination with Bank's IBA (Indian Banks' Association). RBI itself aims to encourage environmental sustainability, lower carbon emissions and stronger green economic growth through the mainstreaming of green banking principles (RBI, 2019.

7.6 Green Finance Cell within RBI

The Green Finance Cell was established by the RBI under its Sustainable Banking Division to promote and undertake initiatives with respect to green financing, sustainable development, and climate resilience. This includes, in particular: Promoting policies for green finance by collaborating with stakeholders like banks and financial institutions as well as government agencies; development of guidelines on Green Finance Recognition Criteria (GFRC); developing capacity-building programs.

8. EXPLORING FUTURE IMPERATIVES OF GREEN FINANCE

Increased awareness around environmental issuers and climate change is resulting in a rise of investors, asset managers and Financial Institutions looking for sustainable investments. Green financing provides potential to meet these demands while adapting with changing market trends (Brown, 2015). In recent years, companies that have issued green bonds and raised billions of dollars in projects around the globe include government entities and financial institutions. In 2020, for its part Apple issued a green bond of $1.5 billion to finance projects related to the production and efficiency of renewable energy (Apple, 2020).

For nations, their central banks and financial systems empowering green financing at massive scale & impact must take these players 'out of their comfort zones' in long established ways. To share best practices and mimic the technological advancements that can scale green financing growth as fast or faster than we need to meet sustainability goals while driving increased economic output without contributing more to climate change.

There are five pillars at the heart of our future approach to green finance:

8.1 Financial Innovation and Research & Extension: Advancement of pro-climate technologies combined with enhanced opportunities to access finance that is friendly towards the environment (e.g., green bonds, sustainability - linked loans) would facilitate pioneering advancements in areas such as water management for agriculture, cleaner urban air quality through mass transportation reforms etc.), natural resource use efficiency improvement practices such large scale carbon capture storage mechanisms are just a few examples. In addition, fintech products and digital finance platforms are becoming driving forces of inclusive green investment by lowering the costs of transactions and enhancing access by small-scale investors (Tang et al., 2020). Research-informed policies that drive innovations such as green fintech and carbon credit marketplaces are also crucial to driving sustainable finance across the world (OECD, 2024).

8.2 Corporate Responsibility: With ever-increasing focus on planet-building by corporates, green finance is a means to help corporates move their operations and supply chains onto sustainable pathways thereby contributing to the cause of low-carbon economy. Firms are incorporating ESG (Environmental, Social, and Governance) metrics into investment decisions, which raises investor confidence in sustainable companies. Moreover, major multinationals are making net-zero carbon commitments by making use of sustainability-linked loans and issuing green bonds. These efforts reflect a transition to climate responsibility led by corporations that aligns financial performance with sustainable outcomes (World Bank, 2023).

8.3 Policy Climate: Product Linked Incentives and other regulatory measures that lure investment in environmentally sustainable projects will be appropriate to long term view of the policies and framework that foster green finance. Governments across the globe are bringing in tax credits for green projects, carbon pricing regimes, and obligatory climate reporting by listed companies. These initiatives ensure private sector investment keeps pace with country-level pledges under the Paris Agreement. Green projects are also less risky and hence better suited for investment due to a positive policy environment (OECD, 2024).

8.4 Global Agreements: Global agreements and partnerships based on collaborative action among member nations, central banks, civil society, inter alia are of crucial importance in addressing the financial domains of green initiatives. Efforts such as the Network for Greening the Financial System (NGFS) consolidate central banks to incorporate climate risks into monetary policy. Furthermore, multilateral climate funds and blended finance models assist in facilitating green transitions within developing economies. These frameworks establish that green finance becomes an all-encompassing global priority and not a scattered effort (NGFS, 2020, 2023).

8.5 Clear and credible information: Transparency, credibility and comparability of green finance investments rests on the adoption of sustainability standard metrics and frameworks that certify the merit of investment in this sphere. International standards like the Task Force on Climate-related Financial Disclosures (TCFD) and International Sustainability Standards Board (ISSB) standards are increasingly becoming the accepted yardsticks. Transparent reporting reduces the risk of greenwashing and generates stakeholder trust, ensuring that the funds truly make a difference to the environment. Additionally, the inclusion of third-party verification mechanisms promotes accountability within the ecosystem of green finance. (Assidi et. al., 2025).

The shift to renewables is very evident in India; solar and wind energy projects have been the recipients of hefty investments from both local and overseas financiers. This financing is enabled by green finance which offers the support to these projects. However, the emergence of green finance in India is both exciting and fraught with challenges. India does not too have much insurance penetration and these funds are risky because green projects bear even higher weight of climate risks leading to economy, public finances and the financial sector doing most of lifting. Collectively when nations, corporates, investors and policymakers come together-it is an investment that soon ensures the destiny of renewable energy projects financing in India to not only thrive but also help make a better planet while supporting sustainable economic growth.

9. RECOMMENDATIONS FOR POLICYMAKERS AND FINANCIAL INSTITUTIONS

The aforesaid discussion makes it clear that development of Green Finance in the economy is both necessary and beneficial. To make it more effective, the policymakers and financial systems can come up with a toolkit for funding schemes aimed at addressing climate concerns pointing the way forward for stakeholders in this area. Governments need to come up with sops and grants incentivising environmental friendly projects given that the political environment of a country plays a crucial role in environmental and social performance of green initiatives.

Emerging economy central banks should also make proactive climate resilience a part of monetary frameworks by introducing specific green finance targets, some of which can be addressed through long-term and affordable international public finance (including grants particularly to avoid debt dependency and fiscal exposures). Policymakers should make climate finance accessible in a timely manner through streamlined processes, effective allocation, and prioritize specific windows for climate assistance (e.g. the Loss and Damage Fund) with emphasis on expeditious disbursement and the targeting of the needs of developing countries.

Southeast Asian countries have been gradually developing resilience to such shocks, and may further enhance sustainability toolkits by setting regional green taxonomies into common place, scaling up a green bond market and aligning the collateral framework and reserve management with climate imperatives. These include: closing critical information gaps in climate data; raising transparency and mutual accountability between tribes and states and regionally and internationally to help achieve greater harmonization. (Durrani et, al., 2020).

Overall, improving liquidity, prioritising lending programs that support sustainable investments, pushing research that ascertains implications of environmental risks, soliciting international collaboration to foster sustainable investments across borders, coordinating efforts to ensure transparency of green investments; are some of the ways central banks can potentially catalyse and accelerate transition to a more climate resilient monetary and economic systems. Financial Systems need to introduce creative instruments and regulatory frameworks tailored to the needs of such projects and prioritise research and development in cleaner technologies. Lastly, collaboration among international bodies, organizations and enabling nations is essential for sharing the best practices and intensifying renewable energy solutions so as to invest in region specific training programs and manpower development to bolster insights for responsible investing (Carè, Fatima, & Boitan, 2024).

In short, financial institutions and central banks need to combine context-aware tools, accessible financing, and deep partnerships to make green finance truly effective. A crucial domain where central banks can play an active role is to classify economic activities on the basis of their environmental sustainability and adopt green taxonomy to facilitate the use of blended finance approaches rooted in Public-Private Partnerships (PPP) consequently managing systemic risks to align financial system with green policies.

10. CONCLUDING REMARKS

Several key dimensions emerged in exploring the impact of green finance. First, sustainable investments not only generate economic gains but also renders resilience to financial system of the economy and enhances long-term profitability prospects for governments and corporates alike. Green finance lays the ground work for sustainable economic growth by creating jobs and driving innovation in green technologies on one hand and bolsters economic well-being of the country by improving access to capital ventures that prioritise environmental, social and community development.

The future of green finance has the potential to transform a sustainable world economy. With climate change, depletion of resources, and environmental degradation continuing to be major issues, green finance can act as a strategic means of balancing economic development with ecological responsibility. Financial markets are now incorporating environmental, social, and governance (ESG) factors, which is an indication of a shifting paradigm towards sustainable investment strategies. This transformation is an expression of increasing awareness that long-term profitability and robustness rely on minimizing environmental risk and enhancing sustainability.

Technology advancements, especially in the area of renewable energy, clean transport, and energy efficiency, will be the driving force for increasing green finance channels. With the help of enabling regulatory systems, public-private cooperation, and global climate deals, green financing can speed up capital mobilization for large-sized infrastructure and eco-friendly development initiatives. In the future, innovative financial products like green bonds, sustainability-linked loans, and carbon credits will become conventional investment instruments.

However, the emergence or identification of new risks also triggers new opportunities for the financial system. The transition to a low-carbon economy is very capital-intensive, requiring the support of private entities, thus generating opportunities for financial services firms. Opportunities are created for portfolio investment, the application of FinTech services for green financial products and services, and artificial intelligence for data analysis and interpretation. Institutional and societal pressure may accelerate awareness of other possible disasters, which should facilitate the implementation of measures to combat climate change and awareness and acceptance of the green finance principles needed to encourage the transition to a low carbon emission economy.

Central banks may provide incentives and support mechanisms to encourage green investments and financing, such as preferential treatment for green assets, concessional financing facilities, and liquidity support for green projects. They create favorable conditions for green finance activities, aligning monetary policy objectives with environmental sustainability goals.

Looking ahead, the prospects of success of green financing initiatives hinges on strong co-operation among stakeholders, innovation in cleaner technologies and failproof regulatory frameworks. Central Banks need to integrate environmental considerations into monetary policies as much as the governments need to re-align fiscal policy objectives with growing environmental concerns. Capacity building, international cooperation, transparency and relevant disclosure mechanisms are some of the pre conditions that are capable of bringing a paradigm shift towards a financial system that safeguards environment and ensures inclusivity for all. Thus, a dynamic nexus of technological innovations, investor preferences and heightened attention towards climate- based risks is needed to expand green finance market in India.

REFERENCES

Agrawal, R., Agrawal, S., Samadhiya, A., Kumar, A., Luthra, S., & Jain, V. (2023). Adoption of green finance and green innovation for achieving circularity: An exploratory review and future directions. *Geoscience Frontiers, 101669*. Advance online publication. DOI: 10.1016/j.gsf.2023.101669

Anand, S. (2024, January 13). REC forays into Yen market with JPY 61.1 billion green bonds *ETEnergyworld.com*. https://energy.economictimes.indiatimes.com/news/power/rec-forays-into-yen-market-with-jpy-61-1-billion-green-bonds/106796345

Apple Inc. (2020). Apple issues $1.5 billion green bond. Retrieved from https://www.apple.com/newsroom/2020/09/apple-issues-1-5-billion-green-bond/

Asian Development Bank (ADB). (2018). Sustainable Infrastructure for Low-Carbon Development in India. Retrieved from https://www.adb.org/publications/sustainable-infrastructure-low-carbon-development-india

Assidi, S., Omran, M., Rana, T., & Borgi, H. (2025). Climate change and Task Force on Climate-related Financial Disclosures (TCFD) reports: A comparison between Italy and Spain. *Journal of Accounting & Organizational Change*, *21*(7), 1–28. DOI: 10.1108/JAOC-05-2024-0172

Bank for International Settlements (BIS). (2020). Green bond finance and central banks. Retrieved from https://www.bis.org/fsi/publ/insights27.htm

Bank Indonesia. (2019). Sustainable Finance Roadmap. Retrieved from https://www.bi.go.id/id/moneter/keuangan-berkelanjutan/tujuan-kebijakan/pages/rujukan-strategi-keuangan-berkelanjutan.aspx

Bank of Canada. (2021). Research on Climate-Related Stress Testing. Retrieved from https://www.bankofcanada.ca/2021/01/discussion-papers/climate-stress-testing-canadian-financial-system/

Bank of Canada (BoC). (2021). Climate-related Stress Testing. Retrieved from https://www.bankofcanada.ca/2021/01/discussion-papers/climate-stress-testing-canadian-financial-system/

Bank of England. (2021). Climate Biennial Exploratory Scenario. Retrieved from https://www.bankofengland.co.uk/climate-hub/climate-biennial-exploratory-scenario-cbes

Bank of England (BoE). (2020). Green Finance Guidelines. Retrieved from https://www.bankofengland.co.uk/prudential-regulation/green-finance

Bloomberg, N. E. F. (2022, June 29). Financing India's 2030 renewables ambition Retrieved from https://about.bnef.com/blog/financing-indias-2030-renewables-ambition/

Business Standard. (2018). SBI targets 15,000 MW solar power projects by 2022 under priority sector lending. Retrieved from https://www.business-standard.com/article/companies/sbi-targets-15-000-mw-solar-power-projects-by-2022-under-priority-sector-lending-118021300009_1.html

Carè, R., Fatima, R., & Boitan, I. A. (2024). Central banks and climate risks: Where we are and where we are going? *International Review of Economics & Finance*, *92*, 1200–1229. DOI: 10.1016/j.iref.2024.01.057

Central Bank of Brazil (BCB). (2020). Green Finance Guidelines. Retrieved from https://www.bcb.gov.br/en/financialstability/greenfinance

Central Bank of Kenya (CBK). (2021). Climate-related Stress Testing. Retrieved from https://www.centralbank.go.ke/stress-testing/

Central Bank of Nigeria (CBN). (2020). Capacity-building Program on Green Finance. Retrieved from https://www.cbn.gov.ng/Out/2020/FMD/FMD%20ED-TRG%20on%20GF.pdf

Durrani, A., Rosmin, M., & Volz, U. (2020). The Role of Central Banks in Scaling Up Sustainable Finance – What do Monetary Authorities in the Asia-Pacific Region Think? *Journal of Sustainable Finance & Investment*, *10*(2), 92–112. DOI: 10.1080/20430795.2020.1715095

Economic Times. (2017). IRFC to raise Rs 1,000 crore via first green bond issue. Retrieved from https://economictimes.indiatimes.com/industry/transportation/railways/irfc-to-raise-rs-1000-crore-via-first-green-bond-issue/articleshow/59377521.cms

Economic Times. (2019). Azure Power raises $350 million green bond. Retrieved from https://economictimes.indiatimes.com/industry/energy/power/azure-power-raises-350-million-green-bond/articleshow/68305970.cms

European Central Bank. (2016). Corporate Sector Purchase Programme. Retrieved from https://www.ecb.europa.eu/mopo/implement/omt/html/corporate_sector_purchase_programme.en.html

European Central Bank (ECB). (2021). Asset Purchase Program. Retrieved from https://www.ecb.europa.eu/mopo/implement/omt/html/index.en.html

European Commission. (2021). Sustainable Finance Action Plan. Retrieved from https://ec.europa.eu/info/publications/sustainable-finance-action-plan_en

European Investment Bank. (2022). The EIB Environment Framework. https://www.eib.org/attachments/lucalli/20220213_eib_environment_framework_en.pdf

Federal Reserve System. (2021). Supervisory Guidance on Climate Risk Management. Retrieved from https://www.federalreserve.gov/supervisionreg/srletters/sr21-8.htm

Federal Reserve System (FRS). (2020). Capacity-building Program on Green Finance. Retrieved from https://www.federalreserve.gov/supervisionreg/srletters/sr20-19.htm

Green Climate Fund (GCF). (2021). Capacity-building. Retrieved from https://www.greenclimate.fund/how-we-work/capacity-building

Indian Renewable Energy Development Agency (IREDA). (2021). Bhadla Solar Park. Retrieved from https://www.ireda.in/Home/SolarProjects

International Energy Agency (IEA). (2020). India Energy Outlook 2020. Retrieved from https://www.iea.org/reports/india-energy-outlook-2020

International Energy Agency (IEA). (2021). World Energy Outlook 2021. Retrieved from https://www.iea.org/reports/world-energy-outlook-2021

International Finance Corporation (IFC). (2021). Climate Business Department. Retrieved from https://www.ifc.org/wps/wcm/connect/industry_ext_content/ifc_external_corporate_site/industries/climate-business

International Renewable Energy Agency (IRENA). (2023) World Energy Transitions Outlook 2023. Retrieved from https://www.irena.org/Digital-Report/World-Energy-Transitions-Outlook-2023

Japan Green Bond Labeling (JGBL). (2017). Green Bond Guidelines. Retrieved from https://www.japanbond.jp/english/greenbond/guideline.html

Kemp-Benedict, E. (2012). *Green finance and investment: Mapping actors and initiatives*. Stockholm Environment Institute.

Kochi Metro Rail Limited (KMRL). (2021). About Us. Retrieved from https://www.kochimetro.org/about-us/

Kumar, J., & Majid, M. A. (2020). Renewable energy for sustainable development in India: Current status, future prospects, challenges, employment, and investment opportunities. *Energy, Sustainability and Society*, *10*(2). Advance online publication. DOI: 10.1186/s13705-019-0232-1

Liu, C., & Xiong, M. (2022). Green finance reform and corporate innovation: Evidence from China. *Finance Research Letters*, *48*, 102993. DOI: 10.1016/j.frl.2022.102993

Ministry of Mines and Energy (MME). (2021). Renewable Energy Incentive Program. Retrieved from http://www.mme.gov.br/documents/1138775/0/Programa+de+Incentivo+às+Energias+Renováveis/06754788-7409-4f9b-9f8b-1311e7bc92e4?version=1.0

Ministry of New and Renewable Energy (MNRE). (2020). National Solar Mission. Retrieved from https://mnre.gov.in/schemes/decentralized-systems/solar-off-grid-2/

Network for Greening the Financial System (NGFS). (2020). A call for action: Climate change as a source of financial risk. Retrieved from https://www.ngfs.net/en/call-action-climate-change-source-financial-risk

Network for Greening the Financial System (NGFS). (2023). *Network for Greening the Financial System: Annual Report 2023*. Retrieved from https://www.ngfs.net

OECD. (2024). *Development Co-operation Report 2024: Tackling Poverty and Inequalities through the Green Transition*. OECD Publishing., DOI: 10.1787/357b63f7-

People's Bank of China. (2016). Green Finance Guidelines. Retrieved from https://www.pbc.gov.cn/english/130919/3164453/index.html

People's Bank of China (PBOC). (2019). Implementation of Green Finance Policies. Retrieved from https://www.pbc.gov.cn/en/3687297/index.html

People's Bank of China (PBOC). (2020). Green finance guidelines. Retrieved from https://www.greenfinance.org.cn/index.php/Home/Index/englishdetail/id/357

Reserve Bank of India. (2018). Framework for Sustainable Development Goals Financing. Retrieved from https://www.rbi.org.in/Scripts/BS_PressReleaseDisplay.aspx?prid=44168

Reserve Bank of India. (2019). National Strategy for Green Banking. Retrieved from https://www.rbi.org.in/Scripts/BS_ViewBulletin.aspx?Id=17989

Reserve Bank of India. (2020). Green Finance Cell within RBI. Retrieved from https://www.rbi.org.in/Scripts/BS_PressRele

Reserve Bank of India. (2021). Guidelines on ESG Risk Management for Banks and Financial Institutions. Retrieved from https://www.rbi.org.in/Scripts/NotificationUser.aspx?Id=12006&Mode=0

Reuters. (2018). India's ReNew Power issues $475 million green bond. Retrieved from https://www.reuters.com/article/us-renew-power-bonds/indias-renew-power-issues-475-million-green-bond-idUSKBN1HN12G

SEACEN. (2024). *Green finance and central banking: Roles, perspectives and experiences of SEACEN members*. The SEACEN Centre. Retrieved from https://www.seacen.org/publications/RePEc/702001-100499-PDF

South African Reserve Bank. (2020). Climate Risk Prudential Practice Guide. Retrieved from https://www.resbank.co.za/Publications/Detail-Item-View/Pages/Publications.aspx?sarbweb=6aa80196-3909-40e8-80d3-b5f698f33564&d=Climate%20Risk%20Prudential%20Practice%20Guide&l=CLIMATE%20RISK%20PRUDENTIAL%20PRACTICE%20GUIDE&per=2020&of=0&sc=0&fl=climate%20risk%20prudential%20practice%20guide

Stern, N., Unsworth, S., Valero, A., Zenghelis, D., Rydge, J., and N. Robins (2020). *Strategy, investment, and policy for a strong and sustainable recovery: An action plan*. Centre for Economic Performance, London School of Economics and Political Science, London, July.

Suzlon Energy Limited. (2021). Wind Energy. Retrieved from https://www.suzlon.com/business/wind-energy/

Tang, D. Y., & Zhang, Y. (2020). Do shareholders benefit from green bonds? *Journal of Corporate Finance*, *61*, 101427. DOI: 10.1016/j.jcorpfin.2018.12.001

Task Force on Climate-related Financial Disclosures (TCFD). (2017). Recommendations of the Task Force on Climate-related Financial Disclosures. Retrieved from https://www.fsb-tcfd.org/publications/final-recommendations-report/

Tata Steel Limited. (2021). Sustainability. Retrieved from https://www.tatasteel.com/sustainability/

Treasury, H. M. (2019). Green Finance Strategy. Retrieved from https://assets.publishing.service.gov.uk/government/uploads/system/uploads/attachment_data/file/791618/green_finance_strategy_web.pdf

UNCTAD. (2023). *The Least Developed Countries Report 2023: The low-carbon transition and its daunting implications for structural transformation*. United Nations Conference on Trade and Development. Retrieved from https://unctad.org/system/files/official-document/ldc2023_ch4_en.pdf

United Nations Development Programme (UNDP). (2020). Sustainable Development Goals Knowledge Platform. Retrieved from https://sustainabledevelopment.un.org/

United Nations Environment Programme Finance Initiative (UNEP FI). (2021). Positive Impact Finance: From Theory to Practice. Retrieved from https://www.unepfi.org/positive-impact-finance-from-theory-to-practice

United Nations Environment Programme (UNEP). (2018). Adaptation Finance Gap Report 2018. Retrieved from https://www.unep.org/resources/adaptation-finance-gap-report-2018

World Bank. (2023). FY23 Climate-Related Financial Disclosures. https://thedocs.worldbank.org/en/doc/23a63a4bde452fe676c0843ab879405a-0340022023/original/World-Bank-FY23-Climate-Related-Financial-Disclosure.pdf

KEY TERMS AND DEFINITIONS

Green Finance: Green finance refers to financing initiatives supporting environmental sustainability like renewable energy, conservation, and climate change reduction, contributing towards a greener and more robust economy.

Financial Innovation: Financial innovation is a process of introducing new financial processes, products, or services improving access to finance, risk handling, and making the financial system more efficient and inclusive.

Climate Change: Climate change is the term used to describe long-term changes in weather and temperatures, primarily due to human activities such as the burning of fossil fuels, resulting in global environmental disturbances.

Renewable Energy: Renewable energy is derived from natural, renewable sources such as sunlight, wind, and water, providing sustainable alternatives to fossil fuels and reducing carbon emissions and pollution.

Green Bonds: Green bonds are special financial instruments for the express purpose of raising funds for green projects like clean energy, pollution prevention, sustainable agriculture, and restoring ecosystems.

Sustainability: Sustainability is to satisfy current needs without sacrificing future generations' capability to satisfy their own, finding a balance between environmental health, economic development, and social equity for long-term welfare.

Green Equity: Green equity is investments in businesses or ventures that are environmentally sustainable, investing in companies that emphasize renewable energy, conservation, and green innovations.

Green Loans: Green loans are lending specifically for projects that have definite environmental advantages, like renewable energy systems, energy efficiency improvements, or sustainable agriculture projects.

Chapter 10
The Role of Green Consumer Finance Products in Advancing Sustainable Development

Jyoti Rani
https://orcid.org/0000-0002-5577-7808
Parul University, India

Shashiranjan Kumar Yadav
Lovely Professional University, India

Bhaskar Mitra
Parul University, India

ABSTRACT

The increasing urgency of addressing climate change has spurred the rise of green consumer finance products, designed to promote sustainable consumption and investment. This chapter explores green loans, credit cards, insurance, and investment options that prioritize environmental sustainability, analyzing their drivers consumer demand, government policies, and financial institutions' roles. The benefits, including environmental impact, financial savings, and social responsibility, while acknowledging challenges such as low awareness, accessibility barriers, and cost concerns. Through case studies and best practices, the chapter showcases successful initiatives and outlines the future of green finance, emphasizing innovation and cross-sector collaboration. Aimed at policymakers, investors, and financial institutions, it provides insights into aligning financial strategies with sustainable

DOI: 10.4018/979-8-3373-1240-8.ch010

development goals to foster a greener economy. By addressing barriers and leveraging opportunities, green consumer finance can play a pivotal role in advancing global sustainability efforts.

INTRODUCTION

Sustainable development has become a global necessity due to the pressing challenges of environmental degradation, climate change and social inequality. Consumer finance with the spending it often entails has also been contributing to an environmental disaster, with overconsumption a source of growing carbon emissions and resource deficits. As a reflection of this need, green finance and green consumer finance are emerging as essential instruments to help advance financial systems towards sustainable development objectives. We aim to address at this intersection in this chapter; we explore the contribution of green finance towards sustainability and how consumer finance impacts on the environment. This dilemma opened the door to green finance, and green consumer finance in particular. Green consumer finance is financial products which is like a green loans eco-credit cards sustainable investment funds and eco-banking services which encourage consumers to act in a more sustainable manner in terms of consumption. These products can redirect capital towards environmental- friendly activities, change consumer behavior and lower the negative externalities of traditional finance by embedding sustainability principles in everyday money management decisions.

Overview of Sustainable Development and Global Urgency

- Sustainable development is development that meets the needs of the present without compromising the ability of future generations to meet their own needs. It has economic and environmental and social vectors, and that these are interdependent and necessary for sustainable and enduring prosperity (Akhtar & Rashid, 2024).
- The need for sustainable development is highlighted by a collective response to global challenges, which include climate change, biodiversity loss and resource scarcity, so there is a need to move towards more sustainable economic models (Atkisson, 2013).

Rise of Consumer Finance and Environmental Implications

- Consumer finance has grown greatly, making for greater consumption and growth. But such development is also frequently unsustainable environmentally, resulting in greater carbon footprints and resource exhaustion (D'Orazio et al., 2023).

- Today's financial system is not suitable for funding sustainable development, and it requires reformation to deal with these environmental externalities.

Emergence of Green Finance and Green Consumer Finance

- Green finance are financial contributions that support environmentally beneficial projects, like renewable energy and green infrastructure. It has the object of promoting flows of funds towards sustainable development goals, while limiting the environmental and social risks (Ali et al., 2024).
- Green consumer finance comprises financial products and services which facilitate consumer actions in favor of the environment, e.g. green loans and green investment products (Raman et al., 2025).
- Innovations in green finance, including green fintech and social impact bonds, are important for financing renewables and reducing negative impacts on the environment.

Purpose and Scope of the Chapter

The purpose of this chapter is to critically examine the role of green consumer finance products in advancing sustainable development. In doing so, it seeks to answer three central questions:

- How do green consumer finance products contribute to sustainable consumption and the achievement of Sustainable Development Goals (SDGs)?
- What are the key drivers and barriers influencing their adoption?
- What policy and market interventions are needed to scale their impact globally?

The chapter relates theory to practice and provides a thorough but concise treatment of these questions. The analysis also reflects literature review, global examples, and new initiatives in green finance to show potential and caveat. Finally, the chapter concludes by stating that green consumer finance represents a massive promise that can drive sustainability, once hurdles can be overcome—greenwashing, green consumer ignorance, broken/missing regulation, and lack of availability. In this regard, the chapter underscores that while green finance holds great potential, right reforms and cooperation are essential to ensure that green finance is a game-changer for sustainable development (Akhtar & Rashid, 2024) (Ahmed et al., 2024). Furthermore, nascent legal system and market obstacles in many places have prevented green finance to be incorporated into the mainstream, requiring sound legal system and international cooperation to resolve the above issues.

CONCEPTUAL FRAMEWORK

The theoretical framework of green consumer finance products includes a range of financial products aimed at enhancing environmental protection. These are products like green loans, green credit cards and the opportunity to invest in sustainable futures that all play a specific role in incentivising eco-friendly consumer behaviour and supporting sustainable development goals. The link between consumer behavior, finance and sustainability is rooted in theories such as stakeholder theory, behavioral economics, and ESG (Environmental, social, and governance) frameworks. These theories contribute to the understanding of consumer financial decision-making and the role financial products play on sustainable behavior.

Types of Green Consumer Finance Products

- Green Loans: Green loans support eco-friendly projects such as solar panels and energy-efficient homes. However, their uptake is often limited by higher upfront costs and the reluctance of banks to extend credit to low-income groups, raising questions about inclusivity. These are loan products provided by financial institutions to help fund projects that are environmentally friendly, like adding renewable energy systems or energy-efficient improvements to your home. Green loans tend to carry lower cost of funds and more favorable terms in order to promote sustainable actions (X. Huang et al., 2022).
- Green Credit Cards: Beyond a mere financial instrument, green credit cards also have the potential to serve as behavioral nudges facilitating sustainable consumption. These products can bring individual consumption in line with climate change targets by offering rewards in the form of carbon offsetting or giving to environmental projects. Their effectiveness, however, is contingent upon consumer knowledge and market confidence, which are both still often lacking in certain parts of the world (Brühl, 2022a).
- Sustainable Investment Options: This category includes ESG investments and green bonds, which guide capital into projects and companies that reach certain environmental and social benchmarks. Green bonds, for example, are intended to fund projects with positive environmental spillovers such as renewable energy and pollution reductions (Z. Huang et al., 2024; Mavlutova et al., 2023).

Link Between Consumer Behavior, Finance, and Sustainability

- Consumer Behavior: Consumer decision making related to green product purchase is affected by environmental concerns, social drivers, and personal values. The PSICHE model emphasizes the effects of product-related variables, social influences/references, and individual concerns on green purchase behaviors (Nascimento & Loureiro, 2024).
- Finance and Sustainability: Financial instruments (e.g. green loans, green bonds) are essential to enabling sustainable development and delivering the capital required for green innovations and projects. By including ESG factors in investment decisions, financial operations are increasingly in line with sustainable objectives (Roy, 2023).
- Theoretical Foundations: Analytically, the traditional stakeholder theory argues that financial institutions interact with a variety of stakeholders as a means of environmentally governing. Behavioral economics offers insights into the ability of financial incentives to nudge consumer behaviour towards more sustainable options (X. Huang et al., 2022) (Duque Oliva et al., 2024).

Theoretical Foundations

- Stakeholder Theory: The premise of this theory is that financial institutions must take into consideration the well-being of all of their stakeholders, not just shareholders, and the environment when making decisions regarding lending and investment. This process will contribute in building up more support for green innovations and sustainable lifestyles (X. Huang et al., 2022).
- Behavioral Economics: This is the discipline that studies how psychological factors affect economic decision making. From the perspective of green finance, an understanding of consumer behavior is vital to develop financial products that are efficient in promoting sustainable consumption.
- ESG Frameworks: ESG standards are being increasingly used to assess the sustainability and ethical impact of investment. Such instruments help financial institutions to evaluate the environmental and social performance of potential investments, effectively contributing to sustainable finance.

Despite GCFPs having an intention to encourage more sustainability, there are challenges technologically and in its practicality. Elaborated regulatory schemes and the lack of transparency in ESG reporting can obstruct moving private capital into sustainable investment. Consumer skepticism about greenwashing and potentially greater cost of green products is also a factor that can influence the consideration of such financial instruments. Regular work still needs to be done to improve the credibility and accessibility of green finance products in order to address these challenges.

DRIVERS OF GREEN CONSUMER FINANCE

Drivers of green consumer finance are diverse, including consumer interest, regulatory encouragement, corporate responsibility and technological progress. These combined factors create an environment that is conducive to fiscal sustainability. Consumer demand is essential and by motivating, driving market and increasing green products. Regulations such as the EU Taxonomy offer some direction for green finance. The CSR and financial innovation also push the sector by integrating business practices with environmental aims. Technology development, fintech especially, is highly vital in terms of making green finance more available and efficient. These drivers are considered in more detail in the following sections.

Consumer Demand and Environmental Awareness

- As consumers up the ante on the climate change, resource scarcity awareness, they've come even more keenly interested in sustainable products. Whatsoever the nature, especially a younger one, likes for its products to match their values, from green loans to ESG investing (Ledo et al., 2020; Testa et al., 2021); however, such acceptance may not be expressed in actual purchases and consumptions because of a number of obstacles (Testa et al., 2021).
- Behavioral determinants, socio demographic characteristics and personal values have significant impact on green consumption behavior.
- The growing environmental awareness is an important driver for increasing the need for sustainable financial products, thereby pressuring financial institution to generate and supply green finance products (Ali et al., 2024).

Regulatory and Policy Support

- Regulation is key to standardizing and promoting green finance by providing clear guidance and criteria for sustainable investment, such as the EU Taxonomy.
- Governments and institutions have launched standards like the EU Taxonomy and Paris Agreement to harmonize sustainability measures. These offer criteria to classify green investments and make them transparent to investors (Zhang et al., 2022).

- In China, environmental regulations have been known to drive regional green innovation, particularly in combination with fintech solutions.

Corporate Social Responsibility and Financial Innovation

- The corporate world has made CSR an integral part of business strategy, and financial institutions are testing the water with cutting-edge products such as green bonds, climate-linked loans and ESG funds. This supports business expansion while aligning it with environmental goals, sending a clear message to consumers that companies are serious about sustainability (Chen, 2024).
- Economic restructuring like green financial products, such as green bonds and climate finance, finance and underpin the transition to a sustainable economy (Ali et al., 2024).
- The collaborative relations between the fintech and green finance are significant to meet the goals of carbon neutrality by exemplifying the case of Australia (Anwar et al., 2024).

Technological Advancements

- Fintech has been touted as crucial to broadening the reach to GCF. Green finance is becoming more easily accessible, more efficient, more transparent, using digital platforms, mobile banking and Blockchain tools (Chueca Vergara & Ferruz Agudo, 2021). Carbon-tracking apps and other technologies also give consumers the power to track their footprints and change behavior accordingly.
- Digital platforms enable the consolidation of green finance to the conventional financial system, and make it more accessible the general populace and enterprises (Hossain et al., 2024).
- Technological innovation, including digital finance can exert a positive influence on green innovation, especially in countries with low level of green innovation.

But there are still challenges, despite the strength of the green consumer finance drivers. Complex regulatory regimes also have the potential to make the mobilization of private capital into sustainable investments more difficult, which indicates that a simplified green rating could support investors. Second, fintech and environmental regulations may contribute to green innovation, but their impacts may differ widely in different regions and for different types of innovation. These all point to the importance of adaptation and cooperation among the relevant parties so that green financial initiatives have the desired impact.

Role of fintech in expanding access and impact

FinTech is core in unlocking financial services and enabling sustainability. Through the use of digital tools and platforms, FinTech promotes financial inclusion, facilitates sustainable business and supports environmentally-sustainable operations. As explained in several research, inclusive FinTech integration in a number of industries have the potential to accelerate sustainable development. This response discusses the multiple dimensions of FinTech's role in deepening access and its implications for sustainability, in light of the research papers provided.

Enhancing Financial Accessibility and Inclusion

- FinTech is a game-changer in providing access to finance, which is key to the sustainability of businesses. FinTech is also supposed to have positive effects on the credit availability in Indian apparel industry, which result in the sustainable future of the firms (Sreenu, 2024).
- FinTech makes financial services more available to a larger population; such services are no longer completely reliant on banking systems. Mobile channels allow for access to green loans, micro-investments, or digital savings products, particularly by individuals and small businesses in emerging markets. For instance, in Bangladesh FinTech is believed to lead to enhanced credit availability for SMEs, promoting circular economy practice (Siddik et al., 2023).
- The concept of FinTech's existence in the market is emphasized on its provision of digital financial services in combatting poverty, income inequality and fostering economic development (Afjal, 2023).

Promoting Environmental Sustainability

- FinTech contributes to the environment by integrating sustainability into financial instruments. Examples include apps that monitor carbon footprints, sites that sell green loans with lower interest rates and carbon trading systems on blockchains. In China, research reveals that the FinTech factor has greatly reduced urban carbon emissions (Li et al., 2025).
- Green FinTech promotes investments in renewable energy and gives financial incentives such as discounts on interest rates for environmentally friendly behavior. It is sustainable, protects the environment and offers financial inclusion for small size businesses and startups too (Aboalsamh et al., 2023).

- FinTech credit is also instrumental in monitoring and minimizing corporate greenwashing, that will in turn enhance green urban development (Pata et al., 2024).

Supporting Sustainable Business Practices

- FinTech supports businesses in aligning themselves with sustainability by providing tools for impact assessment, green investment and ESG reporting. Startups in both Europe and North America, like Clarity AI, have introduced platforms for tracking greenwashing and measuring the true sustainability impact of financial products. FinTech enrolment enhances organizational ecological performance through enabling circular economy operations. This is done through increased financial access and strengthened absorptive capacity that act as a mediation mechanism in the relationship of FinTech adoption and sustainability performance (Siddik et al., 2023).
- In sustainable finance, FinTech can contribute to reshaping and (re-)distributing financial services and consequently give brown companies the necessary support to protect the environment. This reallocation is particularly potent under competitive banking (Zhou & Wang, 2024).

Challenges and Considerations

Market risk It is more difficult to assign risk to the segment than it is to the asset-based lending sub-sector, since growth companies are inherently riskier to invest in and there is little history or data in the area of green consumer finance. Fast growth without vigilant supervision can leave consumers vulnerable to fraud, data breaches or exploitation. Finally, varying regulatory environment also means that FinTech-enabled sustainability solutions can be flourishing in some parts of the world and struggling in other. For example, despite the fact that Switzerland and EU have harmonized their fintech regulation with their sustainability policy, developing countries do not have the regulatory capability to ensure that consumers are protected. While FinTech has a lot to give to the sustainability, there are indeed challenges and issues to be discussed. Regulatory mandates may prevent the widespread spread of green FinTech solutions; therefore, regulatory policies are needed to encourage innovation while protecting consumers. Furthermore, the explosive expansion of FinTech requires close watch not to get side swiped by potential side effects on financial and energy markets (Dunbar et al., 2024). In addition, the influence of FinTech on sustainable development may differ greatly from region to region, as reflected by the regional differences in China. In summary, FinTech is a key enabler of financial inclusion and sustainable development. Through increased financial inclusion, sustainable business support and environmental sustainability, FinTech can also be a force for significant good. Yet, confronting regulatory hurdles and equitable dissemination across regions are critical to optimising its effects.

Regulatory and Policy Support

International agreements, including the EU Taxonomy and Paris Agreement, are influential in the development of green consumer finance, reflecting the value of setting standards and improving transparency and incentives for sustainable investments. Agreements like these establish the building blocks that lead financial markets in the direction of environmental sustainability and ultimately influence consumer habits and corporate decision making. In particular, the Paris Agreement has been helping to raise environmental awareness worldwide, which in turn will influence consumer preferences and eco-investment tendency. The EU Taxonomy goes a step further in this direction with a precision classification of sustainable activities and thus contributes to limit greenwashing and to ensure that investors' incentives are consistent with sustainability objectives. Following are some key points of how these treaties influence green consumer finance.

Impact of the Paris Agreement

- Consumer Awareness and Investment: The Paris Agreement has greatly increased consumer awareness of environmental issues and reduced demand for products from companies that have low environmental rankings. Such changing consumption patterns have compelled companies to enhance their environmental performance in order to stay competitive (Chang et al., 2024).
- Investor Confidence and Sovereign Bonds: Sovereign bond yields are lower for countries that have ratified the Paris Agreement, since investors value taking action to reduce greenhouse gas emissions. This monetary reward motivates countries to comply with the climate agreements and create a cooperative international environment for climate actions. Raising environmental consciousness has made consumers and investors more aware that the global economy must shift to low-carbon. Sovereign bonds from countries that approved the agreement have been enjoying higher investor confidence, which points to the monetary value of climate conformity (Saxena & Singh, 2024). In the same vein, the EU Taxonomy introduces an exhaustive classification system for sustainable economic activities and establishes a shared understanding for green finance.

Role of the EU Taxonomy

- Standardization and Transparency: The EU Taxonomy offers a comprehensive system for classifying environmentally sustainable activities, and helps to ensure the standardization of disclosures and minimization of greenwashing. This visibility is essential for the behaviour of institutional investors to be made consistent with the sustainability wishes of their beneficiaries (Pacces, 2021).
- Facilitating Sustainable Investments: The EU Taxonomy provides a transparent and detailed classification system of sustainable activities, helping companies determine whether economic activities are environmentally sustainable in all market sectors, informing investors and the public. This has the potential to increase private capital in sustainable investment however the framework may complicate the mobilization of such a capital (Zetzsche et al., 2022).

Integration with Trade and Finance

- One advantage of regulatory frameworks is their potential to fight greenwashing through mandates for consistent reporting and impact measurement. Clarity is provided to a certain extent by the EU Taxonomy, which has mostly defined what constitute as sustainable activities and discouraged greenwashing. Trade Agreements and Climate Governance: The EU has made Paris Agreement commitments an integral part of its trade agreements, rendering them binding under law. Such coupling serves to weaponize the cost of exit of the Paris Agreement and to reinforce procedural obligations and climate pledges – raising the bar for climate governance (Bertram & Van Coppenolle, 2024).
- Green Bonds and Sustainable Development: Green bonds, following in line with the Paris Agreement and Sustainable Development Goals, have become increasingly popular for financing projects that mitigate carbon emissions and encourage renewable energy. These bonds appeal to institutional and social responsible investors and are furthering development of sustainable finance markets (Tolliver et al., 2019a).

Although the Paris Agreement and the EU Taxonomy are major advances made in green consumer finance through international cooperation, there are still challenges. The regulatory burden can also put some firms off fully engaging with such regulation and the potential for increased costs. Also, the impact of these agreements in leveraging the private capital for sustainable investments is under debate as the existing regulatory framework might not prove to be strong enough to ensure the needed investment volume (Brühl, 2022b). However, these are significant contracts linking global financial systems to sustainability objectives and thus promoting environmental considerations for both nations and businesses in their financial planning.

CATEGORIES OF GREEN CONSUMER FINANCE PRODUCTS

Green consumer finance products encourage environmentally benign effects of consumer behavior by using financial incentives to stimulate green consumer behavior. These are green loans, green credit cards, green investment funds, eco-banking products. Every category plays its own part in motivating people to buy and invest in sustainable projects, playing a roll in the shift towards the save the environment and sustainability category. The various types are then discussed in terms of their characteristics and effects.

Green Loans

- Green loans fund environmentally friendly projects like solar panels, electric cars or energy-efficient retrofits for homes. They offer below-market interest rates or advantageous terms in a bid to drive the adoption of sustainable consumer behaviors. Green loans are financial products designed to finance environmentally conscious projects like solar panels, electric cars and energy-efficient home upgrades. A portion of these loans is provided by banks who commit to the Equator Principles for banks them to assure the financed schemes satisfy certain environment and social norms (X. Huang et al., 2022).
- Green loans in China significantly foster green innovations, especially in industries with high levels of pollution and market competition. This is accomplished through the reduction of financial frictions and the acceptance of strict monitoring of corporate finance projects.

Green Credit Cards

- Green credit cards entitle you to cashback on eco-friendly purchases, and participation in carbon offset programs. These cards motivate members of the public as they shop to make more environmentally friendly choices by paying them to act in a sustainable way.
- Such solutions encourage customers to spend responsibly by providing incentives such as cash-back for green sustainable shopping, adding carbon-

offset contributions or donations to ecologically oriented charitable institutions (Brühl, 2022a). All of these serve as behavioral nudges that drive up everyday consumption toward sustainability. There is limited research on green credit cards, but green finance more broadly indicates that this type of products may contribute to promoting sustainable behavior, by aligning financial incentives with environmental objectives (Brühl, 2022a). While novel, green credit cards typically attract only those who are already environmentally aware. They are not widely accepted yet, especially in the developing world, as people are not fully aware and are doubtful about their true environmental benefit. Furthermore, without standardised reporting, there's a danger that green credit cards act as advertising, not actual sustainability workhorse. And so their disruptive potential remains chained to customer confidence and market credibility.

Green Investment Funds

- Sustainable investment tools such as ESG funds and green bonds direct capital towards projects that are beneficial environmentally and socially, for example renewable energy, pollution mitigation and sustainable infrastructure. Green investment funds, such as ESG mutual funds and green bonds, are intended to direct investments to sustainable, projects. This type of funds are used more and more frequently by investors who desire to adjust their portfolio to ESG (environmental, social, governance) criteria (Popescu et al., 2024) (Roy, 2023). These instruments have been successful in leveraging such large-scale investment for sustainability. For example, green bonds have helped to fund renewable energy projects throughout Europe and Asia. But worries about greenwashing remain, as some issuers overstate the environmental credentials of their bonds to lure buyers. In addition, ESG ratings are not consistent across the world, which causes confusion and undermines investor trust. These resources of development funds are instrumental to the advancement of Sustainable Development Goals (SDGs), and the accountability structure on these funds highly rely on transparency of reporting and international standardization.
- For all the hand-wringing over greenwashing, sustainable investment funds have delivered outperformance on conventional funds in some impact categories, albeit with trade-offs. Green bonds, in particular, have served as a catalyst to green innovation and carbon emission reductions towards supporting the Sustainable Development Goals (SDGs) (Tolliver et al., 2019b) (Alamgir & Cheng, 2023).

Eco-Banking Products

- Eco-banking features green savings accounts, mobile apps with carbon tracking, and digital banking services where you more easily can become more climate-smart with your money. These services enable people to keep an eye on their carbon footprint as they juggle personal finances. Eco-banking offerings feature sustainable savings accounts and digital banking that comes with carbon tracking capabilities. These products have been designed to help consumers track and minimize their carbon footprint while managing their money. Eco-banking is a growing trend, especially in Europe where banks have begun incorporating carbon calculators into mobile apps. Yet, uptake in non-advanced economies is hampered by digital infrastructure shortcomings and weak consumer awareness. Besides, if as long as they don't come with actual motivations (e.g. discounts or payments) that motivate users to really use them, users don't actually use them at all. With this, the effect of eco-banking is mostly symbolic, rather than transformational in many cases.
- Eco-banking products are part of a larger trend in the financial industry to facilitate the green transformation of the economy. Regulations and the standardization of indicators are still bottlenecks in the mobilization of private capital for sustainable investments (Brühl, 2022a).

Green consumer finance products have potential to provide avenues to promote sustainability, however there are challenges including greenwashing and complexity in regulation. The value of these products will also depend upon transparent reporting and good impact assessments: we need to make sure that these products really do help deliver on environmental goals. Furthermore, the price and availability of green financial products could impact the uptake of consumers and investors. As the green finance space continues to develop, further research and policy formulation will be also important in overcoming these challenges and ensuring the efficacy of green consumer finance.

IMPACT ON SUSTAINABLE DEVELOPMENT GOALS (SDGS)

The SDGs are a call to action to end poverty, protect the planet and ensure peace and prosperity for all. Among them, SDG 7 (Affordable and Clean Energy), SDG 11 (Sustainable Cities and Communities), SDG 12 (Responsible Consumption and Production) and SDG 13 (Climate Action) are closely interrelated, where energy transformation acts as a driver for their attainment. Different case studies and indicators have been used to assess potential synergies and conflicts in reaching the goals.

SDG 7: Affordable and Clean Energy

Green loans and funds provide financing for energy efficiency and renewable energy technology on a household level, such as solar panels, electric cars and smart energy grids. Such efforts will mean less reliance on finite fossil fuels and speed the cleaner future. The ability of GCF to make progress toward SDG 7 is profoundly contextual. Subsidies and concessional loan terms have been effective in promoting renewable uptake in high-income nations. But participants are held back in emerging markets by the high cost of entry and a lack of credit. This opens another can of worms in that green finance will further exacerbate inequality if it predominantly serves rich households and the poor still depends on old energy sources.

- Positive Energy Districts (PEDs) are a potential way to SDG 7 by not only generating renewable surplus energy that can be transferred, in a form of shared economy, to low-income houses to alleviate energy poverty (and inspire social equity) (Cellura et al., 2025).
- CSP systems directly contribute to SDG7 by being an environmentally sustainable source of energy, the combination of CSP technologies with other renewable energy sources can have large crossover impacts, through hybridization of CSP technology for achieving higher efficiency and performance benefits (Yousef et al., 2024).
- Sustainable energy system approaches by European citizen-led energy initiatives are stimulating resource conservation and social resilience and thereby contributing to SDG 7 (Schwanitz et al., 2024).

SDG 11: Sustainable Cities and Communities

Eco-banking and green bonds fund urban sustainability projects, which include energy-conscious housing, sustainable transportation and smart infrastructure. Consumer-facing platforms such as those in the FinTech sector allowing citizens to monitor their carbon footprints Thereby changing behaviour at a city level. As GCF contributes to greener urban development, it also raises issues of equity. "The smart city projects driven by green bonds are often not developed in rural areas but in cities". Economic costs of implementation also may be high as they could be translated into higher housing prices with all attendant affordability consequences. Therefore, note that although the GCF mission is to enhance sustainable cities,its positive effects may not be equitably shared among urban and rural communities.

- Smart city technologies can contribute to the achievement of SDG 11 through enhancing efficiency of cities, stimulating innovation, and increasing citizen

awareness. But there are some challenges that should be well addressed such as privacy issues and infrastructure costs (Sharifi et al., 2024).
- European Energy Communities are advancing energy democracy by involving citizens and protection of the landscape and cultural heritage in cities (Schwanitz et al., 2024).

SDG 12: Responsible Consumption and Production

Green credit cards, eco-banking services and ESG investment funds are designed to nudge consumers towards more sustainable consumption and reward environmentally-friendly corporations. These products aim to curb unsustainable consumption behaviours by associating incentives (e.g. rewards or lower fees) with environmentally more friendly practices. Despite their potential, these products are confronted with the attitude–behavior gap as consumers can have pro-environmental attitudes but still engage in unsustainable consumption due to convenience, price, or disbelief in impact claims. Furthermore, in the absence of clear and strict reporting guidelines, companies can overstate their sustainability accomplishments, eroding the confidence of the consumer. As such, the GCF contribution to SDG 12 is substantial (even if precarious), hinging on credibility and consumer buy-in.

- Transnational climate policies often respond to SDG 12 by encouraging responsible consumption and production patterns, and filling the governance gaps that states performance has left unclosed (Coenen et al., 2022).
- The adoption of smart city solutions can help to foster responsible consumption through better resource use and lower waste, if trade-offs such as the digital divide are addressed (Sharifi et al., 2024).

SDG 13: Climate Action

By channeling capital into low-carbon technologies and incentivizing eco-friendly consumption, GCF directly supports climate action efforts. Green bonds and ESG funds, in particular, have mobilized significant investment for renewable energy, pollution reduction, and climate resilience projects. Although GCF strengthens climate financing, it is not a substitute for systemic reforms. The persistence of fossil fuel subsidies and lobbying undermines the impact of green finance, creating policy contradictions. Furthermore, without global coordination, carbon-intensive industries may simply shift operations to regions with weaker regulation ("carbon leakage"). Thus, GCF contributes to SDG 13 but cannot achieve climate goals alone—it must complement broader policy measures.

- Energy transitions are fundamental to SDG 13, and different prognoses from across the world differ by level of development. Radical transition scenarios are significant for fulfilling climate action targets (Ruan et al., 2024).
- Solar PV power plants have a major impact on SDG 13 by reducing the emission of greenhouse gases and reliance on fossil fuels in relation to climate action (Nooman AlMallahi et al., 2024).
- The interlinkages between SDG 13 and other goals support the notion of holistic approaches to climate action, and underscore the relevance for synergies between relevant goals (Filho et al., 2023).

Although such policy actions and technology components hold promise to provide thrust to the SDGs, realistic catch remains. For example, the focus of energy transition policies have been proven to be insufficient for the realisation of SDGs 7 and 13, which means they require an overarching approach that involves all sectors (Ruan et al., 2024). Furthermore, the trade-offs involved in the deployment of smart city solutions need to be addressed in a way that any negative outcome, including privacy intrusion and negative social bias, the solution may bring about can be eaten up in favour of sustainable development (Sharifi et al., 2024). Overcoming these obstacles will be essential for maximizing the impact of these efforts on the SDGs.

CHALLENGES AND BARRIERS

The obstacles and issues with the archivable of true sustainability in conventional consumer markets are numerous, greenwashing, lack of standardization, low consumer awareness, market fragmentation and lack of insight to sustainability impact etc. These barriers slow down the change towards sustainable choices and items, and it is at the level of both consumer attitudes and corporate strategies. These barriers are discussed in the next sections on the basis of the provided research papers.

Greenwashing and Lack of Standardization

One of the biggest impediments, though, is the potential for greenwashing, which is when financial products are branded as "green" but fail to provide any measurable sustainability benefit. Such a practice would be harmful to consumers' confidence and not incentivise participation in GCF. Despite regulatory efforts like the EU Taxonomy, greenwashing is still rampant because disclosure mandates are still inconsistent amongst countries. Banks might greenwash sustainable claims to draw investors as they go about unsustainable business as usual elsewhere. Without strict global standards, green finance risks just ending up as a branding issue, rather than a real sustainability tool.

- Greenwashing, when companies inaccurately promote their products as environmentally safe, is a major obstacle. It confuses consumers and erodes trust in actually sustainable products. This practice is widespread across sectors, such as in the fossil fuel industry, in which the term greenwashing is used to ensure a good public image while still acting environmentally destructive (Inês et al., 2023) (Makhoul et al., 2024).
- No consistent sustainability metrics and reporting adopts a greenwashing syndrome. Many organizations follow their own approach in sustainability reporting, leading to incongruent and non-comparable data. This lack of standardization imposes barriers for consumers to recognize sustainable production in contrast to non-sustainable production (Gonçalves & Silva, 2021).

Limited Consumer Awareness and Financial Literacy

A lack of commonly-agreed definitions of what constitutes "green" leads to inconsistency in product labelling. There's also wide variation in ESG ratings offered by providers, confusing investors and consumers alike. Lack of a unified metrics specification makes it impossible to compare and reduces the credibility of GCF. For example, one rating agency might give the same company a "highly sustainable" rating, while another might give that company a "moderate" score, leading to confusion. Smaller companies also struggle with the cost and complexity of reporting requirements intended for large companies. This is an impediment to inclusiveness and participation, especially from SMEs. There are still many consumers who don't know about or who are suspicious of GCF goods. Even if informed, the attitude-behavior gap frequently hinders consumers in making sustainable financial decisions. Awareness campaigns have sparked interest in green finance, particularly among younger generations, but it has failed to take off as sustainable products are usually more expensive. Without focused education and monetary incentives consumers may not show a real shift in behavior despite awareness being raised. This problem is particularly acute in less developed countries with lower levels of financial education.

- Most consumers don't know about sustainability concerns, packaging requirements and can't discern the difference between products that are really sustainable or 'greenwashed.' This ignorance is further fueled by a poor financial education impacting how people consider buying things.

- Education programs are required to increase consumer awareness of sustainability labels and environmental costs of their consumption. Without this information consumers are at risk of misleading marketing.

Market Fragmentation and Product Accessibility

It is known that GCF products tend to be highly "clustered" in developed territories, while lagging in LIDCs. In most countries, the access is confined to the middle-income and high-income groups. The price of green loans, the higher fees on sustainable investment funds and the dependence on digital platforms are all barriers for those without an income or without internet access. This exacerbates inequality as the rich can avail themselves of incentive to be sustainable, whereas the poorest groups must continue to rely on unsustainable consumption. Without intervention, GCF could exacerbate social and economic divisions.

- The sustainable-products market is fragmented, and consumers' access to it is limited. This phenomena arises because of the absence of integrated supply chain strategies and the complexity in the value chain that might demotivate firms from the sustainable efforts (Boz et al., 2020).
- Sustainable products are usually more expensive, putting them out of reach for much of the market. This price gap restricts the availability of sustainable products in the market.

Measuring Actual Sustainability Impact

So, there are policies on the books, but enforcement is spotty at best. The powerplay, inexperienced institutions and lack of international co-ordination are long-term threats to GCF market stability. For instance, the EU may have established effective regulations, but in many developing countries the institutional mechanisms to ensure compliance with sustainability standards do not exist. Add the political cycles to that complexity – because governments may prioritize other things over sustainability. This sort of (regulatory) uncertainty dampens investment and stunts the expansion of GCF.

- It is difficult to calculate and quantify the impact on sustainability of products because of the complexity of the life cycle assessments and the diversity of methodologies applied. This complexity makes it complex to develop benchmarks and compare products in an effective manner (Gonçalves & Silva, 2021).

- Lack of robust metrics and key performance indicators "(KPIs)" on sustainability deter companies from disclosing transparent environmental performance. This opaqueness breeds mistrust amongst customers and partners.

These are serious issues, but they are being addressed. For example regularising sustainability reporting frameworks and certification programmes help in reducing greenwashing and achieving transparency. Also, developing customer knowledge and understanding might help empower people to make better decisions, which will help demand for truly sustainable products incentivize change. But it is incumbent upon both policy makers and businesses, as well as consumers, to work together in improving the market transparency and its sustainability.

CASE STUDIES AND GLOBAL BEST PRACTICES

The combination of fintech and green finance is being recognized as a key tool to advance sustainable development in many regions, such as Europe, Asia, and North America. These are areas in which fintech is already having considerable success and which highlight its potential to scale green finance, especially in the context of emerging economies, where technology can help to increase financial access and sustainability. Public-private partnerships are equally essential for the development of green consumer products, leveraging resources and know-how of both sectors to advance innovation and uptake. This response considers country cases, best practices, the contribution of fintech (financial technology) to green finance initiatives in developing countries and the role of public–private partnership in the development of green consumer products.

Case Studies and Global Best Practices

- Europe: Switzerland has led the way with green fintech innovation, home to many start-ups in sustainable finance services. This matters because from customer-tocustomer to businessto-business service businesses to the firm value chain, experimentation on green fintech across the financial value chain has been wide and the impact has been significant (Puschmann et al., 2020). witzerland has become a center for sustainable FinTech startups, bringing a new generation of digital platforms which enable consumers to measure their carbon footprint, invest in ESG funds, and track the sustainability of their portfolio. The country's robust regulatory framework, transparent financial culture and high penetration digital landscape has laid the fertile ground for green consumer finance innovation. The Swiss example is proof of the strength of leveraging technology and financial institutions' trust. However, its success is context-dependent. The high degree of financial literacy, the strength of institutions and consumers' trust in them are not often to be found in the emerging economies, which are still distrustful of their financial institutions. And so, as we have seen, even though Switzerland presents a best practice model, it may not be applicable into countries with poor governance or those which have low digital adoption.

- Asia: The implementation of Turkey fintech has improved the financial inclusion rate, especially for the underbanked people and small businesses. The nation has harnessed fintech to stimulate responsible consumption and contribute to sustainable development goals through enhancements in payment systems and educational content (Bayram et al., 2022). In Turkey, the central bank has taken measures to promote the incorporation of green financial systems into the banking system by adopting practices to integrate sustainability into lending operations. A few commercial banks offer environmentally friendly (green) loan products for small businesses towards energy efficiency and renewables. The case of Turkey demonstrates how the expansion of GCF requires support for GCF at the policy level. But regulatory turbulence and macroeconomic turbulence reduce long-term efficacy. Continuous policy flip-flops keep investors on tenterhooks and diminish consumer confidence in green products. Turkey shows that mere regulatory intentions are not enough without a stable institutional environment in the long run.
- North America: In the United States, a growing trend is the emergence of fintechs with a focus on sustainability, such as Clarity AI and Pensumo, which seek to enhance transparency and the identification of greenwashing in financial products (Chueca Vergara & Ferruz Agudo, 2021). In the US, platforms that track the real sustainability impact of financial products such as Clarity AI and Aspiration are gaining traction. The tools tackle greenwashing and enable investors to match investments to personal values. The experience of the US indicates how private sector innovation can enforce accountability in GCF. But an excessive reliance on market-led responses threatens to shut out consumers who lack adequate financial literacy or access to digital means. Furthermore, without federal-level regulation, these platforms are fragmented and are only reaching eco- and techno-savvy consumers.

Fintech Solutions for Green Finance in Developing Countries

- Boosting Green Innovation: Green finance can effectively promote the number of green patent applications in developing countries, which is an important factor in the promotion of green development. The former is more obvious in the country with poor environmental performance, and the influence of green finance is more significant (Yang, 2024) (Ma & Chang, 2023).

- Role of Fintech: In emerging markets, new financial technology (Fintech) solutions have played a significant role in advancing sustainable finance through innovative financial products and services. For example, in the BRICS countries, fintech and green finance have been unveiled to be central tools to support environmental sustainability and reach carbon neutrality targets (Udeagha & Muchapondwa, 2023).

Public-Private Partnerships in Promoting Green Consumer Products

- Blended Finance: A combination of public, philanthropic and private capital, blended finance has the potential to scale green consumer product investments. This, in turn, breaks the investment gridlock and facilitates movement towards the SDGs.
- Collaborative Efforts: It is understood how joint efforts of the public and private sectors help in the creation and distribution of green consumer products by combining knowledge and resources together. It is this kind of partnership that is required so that the green industry can get the support it needs to innovate and be implemented.
- Although fintech and green finance actions appear promising, efforts are still required to ensure uptake and effects at scale. Fintech solutions may encounter difficulties being rolled out as a result of regulatory issues, especially in emerging markets. Furthermore, the threat of greenwashing and misleading practices in financial markets justify stringent regulatory frameworks to shield consumers and provide transparency (Kwong et al., 2023) (Chueca Vergara & Ferruz Agudo, 2021). Yet despite these obstacles, the enduring partnership between governments and the private sector, as well as innovations in fintech, can pave a way forward for ambitious green finance and sustainable development around the world.

POLICY RECOMMENDATIONS AND STRATEGIC INTERVENTIONS

Encouraging green financial products and sustainable finance is so multi - dimensional that it must be done simultaneously through tax incentives, transparency, consumer education, and the policy guidance of the central banks as well as international financial organizations. These are essential factors in promoting a financial system that is friendly to the environment and combats climate change. The next sections elaborate on these factors, referring to the included papers for more community-based research.

Incentivizing Green Financial Products

- Tax Benefits and Subsidies: Providing tax benefits and subsidy may largely attract investment in green finance products. These financial subsidies can reduce the capital cost of green projects, thus stimulating investors' investment interests. For example, central banks can offer preferential interest rates and subsidies to stimulate investments in green bonds and renewable energy projects.
- Green Bonds and Loans: Financial institutions are increasingly tapping green bonds and sustainability-linked loans to finance eco-friendly projects. Green bonds recycle markets capital for green projects and returns for the investors, respectively aligning both the market and environmental objectives (Aumbur Kwaghter Sule et al., 2024).

Promoting Transparency and Standardization

- Standardization of Green Finance: It is crucial to have clear definitions and standards for what makes a financial product "green." This has entailed the creation of: a green finance taxonomy, with associated disclosure obligations to make the taxonomy actionable, and to avoid greenwashing (Brühl, 2022a).
- Regulatory Frameworks: Sound regulation can increase the credibility of green finance. This includes providing guidelines for disclosure, and reporting to enable investors to make informed decisions, and to facilitate the flow of private capital in green investments.

Enhancing Consumer Education and Trust

- Public Awareness Campaigns: Promoting and raising awareness of the benefits of green finance will be critical to its successful promotion and investment. Education programs can enable consumers to make informed decisions about green financial products, thereby building trust and engagement.
- Simplified Green Ratings: In order to help consumers to compare green financial products, simplified green ratings can be established using taxonomy ratios. This would make it easier for investors to recognize truly sustainable products.

Role of Central Banks and International Financial Institutions

- Central Banks' Influence: Central banks are crucial drivers of green finance as they are integrating sustainability into their monetary policy and prudential regulation. They have the ability to encourage financial institutions to adopt green measures through climate risk assessment and sustainable investment approaches (Faruq & Huq, 2024).
- International Cooperation: There's a crucial need to bring the world's central banks, governments, and international financial institutions together – if we're to have financial systems that are compatible with the goals of sustainability. This involves sharing best practices and planning how to overcome obstacles to green financing.

Although these measures provide a holistic structure for the development of green finance, there are still shortcomings. Complicated legal regimes and the temptation to greenwash can be obstacles. Further, investments by the private sector are needed on a large scale for the transition to a sustainable financial system, but may be hindered by information asymmetry and insufficient analytic ability (Brühl, 2022a). Overcoming these challenges requires sectoral and cross-border cooperation to make financial systems resilient and supportive of global sustainability objectives.

FUTURE OUTLOOK

The prospects of green finance are also closely connected with the development of artificial intelligence (AI), blockchain and digital identity technologies. These advances are key to increasing efficiency, transparency and access to sustainable financial products and services. AI, for example is shaking up risk assessment and investment strategies and blockchain is guaranteeing trust in transactions. Secure and inclusive access to financial services is promoted by digital identity systems. Trends in sustainable consumer behavior and innovative opportunities in designing products are also driving the green finance space. These are indeed developments important to meet the sustainable development goals and promote resilient financial ecosystem.

Role of AI, Blockchain, and Digital Identity in Green Finance

Artificial Intelligence (AI):

- AI can play a crucial role in enhancing risk assessment, and supporting the identification of green finance investment options. They met development of far-reaching accuracy and can facilitate better allocation and decisions which are consistent with the goals of sustainability (Shajar et al., 2024) (Ikechukwu Obinyeluaku et al., 2023).
- Tools based on AI are an imperative for predicting and creating new financial instruments in support of green norms and bonds of sustainable investment.

Blockchain Technology:

- Blockchain can increase the transparency and accountability of financial transactions, a critical issue for sustainable finance. It promotes the democratization of green investment access and enhances ESG reporting(Hasan et al., 2024).
- The technology is also used in carbon trading and funding for renewable energy, encouraging inclusion and sustainability.

Digital Identity:

- For increasing the participation in green finance, due to green bonds representing higher risk and rewarding rates than traditional bonds -Particularly, for foreign investors Information on environmental, social and corporate governance (Saeedi & Ashraf, 2024).
- These systems assist in addressing concerns with respect to data privacy and regulatory compliance, thus enabling a more inclusive financial system (Ramadugu et al., 2022).

Emerging Trends in Sustainable Consumer Behavior

Conscious Consumerism:

- Compliance with ethical values among consumers is increasing, for example, consumers have been practicing green budgeting and making green investments (Wen et al., 2024).
- Green financial products, such as environmentally friendly credit cards and green loans, encourage sustainable behavior and stimulate investment in green sectors.

Technological Adoption:

- Technology-focused consumers are using new innovations such as IoT and virtual/augmented reality to help them make wise decisions on sustainable finance.
- These technologies aid the transparency and efficiency of sustainable finance, making eco-conscious financial services more accessible to a larger demographic of consumers.

Opportunities for Innovation in Financial Product Design

Innovative Financial Products:

- The combination of AI and blockchain can be useful in designing financial products which in turn will help in generating novel green financial products like sustainable policies of insurance and green bonds (Saeedi & Ashraf, 2024).
- FinTech is breaking down barriers to entry for new financial products that meet the demand for environmental products, for example renewable energy crowdfunding and ESG risk assessment tools.

Regulatory and Policy Support:

- Enabling regulation and international standards are key for unlocking the potential of FinTech for sustainable development.
- A joint effort by policy makers, the financial industry in the region, and FinTech entrepreneurs is necessary to encourage the development of new products within the financial sector.

The combination of AI, blockchain, and digital identity with green finance application has huge potentials yet challenges exist, like data sovereignty, regulatory supervision, and digital gap. Solving them requires continuous innovation, cooperation, and favourable policy environment. The carbon footprint of new technologies, including cryptocurrencies, is also a growing issue that must be resolved for digital financial solutions to be sustainable(Saeedi & Ashraf, 2024).

CONCLUSION

The rapid development of green consumer finance has been changing the world's financial system by shaping personal finance to broader environmental and social objectives. This chapter has demonstrated how green loans, credit cards, sustainable investment and eco-banking products can contribute to achieving the (SDGs), particularly the SDGs for clean energy, sustainable cities, responsible consumption and climate action. It is not until consumer finance is viewed theoretically through the lenses of stakeholder theory, behavioral economics, and ESG integration that we see that it can function as a highly effective lever of sustainability practice when designed adequately and applied. While the landscape is improving, various obstacles need to be overcome including greenwashing, regulation, lack of knowledge, and access issues. These are barriers that can affect the generalization of the green financial instruments and which may weaken the credibility and the efficiency of this instruments. But, as we show with global examples and emergent best practices, the combination of fintech, enabling regulatory environments, and smart public–private partnerships can help to overcome many of these constraints – and facilitate large-scale, inclusive and transparent green finance solutions. In the future, innovations like AI, blockchain, and digital identity systems will be key for generating investment ideas, push innovation, and guarantee the accountability of innovative financial products in sustainable finance. Such instruments not only add value in terms of efficiency and security; they also educate customers to make informed "green" purchasing choices. Meanwhile, those surging trends in socially conscious consumerism and sustainable investing are an indication of a maturing market that is starting to prize ethical and environmental considerations more highly. In order to unlock the potential of green consumer finance, governments, financial institutions, fintechs and consumers all need to work together. Policy interventions that encourage, enable, and accelerate will be key to transforming the financial system into a driver of sustainable development. Ultimately, green consumer finance is more than a suite of financial products – it's a powerful way forward to realizing a resilient, equitable and environmentally sustainable future.

REFERENCES

Aboalsamh, H. M., Khrais, L. T., & Albahussain, S. A. (2023). Pioneering Perception of Green Fintech in Promoting Sustainable Digital Services Application within Smart Cities. *Sustainability, 15*(14), 11440. DOI: 10.3390/su151411440

Afjal, M. (2023). Bridging the financial divide: A bibliometric analysis on the role of digital financial services within FinTech in enhancing financial inclusion and economic development. *Humanities & Social Sciences Communications, 10*(1), 645. DOI: 10.1057/s41599-023-02086-y

Ahmed, D., Hua, H. X., & Bhutta, U. S. (2024). Innovation through Green Finance: A thematic review. *Current Opinion in Environmental Sustainability, 66*, 101402. DOI: 10.1016/j.cosust.2023.101402

Akhtar, N., & Rashid, A. (2024). Financial development and sustainable development: A review of literature. *Sustainable Development, 32*(6), 7114–7139. DOI: 10.1002/sd.3068

Alamgir, M., & Cheng, M.-C. (2023). Do Green Bonds Play a Role in Achieving Sustainability? *Sustainability, 15*(13), 10177. DOI: 10.3390/su151310177

Ali, F., Sayal, A., Suri, P., Ahmad, V., Chauhan, S. S., & Panwar, D. (2024). The emergence of green finance a conceptual framework for environmental sustainability: Innovation viewpoint. *F1000 Research, 13*, 1312. DOI: 10.12688/f1000research.157894.1

Anwar, H., Waheed, R., & Aziz, G. (2024). Importance of FinTech and green finance to achieve the carbon neutrality targets: A study of australian perspective. *Environmental Research Communications, 6*(11), 115007. DOI: 10.1088/2515-7620/ad853d

Atkisson, A. (2013). A Fresh Start for Sustainable Development. *Development, 56*(1), 52–57. DOI: 10.1057/dev.2013.2

Bayram, O., Talay, I., & Feridun, M. (2022). Can Fintech Promote Sustainable Finance? Policy Lessons from the Case of Turkey. *Sustainability, 14*(19), 12414. DOI: 10.3390/su141912414

Bertram, C., & Van Coppenolle, H. (2024). Strengthening the Paris Agreement through trade? The potential and limitations of EU preferential trade agreements for climate governance. *International Environmental Agreement: Politics, Law and Economics, 24*(4), 589–610. DOI: 10.1007/s10784-024-09653-x

Boz, Z., Korhonen, V., & Koelsch Sand, C. (2020). Consumer Considerations for the Implementation of Sustainable Packaging: A Review. *Sustainability*, *12*(6), 2192. DOI: 10.3390/su12062192

Brühl, V. (2022a). Green Financial Products in the EU — A Critical Review of the Status Quo. *Inter Economics*, *57*(4), 252–259. DOI: 10.1007/s10272-022-1057-2

Brühl, V. (2022b). Green Financial Products in the EU — A Critical Review of the Status Quo. *Inter Economics*, *57*(4), 252–259. DOI: 10.1007/s10272-022-1057-2

Cellura, M., Fichera, A., Guarino, F., & Volpe, R. (2025). Leveraging Positive Energy Districts Surplus for the Achievement of the Sustainable Development Goals. *Energies*, *18*(3), 506. DOI: 10.3390/en18030506

Chang, Y.-K., Cheung, W. M. Y., Chung, M.-H., & Tan, H. (2024). The Paris Agreement effect of consumer awareness and sustainable investing: Some international evidence. *Pacific-Basin Finance Journal*, *85*, 102394. DOI: 10.1016/j.pacfin.2024.102394

Chen, L. (2024). Exploring Innovative Practices and Challenges in the Ecological Development of Art Industry Driven by Digital Technology. *Applied Mathematics and Nonlinear Sciences*, *9*(1), 20242975. DOI: 10.2478/amns-2024-2975

Chueca Vergara, C., & Ferruz Agudo, L. (2021). Fintech and Sustainability: Do They Affect Each Other? *Sustainability*, *13*(13), 7012. DOI: 10.3390/su13137012

Coenen, J., Glass, L.-M., & Sanderink, L. (2022). Two degrees and the SDGs: A network analysis of the interlinkages between transnational climate actions and the Sustainable Development Goals. *Sustainability Science*, *17*(4), 1489–1510. DOI: 10.1007/s11625-021-01007-9

D'Orazio, P., Scholtens, B., De Mariz, F., González-Ruiz, J. D., Ullah, S., Adegbite, O., Thompson, B. S., Liu, F. H. M., Harris, J. L., Bigger, P., Pill, M., Hammersley, G., & Berg, M. (2023). Catalyzing the transformation to sustainable finance. *One Earth*, *6*(10), 1271–1276. DOI: 10.1016/j.oneear.2023.09.011

Duque Oliva, E. J., Sánchez-Torres, J. A., Arroyo-Cañada, F.-J., Argila-Irurita, A., Fuente, J. G.-L., Palacio-López, S.-M., & Arrubla-Zapata, J.-P. (2024). Green Buying Behaviour: An Integrated Model. *Sustainability*, *16*(11), 4441. DOI: 10.3390/su16114441

Faruq, A. T. M. O., & Huq, M. T. (2024). *The Role of Central Banks in Advancing Sustainable Finance* (Version 1). arXiv. https://doi.org/DOI: 10.48550/ARXIV.2411.13576

Filho, W. L., Wall, T., Salvia, A. L., Dinis, M. A. P., & Mifsud, M. (2023). The central role of climate action in achieving the United Nations' Sustainable Development Goals. *Scientific Reports, 13*(1), 20582. DOI: 10.1038/s41598-023-47746-w PMID: 37996539

Gonçalves, A., & Silva, C. (2021). Looking for Sustainability Scoring in Apparel: A Review on Environmental Footprint, Social Impacts and Transparency. *Energies, 14*(11), 3032. DOI: 10.3390/en14113032

Hasan, M. H., Hossain, M. Z., Hasan, L., & Dewan, M. A. (2024). FinTech and Sustainable Finance: How is FinTech Shaping the Future of Sustainable Finance? *European Journal of Management. Economics and Business, 1*(3), 100–115. DOI: 10.59324/ejmeb.2024.1(3).09

Hossain, M. T., Shahid, M. A., Limon, M. G. M., Hossain, I., & Mahmud, N. (2024). Techniques, applications, and challenges in textiles for a sustainable future. *Journal of Open Innovation, 10*(1), 100230. DOI: 10.1016/j.joitmc.2024.100230

Huang, X., Guo, Y., Lin, Y., Liu, L., & Yan, K. (2022). Green Loans and Green Innovations: Evidence from China's Equator Principles Banks. *Sustainability, 14*(20), 13674. DOI: 10.3390/su142013674

Huang, Z., Zhang, Z., Hua, C., Liao, B., & Li, S. (2024). Leveraging enhanced egret swarm optimization algorithm and artificial intelligence-driven prompt strategies for portfolio selection. *Scientific Reports, 14*(1), 26681. DOI: 10.1038/s41598-024-77925-2 PMID: 39496781

Ikechukwu Obinyeluaku, M., Mobolaji Abioye, K., Ibukun Babalola, F., Zamanjomane Mhlongo, N., & Daraojimba, C. (2023). A COMPREHENSIVE REVIEW OF AI APPLICATIONS IN FINANCE FOR ACCELERATING CLEAN ENERGY TRANSITION. *Information Management and Computer Science, 6*(1), 41–49. DOI: 10.26480/imcs.01.2023.41.49

Inês, A., Diniz, A., & Moreira, A. C. (2023). A review of greenwashing and supply chain management: Challenges ahead. *Cleaner Environmental Systems, 11*, 100136. DOI: 10.1016/j.cesys.2023.100136

Kwong, R., Kwok, M. L. J., & Wong, H. S. M. (2023). Green FinTech Innovation as a Future Research Direction: A Bibliometric Analysis on Green Finance and FinTech. *Sustainability, 15*(20), 14683. DOI: 10.3390/su152014683

Li, R., Zhang, S., Wang, Q., & Hu, S. (2025). Fintech and urban environmental sustainability: Exploring the impact of financial technology on urban carbon emissions. *Sustainable Development, 33*(2), 2118–2136. DOI: 10.1002/sd.3212

Ma, J., & Chang, C.-P. (2023). The Role of Green Finance in Green Innovation: Global Perspective from 75 Developing Countries. *Emerging Markets Finance & Trade, 59*(10), 3109–3128. DOI: 10.1080/1540496X.2023.2210720

Makhoul, J., Talhouk, N., Loutfi, J., & Al-Madhwahi, A. (2024). Greenwashing by the fossil fuel industry: Impediments to SDGs. *European Journal of Public Health, 34*(Supplement_3), ckae144.420. https://doi.org/DOI: 10.1093/eurpub/ckae144.420

Mavlutova, I., Spilbergs, A., Verdenhofs, A., Kuzmina, J., Arefjevs, I., & Natrins, A. (2023). The Role of Green Finance in Fostering the Sustainability of the Economy and Renewable Energy Supply: Recent Issues and Challenges. *Energies, 16*(23), 7712. DOI: 10.3390/en16237712

Nascimento, J., & Loureiro, S. M. C. (2024). The PSICHE framework for sustainable consumption and future research directions. *EuroMed Journal of Business, 19*(3), 571–611. DOI: 10.1108/EMJB-12-2021-0199

Nooman AlMallahi, M., Al Swailmeen, Y., Ali Abdelkareem, M., Ghani Olabi, A., & Elgendi, M. (2024). A path to sustainable development goals: A case study on the thirteen largest photovoltaic power plants. *Energy Conversion and Management: X, 22*, 100553. https://doi.org/DOI: 10.1016/j.ecmx.2024.100553

Pacces, A. M. (2021). Will the EU Taxonomy Regulation Foster Sustainable Corporate Governance? *Sustainability, 13*(21), 12316. DOI: 10.3390/su132112316

Pata, U. K., Si Mohammed, K., Nassani, A. A., & Ghosh, S. (2024). Discovering the sustainable development role of fintech credit and the pilot low carbon project on greenwashing in China. *Environment, Development and Sustainability*. Advance online publication. DOI: 10.1007/s10668-024-04919-5

Popescu, I.-S., Schaubroeck, T., Gibon, T., Petucco, C., & Benetto, E. (2024). Investment funds are responsible for substantial environmental and social impacts. *Communications Earth & Environment, 5*(1), 355. DOI: 10.1038/s43247-024-01479-4

Puschmann, T., Hoffmann, C. H., & Khmarskyi, V. (2020). How Green FinTech Can Alleviate the Impact of Climate Change—The Case of Switzerland. *Sustainability, 12*(24), 10691. DOI: 10.3390/su122410691

Ramadugu, R., Doddipatla, L., & Stone, J. (2022). Leveraging Artificial Intelligence and Machine Learning for Sustainable Financial Technologies: Innovations, Challenges, and Future Prospects. [IJSRM]. *International Journal of Scientific Research and Management, 10*(08), 942–959. DOI: 10.18535/ijsrm/v10i8.ec01

Raman, R., Ray, S., Das, D., & Nedungadi, P. (2025). Innovations and barriers in sustainable and green finance for advancing sustainable development goals. *Frontiers in Environmental Science, 12*, 1513204. DOI: 10.3389/fenvs.2024.1513204

Roy, P. K. (2023). Enriching the green economy through sustainable investments: An ESG-based credit rating model for green financing. *Journal of Cleaner Production, 420*, 138315. DOI: 10.1016/j.jclepro.2023.138315

Ruan, W., Guo, Z., Yang, J., Gao, L., Dong, Y., & Liu, Q. (2024). Assessing the progress toward achieving energy- and climate-related sustainable development goals under four global energy transition outlooks. *Sustainable Development, 32*(4), 3695–3707. DOI: 10.1002/sd.2873

Saeedi, M., & Ashraf, B. N. (2024). The Role of Technology in Promoting Green Finance: A Systematic Literature Survey and the Development of a Framework. *Journal of Risk and Financial Management, 17*(10), 472. DOI: 10.3390/jrfm17100472

Saxena, K., & Singh, M. (2024). Investors reward countries for participating in climate agreements. *Nature Communications, 15*(1), 8908. DOI: 10.1038/s41467-024-53012-y PMID: 39414786

Schwanitz, V. J., Paudler, H. A., & Wierling, A. (2024). The contribution of European citizen-led energy initiatives to sustainable development goals. *Sustainable Development, 32*(4), 3313–3328. DOI: 10.1002/sd.2844

Shajar, S. N., Kashif, M., George, J., & Nasir, S. (2024). The Future of Green Finance: Artificial Intelligence-Enabled Solutions for a More Sustainable World. In Jafar, S. H., Rodriguez, R. V., Kannan, H., Akhtar, S., & Plugmann, P. (Eds.), (pp. 316–328). Advances in Finance, Accounting, and Economics. IGI Global., DOI: 10.4018/979-8-3693-1878-2.ch013

Sharifi, A., Allam, Z., Bibri, S. E., & Khavarian-Garmsir, A. R. (2024). Smart cities and sustainable development goals (SDGs): A systematic literature review of co-benefits and trade-offs. *Cities (London, England), 146*, 104659. DOI: 10.1016/j.cities.2023.104659

Siddik, A. B., Yong, L., & Rahman, M. N. (2023). The role of Fintech in circular economy practices to improve sustainability performance: A two-staged SEM-ANN approach. *Environmental Science and Pollution Research International, 30*(49), 107465–107486. DOI: 10.1007/s11356-023-25576-7 PMID: 36735123

Sreenu, N. (2024). The influence of fintech and financial knowledge on sustainable business success: Exploring the mediating effect of financial accessibility in Indian. *Benchmarking*. Advance online publication. DOI: 10.1108/BIJ-12-2023-0875

Sule, A. K., Eyo-Udo, N. L., Onukwulu, E. C., Agho, M. O., & Azubuike, C. (2024). Green finance solutions for banking to combat climate change and promote sustainability. *Gulf Journal of Advance Business Research*, *2*(6), 376–410. DOI: 10.51594/gjabr.v2i6.54

Testa, F., Pretner, G., Iovino, R., Bianchi, G., Tessitore, S., & Iraldo, F. (2021). Drivers to green consumption: A systematic review. *Environment, Development and Sustainability*, *23*(4), 4826–4880. DOI: 10.1007/s10668-020-00844-5

Tolliver, C., Keeley, A. R., & Managi, S. (2019a). Green bonds for the Paris agreement and sustainable development goals. *Environmental Research Letters*, *14*(6), 064009. DOI: 10.1088/1748-9326/ab1118

Tolliver, C., Keeley, A. R., & Managi, S. (2019b). Green bonds for the Paris agreement and sustainable development goals. *Environmental Research Letters*, *14*(6), 064009. DOI: 10.1088/1748-9326/ab1118

Udeagha, M. C., & Muchapondwa, E. (2023). Green finance, fintech, and environmental sustainability: Fresh policy insights from the BRICS nations. *International Journal of Sustainable Development and World Ecology*, *30*(6), 633–649. DOI: 10.1080/13504509.2023.2183526

Wen, Z., Chen, Y., Liu, H., & Liang, Z. (2024). Text Mining Based Approach for Customer Sentiment and Product Competitiveness Using Composite Online Review Data. *Journal of Theoretical and Applied Electronic Commerce Research*, *19*(3), 1776–1792. DOI: 10.3390/jtaer19030087

Yang, M. (2024). Research on Teaching Methods of Integrating Watercolor Techniques and Information Technology in Higher Education Art Education. *Applied Mathematics and Nonlinear Sciences*, *9*(1), 20242803. DOI: 10.2478/amns-2024-2803

Yousef, B. A. A., Obaideen, K., AlMallahi, M. N., Alajmi, N., Radwan, A., Al-Shihabi, S., & Elgendi, M. (2024). On the contribution of concentrated solar power (CSP) to the sustainable development goals (SDGs): A bibliometric analysis. *Energy Strategy Reviews*, *52*, 101356. DOI: 10.1016/j.esr.2024.101356

Zetzsche, D. A., Bodellini, M., & Consiglio, R. (2022). The EU Sustainable Finance Framework in Light of International Standards. *Journal of International Economic Law*, *25*(4), 659–679. DOI: 10.1093/jiel/jgac043

Zhang, K. Q., Chen, H. H., Tang, L. Z., & Qiao, S. (2022). Green Finance, Innovation and the Energy-Environment-Climate Nexus. *Frontiers in Environmental Science*, *10*, 879681. DOI: 10.3389/fenvs.2022.879681

Zhou, B., & Wang, Q. (2024). FinTech matters in sustainable finance: Does it redistribute the supply of financial services? *Journal of International Financial Markets, Institutions and Money*, *91*, 101913. DOI: 10.1016/j.intfin.2023.101913

Chapter 11
European Green Financial Strategies and Their Role in Sustainable Growth

Weirong He
University of Malaya, Malaysia

Sameer Kumar
https://orcid.org/0000-0002-6425-278X
University of Malaya, Malaysia

ABSTRACT

The chapter comprehensively discusses the impact of European green finance policies on sustainable development. As an important tool for addressing climate change and promoting the green transformation of the economy, green finance has become a core component of the European policy system. First, the chapter points out that the impact of climate change and environmental pollution on the economic system is becoming increasingly prominent, including physical risks and transition risks. Secondly, the chapter elaborates on the green finance practices of major European countries through case analysis, covering the innovation and application of tools such as green bonds, green credit, and carbon trading markets. These policies have effectively promoted the development of renewable energy and significantly improved the competitiveness of the green economy. At the same time, green finance policies promote the green transformation of the economy through mechanisms such as internalizing environmental costs and promoting technological innovation.

DOI: 10.4018/979-8-3373-1240-8.ch011

INTRODUCTION

Many scholars, international organizations and government agencies have defined the concept of green finance, but no unified international consensus has been reached so far (Palmaccio et al., 2023). In 2000, The American Heritage Dictionary defined green finance as "environmental finance", which put the financial industry and environmental protection in a unified framework and required the financial industry to introduce environmental protection concepts to form a new financial development model that is conducive to saving resources and reducing environmental pollution; it emphasized that while promoting economic development, the financial industry should also pay attention to pollution problems in the production process to achieve a win-win situation between environmental protection and economic development. In short, green finance is the innovation of financial products and services developed for ecological environmental protection (Fu et al., 2023). With the continuous development and maturity of the financial market, the relevant tools of green finance have continued to develop. These products and services have had a multi-faceted impact on the ecological environment and economic development in practice (Zheng et al., 2025).

There are many problems with the current status of green finance. After the Paris Agreement, there has been a huge demand for investment in the climate field. According to the latest data from the Climate Policy Initiative, the scale of climate investment and financing exceeded US$600 billion for the first time in 2020, and the total amount of financing has increased year by year in the past decade, with a growth rate of 15% in 2020. Although the scale is increasing, there are still many problems. For example, first, the gap in the entire climate investment is still expanding year by year. Global carbon emissions have not yet peaked, and the annual scale of climate investment is far from the expected demand. According to conservative estimates, the annual scale of climate investment and financing should be between 4.5 trillion and 5 trillion US dollars. If the 1.5°C climate target is successfully achieved by 2030, climate financing needs to be increased by at least 590% each year. Second, capital investment mainly depends on the government public sector, and the enthusiasm of enterprises and the private sector needs to be improved. In 2020, climate investment from the public sector accounted for 51%, and market-oriented financial institutions still have great room for improvement. Third, the form of climate financing is too single, and diversified methods need to be expanded. In 2020, the main form of climate financing, debt financing, accounted for 61%, while equity financing and innovative finance accounted for 39%. Fourth, regional cooperation is insufficient, and more than 75% of climate investment and financing flows within the country (Zheng et al., 2025).

RESEARCH QUESTIONS

Based on the two dimensions of the financial system's own climate and environmental risk prevention and financial support for economic transformation, there are a series of issues worth thinking about. This article intends to conduct in-depth discussions around three key issues, as follows:

First, how should financial policies prevent climate and environmental risks? When climate change and environmental risk prevention have become an important part of global financial regulation, European financial regulators (such as the EU's Sustainable Finance Action Plan) have begun to take measures to identify and respond to these issues. Among them, the role of banks and the optimization of monetary policy are key, especially whether monetary policy should pay attention to climate factors and environmental governance, and whether it can prevent climate and environmental risks by optimizing policy rules to improve the overall welfare of society? The ultimate goals of traditional monetary policy include stable prices, economic growth, full employment and balance of international payments. However, at present, the impact of climate change uncertainty on the real economy is increasingly concerned, and the implementation of green financial policies, as well as the economic transformation pressure of various climate and environmental policies and regulatory policies may also affect economic stability. This article focuses on whether monetary policy has room for adjustment to adapt to climate and environmental institutions (Schoenmaker, 2021; Desalegn et al., 2022).

Second, from a theoretical mechanism perspective, how can policy finance support the green transformation of the economic system? Green transformation is an important goal of European policy, especially under the framework of the Green Agreement, the EU has proposed the financial support and policy guidance needed to achieve the carbon neutrality target economy. Financial policies play a key role in this process, including the promotion of green financial products, support for green investment, and policy tools to promote corporate green transformation. Based on this, this paper focuses on how to promote economic green transformation more effectively through green financial transformation policies at a lower policy cost, thereby promoting the greening of economic development (Fu et al., 2023).

Third, from the practical test, how effective is the green financial policy in supporting the green transformation of the economy? This is not only a theoretical question, but also a practical question. The effectiveness of green financial policies is directly related to whether the green transformation can be successfully achieved. In Europe, with the gradual advancement of green financial policies, some identifiable results have emerged (such as the growth of the green bond market, the increase in green investment, etc.). By analyzing these actual effects, we can show the actual impact of green financial policies on economic transformation and test whether green financial policies have played an incentive effect on the green transformation of the economy (Yu et al., 2025).

LITERATURE REVIEW

The concept of "sustainable development" can be traced back to 1980, when the International Union for Conservation of Nature (IUCN), the World Wildlife Fund (WWF) and the United Nations Environment Programme (UNEP) first proposed the concept of sustainable development in the World Conservation Program. In 1987, the World Commission on Environment and Development (WCED) published *Our Common Future*, which formally defined "sustainable development" as "development that meets the needs of the present without threatening the ability of future generations to meet their needs." The origin of the concept of "sustainable development" and pointed out that many scholars believe that the realization of sustainable development depends on the green transformation of technology, that is, by turning to research and development and applying greener and more efficient technologies, with the help of technologies that can achieve zero emissions, the efficiency of energy and resource use can be improved as much as possible, and the waste and pollutants generated can be reduced (Söderholm, 2020). This means that in order to achieve sustainable development of mankind, the green transformation of the economy is essential. The World Commission on Environment and Development (WCED) believes that the concept of green growth is closely related to the concept of sustainable development. From the perspective of the three pillars of sustainable theory (economic growth, social equity, and environmental sustainability), green growth is closely related to the economic and environmental pillars of sustainable development (Fu, Lu & Pirabi, 2023). To achieve green growth, an effective measurement framework and indicators are needed to track the progress of key issues (Zournatzidou, 2025). Existing research has already conducted some discussions on green transformation. Regarding the necessity and strategy formulation of economic green transformation, the formation of green transformation depends on the expansion of the market.

RESEARCH METHODS

The research methods of this paper will mainly adopt a qualitative and quantitative analysis framework, combining literature review, case analysis, statistical data analysis and policy evaluation and other research methods to comprehensively explore the impact of European green finance on sustainable development. The following is a detailed discussion of the research methods.

The literature review is the basis of this study. The main purpose is to sort out the existing academic research results, understand the theoretical background and policy practice of green finance, and the current status of relevant research in this field in Europe. By systematically reviewing domestic and foreign literature related to green finance, sustainable development and policy implementation effects, it can help researchers identify the shortcomings of existing research and provide theoretical support and methodological guidance for subsequent research (Raman, Ray, Das & Nedungadi, 2025). The goal of the literature review is to lay a solid theoretical foundation for this study, clarify research gaps, and provide a basis for the selection of research methods and research design.

Case analysis is one of the core methods of this study. It aims to reveal the actual effects of green finance policies and their role in promoting sustainable development through in-depth analysis of green finance practices in specific countries and regions. By selecting representative European country cases, this study will explore the policy design, implementation process and effectiveness of these countries in the field of green finance. Taking France and the United Kingdom as representatives, this paper explores the establishment and development process of green bond markets in these countries, analyzes how green bonds provide financing support for green projects, and evaluates the contribution of green bond markets to promoting green economic transformation. Taking Germany's green credit policy as an example, this paper analyzes how financial institutions support environmental protection projects through green loans and green financial products, and explores the implementation effect of green credit policies. Analyze the synergy of member states in implementing green financial policies under the EU green financial policy framework, especially the integration of green financial markets, the unification of green standards, and the cross-border flow of green investment (Zheng, Wu, Feng & Chang, 2025). Through case analysis, this study can specifically demonstrate the implementation effects of different green financial policies, compare the differences in the design and implementation of green financial policies in different countries, and further reveal the actual effectiveness of green finance in promoting sustainable development.

Another important method of this study, which evaluates the actual impact of green financial policies on sustainable development through statistical data and empirical analysis. Quantitative analysis will help us evaluate the implementation effect of green financial policies at the macro level, especially its impact on indicators such as economic growth, employment, environmental protection and carbon emissions (Liu et al., 2025). Specific methods include collecting relevant data on green finance and sustainable development, including historical data on green bonds, green loans, green investments, etc. of the European Union and its member states, economic growth data, environmental indicators (such as carbon emissions, energy consumption, etc.), and social development indicators (such as employment rate, poverty rate, etc.). Quantify the impact of green finance policies on these variables through data analysis and other methods. And policy effect analysis, analyze the impact of green finance policies on economic transformation, and evaluate how green finance can play a role in promoting low-carbon economy, energy transformation, and improving resource utilization efficiency. At the same time, analyze the potential impact of green finance policies on social aspects such as employment and income distribution to ensure the comprehensive effect of policy implementation.

Policy evaluation is another important part of this study. Its main purpose is to provide theoretical basis and practical suggestions for future policy optimization through the evaluation of the implementation effect of green finance policies. Policy evaluation not only focuses on the short-term effects of green finance policies, but also their long-term environmental and social benefits. By evaluating the direct and indirect effects of green finance policies on the environment, economy and society, understand the overall effect of policy implementation (Hu, & Gan, 2025). By comparing the green finance policies of different European countries, evaluate their differences in policy design, implementation effect and market response. Comparative analysis will help reveal the common characteristics of successful policies and further provide reference for policy optimization. Policy evaluation and comparative analysis will provide important policy recommendations for the future development of European green finance policies and provide reference for green finance policies in other countries or regions.

By adopting a variety of research methods, especially literature review, case analysis, quantitative analysis and policy evaluation, this paper will be able to comprehensively analyze and evaluate the impact of European green finance policies on sustainable development. The organic combination of these methods can not only ensure reliability of the research results, but also provide valuable decision-making basis for policymakers, and provide theoretical support and practical guidance for the future development of green finance.

RESULTS AND DISCUSSION

Europe is a global leader in promoting green economic development, and its environmental protection has achieved rich results after decades of development. In the EU's green development model, ecological environmental pollution control, ecological and environmental protection industry development, new energy development and utilization, carbon emission reduction, etc. are all included in a unified framework. In 2009, the EU announced the launch of a green development plan within the region as a whole, and announced that the plan would be actively promoted in all EU member states. In order to help EU member states implement EU environmental protection laws and regulations and research and innovate to improve the treatment technology of polluted waste, the EU proposed a support plan of more than 100 billion euros. The plan aims to promote green employment and green economic growth in EU member states, so that the development of EU green industries has international advanced levels and global competitiveness. Due to the development of the economy and the transformation of the post-industrial society, green consumption in the EU has also become popular, and consumers prefer to buy green products with green labels. In addition, the EU also has the world's largest and most mature carbon trading market, leading the world in many aspects such as green standard setting, financial operation supervision, and market mechanism design (Leitão et al., 2021). Among the green development of EU member states, the development of the United Kingdom, Germany and France is relatively typical (Oyebanji & Kırıkkaleli, 2022).

UK's Green Economic Transformation

The UK's green development mainly includes three aspects: green energy, green finance and green consumption. Its characteristics are that the green financial system is very complete and leading in the world (Zhang et al., 2022).

In 2009, the UK successively promulgated two green economy-related bills, namely the UK Low Carbon Transformation Plan and the UK Renewable Energy Strategy. These two bills clearly require the UK government to put carbon emission management planning within the government budget framework, making the UK the first country in the world to set up a special carbon emission budget. According to the bill, the UK government plans to increase the proportion of clean energy in the entire energy structure, while increasing the green transformation of coal-based thermal power generation, and requiring the proportion of green energy such as wind power to reach two-fifths. In addition, the UK government also implements industrial policies for green manufacturers, providing direct financial and policy support to low-carbon industries (Chenic et al., 2022). For the green transformation of British family life, the British government has introduced a family compensation system, which mainly encourages people to renovate their houses to install clean energy equipment to replace old energy-consuming equipment.

In cities and towns in the UK, there are charity shops everywhere, which indicates that the concept of green consumption has penetrated into the daily life of ordinary British people. Such shops are called charity shops, thrift shops or hospice shops in the UK. They are a kind of socialized enterprises with typical public welfare nature. These charity shops receive second-hand items donated by British citizens for free, and then sell them at low prices after necessary processing. All the income from the sales is used for charity. In the 1990s, the number of such charity retail shops in the UK began to double, and this growth entered a golden age in the 21st century. In 2002, the number of charity shops in the UK increased from 3480 in 1992 to 6220. Today, the charity retail industry in the UK has become a huge industry, and its retail sales are also increasing rapidly. In 1992, the retail sales of the charity retail industry in the UK were 183 million pounds, and in 2002 it reached 426 million pounds. In 2012, the annual transaction volume of charity shops in the UK was between 350 million and 450 million pounds, with an annual income of about 100 million pounds, accounting for 2% of the total annual retail industry in the UK (Owen et al., 2020).

The UK has made a lot of investments in the field of climate change by taking advantage of its financial innovation and actively promoting low-carbon production. For example, the British Green Investment Bank (GIB), established in 2012, aims to encourage private capital to invest in the green economy. Although GIB is wholly owned by the British government, it is fully market-oriented. In making green investments, GIB has achieved good economic and social benefits. In just two years since GIB was established, the assets obtained from green investments have exceeded 140 million pounds, and dozens of green investment projects have been carried out in more than 200 places in the UK. The greenhouse gas reduction from GIB's green investment is equivalent to the exhaust emissions of 1.6 million cars, and 150 tons of waste on land have been reduced. The renewable electricity it creates can be used by 3.1 million households. In order to strengthen the top-level design, in 2019, the UK launched the Green Finance Strategy, which comprehensively planned the development path of UK green finance from three levels: macro, micro and international cooperation. In order to implement this strategy, the UK issued the UK Government Green Financing Framework and the Green Bond Principles in 2021, aiming to make further detailed provisions on the evaluation, management, and operation of green projects. At the same time, the UK has continued to strengthen the construction of green financial institutions. For example, in 2019, the UK established the Green Finance Institute to provide policy recommendations for the government's green financial development. At present, the UK has formed a standardized green financial system represented by green bonds, green credit, green insurance, green funds and carbon markets (Peck et al., 2022). In terms of international green financial cooperation, the 26th United Nations Climate Change Conference of the Parties (COP26) hosted by the UK in 2021 reached the Glasgow Climate Convention. One of the important contents of the convention is to enable countries to achieve their climate goals through finance. At the same time, at COP26, the UK also announced its goal of becoming the world's first net zero financial center. As the host of COP26, the UK led the establishment of the Glasgow Net Zero Finance Alliance (GFANZ), and more than 450 financial institutions from 45 countries announced that 40% of the world's financial assets, or more than $130 trillion in assets, would be aligned with the goals of the Paris Agreement on climate (Cohen et al., 2022; Cadman & Hales, 2022).

Germany's Green Economic Transformation

The development of Germany's green economy is mainly due to three reasons. First, it is influenced and affected by the overall strategy of the European Union; second, the government plays a key "intermediary" role in green development; third, it is promoted by the German Green Party and supported by the majority of the people (Lutz et al., 2017).

Since the 1970s, in order to effectively solve various pollution problems such as air, water, noise, and waste, the German government has begun to introduce specific laws and relevant regulations. In 1972, the German government introduced the Waste Disposal Act, which clarified the "end-of-pipe treatment" principles and methods of waste treatment. In 1974, the German government introduced the Air Pollution Prevention and Control Act, which clearly required German companies to update their filtration devices within a specified time and set very strict emission standards for companies. In 1976, the German government issued the Water Pollution Prevention and Control Law, which established a pollution discharge fee system for enterprises. In 1983, the German government issued the Combustion Pollution Control Law, which made clear requirements on how enterprises should discharge flue gas. In order to supervise the implementation of these plans, the German government also established the Federal and State Environmental Protection Bureaus in 1986 to be fully responsible for the formulation and implementation of environmental protection laws and policies. Although Germany began to pay attention to specific environmental issues at this stage, it lacked an overall program and legal policy system. Its focus was on "end-of-pipe treatment" and it still took the approach of "first pollution and then treatment". But overall, the German government has begun to pay more attention to and attach importance to green economy and ecological environment at this stage. In the field of green finance, a special ecological bank appeared in Germany during this period. In 1988, Frankfurt established the world's first bank for the purpose of ecological environment protection. The bank mainly operates natural and environmental protection credit business (Dröge et al., 2004).

In 1994, Germany issued the world's first bill on circular economy-the "Circular Economy and Waste Disposal Law". In 1997, the German government formulated the overall framework of the green economy strategy and specific steps in steps. In order to promote the implementation of the green economic development strategy, the German government has formulated highly operational laws and regulations such as the “Ecological Tax Reform Implementation Law” and the “Renewable Energy Law”. In 1999, Germany officially imposed ecological taxes on gasoline, diesel, fuel gas and electricity. Unlike the previous stage, the German government's emphasis on the green economy has begun to be reflected in the fact that both laws and green economic policies have begun to rise to the level of national strategy. The key themes of Germany's relevant green economic laws and policies have shifted from passive “prevention and treatment” characterized by end-of-pipe governance to actively guiding the development of the green economy. In 2002, Germany began to shut down the existing 19 nuclear power plants one after another. In order to ensure the country's electricity safety, Germany began to enter a period of rapid development of rapid renewable energy. For this reason, the German government has revised the “Renewable Energy Law” four times. The revised bill clearly requires Germany to become the world's first industrialized country to complete the transition to clean energy. In 2014, Germany launched the “Green Economy Research Agenda” to innovate and vigorously develop the green economy. In 2019, the German government issued the German Federal Climate Protection Act, which imposed rigid constraints on the carbon emission targets of various industries. In May 2021, Germany passed legislation to achieve the zero emission target of “carbon neutrality” by 2045 (Baran, 2015; Mohajan, 2021). After the new German government came to power, it also paid great attention to the development of the green economy, especially in the context of the epidemic, this development has become the key to economic recovery. During this period, the role of green financial leverage has been further exerted. The German government supports the national policy bank, the German Reconstruction Credit Bank (KFW), which mainly operates green credit products. The main purpose is to provide enterprises with green financial products and services that support environmental protection, energy conservation and greenhouse gas emission reduction. The government assists financial institutions in the form of interest subsidies. At present, KFW has become a key financial institution that plays a fundamental role in the field of green finance in Germany. Every year, the institution issues special loans for ecological environmental protection and renewable energy development of tens of billions of euros. For example, the German government has made special subsidies for energy-saving renovation of residential housing. This government implements preferential policies by establishing a federal energy-saving building fund. KFW can give long-term loan interest rate discounts to good projects with outstanding environmental protection and energy-saving performance. The German government plays a subsidizing role here to support financial institutions. At the same time, some international financial institutions also settled in Frankfurt during this period to provide financial support for the development of the green economy (Flögel et al., 2023; Ringel & Mjekic, 2023).

France's Green Development Path

France is one of the main parties to the United Nations Convention on Biological Diversity in 1992. In 2011, the French government announced a national biodiversity strategy with six major directions, incorporating ecological civilization construction into the national strategic framework (Fang et al., 2022).

In May 2007, the Sarkozy government established the Ministry of Environmental Protection and Sustainable Development. The establishment of this agency shows that the government attaches great importance to ecological environmental protection. A new environmental protection bill was introduced. In July 2009, France formulated and promulgated a draft of a new environmental protection law. The bill makes clear provisions for energy conservation and emission reduction in different industries. In order to achieve the goal of carbon peak, the bill requires that France's CO2 emissions must be reduced by at least three quarters by 2050. For agriculture, it strives to increase the proportion of farmland planted with ecological agricultural products to 20% by 2020. And France is the first country in the EU to establish a carbon tax. France imposes strict carbon tax on enterprises, and enterprises must pay taxes accordingly. The government reserves the right to dynamically adjust the carbon tax rate and will adjust and increase the tax rate in a timely manner. At the end of 2008, the French government established the "Renewable Energy Fund". The government plans to increase the total amount of geothermal energy utilization fivefold by 2020. For solar energy, the French government plans to build at least one solar power station in each administrative region, thus becoming one of the world's advanced countries. At the same time, the government also encourages the installation of solar panels on the roofs of commercial and industrial and agricultural facilities, and provides national subsidies for this (Ayodele et al., 2023)

In 2017, the French government issued the "Green Treasury Framework Document", proposing that green bonds help green development. In January, the French Treasury issued the first green bond. At present, France's green bond market is the largest in Europe and the third largest in the world. France is the first country in the world to legalize green finance. In 2015, France promulgated the "Green Development Energy Transition Law", which is regarded as a landmark document for France's green transformation. This document stipulates the basic framework of green development from a legal perspective, which is equivalent to laying a solid legal foundation for the development of green finance. France has established various public mechanisms led by local governments, public institutions and financial institutions to subsidize corporate energy transformation under the legal framework established by the government. In 2020, France launched a special fund of 16 billion euros to subsidize the energy transformation of French companies. To support research related to green finance, the French government has helped major research institutions, think tanks, and other academic teams to form an academic ecosystem, laying a solid academic and theoretical foundation for the green finance practice of France and the European Union.

Affected by various factors such as the new crown pneumonia epidemic, the French economy has stagnated or even regressed. In order to restore economic vitality as soon as possible, the French government issued a green economic recovery plan in September 2020 and early 2021. The green recovery plan includes four important measures: First, decarbonization of the industrial sector. The French government plans to invest a large amount of fiscal funds to provide government subsidies for enterprises to carry out green and low-carbon technology innovation and purchases. Second, attach importance to hydrogen energy development. The French government plans to invest 7 billion euros in the development of renewable and low-carbon hydrogen energy by 2030, and subsidize hydrogen energy solutions for enterprises. Third, promote green travel. The French government plans to invest 1.2 billion euros to meet the infrastructure construction needs for energy conservation, emission reduction and green travel. Fourth, green transformation of buildings. The French government has invested 6.7 billion euros in green transformation of residential buildings, corporate plants and various public infrastructure.

Critical Comparison and Discussion of Green Finance Policies in the UK, Germany and France

The UK, Germany and France reflect their respective economic and institutional characteristics in the design and implementation of green finance policies, but also expose obvious advantages and disadvantages in the implementation process. First, Germany, represented by the green credit policy of policy banks (such as KfW), supports the green transformation of small and medium-sized enterprises through low- interest loans. This model is outstanding in terms of financing convenience and policy guidance, but its limitations lie in the high concentration of funds. Green credit mostly flows to enterprises with strong capital strength, while the scope of benefit for small and medium-sized enterprises with limited resources and local green projects is relatively limited. In addition, although Germany's green credit policy has made significant contributions to energy transformation, such as the rapid expansion of renewable energy projects, the policy is overly dependent on the dominance of traditional financial institutions, which may also limit the innovation capacity of private capital. In contrast, France has become one of the world's leading green bond markets through its green bond policy. In 2017, the French government issued the world's first sovereign green bond, raising considerable funds for large-scale infrastructure and low- carbon projects. However, this green finance policy that relies on the bond market is still limited in stimulating private investment, especially in attracting small and medium-sized enterprises to participate in green transformation. More importantly, France's green bond market needs to deal with the transparent management of project funds and the unification of green standards. Some investors have questioned the actual use of funds and environmental impact.

The UK has adopted a more market-oriented approach in its green finance policy, such as promoting green funds and private capital to participate in green investment. The UK's advantage lies in its flexible financial market structure and open capital liquidity, which makes it easier for private capital to participate in green projects. However, the market-oriented mechanism also brings some potential risks, such as the problem of “greenwashing”, that is, some companies use false propaganda to obtain green financing, while the actual environmental benefits of the project are limited. In addition, the UK government's supervision in green finance policy is weak, which may lead to uneven quality of green projects.

From an overall comparison, Germany's green credit policy is more suitable for promoting energy-saving transformation of small and medium-sized enterprises, while France's green bond market performs well in promoting large-scale infrastructure projects. Although the UK's market-oriented green finance policy is flexible, weak supervision may affect the long-term effect of the policy. These three policy models show the advantages and disadvantages of different paths, and also provide important reference for other countries and regions. In the future, these policies can achieve better complementarity through strengthening cross-border cooperation. For example, Germany's green credit model can be combined with France's green bond standardization experience to meet the financing needs of large projects and small and medium-sized enterprises at the same time. In addition, when promoting green financial policies, countries also need to pay more attention to transparency, regulatory effectiveness, and fairness in the use of funds. Therefore, the green financial policies of various countries not only need diversified paths, but also need to emphasize the balance between regional adaptation and policy effects in policy design. These experiences and lessons can provide guidance for the implementation of green financial policies in other countries, especially in developing countries with limited resources but urgent needs for green transformation.

How Should Financial Policies Guard Against Climate and Environment- Related Risks

Should central banks pay attention to climate and environment-related issues? In 2015, a report released by the Bank of England suggested that climate change could pose risks to financial stability and economic development. Especially after the signing of the Paris Agreement, climate change and broader environmental issues have become factors for central banks to consider. Under the advocacy of the

Central Bank and Green Finance Supervisory Network (NGFS) established in 2017 and the International Platform on Sustainable Finance (IPSF) established in 2019, more and more central banks have begun to study ways to manage climate change risks to support the green economic transition. However, these views and actions do not prove that it is completely reasonable for central banks to unconditionally participate in climate change issues. Some experts worry that such participation will not only deviate from the market neutrality and basic goals of central banks, but also overburden their policy tools. The development of policy practice and the debate on the feasibility of participation have derived the necessity of studying monetary policy under the consideration of climate change.

In terms of theoretical mechanism, on the one hand, monetary policy is first of all a countercyclical adjustment policy, and its ultimate goal is to maintain inflation and price stability. Therefore, in terms of how climate and environment-related factors affect monetary policy, there are two aspects of influence: physical risk and transition risk. Physical risk refers to the output loss caused by climate change and environmental pollution itself, such as the increase in the frequency of extreme weather leading to more disaster losses, the greater instability of precipitation leading to a higher probability of agricultural failure, the frequent occurrence of heat and cold waves leading to shutdowns and higher demand for energy, all of which may reduce output and increase the price level (inflation). Transition risk means climate policy, environmental policy or stricter environmental supervision, although aimed at reducing long-term physical risks, it requires companies to put forward higher environmental protection standards and emission reduction standards. This means that in order to reduce the emission of greenhouse gases or other pollutants, companies either reduce production or increase costs to reduce emissions, which will also reduce output and increase prices. Therefore, there must be an appropriate intensity for climate and environmental policies to achieve a compromise between physical risk and transition risk, that is, generally speaking, the real economy will have these two risks at the same time, affecting the stability of the macroeconomy (prices, output). Therefore, monetary policy will be more or less indirectly affected by climate and environmental policies, but the specific form of influence is uncertain. When there are losses, due to output losses, a looser monetary policy is required to combat the risk of economic downturn. At this time, because economic losses may increase prices, it means that monetary policy should be tightened to prevent inflation.

On the other hand, considering the impact of climate and environmental factors on monetary policy, does monetary policy need to pay attention to or even actively adjust the rules to some extent to deal with previously ignored climate and environmental factors? In reality, relatively stricter climate and environmental policies mean that they may increase short-term transition risks, leading to higher output losses and price levels. Therefore, as a countercyclical adjustment policy, monetary policy should appropriately adjust the weights of its different goals to offset the impact of the policy. Intuitively, it seems that under a stricter environmental system, monetary policy only needs to increase the weight of inflation and reduce the weight of output stability. However, considering the various types of shocks faced by the economy, this adjustment method is incomplete. For example, under supply-side shocks, output and prices will rise and fall together, so the impact of environmental policies on prices may offset the impact of shocks to a certain extent. Therefore, the way monetary policy responds to climate and environmental factors may be sensitive to the type of economic shock source and other economic parameters. When formulating appropriate monetary policies, it is necessary for central banks to take these factors into consideration so as to correctly play a role in stabilizing the economy.

In addition, environmental-related goals may affect social welfare in two ways, thereby affecting the effectiveness of monetary policy. First, environmental goals themselves (through output losses and thus affecting residents' consumption and employment) will affect social welfare, and second, achieving certain environmental goals (because the effects of climate and environmental policies and regulatory policies affect corporate emission reduction and other behaviors, resulting in the transformation costs squeezing out social resources and reducing corporate profits and consumption) will affect social welfare. Therefore, this article incorporates environmental goals into monetary policy as a theoretical discussion of the current debate on "green monetary policy". It not only involves practical issues of monetary policy, but also involves in- depth thinking on the economic significance of monetary policy.

In summary, on the issue of how monetary policy can prevent climate and environmental risks, this article believes that climate change and environmental pollution themselves and the transformation policies to address climate and environmental issues will have an impact on the most basic macroeconomic goals - inflation and output. Therefore, in the process of formulating monetary policy, these previously ignored factors need to be taken into account to play a better role in economic stability.

How Financial Policies Support the Green Transformation of the Economic System

Theoretically, the reason why green financial policies are needed to promote the green transformation of the economy is that, on the one hand, there are imperfections in the financial market, which makes it impossible for the financial system to correctly price the green sector (and environmental consequences), resulting in relatively insufficient investment in the green sector and relatively excessive investment in the non-green sector, and the environmental consequences are borne by the public and community residents. Therefore, correctly understanding how monetary and financial factors affect the green transformation process of the economy is a prerequisite for the rational use of financial policies. In reality, investment projects with good environmental benefits are often costly, have a long payback period, and low economic returns. Therefore, the financing risks and costs of investments in the green sector are relatively high in the short term, and their capital costs push up the total cost of green sector products, resulting in relatively low market attractiveness. The goal of green financial policies is to try to correct the problem of high financing risks and costs in the green sector, thereby increasing the market attractiveness of products and services in this sector and attracting social capital to enter this sector.

On the other hand, the reason why green financial policies are needed rather than more traditional fiscal policies is that the efficiency of fiscal policy in the use of funds is relatively low. Although fiscal investment in the green sector has a strong direct effect and is indispensable, the use of public fiscal funds faces complex administrative procedures and has high operating costs. Since public finance is not a profit-oriented economic entity, it is difficult to ensure the economic efficiency of the investment of funds, and it is easy to be inefficient and wasteful, and it is difficult to assess the benefits. In addition, government-led investment or subsidies are also prone to rent- seeking space and high monitoring costs. Therefore, through financial price levers (such as interest rate discounts), it is a potential option to achieve stronger policy effects with less policy costs (Feng, 2024; Ljubičić, 2025). From the perspective of economic roles, the positioning of green financial policies is not to completely replace traditional fiscal expenditures or subsidy policies, but to complement these policies, so that when achieving the same policy effect, it can reduce policy costs, thereby leaving more economic resources to market entities and exerting higher capital operation efficiency (Zhu, 2022).

In addition, from the perspective of economic green transformation, the key point lies in technological progress. Only by accelerating technological progress in the green field, and even its productivity can surpass the non-green field, can the market attractiveness of green field-related products be improved in the long run. A typical example is that the recent intelligent driving technology in the new energy vehicle field is surpassing traditional energy vehicles. Therefore, whether green financial policies help promote accelerated technological progress in the green field is also an important aspect of its long-term effect. If green finance policies can reduce the costs related to the green field to a certain extent, there is a potential possibility to encourage the power of scientific and technological research and development to shift to this field, thereby accelerating technological progress in this field (Ma & Zhao, 2024; Song & Gao, 2025; Zhang, 2024)

CONCLUSION

On the one hand, economic and financial stability requires policymakers to pay more attention to the impact of climate and environmental factors. From the perspective of the financial industry and financial policymakers, finance is not a field that has nothing to do with environmental issues. From a macro perspective, climate change and environmental pollution will bring direct damage to economic production activities (such as more frequent extreme weather disasters and shutdowns caused by environmental pollution) and more other uncertainties. This uncertainty poses a challenge to traditional macroeconomic goals (price stability, economic growth, etc.) (physical risk); from the perspective of enterprises, the green transformation of enterprises will face increasingly stringent policy efforts (transformation risk). These risks will be transmitted to the financial sector and have a significant impact on macro- financial stability and economic stability, so risk prevention is also very important. To this end, the central bank should introduce climate and environmental risks into the important factors of financial stability supervision and micro-regulation.

On the other hand, financial policies should play an active guiding role in promoting the green transformation of the economy. Paying attention to the role and responsibility of financial policies in the green transformation of the economy does not mean denying the original economic means and administrative and legal means. Traditionally, administrative and legal means are used to restrict and combat polluting behaviors, and environmental governance is carried out through government investment and other means. The current environmental governance and economic green transformation not only need to improve the enforcement of climate policies and regulations, but also need to pay attention to how to more widely mobilize the funds, human and material resources of the whole society to invest in the environmental field, provide financial support for the green transformation of the economy, improve the efficiency of economic resource allocation, and make up for the shortcomings of administrative means.

European green finance policies have had a profound impact on sustainable development goals by promoting the greening of capital markets, promoting low-carbon technology innovation, improving ecological environmental quality, optimizing economic structure, and enhancing social equity. These policies effectively guide funds to low-carbon economy and sustainable projects, improve resource allocation efficiency, reduce carbon emissions, and promote technology cost reduction and employment opportunities. Provide a strong driving force for the green transformation of the economy. In addition, Europe's leading role in the formulation of global green finance standards and international cooperation has not only consolidated its own sustainable development process, but also provided a model for the improvement of the global green financial system. However, these policies still face challenges such as regional differences, green whitewashing, and insufficient financing coverage in the implementation process, and need to be further improved and innovated to better achieve the coordination and unification of economic, social and environmental goals.

REFERENCES

Ayodele, F. O., Mustapa, S., & Ayodele, B. (2023). The potential of renewable energy green financing through carbon taxation to achieve net-zero emissions target. *International Journal of Energy Economics and Policy, 13*(5), 145–155.

Baran, B. (2015). Support for renewable energy in Germany as an example of effective public policy. *Oeconomia Copernicana, 6*(3), 143–158.

Cadman, T., & Hales, R. (2022). COP26 and a framework for future global agreements on carbon market integrity. *The International Journal of Social Quality, 12*(1), 97–118.

Chenic, A. S., Cre u, A., Burlacu, A., Moroianu, N., Vîrjan, D., Huru, D., Stanef-Puică, M., & Enăchescu, V. (2022). Logical analysis on the strategy for a sustainable transition of the world to green energy—2050. *Sustainability, 14*(14), 8622.

Cohen, R., Eames, P., Hammond, G. P., Newborough, M., & Norton, B. (2022). The 2021 Glasgow Climate Pact – Steps on the transition pathway towards a low carbon world. *Proceedings of the Institution of Civil Engineers – Energy, 175*(4), 123–136.

Desalegn, G., Fekete-Farkas, M., & Tangl, A. (2022). The effect of monetary policy and private investment on green finance: Evidence from Hungary. *Journal of Risk and Financial Management, 15*(3), 117.

Dröge, S., Trabold, H., Biermann, F., Böhm, F., & Brohm, R. (2004). National climate change policies and WTO law: A case study of Germany's new policies. *World Trade Review, 3*(2), 161–187.

Fang, Z., Yang, C., & Song, X. (2022). How do green finance and energy efficiency mitigate carbon emissions without reducing economic growth in G7 countries? *Frontiers in Psychology, 13*, 879741. PMID: 35592175

Feng, M. (2024). Green loan interest subsidy policy, green technological innovation, and high-quality enterprise development. *Asia Pacific Economic and Management Review, 1*(5), 74.

Flögel, F., Schepelmann, P., Zademach, H. M., & Zörner, M. (2023). Injecting climate finance into SME lending in Germany. *ZFW - Advances in Economic Geography, 0*, 1–21.

Fu, C., Zhang, Y., & Wu, J. (2023). Advancing green finance: A review of sustainable finance, climate change and decarbonization. *Business Strategy and the Environment, 32*(1), 49–68.

Hu, D., & Gan, C. (2025). Green finance development and its origin, motives, and barriers: An exploratory study. *Environment, Development and Sustainability*, •••, 1–25.

Leitão, J. C., Ferreira, J. J. M., & Santibañez-González, E. (2021). Green bonds, sustainable development and environmental policy in the EU carbon market. *Business Strategy and the Environment*, *30*(4), 2077–2090.

Liu, M., Yaacob, M. H., Ma, Q., & Ding, S. (2025). Green finance and corporate green innovation: A systematic literature review. *SAGE Open*, *15*(3), 21582440251370800.

Ljubičić, I. (2025). Tax instruments as a key driver of the green transition. *Journal of Agronomy, Technology and Engineering Management*, *8*(1), 45–63.

Lutz, C., Zieschank, R., & Drosdowski, T. (2017). Measuring Germany's transition to a green economy. *Low Carbon Economy*, *8*(1), 1–19.

Ma, Y., & Zhao, H. (2024). Green technology innovation guiding policies under the synergy of government and financial institutions. *Sustainable Operations and Computers*, *5*(2), 88–103.

Mohajan, H. (2021). Germany is ahead to implement sustainable circular economy. *Journal of Economic Development. Environment and People*, *10*(2), 46–64.

Oyebanji, M. O., & Kırıkkaleli, D. (2022). Green technology, green electricity, and environmental sustainability in Western European countries. *Environmental Science and Pollution Research International*, *30*(45), 38525–38534. PMID: 36580250

Palmaccio, M., Galeone, G., Shini, M., & Campobasso, F. (2023). Green finance: Past, present and future studies. *Journal of Financial Management. Markets and Institutions*, *11*(2), 1–19.

Peck, G., Rosenbaum, H., Hudon, I., Yoon, J.-W., Kamal-Chaoui, L., & Lagarde, P. (2022). Financing SMEs for sustainability. *OECD SME and Entrepreneurship Papers*, *31*, 1–38.

Raman, R., Ray, S., Das, D., & Nedungadi, P. (2025). Innovations and barriers in sustainable and green finance for advancing sustainable development goals. *Frontiers in Environmental Science*, *14*, 1513204.

Ringel, M., & Mjekic, S. (2023). Analyzing the role of banks in providing green finance for retail customers: The case of Germany. *Sustainability*, *15*(11), 8745.

Schoenmaker, D. (2021). Greening monetary policy. *Climate Policy*, *21*(6), 735–750.

Söderholm, P. (2020). The green economy transition and sustainable technological change. *Sustainable Earth Reviews*, *1*(1), 1–17.

Song, J., & Gao, X. (2025). Does China's green credit interest subsidies policy promote enterprises' green technology innovation quality? *Journal of Environmental Management*, *390*, 126366. PMID: 40577875

Yu, X., Li, W., Wang, Y., & Chen, H. (2025). The impact of green finance policy on environmental performance of firms. *Sustainability*, *17*(17), 7589.

Zhang, D., Zhao, Z., & Lau, C. (2022). Sovereign ESG and corporate investment: New insights from the UK. *Technological Forecasting and Social Change*, *182*, 121899.

Zhang, Y. (2024). The impact of green finance on the sustainable development of new energy enterprises. *Highlights in Business. Economics and Management*, *4*(3), 59–74.

Zheng, M., Wu, L., Feng, G. F., & Chang, C. P. (2025). The impact of green finance on sustainable development: An investigation into national ESG performance. *Journal of Applied Econometrics*, *28*(1), 2528672.

Zhu, R. (2022). Research on fiscal policy support for green finance development in the context of green recovery. *BCP Business & Management*, *30*(1), 102–114.

Zournatzidou, G. (2025). Green finance and sustainable development: Investigating greentech ecosystems through PRISMA analysis. *Administrative Sciences*, *15*(4), 150.

ADDITIONAL READING

Batten, S., Sowerbutts, R., & Tanaka, M. (2016). Let's talk about the weather: The impact of climate change on central banks. Bank of England Staff Working Paper No. 603.

Bolton, P., Despres, M., Pereira Da Silva, L., Samama, F., & Svartzman, R. (2020). *The green swan: Central banking and financial stability in the age of climate change*. Bank for International Settlements.

Campiglio, E. (2016). Beyond carbon pricing: The role of banking and monetary policy in financing the transition to a low-carbon economy. *Ecological Economics*, *121*, 220–230. DOI: 10.1016/j.ecolecon.2015.03.020

D'Orazio, P., & Popoyan, L. (2019). Fostering green investments and tackling climate-related financial risks: Which role for macroprudential policies? *Ecological Economics*, *160*, 25–37. DOI: 10.1016/j.ecolecon.2019.01.029

Flammer, C. (2021). Corporate green bonds. *Journal of Financial Economics*, *142*(2), 499–516. DOI: 10.1016/j.jfineco.2021.05.008

Heede, R. (2014). Tracing anthropogenic carbon dioxide and methane emissions to fossil fuel and cement producers, 1854–2010. *Climatic Change*, *122*(1–2), 229–241. DOI: 10.1007/s10584-013-0986-y

OECD. (2017). *Investing in climate, investing in growth*. OECD Publishing., DOI: 10.1787/9789264273528-

UNEP. (2016). *The financial system we need: Aligning the financial system with sustainable development* (2nd ed.). United Nations Environment Programme.

Volz, U. (2018). *Fostering green finance for sustainable development in Asia*. Asian Development Bank Institute.

KEY TERMS AND DEFINITIONS

Green Finance: Financial activities that support environmental sustainability, including green loans, bonds, and investment in eco-friendly projects.

Climate Finance: Funding aimed specifically at initiatives that address climate change mitigation and adaptation.

Sustainable Development: A model of growth that meets present needs without compromising the ability of future generations to meet theirs, balancing economic, environmental, and social goals.

Green Bonds: Fixed-income financial instruments designed to fund projects with positive environmental or climate benefits.

Transition Risk: Financial risks associated with the economic shift from a high-carbon to a low-carbon economy, including regulatory, technological, and market changes.

Physical Risk: Risks to the financial system and economy arising from climate-induced natural disasters and environmental degradation.

Carbon Pricing: An economic tool that charges emitters for their carbon dioxide emissions to incentivize lower emissions.

Greenwashing: Misleading claims by firms or institutions that exaggerate or falsify their environmental efforts to appear sustainable.

Monetary Policy and Climate Risk: The evolving understanding that central banks may need to adjust their monetary frameworks to account for climate and environmental-related risks.

Circular Economy: An economic system that aims to minimize waste and make the most of resources by promoting reuse, repair, refurbishment, and recycling.

Compilation of References

Abera, M., Marvadi, C., & Suthar, D. (2025). Digitization strategy and innovation performance of microfinance institutions: Mediating role of innovation capability. *Journal of Accounting & Organizational Change*, *21*(2), 250–277. DOI: 10.1108/JAOC-12-2023-0241

Ablender, M. S. (2011). Corporate social responsibility as subsidiary co-responsibility: A macroeconomic perspective. *Journal of Business Ethics*, *99*, 115–128.

Aboalsamh, H. M., Khrais, L. T., & Albahussain, S. A. (2023). Pioneering Perception of Green Fintech in Promoting Sustainable Digital Services Application within Smart Cities. *Sustainability*, *15*(14), 11440. DOI: 10.3390/su151411440

Aboutorabifard, H. (2016). Equator Principles and Climate Change Issues: Examining the EPs' Climate Change Policies and Analyzing the Likely Effectiveness of these Policies. UWSpace. http://hdl.handle.net/10012/10361

Adem, M., & Dsouza, P. K. (2024). Impact of board characteristics on firm performance: Evidence from Ethiopian microfinance institutions. *Global Business Review*. Advance online publication. DOI: 10.1177/09721509241276957

Afanasiev, M. P., & Belenchuk, A. A. (2021). Towards to the first green federal budget of Russia: Basis and elaboration. *Voprosy Ekonomiki*, *11*, 71–88. DOI: 10.32609/0042-8736-2021-11-71-88

Afjal, M. (2023). Bridging the financial divide: A bibliometric analysis on the role of digital financial services within FinTech in enhancing financial inclusion and economic development. *Humanities & Social Sciences Communications*, *10*(1), 645. DOI: 10.1057/s41599-023-02086-y

Afriyie, E. Y. (2022). The impact of custom-made internal risk control systems on bank performance in Ghana. *Forum Scientiae Oeconomia*, *4*, 151–174. DOI: 10.23762/FSO_VOL10_NO4_8

Aftab, J., Veneziani, M., Sarwar, H., & Abid, N. (2024). Do green practices drive business excellence in SMEs? Investigating how green entrepreneurial orientation improves firm's performance. *Total Quality Management & Business Excellence, 35*(5–6), 529–558. DOI: 10.1080/14783363.2024.2315442

Afum, E., Zhang, R., Agyabeng-Mensah, Y., & Sun, Z. (2021). Sustainability excellence: The interactions of lean production, internal green practices and green product innovation. *International Journal of Lean Six Sigma, 12*(6), 1089–1114.

Agathou, N., & Schuite, G. J. (2015). Environmental performance of African microfinance institutions: Using the Green Performance Agenda framework to assess and build the business case for sustainability. *Enterprise Development & Microfinance, 26*(3), 230–247.

Agrawal, R., Agrawal, S., Samadhiya, A., Kumar, A., Luthra, S., & Jain, V. (2023). Adoption of green finance and green innovation for achieving circularity: An exploratory review and future directions. *Geoscience Frontiers, 101669*. Advance online publication. DOI: 10.1016/j.gsf.2023.101669

Ahmad, M., Khattak, S. I., Khan, A., & Rahman, Z. U. (2020). Innovation, foreign direct investment (FDI), and the energy–pollution–growth nexus in OECD region: A simultaneous equation modeling approach. *Environmental and Ecological Statistics, 27*(2), 203–232. DOI: 10.1007/s10651-020-00442-8

Ahmed, D., Hua, H. X., & Bhutta, U. S. (2024). Innovation through Green Finance: A thematic review. *Current Opinion in Environmental Sustainability, 66*, 101402. DOI: 10.1016/j.cosust.2023.101402

Akhtar, N., & Rashid, A. (2024). Financial development and sustainable development: A review of literature. *Sustainable Development, 32*(6), 7114–7139. DOI: 10.1002/sd.3068

Alamgir, M., & Cheng, M.-C. (2023). Do Green Bonds Play a Role in Achieving Sustainability? *Sustainability, 15*(13), 10177. DOI: 10.3390/su151310177

Albuquerque, R., Koskinen, Y., Yang, S., & Zhang, C. (2020). Resiliency of environmental and social stocks: An analysis of the exogenous COVID-19 market crash. *The Review of Corporate Finance Studies, 9*(3), 593–621. DOI: 10.1093/rcfs/cfaa009 PMID: 40504189

Ali, F., Sayal, A., Suri, P., Ahmad, V., Chauhan, S. S., & Panwar, D. (2024). The emergence of green finance a conceptual framework for environmental sustainability: Innovation viewpoint. *F1000 Research, 13*, 1312. DOI: 10.12688/f1000research.157894.1

Ali, M., Seraj, M., Turuc, F., Tursoy, T., & Uktamov, K. F. (2024). Green finance investment and climate change mitigation in OECD-15 European countries: RALS and QARDL evidence. *Environment, Development and Sustainability, 26*(11), 27409–27429. DOI: 10.1007/s10668-023-03765-1

Allet, M. (2014). Why do microfinance institutions go green? An exploratory study. *Journal of Business Ethics, 122*(3), 405–424.

Alshebami, A. S. (2023). Green innovation, self-efficacy, entrepreneurial orientation and economic performance: Interactions among Saudi small enterprises. *Sustainability, 15*(3), 1961.

Altaf, A., Anwar, M. A., Shahzad, U., & Bilan, Y. (2025). Exploring the nexus among green finance, renewable energy and environmental sustainability: Evidence from OECD economies. *Renewable Energy, 244*. Advance online publication. DOI: 10.1016/j.renene.2025.122589

Alvi, S., Ahmad, I., Naeem Nawaz, S. M., Connell, W., Anser, M. K., & Ul Hassan, M. (2025). The role of green finance, energy transition, and digitalization in OECD greenhouse gas emissions. *Journal of Cleaner Production, 518*. Advance online publication. DOI: 10.1016/j.jclepro.2025.145865

Amalric, F. (2005). The Equator Principles : A Step Towards Sustainability? *CCRS Working Paper Series Working Paper No. 01 / 05*

Ameli, N., Drummond, P., Bisaro, A., Grubb, M., & Chenet, H. (2021). Climate finance and disclosure for institutional investors: Why transparency is not enough. *Climate Policy, 21*(4), 495–512.

Amersdorffer, F., Buchenrieder, G., Bokusheva, R., & Wolz, A. (2015). Efficiency in microfinance: Financial and social performance of agricultural credit cooperatives in Bulgaria. *The Journal of the Operational Research Society, 66*(1), 57–65.

Anand, S. (2024, January 13). REC forays into Yen market with JPY 61.1 billion green bonds *ETEnergyworld.com*. https://energy.economictimes.indiatimes.com/news/power/rec-forays-into-yen-market-with-jpy-61-1-billion-green-bonds/106796345

Anwar, H., Waheed, R., & Aziz, G. (2024). Importance of FinTech and green finance to achieve the carbon neutrality targets: A study of australian perspective. *Environmental Research Communications, 6*(11), 115007. DOI: 10.1088/2515-7620/ad853d

Apple Inc. (2020). Apple issues $1.5 billion green bond. Retrieved from https://www.apple.com/newsroom/2020/09/apple-issues-1-5-billion-green-bond/

Aras, G., Tezcan, N., & Kutlu Furtuna, O. (2018). Multidimensional comprehensive corporate sustainability performance evaluation model: Evidence from an emerging market banking sector. *Journal of Cleaner Production, 185*, 600–609. DOI: 10.1016/j.jclepro.2018.01.175

Ardyan, E., Nurtantiono, A., Istiyanto, B., & Rahmawan, G. (2017). Green innovation capability as driver of sustainable competitive advantages and smes marketing performance. *Technology*, *8*(8), 1114–1122.

Aria, M., Cuccurullo, C., D'Aniello, L., Misuraca, M., & Spano, M. (2022). Thematic analysis as a new culturomic tool: The social media coverage on COVID-19 pandemic in Italy. *Sustainability*, *14*(6), 3643.

Armendáriz, B., & Morduch, J. (2010). *The economics of microfinance* (2nd ed.). MIT Press.

Arner, D. W., Barberis, J., & Buckley, R. P. (2016). The evolution of fintech: A new post-crisis paradigm? *Georgetown Journal of International Law*, *47*(4), 1271–1319.

Arora, R. U., & Sarker, T. (2023). Financing for Sustainable Development Goals (SDGs) in the Era of COVID-19 and Beyond. *European Journal of Development Research*, *35*, 1–19. https://link.springer.com/article/10.1057/s41287-022-00571-9 PMID: 36620200

Arrègle, J. L. (2006). "Resource Based" analysis and identification of strategic assets. *French Management Journal*, *160*, 241–259.

Asad, M., Aledeinat, M., Majali, T., Almajali, D. A., & Shrafat, F. D. (2024). Mediating role of green innovation and moderating role of resource acquisition with firm age between green entrepreneurial orientation and performance of entrepreneurial firms. *Cogent Business & Management*, *11*(1), 2291850. DOI: 10.1080/23311975.2023.2291850

Asian Development Bank (ADB). (2018). Sustainable Infrastructure for Low-Carbon Development in India. Retrieved from https://www.adb.org/publications/sustainable-infrastructure-low-carbon-development-india

Assidi, S., Omran, M., Rana, T., & Borgi, H. (2025). Climate change and Task Force on Climate-related Financial Disclosures (TCFD) reports: A comparison between Italy and Spain. *Journal of Accounting & Organizational Change*, *21*(7), 1–28. DOI: 10.1108/JAOC-05-2024-0172

Atkisson, A. (2013). A Fresh Start for Sustainable Development. *Development*, *56*(1), 52–57. DOI: 10.1057/dev.2013.2

Ayal, B. A., Tassew, D. T., Alem, Y. T., & Kebede, A. T. (2025). The impact of the Federal Government–Amhara Fano conflict on microfinance and economic outcomes in the Amhara Region, Ethiopia. *Public Organization Review*. Advance online publication. DOI: 10.1007/s11115-025-00863-8

Ayayi, A. G., & James, A. P. (2018). Cost implications of microfinance regulation: Lessons from Ghana. *Journal of Sustainable Finance & Investment*, *8*(3), 259–274.

Ayodele, F. O., Mustapa, S., & Ayodele, B. (2023). The potential of renewable energy green financing through carbon taxation to achieve net-zero emissions target. *International Journal of Energy Economics and Policy*, *13*(5), 145–155.

Bai, C., Quayson, M., & Sarkis, J. (2021). COVID-19 pandemic digitization lessons for sustainable development of micro-and small- enterprises. *Sustainable Production and Consumption*, *27*. Advance online publication. DOI: 10.1016/j.spc.2021.04.035 PMID: 34722843

Bakhsh, S., Alam, M. S., & Zhang, W. (2024). Green finance and Sustainable Development Goals: Is there a role for geopolitical uncertainty? *Economic Change and Restructuring*, *57*(4). Advance online publication. DOI: 10.1007/s10644-024-09719-5

Bakkensen, L. A., & Ma, L. (2020). Sorting over flood risk and implications for policy reform. *Journal of Environmental Economics and Management*, *104*, 102362. DOI: 10.1016/j.jeem.2020.102362

Balsalobre-Lorente, D., Driha, O. M., Bekun, F. V., & Osundia, O. A. (2019). Do Agricultural Activities Induce Carbon Emissions? The BRICS Experience. *Environmental Science and Pollution Research International*, *26*, 25218–25234. https://link.springer.com/article/10.1007/s11356-019-05737-3 PMID: 31256399

Banga, J. (2019). The green bond market: A potential source of climate finance for developing countries. *Journal of Sustainable Finance & Investment*, *9*(1), 17–32.

Bank for International Settlements (BIS). (2020). Green bond finance and central banks. Retrieved from https://www.bis.org/fsi/publ/insights27.htm

Bank Indonesia. (2019). Sustainable Finance Roadmap. Retrieved from https://www.bi.go.id/id/moneter/keuangan-berkelanjutan/tujuan-kebijakan/pages/rujukan-strategi-keuangan-berkelanjutan.aspx

Bank of Canada (BoC). (2021). Climate-related Stress Testing. Retrieved from https://www.bankofcanada.ca/2021/01/discussion-papers/climate-stress-testing-canadian-financial-system/

Bank of Canada. (2021). Research on Climate-Related Stress Testing. Retrieved from https://www.bankofcanada.ca/2021/01/discussion-papers/climate-stress-testing-canadian-financial-system/

Bank of England (BoE). (2020). Green Finance Guidelines. Retrieved from https://www.bankofengland.co.uk/prudential-regulation/green-finance

Bank of England. (2021). Climate Biennial Exploratory Scenario. Retrieved from https://www.bankofengland.co.uk/climate-hub/climate-biennial-exploratory-scenario-cbes

Baran, B. (2015). Support for renewable energy in Germany as an example of effective public policy. *Oeconomia Copernicana*, *6*(3), 143–158.

Barbot, G. (2010). The social utility of the bank in question. Some reflections for the post-crisis period. *Life & Economic Sciences, 3-4* (185-186).

Barrell, R. J., & Nahhas, A. (2022). Regional integration and bilateral FDI stocks in the OECD. *International Journal of Finance & Economics*, *27*(3), 3032–3050. DOI: 10.1002/ijfe.2311

Basha, S., Elgammal, M. M., & Abuzayed, B. M. (2021). Online peer-to-peer lending: A review of the literature. *Electronic Commerce Research and Applications*, *48*, 101069. DOI: 10.1016/j.elerap.2021.101069

Batae, O. M., Dragomir, V., & Ionescu-Feleaga, L. (2021). The Relationship between Environmental, Social, and Financial Performance in the Banking Sector: A European Study. [January.]. *Journal of Cleaner Production*, *290*, 125791.

Bayram, O., Talay, I., & Feridun, M. (2022). Can Fintech Promote Sustainable Finance? Policy Lessons from the Case of Turkey. *Sustainability*, *14*(19), 12414. DOI: 10.3390/su141912414

Beisland, L. A., Zamore, S., & Mersland, R. (2023). Does it pay to be green? A study of the global microfinance industry. *Nonprofit and Voluntary Sector Quarterly*, *52*(3), 631–653. DOI: 10.1177/08997640221110209

Beljić, M., Glavaški, O., Beker Pucar, E., Stojkov, S., & Pejčić, J. (2023). Asymmetric Effects of Tax Competition on FDI vs. Budget Balance in European OECD Economies: Heterogeneous Panel Approach †. *Risks*, *11*(12). Advance online publication. DOI: 10.3390/risks11120219

Ben Abdelkader, I., & Mansouri, F. (2019). Performance of microfinance institutions in the MENA region: A comparative analysis. *International Journal of Social Economics*, *46*(1), 47–65.

Ben Emukufia, A. O., & Aduloju, S. A. (2020). Adoption of Voluntary Global Governance Initiatives: Equator Principles and Banks In Nigeria. Facta Universitatis, Series: Economics and Organization, 249-260.https://doi.org/DOI: 10.22190/FUEO2004160160

Berg, F., Koelbel, J. F., & Rigobon, R. (2022). Aggregate confusion: The divergence of ESG ratings. *Review of Finance*, *26*(6), 1315–1344. DOI: 10.1093/rof/rfac033

Berrou, R., Dessertine, P., & Migliorelli, M. (2019). An Overview of Green Finance. M. Migliorelli & P. Dessertine (Eds.), *The Rise of Green Finance in Europe: Opportunities and Challenges for Issuers, Investors, and Marketplaces* (pp. 3-19). Palgrave Macmillan.

Bertram, C., & Van Coppenolle, H. (2024). Strengthening the Paris Agreement through trade? The potential and limitations of EU preferential trade agreements for climate governance. *International Environmental Agreement: Politics, Law and Economics*, *24*(4), 589–610. DOI: 10.1007/s10784-024-09653-x

Bhatnagar, S., & Sharma, D. (2022). Evolution of Green Finance and Its Enablers: A Bibliometric Analysis. *Renewable & Sustainable Energy Reviews*, *162*, 112405. https://www.sciencedirect.com/science/article/abs/pii/S1364032122003136

Bhattacharya, A., & Kojima, S. (2012). Power sector investment risk and renewable energy: A Japanese case study using portfolio risk optimization method. *Energy Policy*, *40*, 69–80. DOI: 10.1016/j.enpol.2010.06.044

Bhattacharya, A., Nand, A., & Castka, P. (2019). Lean-green integration and its impact on sustainability performance: A critical review. *Journal of Cleaner Production*, *236*, 117697.

Bhushan, M., & Singh, R. (2024). Talent Management Facilitates Net-Zero Transition through Employee Green Behavior. In Singh, R., Khan, S., Kumar, A., Luthra, S., & Chokshi, H. (Eds.), *Net Zero Economy, Corporate Social Responsibility and Sustainable Value Creation: Exploring Strategies, Drivers, and Challenges* (pp. 117–129). Springer.

Bibi, U., Balli, H. O., Matthews, C. D., & Triple, T. W. L. (2018). New approaches to measure the social performance of microfinance institutions (MFIs). *International Review of Economics & Finance*, *53*, 88–97.

BlackRock. (2020). *Sustainability as BlackRock's new standard for investing*. https://www.blackrock.com/corporate/investor-relations/blackrock-client-letter

Bloomberg, N. E. F. (2022, June 29). Financing India's 2030 renewables ambition Retrieved from https://about.bnef.com/blog/financing-indias-2030-renewables-ambition/

Boffo, R., & Patalano, R. (2020). *ESG investing: Practices, progress and challenges*. OECD., DOI: 10.1787/67cbbb88-

Bolton, P., Després, M., Pereira da Silva, L. A., Samama, F., & Svartzman, R. (2020). *The green swan: Central banking and financial stability in the age of climate change*. Bank for International Settlements.

Boubacar, I. (2016). Spatial determinants of U.S. FDI and exports in OECD countries. *Economic Systems*, *40*(1), 135–144. DOI: 10.1016/j.ecosys.2015.04.005

Boubaker, S., Karim, S., Naeem, M. A., & Rahman, M. R. (2023). On the prediction of systemic risk tolerance of cryptocurrencies. *Technological Forecasting and Social Change*, *198*, 122963. DOI: 10.1016/j.techfore.2023.122963

Bourlès, R., & Cozarenco, A. (2018). Entrepreneurial motivation and business performance: Evidence from a French microfinance institution. *Small Business Economics*, *51*(4), 943–963.

Boz, Z., Korhonen, V., & Koelsch Sand, C. (2020). Consumer Considerations for the Implementation of Sustainable Packaging: A Review. *Sustainability*, *12*(6), 2192. DOI: 10.3390/su12062192

Bratu, D., & Jacquin, M. P. (2007). Communicating around CSR and sustainable development: The case of the savings bank. *CEREN Notebook*, *21*, 52–63.

Broadstock, D. C., Chan, K., Cheng, L. T. W., & Wang, X. (2021). The role of ESG performance during times of financial crisis: Evidence from COVID-19 in China. *Finance Research Letters*, *38*, 101716. DOI: 10.1016/j.frl.2020.101716 PMID: 32837385

Brühl, V. (2022a). Green Financial Products in the EU — A Critical Review of the Status Quo. *Inter Economics*, *57*(4), 252–259. DOI: 10.1007/s10272-022-1057-2

Buisson, M. L. (2008). Legitimacy and management sciences: State of play and perspectives. *Humanism and Business*, *289*, 29–57.

Business Roundtable. (2019). *Statement on the purpose of a corporation*. https://opportunity.businessroundtable.org/ourcommitment/

Business Standard. (2018). SBI targets 15,000 MW solar power projects by 2022 under priority sector lending. Retrieved from https://www.business-standard.com/article/companies/sbi-targets-15-000-mw-solar-power-projects-by-2022-under-priority-sector-lending-118021300009_1.html

Cadman, T., & Hales, R. (2022). COP26 and a framework for future global agreements on carbon market integrity. *The International Journal of Social Quality, 12*(1), 97–118.

Caldecott, B., Howarth, N., & McSharry, P. (2016). *Stranded assets in agriculture: Protecting value from environment-related risks*. Smith School of Enterprise and the Environment, University of Oxford.

Caldera, H. T. S., Desha, C., & Dawes, L. (2017). Exploring the role of lean thinking in sustainable business practice: A systematic literature review. *Journal of Cleaner Production, 167*, 1546–1565.

Campiglio, E., Dafermos, Y., Monnin, P., Ryan-Collins, J., Schotten, G., & Tanaka, M. (2018). Climate change challenges for central banks and financial regulators. *Nature Climate Change, 8*(6), 462–468.

Can, U., & Can, Z. G. (2025). *Financing or taxation? Assessing the effectiveness of carbon emissions reduction programs*. Borsa Istanbul Review., DOI: 10.1016/j.bir.2025.03.005

Capron, M., & Quairel-Lanoizelée, F. (2007). *Corporate social responsability*. Repères Collection.

Carè, R., Fatima, R., & Boitan, I. A. (2024). Central banks and climate risks: Where we are and where we are going? *International Review of Economics & Finance, 92*, 1200–1229. DOI: 10.1016/j.iref.2024.01.057

Carney, M. (2015). *Breaking the tragedy of the horizon—climate change and financial stability*. Speech at Lloyd's of London.

Carpentier, C. L., & Braun, H. (2020). Agenda 2030 for Sustainable Development: A Powerful Global Framework. *Journal of the International Council for Small Business, 1*(1), 14–23. https://www.tandfonline.com/doi/full/10.1080/26437015.2020.1714356

Casselman, R. M., Sama, L. M., & Stefanidis, A. (2015). Differential social performance of religiously-affiliated microfinance institutions (MFIs) in base of pyramid (BoP) markets. *Journal of Business Ethics, 132*(3), 539–552.

Cellura, M., Fichera, A., Guarino, F., & Volpe, R. (2025). Leveraging Positive Energy Districts Surplus for the Achievement of the Sustainable Development Goals. *Energies*, *18*(3), 506. DOI: 10.3390/en18030506

Central Bank of Brazil (BCB). (2020). Green Finance Guidelines. Retrieved from https://www.bcb.gov.br/en/financialstability/greenfinance

Central Bank of Kenya (CBK). (2021). Climate-related Stress Testing. Retrieved from https://www.centralbank.go.ke/stress-testing/

Central Bank of Nigeria (CBN). (2020). Capacity-building Program on Green Finance. Retrieved from https://www.cbn.gov.ng/Out/2020/FMD/FMD%20ED-TRG %20on%20GF.pdf

Cerchione, R., Centobelli, P., & Shabani, A. (2018). Sustainability orientation, supply chain integration, and SMEs performance: A causal analysis. *Benchmarking*, *25*(9), 3679–3701.

Chai, N., Abedin, M. Z., Yang, L., & Shi, B. (2025). Farmers' credit risk evaluation with an explainable hybrid ensemble approach: A closer look in microfinance. *Pacific-Basin Finance Journal*, *89*, 102612. DOI: 10.1016/j.pacfin.2024.102612

Challoumis, C. (2024, October 3-4). *Financial Literacy in an AI-Driven World: What you need to know* [Presentation]. *16th International Scientific Conference*, Philadelphia, USA.

Chang, Y.-K., Cheung, W. M. Y., Chung, M.-H., & Tan, H. (2024). The Paris Agreement effect of consumer awareness and sustainable investing: Some international evidence. *Pacific-Basin Finance Journal*, *85*, 102394. DOI: 10.1016/j.pacfin.2024.102394

Chaudhury, A. (2020). Role of Intermediaries in Shaping Climate Finance in Developing Countries—Lessons from the Green Climate Fund. *Sustainability*, *12*(14), 5507. https://www.mdpi.com/2071-1050/12/14/5507

Cheberyako, O. V., Varnalii, Z. S., Borysenko, O. A., & Miedviedkova, N. S. (2021). "Green" Finance as a Modern Tool for Social and Environmental Security. IOP Conference Series: Earth and Environmental Science. https://iopscience.iop.org/article/10.1088/1755-1315/915/1/012017

Chekenya, N. S., & Mundava, S. (2025). CEOs' characteristics and the performance of microfinance institutions in Africa: A multitier model approach. *Cogent Business & Management*, *12*(1), 2464224. DOI: 10.1080/23311975.2025.2464224

Chen, S., Wang, K., & Liu, H. (2022). The Impact of the Equator Principle on Carbon Financial Markets: A Case Study Based on China's Green Credit Data. SSRN *Electronic Journal*. https://doi.org/DOI: 10.2139/ssrn.4113787

Chenic, A. S., Cre u, A., Burlacu, A., Moroianu, N., Vîrjan, D., Huru, D., Stanef-Puică, M., & Enăchescu, V. (2022). Logical analysis on the strategy for a sustainable transition of the world to green energy—2050. *Sustainability*, *14*(14), 8622.

Chen, L. (2024). Exploring Innovative Practices and Challenges in the Ecological Development of Art Industry Driven by Digital Technology. *Applied Mathematics and Nonlinear Sciences*, *9*(1), 20242975. DOI: 10.2478/amns-2024-2975

Chen, M., Liang, Y., Zhu, J., & Zheng, S. (2023). A DEA-based ESG performance evaluation framework for sustainable supply chain finance. *Sustainability*, *15*(2), 723.

Chen, M., & Wang, C. (2024). How business model innovation facilitates microcredit in balancing social mission with commercial performance – Evidence from local commercial banks. *Technological Forecasting and Social Change*, *202*, 123287. DOI: 10.1016/j.techfore.2024.123287

Chen, Y., & Volz, U. (2022). Green finance and fintech: Emerging issues and prospects. *Journal of Sustainable Finance & Investment*, *12*(2), 329–347. DOI: 10.1080/20430795.2020.1802815

Cherrafi, A., Elfezazi, S., Govindan, K., Garza-Reyes, J. A., Benhida, K., & Mokhlis, A. (2017). A framework for the integration of Green and Lean Six Sigma for superior sustainability performance. *International Journal of Production Research*, *55*(15), 4481–4515. DOI: 10.1080/00207543.2016.1266406

Chih, H.-L., Chih, H.-H., & Chen, T.-Y. (2010). On the Déterminants of Corporate Social Responsibility: International Evidence on the Financial Industry. *Journal of Business Ethics*, *93*, 115–135.

Chikalipah, S. (2018). Do microsavings stimulate financial performance of microfinance institutions in Sub-Saharan Africa? *Journal of Economic Studies (Glasgow, Scotland)*, *45*(5), 1072–1087.

Chow, W. W., & Fung, M. K. (2025). Relative ESG positions among OECD countries in the presence of international competition for FDI inflow: A gravity model perspective. *Research in International Business and Finance*, *76*. Advance online publication. DOI: 10.1016/j.ribaf.2025.102851

Christiansen, J. K., & Vendelo, M. T. (2003). The Role of Reputation Building in International R&D Project Collaboration. *Corporate Reputation Review*, *5*, 304–329.

Chueca Vergara, C., & Ferruz Agudo, L. (2021). Fintech and Sustainability: Do They Affect Each Other? *Sustainability*, *13*(13), 7012. DOI: 10.3390/su13137012

Chugani, N., Kumar, V., Garza-Reyes, J. A., Rocha-Lona, L., & Upadhyay, A. (2017). Investigating the green impact of Lean, Six Sigma and Lean Six Sigma: A systematic literature review. *International Journal of Lean Six Sigma*, *8*(1), 7–32.

Churchill, S. A., Inekwe, J., Smyth, R., & Zhang, X. (2019). R&D Intensity and Carbon Emissions in the G7: 1870-2014. *Energy Economics*, *80*, 30–37. https://www.sciencedirect.com/science/article/abs/pii/S0140988318305024?via%3Dihub

Citraresmi, A. D. P., Rucitra, A. L., Amalia, F., & Mustaniroh, S. A. (2023). Effect of sustainability readiness on digital transformation adoption in SMEs. *Advances in Food Science. Sustainable Agriculture and Agroindustrial Engineering*, *6*(4). Advance online publication. DOI: 10.21776/ub.afssaae.2023.006.04.2

Clark, G. L., Feiner, A., & Viehs, M. (2015). From the stockholder to the stakeholder: How sustainability can drive financial outperformance. University of Oxford and Arabesque Partners. https://arabesque.com/research/

Climate Bonds Initiative. (2021). *Financing credible transitions: A guide to supporting companies in transition*. https://www.climatebonds.net/resources/reports

Coenen, J., Glass, L.-M., & Sanderink, L. (2022). Two degrees and the SDGs: A network analysis of the interlinkages between transnational climate actions and the Sustainable Development Goals. *Sustainability Science*, *17*(4), 1489–1510. DOI: 10.1007/s11625-021-01007-9

Cohen, R., Eames, P., Hammond, G. P., Newborough, M., & Norton, B. (2022). The 2021 Glasgow Climate Pact – Steps on the transition pathway towards a low carbon world. *Proceedings of the Institution of Civil Engineers – Energy*, *175*(4), 123–136.

Cojoianu, T. F., French, D., Hoepner, A. G. F., Sheenan, L., & Vu, A. (2025). On the Origin of Green Finance Policies. *Journal of Financial Stability*, *79*, 101418. https://www.sciencedirect.com/science/article/pii/S1572308925000476

Conley, J. M., & Williams, C. A. (2011). Global banks as global sustainability regulators?: The equator principles. *Law & Policy*, *33*(4), 542–575. DOI: 10.1111/j.1467-9930.2011.00348.x

Contreras, G., Jaap, W. B., & Kleimeier, S. (2019). Self-regulation in sustainable finance: The adoption of the Equator Principles. *World Development, Elsevier*, *122*(C), 306–324.

Corvellec, H., Stowell, A. F., & Johansson, N. (2022). Critiques of the Circular Economy. *Journal of Industrial Ecology*, *26*, 421–432. https://onlinelibrary.wiley.com/doi/pdf/10.1111/jiec.13187?trk=public_post_comment-text

Coulee, F. & Motte-Baumvol, J. (2018). Rapport de recherche sur l'effectivité des codes de gouvernance d'entreprise, de l'intérêt du droit international pour apprécier l'opportunité d'une réforme législative en France. HAL Science Ouverte. hal-04527939, version 1.

Cullen, J. (2018, August). After "HLEG": EU Banks, Climate Change Abatement and the Precautionary Principle. *Cambridge Yearbook of European Legal Studies*, *20*, 61–87. DOI: 10.1017/cel.2018.7

D'Espallier, B., Hudon, M., & Szafarz, A. (2017). Aid volatility and social performance in microfinance. *Nonprofit and Voluntary Sector Quarterly*, *46*(1), 116–140.

D'Orazio, P., Scholtens, B., De Mariz, F., González-Ruiz, J. D., Ullah, S., Adegbite, O., Thompson, B. S., Liu, F. H. M., Harris, J. L., Bigger, P., Pill, M., Hammersley, G., & Berg, M. (2023). Catalyzing the transformation to sustainable finance. *One Earth*, *6*(10), 1271–1276. DOI: 10.1016/j.oneear.2023.09.011

Dam, L. (2008). *Corporate social responsibility and financial markets*. Doctoral Thesis, Rijksuniversiteit Groningen, PrintPartners Ipskamp, Nederland.

Danish, B. M. A., Mahmood, N., & Zhang, J. W. (2019). Effect of Natural Resources, Renewable Energy, and Economic Development on CO_2 Emissions in BRICS Countries. *Science of the Total Environment*, 678, 632-638. https://www.sciencedirect.com/science/article/abs/pii/S004896971932039X?via%3Dihub

De Perthuis, C. (2003). La génération future a-t-elle un avenir? Développement durable et mondialisation, Paris: Belin.

Debrah, C., Darko, A., & Chan, A. P. C. (2022). A bibliometric-qualitative literature review of green finance gap and future research directions. *Climate and Development*, *15*(5), 432–455. DOI: 10.1080/17565529.2022.2095331

DEH. A. A., & KHOUMA, N. P. (2023). Performance financière des institutions de microfinance au Sénégal et en Côte d'Ivoire: Quels en sont les déterminants? Revue Africaine de Management, 1(9). https://doi.org/DOI: 10.48424/IMIST.PRSM/RAM-V1I9.40402

Delina, L.L, Lam, Rainbow, Y.H.,Tang, W.S., & Wong, K.Y. (2023). Mapping the actor landscape of a future fintech-funded renewable energy ecosystem in Hong Kong. *Journal of Environmental Studies and Sciences*, *13*(3), 419–427.

Dellis, K. (2024). Financial distance and FDI flows: Evidence from OECD economies. *World Economy*, *47*(6), 2536–2573. DOI: 10.1111/twec.13552

Delmas, M. A., & Burbano, V. C. (2011). The drivers of greenwashing. *California Management Review*, *54*(1), 64–87. DOI: 10.1525/cmr.2011.54.1.64

Derrick, M. (2024). Top 10: Countries Using Renewable Energies. *Energy Digital*. https://energydigital.com/top10/top-10-countries-using-renewable-energies

Desalegn, G., Fekete-Farkas, M., & Tangl, A. (2022). The effect of monetary policy and private investment on green finance: Evidence from Hungary. *Journal of Risk and Financial Management*, *15*(3), 117.

Dey, P. K., Malesios, C., De, D., Chowdhury, S., & Abdelaziz, F. B. (2020). The Impact of Lean Management Practices and Sustainably-Oriented Innovation on Sustainability Performance of Small and Medium-Sized Enterprises: Empirical Evidence from the UK. *British Journal of Management*, *31*(1), 141–161. DOI: 10.1111/1467-8551.12388

Diaz-Serrano, L., & Sackey, F. G. (2018). Microfinance and credit rationing: Does the microfinance type matter? *Journal of Sustainable Finance & Investment*, *8*(2), 114–131.

Digital literacy, digital intelligence and small and medium enterprises' (SMEs) sustainability: The mediating role of digital technology usage—Masud Ibrahim, Elizabeth Wetania Aduah, 2025. (n.d.). Retrieved August 11, 2025, from https://journals.sagepub.com/doi/abs/10.1177/02666669251335001

Dikau, S., & Volz, U. (2020). Central Bank Mandates, Sustainability Objectives and the Promotion of Green Finance. Working Papers 232, Department of Economics, SOAS University of London, UK.

Dimson, E., Karakaş, O., & Li, X. (2015). Active ownership. *Review of Financial Studies*, *28*(12), 3225–3268. DOI: 10.1093/rfs/hhv044

Djoufouet, F. W., & Nzongang, J. (2020). Effets combinés des mécanismes de gouvernance sur la performance des institutions de microfinance au Cameroun. *Journal of Academic Finance*, *11*(1), 22–32. DOI: 10.59051/joaf.v11i1.324

Dogan, E., Luni, T., Majeed, M. T., & Tzeremes, P. (2023). The Nexus between Global Carbon and Renewable Energy Sources: A Step Towards Sustainability. *Journal of Cleaner Production*, *416*, 137927. https://www.sciencedirect.com/science/article/abs/pii/S0959652623020851?via%3Dihub

Domergue, F. (2018). CSR in the banking sector, a tool for regaining confidence in times of crisis? https://hal.archives-ouvertes.fr

Dong, K., Sun, R., Jiang, H., & Zeng, X. (2018). CO_2 Emissions, Economic Growth, and the Environmental Kuznets Curve in China: What Roles Can Nuclear Energy and Renewable Energy Play? *Journal of Cleaner Production, 196*, 51–63. https://www.sciencedirect.com/science/article/abs/pii/S095965261831624X?via%3Dihub

Donou-Adonsou, F. (2025). Financial structure and economic efficiency in Sub-Saharan Africa. *Global Finance Journal, 67*, 101150. DOI: 10.1016/j.gfj.2025.101150

Donthu, N., Kumar, S., Mukherjee, D., Pandey, N., & Lim, W. M. (2021). *H*ow to conduct a bibliometric analysis: An overview and guidelines. *Journal of Business Research, 133*, 285–296.

Dröge, S., Trabold, H., Biermann, F., Böhm, F., & Brohm, R. (2004). National climate change policies and WTO law: A case study of Germany's new policies. *World Trade Review, 3*(2), 161–187.

Duan, K. (2021, August). Green into Gold: The Sustainable Development of Commercial Banks from the Perspective of the Equator Principles. *International Journal of Theoretical and Applied Mathematics., 7*(4), 57–67.

Duque Oliva, E. J., Sánchez-Torres, J. A., Arroyo-Cañada, F.-J., Argila-Irurita, A., Fuente, J. G.-L., Palacio-López, S.-M., & Arrubla-Zapata, J.-P. (2024). Green Buying Behaviour: An Integrated Model. *Sustainability, 16*(11), 4441. DOI: 10.3390/su16114441

Durrani, A., Rosmin, M., & Volz, U. (2020). The Role of Central Banks in Scaling Up Sustainable Finance – What do Monetary Authorities in the Asia-Pacific Region Think? *Journal of Sustainable Finance & Investment, 10*(2), 92–112. DOI: 10.1080/20430795.2020.1715095

Durrani, A., Rosmin, M., & Volz, U. (2020). The role of central banks in scaling up sustainable finance—What do monetary authorities in the Asia-Pacific region think? *Journal of Sustainable Finance & Investment, 10*, 92–112.

Dynamic Capabilities and Green Strategy in Green Entrepreneurship and Circular Economy: A Study—Mondal—Business Strategy and the Environment—Wiley Online Library. (n.d.). Retrieved August 11, 2025, from https://onlinelibrary.wiley.com/doi/abs/10.1002/bse.70030

Dziwok, E., & Jäger, J. (2024). A Critical Overview of Green Finance. In Jäger, J., & Dziwok, E. (Eds.), *Understanding Green Finance: A Critical Assessment and Alternative Perspective* (pp. 2–17). Edward Elgar., https://www.elgaronline.com/edcollchap/book/9781803927558/book-part-9781803927558-8.xml

Eccles, R. G., Ioannou, I., & Serafeim, G. (2014). The impact of a corporate culture of sustainability on corporate behavior and performance. *Harvard Business School Working Paper*, 12-035.

Eccles, R. G., & Klimenko, S. (2019). The investor revolution. *Harvard Business Review*, *97*(3), 106–116.

Economic Times. (2017). IRFC to raise Rs 1,000 crore via first green bond issue. Retrieved from https://economictimes.indiatimes.com/industry/transportation/railways/irfc-to-raise-rs-1000-crore-via-first-green-bond-issue/articleshow/59377521.cms

Economic Times. (2019). Azure Power raises $350 million green bond. Retrieved from https://economictimes.indiatimes.com/industry/energy/power/azure-power-raises-350-million-green-bond/articleshow/68305970.cms

Ehlers, T., & Packer, F. (2017). Green bond finance and certification. *BIS Quarterly Review*, (September), 89–104.

Eisenbach, S., Schiereck, D., Trillig, J., & von Flotow, P. (2014). Sustainable project finance, the adoption of the equator principles and shareholder value effects. *Business Strategy and the Environment*, *23*(6), 375–394. DOI: 10.1002/bse.1789

El Hasanah, L. N. (2025). Exploring Green Research Opportunities Within the Fintech Landscape for Sustainable Growth. *Start-Up and Financial Technology*, *1*(1), 44–56. DOI: 10.70764/gdpu-sft.2025.1(1)-04

El-Kassar, A.-N., & Singh, S. K. (2019). Green innovation and organizational performance: The influence of big data and the moderating role of management commitment and HR practices. *Technological Forecasting and Social Change*, *144*, 483–498. DOI: 10.1016/j.techfore.2017.12.016

Elkington, J. (1994). Towards the sustainable corporation: Win-win-win business strategies for sustainable development. *California Management Review*, *36*(2), 90–100. DOI: 10.2307/41165746

EU Technical Expert Group on Sustainable Finance. (2020). *Taxonomy: Final report of the Technical Expert Group on Sustainable Finance*. European Commission. https://ec.europa.eu/info/publications/sustainable-finance-technical-expert-group_en

EU. (2018). *EU Action Plan on Sustainable Finance*. European Commission.

EU. (2020). *EU Taxonomy Regulation*. Official Journal of the European Union.

European Central Bank (ECB). (2021). Asset Purchase Program. Retrieved from https://www.ecb.europa.eu/mopo/implement/omt/html/index.en.html

European Central Bank. (2016). Corporate Sector Purchase Programme. Retrieved from https://www.ecb.europa.eu/mopo/implement/omt/html/corporate_sector_purchase_programme.en.html

European Commission (2014a). Directive of the European Parliament and of the Council: Amending Directive 2007/36/EC." Proposal. Brussels: European Commission.

European Commission. (2004). Recommendation on remuneration of directors in listed companies (2004/913/EC). Working Document. Brussels: European Commission. www.ec.europa.eu

European Commission. (2014b). European Commission proposes to strengthen shareholder engagement and introduce a 'say on pay' for Europe's largest companies." Press Release (April 9). Brussels: European Commission. www.ec.europa.eu

European Commission. (2014c). EU Audit Directive and Regulation." Factsheet. Brussels: European Commission. www.ec.europa.eu

European Commission. (2020). *EU taxonomy for sustainable activities*. https://finance.ec.europa.eu/sustainable-finance/tools-and-standards/eu-taxonomy-sustainable-activities_en

European Commission. (2021). Sustainable Finance Action Plan. Retrieved from https://ec.europa.eu/info/publications/sustainable-finance-action-plan_en

European Commission. (2021). *Sustainable Finance Disclosure Regulation (SFDR)*. https://finance.ec.europa.eu/sustainable-finance/disclosure-and-reporting/sfdr_en

European Commission. (2021). *Sustainable finance: Commission welcomes the adoption of the European Green Bond Standard*. https://ec.europa.eu/info/publications/210507-sustainable-finance-communication_en

European Investment Bank. (2022). The EIB Environment Framework. https://www.eib.org/attachments/lucalli/20220213_eib_environment_framework_en.pdf

European Union. (2020). *Regulation (EU) 2019/2088 on sustainability-related disclosures in the financial services sector (SFDR).*

Exploring the impact of green entrepreneurial orientation on sustainable performance: Insights from CSR, policy and innovation | Management Decision | Emerald Publishing. (n.d.). Retrieved August 11, 2025, from https://www.emerald.com/md/article-abstract/62/12/3946/1228791/Exploring-the-impact-of-green-entrepreneurial?redirectedFrom=fulltext

Fama, E. F. (1970). Efficient capital markets: A review of theory and empirical work. *The Journal of Finance*, *25*(2), 383–417. DOI: 10.2307/2325486

Fang, Z., Yang, C., & Song, X. (2022). How do green finance and energy efficiency mitigate carbon emissions without reducing economic growth in G7 countries? *Frontiers in Psychology*, *13*, 879741. PMID: 35592175

Faruq, A. T. M. O., & Huq, M. T. (2024). *The Role of Central Banks in Advancing Sustainable Finance* (Version 1). arXiv. https://doi.org/DOI: 10.48550/ARXIV.2411.13576

Fechtelpeter, C., Kuehn, A., Dumitrescu, R., & Ebbesmeyer, P. (2017). Integrated technology transfer concept for fostering innovation in SMEs. *26th Int. Assoc. Manag. Technol. Conf. IAMOT*, 1028–1048. https://www.researchgate.net/profile/Christian-Fechtelpeter/publication/344427721_Integrated_Technology_Transfer_Concept_For_Fostering_Innovation_In_SMEs/links/5f8e9679458515b7cf8dd629/Integrated-Technology-Transfer-Concept-For-Fostering-Innovation-In-SMEs.pdf

Federal Reserve System (FRS). (2020). Capacity-building Program on Green Finance. Retrieved from https://www.federalreserve.gov/supervisionreg/srletters/sr20-19.htm

Federal Reserve System. (2021). Supervisory Guidance on Climate Risk Management. Retrieved from https://www.federalreserve.gov/supervisionreg/srletters/sr21-8.htm

Feng, M. (2024). Green loan interest subsidy policy, green technological innovation, and high-quality enterprise development. *Asia Pacific Economic and Management Review*, *1*(5), 74.

Fernandez-Lores, S., Crespo-Tejero, N., & Fernández-Hernández, R. (2022). Driving traffic to the museum: The role of the digital communication tools. *Technological Forecasting and Social Change*, *174*, 121273.

Fersi, M., & Boujelbène, M. (2022). Overconfidence and credit risk-taking in microfinance institutions: A cross-regional analysis. *The International Journal of Organizational Analysis*, *30*(6), 1672–1693. DOI: 10.1108/IJOA-11-2020-2510

Filho, W. L., Wall, T., Salvia, A. L., Dinis, M. A. P., & Mifsud, M. (2023). The central role of climate action in achieving the United Nations' Sustainable Development Goals. *Scientific Reports*, *13*(1), 20582. DOI: 10.1038/s41598-023-47746-w PMID: 37996539

Fink, L. (2020). *A fundamental reshaping of finance*. BlackRock. https://www.blackrock.com/corporate/investor-relations/larry-fink-ceo-letter

Flaherty, M., Gevorkyan, A., Radpour, S., & Semmler, W. (2017). Financing Climate Policies through Climate Bonds — A Three Stage Model and Empirics. *Research in International Business and Finance*, *42*, 468–479. https://www.sciencedirect.com/science/article/abs/pii/S0275531916301003?via%3Dihub

Flammer, C. (2021). Corporate green bonds. *Journal of Financial Economics*, *142*(2), 499–516.

Flögel, F., Schepelmann, P., Zademach, H. M., & Zörner, M. (2023). Injecting climate finance into SME lending in Germany. *ZFW - Advances in Economic Geography*, *0*, 1–21.

Florini, A. (2003). Business and Global Governance: The Growing Role of Corporate Codes of Conduct. *The Brookings Review*, *21*(2), 4–8.

Freeman, R. E. (1984). *Strategic Management: A Stakeholder Approach*. Pitman Publishing.

Freeman, R. E. (1984). *Strategic management: A stakeholder approach*. Pitman.

Freshfields Bruckhaus Deringer. (2005). *A legal framework for the integration of environmental, social and governance issues into institutional investment*. UNEP FI.

Friede, G., Busch, T., & Bassen, A. (2015). ESG and financial performance: Aggregated evidence from more than 2000 empirical studies. *Journal of Sustainable Finance & Investment*, *5*(4), 210–233. DOI: 10.1080/20430795.2015.1118917

Friedman, M. (1970, September 13). The social responsibility of business is to increase its profits. *The New York Times Magazine*.

Fu, C., Lu, L., & Pirabi, M. (2023). Advancing Green Finance: A Review of Sustainable Development. *Digital Economy and Sustainable Development,* 1(20), 1-19. https://link.springer.com/article/10.1007/s44265-023-00020-3

Fu, C., Zhang, Y., & Wu, J. (2023). Advancing green finance: A review of sustainable finance, climate change and decarbonization. *Business Strategy and the Environment*, *32*(1), 49–68.

G20 Green Finance Study Group. (2016). G20 Green Finance Synthesis Report. https://g20sfwg.org/wp-content/uploads/2021/07/2016_Synthesis_Report_Full_EN.pdf

Gaganis, C. (2016). Assessing the overall performance of microfinance institutions. International Journal of Banking. *Accounting and Finance*, *7*(1), 52–83.

Garza-Reyes, J. A. (2015). Lean and green–a systematic review of the state of the art literature. *Journal of Cleaner Production*, *102*, 18–29.

GCF. (2021). *Green Climate Fund Annual Results Report*. Retrieved from https://www.greenclimate.fund/

Geissdoerfer, M., Savaget, P., Bocken, N. M., & Hultink, E. J. (2017). The Circular Economy—A New Sustainability Paradigm? *Journal of Cleaner Production*, *143*, 757–768. https://www.sciencedirect.com/science/article/abs/pii/S0959652616321023

Ghazilla, R. A. R., Sakundarini, N., Abdul-Rashid, S. H., Ayub, N. S., Olugu, E. U., & Musa, S. N. (2015). Drivers and barriers analysis for green manufacturing practices in Malaysian SMEs: A preliminary findings. *Procedia CIRP*, *26*, 658–663.

Gholami, S. (2011). Value creation model through corporate social responsibility (CSR). *International Journal of Business and Management*, *6*(9), 148–154.

Gholipour, H. F., & Al-Mulali, U. (2014). The interaction between tourism and FDI in real estate in OECD countries. *Current Issues in Tourism*, *17*(2), 105–113. DOI: 10.1080/13683500.2012.733359

Ghosh, M., & Wang, W. (2010). Does FDI accelerate economic growth? the OECD experience based on panel data estimates for the period 1980-2004. *Global Economy Journal*, *9*(4). Advance online publication. DOI: 10.2202/1524-5861.1496

Ghosh, S. (2020). *Financing green recovery in developing Asia*. Asian Development Bank Institute.

Ghosh, S., Dey, S., & Kumar, S. (2023). Fintech for sustainability: Transformative potential of digital innovation in green finance. *Journal of Sustainable Finance & Investment*, *13*(1), 45–63. DOI: 10.1080/20430795.2022.2107093

Giese, G., Lee, L. E., Melas, D., Nagy, Z., & Nishikawa, L. (2019). Foundations of ESG investing: How ESG affects equity valuation, risk, and performance. *Journal of Portfolio Management*, *45*(5), 69–83.

Golesorkhi, S., Mersland, R., Randøy, T., & Shenkar, O. (2019). The performance impact of culture and formal institutional differences in cross-border alliances: The case of the microfinance industry. *International Business Review*, *28*(1), 104–118.

Gomes, S., Pinho, M., & Lopes, J. M. (2024). From environmental sustainability practices to green innovations: Evidence from small and medium-sized manufacturing companies. *Corporate Social Responsibility and Environmental Management, 31*(3), 1677–1687. DOI: 10.1002/csr.2657

Gonçalves, A., & Silva, C. (2021). Looking for Sustainability Scoring in Apparel: A Review on Environmental Footprint, Social Impacts and Transparency. *Energies, 14*(11), 3032. DOI: 10.3390/en14113032

Gond, J. P., & Igalens, J. (2008). Corporate social responsibility. Collection: What do I know? Publisher: Presses Universitaires de France, 128 pages.

Goss, A., & Roberts, G. S. (2011). The impact of corporate social responsibility on the cost of bank loans. *Journal of Banking & Finance, 35*(7), 1794–1810. DOI: 10.1016/j.jbankfin.2010.12.002

Green Climate Fund (GCF). (2021). Capacity-building. Retrieved from https://www.greenclimate.fund/how-we-work/capacity-building

Griffith-Jones, S., Marodon, R., Rochon, L. P., & Xu, J. (2022). Introduction: Unleashing the Potential of Public Development Banks for Achieving Sustainable Development Goals. In *Development and Public Banks* (pp. 1-4). Routledge.

Grigoryan, A., Khachatryan, K., Hartarska, V., & Mersland, R. (2025). Are all deposit products in the microfinance world created equal? *Emerging Markets Finance & Trade, 61*(5), 1160–1176. DOI: 10.1080/1540496X.2024.2413172

Gul, F. A., Podder, J., & Shahriar, A. Z. M. (2017). Performance of microfinance institutions: Does government ideology matter? *World Development, 100*, 1–15.

Gurbanov, S., & Suleymanli, F. (2022). Analytical Assessment of Green Digital Finance Progress in the Republic of Georgia. *Economics, Law, and Institutions in Asia Pacific*, 205 – 222. https://doi.org/DOI: 10.1007/978-981-19-2662-4_10

Gu, X., Alamri, A. M., Ahmad, M., Alsagr, N., Zhong, X., & Wu, T. (2023). Natural resources extraction and green finance: Dutch disease and COP27 targets for OECD countries. *Resources Policy, 81*. Advance online publication. DOI: 10.1016/j.resourpol.2023.103404

Habib, Y., Abd Rahman, N. R., Hashmi, S. H., & Ali, M. (2025). Green finance and environmental decentralization drive OECD low carbon transitions. *Scientific Reports, 15*(1). Advance online publication. DOI: 10.1038/s41598-025-11967-y PMID: 40750618

Hallam, C., & Contreras, C. (2016). Integrating lean and green management. *Management Decision, 54*(9), 2157–2187.

Hamdani, S., & Ibenrissoul, A. (2017). Sustainable microfinance and global performance proposal for a decision-making support tool. *European Journal of Sustainable Development, 6*(3), 253–270.

Han, J., & Gao, H. (2024). Green finance, social inclusion, and sustainable economic growth in OECD member countries. *Humanities & Social Sciences Communications, 11*(1). Advance online publication. DOI: 10.1057/s41599-024-02662-w

Hardenbrook, A. (2007). The Equator Principles : The Private Financial Sector's Attempt at Environmental Responsibility. *Vanderbilt Journal of Transnational Law, 40*(1), 197–232.

Hasan, M. H., Hossain, M. Z., Hasan, L., & Dewan, M. A. (2024). FinTech and Sustainable Finance: How is FinTech Shaping the Future of Sustainable Finance? *European Journal of Management. Economics and Business, 1*(3), 100–115. DOI: 10.59324/ejmeb.2024.1(3).09

Hegab, H., Shaban, I., Jamil, M., & Khanna, N. (2023). Toward Sustainable Future: Strategies, Indicators, and Challenges for Implementing Sustainable Production Systems. *Sustainable Materials and Technologies,* 36, e00617. https://www.sciencedirect.com/science/article/abs/pii/S2214993723000520

Heinkel, R., Kraus, A., & Zechner, J. (2001). The effect of green investment on corporate behavior. *Journal of Financial and Quantitative Analysis, 36*(4), 431–449. DOI: 10.2307/2676219

Hermes, N., & Hudon, M. (2018). Determinants of the performance of microfinance institutions: A systematic review. *Journal of Economic Surveys, 32*(5), 1483–1513.

Hesse, C. (2016). Decentralizing Climate Finance to Reach the Most Vulnerable. *International Institute for Environment and Development*. https://www.iied.org/g04103

Hosmer, L. T. (1995). Trust: The Connecting Link between Organizational Theory and Philosophical Ethics. *Academy of Management Review, 20*, 379–403.

Hossain, M. T., Shahid, M. A., Limon, M. G. M., Hossain, I., & Mahmud, N. (2024). Techniques, applications, and challenges in textiles for a sustainable future. *Journal of Open Innovation, 10*(1), 100230. DOI: 10.1016/j.joitmc.2024.100230

Hossain, S., Hossain, M. M., & Chong, V. K. (2025). Do client protection principles matter for the economic and social performance of microfinance institutions? *The British Accounting Review, 57*(4), 101493. DOI: 10.1016/j.bar.2024.101493

Hu, D., & Gan, C. (2025). Green Finance Development and its Origin, Motives, and Barriers: An Exploratory Study. *Environment, Development, and Sustainability*. https://link.springer.com/article/10.1007/s10668-024-05570-w

Huang, L., Cao, Y., & Zhu, Y. (2023). Is there any recovery power for economic growth from green finance? Evidence from OECD member countries. *Economic Change and Restructuring*, *56*(6), 3909–3926. DOI: 10.1007/s10644-022-09458-5

Huang, X., Guo, Y., Lin, Y., Liu, L., & Yan, K. (2022). Green Loans and Green Innovations: Evidence from China's Equator Principles Banks. *Sustainability*, *14*(20), 13674. DOI: 10.3390/su142013674

Huang, Z., Zhang, Z., Hua, C., Liao, B., & Li, S. (2024). Leveraging enhanced egret swarm optimization algorithm and artificial intelligence-driven prompt strategies for portfolio selection. *Scientific Reports*, *14*(1), 26681. DOI: 10.1038/s41598-024-77925-2 PMID: 39496781

Hu, D., & Gan, C. (2025). Green finance development and its origin, motives, and barriers: An exploratory study. *Environment, Development and Sustainability*, •••, 1–25.

Hudon, M., & Allet, M. (2015). Green microfinance: Characteristics of microfinance institutions involved in environmental management. *Journal of Business Ethics*, *126*(3), 395–414.

Hu, H., Jia, Z., & Yang, S. (2025). Exploring FinTech, green finance, and ESG performance across corporate life-cycles. *International Review of Financial Analysis*, *97*, 103871. DOI: 10.1016/j.irfa.2024.103871

Hussain, M., Rehman, R. U., Bashir, U., & Faisal, F. (2025). Examining employee well-being and financial performance in microfinance institutions: Insights from cross-country analysis. *Journal of Social and Economic Development*. Advance online publication. DOI: 10.1007/s40847-025-00458-5

Ikechukwu Obinyeluaku, M., Mobolaji Abioye, K., Ibukun Babalola, F., Zamanjomane Mhlongo, N., & Daraojimba, C. (2023). A COMPREHENSIVE REVIEW OF AI APPLICATIONS IN FINANCE FOR ACCELERATING CLEAN ENERGY TRANSITION. *Information Management and Computer Science*, *6*(1), 41–49. DOI: 10.26480/imcs.01.2023.41.49

IMF. (2021). *Mobilizing Private Climate Financing in Emerging Market and Developing Economies*. International Monetary Fund.

IMF. (2023). *Fintech and the Sustainable Finance Agenda: Policy Considerations for China and Beyond.* International Monetary Fund. https://www.imf.org/en/Publications

Inderst, G., Kaminker, C., & Stewart, F. (2012). Defining and measuring green investments. *OECD Working Papers on Finance, Insurance and Private Pensions*, No. 24.

Indian Renewable Energy Development Agency (IREDA). (2021). Bhadla Solar Park. Retrieved from https://www.ireda.in/Home/SolarProjects

Inês, A., Diniz, A., & Moreira, A. C. (2023). A review of greenwashing and supply chain management: Challenges ahead. *Cleaner Environmental Systems, 11*, 100136. DOI: 10.1016/j.cesys.2023.100136

Integrating Sustainability in Small Scale Industries: From Environmental Degradation to Cleaner Practices: Environmental Claims Journal: Vol 0, No 0. (n.d.). Retrieved August 11, 2025, from https://www.tandfonline.com/doi/abs/10.1080/10406026.2025.2506658

International Energy Agency (IEA). (2020). India Energy Outlook 2020. Retrieved from https://www.iea.org/reports/india-energy-outlook-2020

International Energy Agency (IEA). (2021). World Energy Outlook 2021. Retrieved from https://www.iea.org/reports/world-energy-outlook-2021

International Finance Corporation (IFC). (2021). Climate Business Department. Retrieved from https://www.ifc.org/wps/wcm/connect/industry_ext_content/ifc_external_corporate_site/industries/climate-business

International Renewable Energy Agency (IRENA). (2023) World Energy Transitions Outlook 2023. Retrieved from https://www.irena.org/Digital-Report/World-Energy-Transitions-Outlook-2023

International Renewable Energy Agency. (2022). *World energy transitions outlook 2022*. IRENA. https://www.irena.org/publications

Isensee, C., Teuteberg, F., Griese, K.-M., & Topi, C. (2020). The relationship between organizational culture, sustainability, and digitalization in SMEs: A systematic review. *Journal of Cleaner Production, 275*, 122944.

Ishaq, M. I., Sarwar, H., Aftab, J., Franzoni, S., & Raza, A. (2024). Accomplishing sustainable performance through leaders' competencies, green entrepreneurial orientation, and innovation in an emerging economy: Moderating role of institutional support. *Business Strategy and the Environment, 33*(2), 1515–1532. DOI: 10.1002/bse.3557

Jackson, E. T., & Harji, K. (2012). *Accelerating impact: Achievements, challenges and what's next in building the impact investing industry*. Rockefeller Foundation.

Jafri, M. A. H., Liu, H., Usman, A., & Khan, Q. R. (2021). Re-evaluating the Asymmetric Conventional Energy and Renewable Energy Consumption-Economic Growth Nexus for Pakistan. *Environmental Science and Pollution Research International, 28*(4), 37435–37447. https://link.springer.com/article/10.1007/s11356-021-13131-1 PMID: 33713265

Jalil, M. F., Marikan, D. A. B. A., & Jais, M. bin, Ayupp, K., & Shukri, M. H. bin M. (2025). A Green Internet of Things (GIoT) Adoption Framework to Enhance Environmental Performance of SMEs Through the Digital Social Networking. *Business Strategy & Development, 8*(3), e70179. DOI: 10.1002/bsd2.70179

Jansson, J., Nilsson, J., Modig, F., & Hed Vall, G. (2017). Commitment to Sustainability in Small and Medium-Sized Enterprises: The Influence of Strategic Orientations and Management Values. *Business Strategy and the Environment, 26*(1), 69–83. DOI: 10.1002/bse.1901

Japan Green Bond Labeling (JGBL). (2017). Green Bond Guidelines. Retrieved from https://www.japanbond.jp/english/greenbond/guideline.html

Jerbi, S. (2009). Business and Human Rights at the UN: What Might Happen Next? *Human Rights Quarterly, 31*(2), 299–320. https://www.jstor.org/stable/20486754

Jeucken, M. (2004). Sustainability in Finance. Banking on the planet. Delft, The Netherlands: Eburon.

Jeucken, M., & Bouma, J. J. (1999). The Changing Environment of Banks. *Greener Management International, 27*, 21–35.

Jeyadevi J, C. (2023). *SUSTAINABLE DEVELOPMENTS THROUGH MSMEs: A PATHWAY TO SELF-RELIANT INDIA SUSTAINABLE DEVELOPMENTS THROUGH MSMEs: A PATHWAY TO SELF-RELIANT INDIA*.

Jin, C., Lv, Z., Li, Z., & Sun, K. (2023). Green finance, renewable energy and carbon neutrality in OECD countries. *Renewable Energy, 211*, 279–284. DOI: 10.1016/j.renene.2023.04.105

Joeliaty, J. (2024). Green Growth and Beyond: The Influence of Environmental Practices, Financial Management, Market Access, and Digital Integration on the Resilience and Sustainability Business Practices of MSMEs in Indonesia. *International Journal of Business, Law, and Education*, *5*(1), 1. Advance online publication. DOI: 10.56442/ijble.v5i1.446

John-Mathews, J. (2021a). Some critical and ethical perspectives on the empirical turn of AI interpretability. *Technological Forecasting and Social Change*, *174*, 121209. DOI: 10.1016/j.techfore.2021.121209

Jokhio, S. M., Fuzail, M., Murtaza, M., Anwar, A., Lodhi, K., & Asif, T. (2025). *FinTech and Green Finance: Assessing the Impact of Financial Technology Adoption on Sustainability Performance in Emerging Economies*. https://www.researchgate.net/publication/392164574

Jørgensen, U. (2001). Greening of Technology and Ecotechnology. In Smelser, N. J., & Baltes, P. B. (Eds.), *International Encyclopaedia of the Social and Behavioural Sciences* (pp. 6393–6396). Elsevier.

Kanie, N., & Biermann, F. (Eds.). (2017). *Governing through Goals: Sustainable Development Goals as Governance Innovation*. MIT Press.

Kar, A. K., & Swain, R. B. (2018). Competition, performance and portfolio quality in microfinance markets. *European Journal of Development Research*, *30*(5), 842–870.

Karuppiah, K., Sankaranarayanan, B., Ali, S. M., Chowdhury, P., & Paul, S. K. (2020). An integrated approach to modeling the barriers in implementing green manufacturing practices in SMEs. *Journal of Cleaner Production*, *265*, 121737.

Kashif, M., Pinglu, C., Ullah, A., & Qian, N. (2025). The Impact of Green Finance and Fintech Mechanisms on Financial Stability: Evidence from advanced emerging economies. *China Finance Review International*. Advance online publication. DOI: 10.1108/cfri-07-2024-0393

Kasturi Rangan, V., Chase, L., & Karim, S. (2015). The Truth about CSR. *Harvard Business Review*, *93*(1/2), 40–49. https://hbr.org/2015/01/the-truth-about-csr

Kazemian, S., Rahman, R. A., Mohd-Sanusi, Z., & Adewale, A. A. (2016). Role of market orientation in sustainable performance: The case of a leading microfinance provider. *Humanomics*, *32*(3), 352–375.

Kemp-Benedict, E. (2012). *Green finance and investment: Mapping actors and initiatives*. Stockholm Environment Institute.

Kemp, R. (1994). Technology and the Transition to Environmental Sustainability: The Problem of Technological Regime Shifts. *Futures, 26*(10), 1023–1046. https://www.sciencedirect.com/science/article/abs/pii/001632879490071X

Ketchoua, G. S., Arogundade, S. T., & Biyase, M. (2024). Revaluating the Sustainable Development Thesis: exploring the moderating influence of Technological Innovation on the impact of Foreign Direct Investment (FDI) on Green Growth in the OECD Countries. *Discover Sustainability, 5*(1). https://doi.org/DOI: 10.1007/s43621-024-00433-w

Khalfaoui, H., Guenichi, H., Nabli, M. A., Belghouthi, H., & Guesmi, M. (2024). Threshold effects of credit risk on renewable energy consumption and green financial policies nexus: Evidence from OECD countries. *Environment, Development and Sustainability*. Advance online publication. DOI: 10.1007/s10668-024-05625-y

Khan, A., Goswami, A., & Choudhury, T. (2025). Technology gaps, social outreach and financial sustainability of South Asian MFIs: Bootstrap DEA meta-frontier approach. *Electronic Commerce Research, 25*(3), 1577–1606. DOI: 10.1007/s10660-023-09747-9

Khana, M. P., Talibb, N. A., & Kowangc, T. O. (2020). The development of a sustainability framework via lean green six sigma practices in SMEs based upon RBV theory. *Development, 12*(5), 135–156.

Khan, F., Din, A. U., Jehangir, M., Farooq, S. H., & Riviezzo, A. (2024). The nexus of technology orientation and green innovation performance: The potential mediating role of innovation capability. *The Journal of High Technology Management Research, 35*(2), 100509.

Khan, M. N., & Omar, A. Bin, Azizan, N. A., & Abidin, S. Z. (2023). The Role of Green Finance and Green Technology in Improving Environmental Performance Across OECD Economies: An in-depth Investigation Using Advanced Quantile Modeling. *Cuadernos de Economía (Santiago, Chile), 46*(132), 157–169. DOI: 10.32826/cude.v46i132.1215

Khan, M., Serafeim, G., & Yoon, A. (2016). Corporate sustainability: First evidence on materiality. *The Accounting Review, 91*(6), 1697–1724. DOI: 10.2308/accr-51383

Khan, Q. R. (2023). From Industrialization to Dehumanization: Understanding the Deriving Forces of Environment and Implications for Sustainable Development. *Environmental Science and Pollution Research International, 30*, 123396–123411. https://link.springer.com/content/pdf/10.1007/s11356-023-30983-x.pdf PMID: 37981608

Kidney, S., Oliver, P., Sonerud, B., & Sullivan, R. (2017). *Unlocking green finance for developing countries*. Climate Bonds Initiative. https://www.climatebonds.net

Kihombo, S., Ahmed, Z., Chen, S., Adebayo, T. S., & Kirikkaleli, D. (2021). Linking Financial Development, Economic Growth, and Ecological Footprint: What is the Role of Technological Innovation? *Environmental Science and Pollution Research International, 28*, 61235–61245. https://link.springer.com/article/10.1007/s11356-021-14993-1 PMID: 34170468

Kim, H. -E. (2011). *The Role of the Patent System in Stimulating Innovation and Technology Transfer for Climate Change: Including Aspects of Licencing and Competition Law*. Nomos Verlagsgesellschaft mbH.

Kingsbury, D., Remenyi, J., McKay, J., & Hunt, J. (2004). *Key Issues in Development*. Palgrave Macmillan.

Kitchenham, B., & Charters, S. (2007). Guidelines for performing systematic literature reviews in software engineering (Technical Report EBSE-2007-01). Keele University and Durham University Joint Report. Retrieved from https://www.cs.auckland.ac.nz/~norsaremah/2007%20Guidelines%20for%20performing%20SLR%20in%20SE%20v2.3.pdf

Klasen, A., & Vassard, J. (2023). The new OECD arrangement on export credits: Breakthrough or bad compromise? *Global Policy, 14*(5), 958–961. DOI: 10.1111/1758-5899.13255

Klewitz, J., & Hansen, E. G. (2014). Sustainability-oriented innovation of SMEs: A systematic review. *Journal of Cleaner Production, 65*, 57–75.

Kochi Metro Rail Limited (KMRL). (2021). About Us. Retrieved from https://www.kochimetro.org/about-us/

Korhonen, J., Honkasalo, A., & Seppälä, J. (2018). Circular Economy: The Concept and Its Limitations. *Ecological Economics, 143*, 37–46. https://www.sciencedirect.com/science/article/abs/pii/S0921800916300325

Kosasih, W., Pujawan, I. N., & Karningsih, P. D. (2023a). Integrated Lean-Green Practices and Supply Chain Sustainability for Manufacturing SMEs: A Systematic Literature Review and Research Agenda. *Sustainability, 15*(16), 12192.

Kotsantonis, S., & Serafeim, G. (2019). Four things no one will tell you about ESG data. *Journal of Applied Corporate Finance, 31*(2), 50–58. DOI: 10.1111/jacf.12346

Kou, G., Akdeniz, Ö. O., Dinçer, H., & Yüksel, S. (2021). Fintech investments in European banks: A hybrid IT2 fuzzy decision-making approach. *Financial Innovation, 7*(1), 1–23. DOI: 10.1186/s40854-020-00218-x PMID: 35024283

Kovilage, M. P. (2021). Influence of lean–green practices on organizational sustainable performance. *Journal of Asian Business and Economic Studies, 28*(2), 121–142.

Kozar, L. K., & Wodnicka, M. (2024). FinTech and Green Finance: Bibliometric Analysis. *Procedia Computer Science, 246*, 2080–2089. DOI: 10.1016/j.procs.2024.09.643

Kreibiehl, S., Battiston, S., & Downing, L.. (2022). *Climate Finance – IPCC Working Group III Sixth Assessment Report*. IPCC.

Krinichansky, K. V., & Rubtsov, B. B. (2022). Financial Sector Regulation on the Agenda of Economic Policy Reforms [Регулирование финансового сектора в повестке реформ экономической политики]. *Finance: Theory and Practice, 26*(5), 6–21. DOI: 10.26794/2587-5671-2022-26-5-6-21

Kukreti, M., Sehajpal, S., Tiwari, R., & Sood, K. (2024a). Driving global health and sustainable development goals with smart technology. In *Driving Global Health and Sustainable Development Goals With Smart Technology*. IGI Global., DOI: 10.4018/979-8-3373-0240-9

Kumar, J., & Majid, M. A. (2020). Renewable energy for sustainable development in India: Current status, future prospects, challenges, employment, and investment opportunities. *Energy, Sustainability and Society, 10*(2). Advance online publication. DOI: 10.1186/s13705-019-0232-1

Kwong, R., Kwok, M. L. J., & Wong, H. S. M. (2023). Green FinTech Innovation as a Future Research Direction: A Bibliometric Analysis on Green Finance and FinTech. *Sustainability, 15*, 14683. DOI: 10.3390/su152014683

Lau, C. K., Padhan, H., Kumar Das, A., Tiwari, A. K., Gozgor, G., & Jain, P. (2025). The role of green bonds on industrial sustainability for achieving carbon neutrality: Evidence from the artificial neural network method. *Research in International Business and Finance, 73*. Advance online publication. DOI: 10.1016/j.ribaf.2024.102659

Lawrence, R. F., & Thomas, W. L. (2004). The Equator Principles and Project Finance: Sustainability in Practice? *Natural Resources and Environment, 19*(2), 20–26.

Le, D. A., Truong, T. H., & Dang, T. C. (2024). *Green Finance Tools Education in Vietnam: A Mixed Method Study*. Vin University.

Ledgerwood, J. (1999). *Microfinance handbook: An institutional and financial perspective*. The World Bank.

Leitão, J. C., Ferreira, J. J. M., & Santibañez-González, E. (2021). Green bonds, sustainable development and environmental policy in the EU carbon market. *Business Strategy and the Environment*, *30*(4), 2077–2090.

Leitner, J., Reichelstein, S., & Zadek, S. (2023). ESG analytics and the future of sustainable investing. *Finance Research Letters*, *54*, 103711. DOI: 10.1016/j.frl.2023.103711

Leydesdorff, L., & Vaughan, L. (2006). Co-occurrence matrices and their applications in information science: Extending ACA to the Web environment. *Journal of the American Society for Information Science and Technology*, *57*, 1616–1628. DOI: 10.1002/asi.20335

Li, B., Liu, Z., Jia, X., & Ma, F. (2024). Digital finance, financing constraints, and green technological innovation: A spatial analysis. *Global Finance Journal*, *61*, 100988. DOI: 10.1016/j.gfj.2024.100988

Li, D. (2024). Green finance, fossil fuel efficiency, and sustainable development in OECD. *Resources Policy*, *98*. Advance online publication. DOI: 10.1016/j.resourpol.2024.105306

Li, G., Gao, D., & Shi, X. X. (2023). How Does Information and Communication Technology Affect Carbon Efficiency? Evidence at China's City Level. *Energy & Environment*, *35*(8), 4272–4293. https://journals.sagepub.com/doi/10.1177/0958305X231156405

Li, J., Gong, Y., Ho, K., & Zhang, C. (2023b). Trust and price efficiency. *Journal of International Financial Markets, Institutions and Money*, *89*, 101855. DOI: 10.1016/j.intfin.2023.101855

Li, J., Xu, L., & Li, X. (2021). Fintech, ESG and sustainable finance: A literature review. *Sustainability*, *13*(15), 8448.

Lin, L., & Hong, Y. (2022). Developing a Green Bonds Market: Lessons from China. *European Business Organization Law Review*, *23*(1), 143–185. DOI: 10.1007/s40804-021-00231-1

Li, R., Zhang, S., Wang, Q., & Hu, S. (2025). Fintech and urban environmental sustainability: Exploring the impact of financial technology on urban carbon emissions. *Sustainable Development*, *33*(2), 2118–2136. DOI: 10.1002/sd.3212

Liu, C., & Xiong, M. (2022). Green finance reform and corporate innovation: Evidence from China. *Finance Research Letters*, *48*, 102993. DOI: 10.1016/j.frl.2022.102993

Liu, H., Yao, P., Latif, S., Aslam, S., & Iqbal, N. (2022). Impact of Green financing, FinTech, and financial inclusion on energy efficiency. *Environmental Science and Pollution Research International, 29*(13), 18955–18966. DOI: 10.1007/s11356-021-16949-x PMID: 34705207

Liu, L., Li, Z., Fu, X., Liu, X., Li, Z., & Zheng, W. (2022). Impact of power on uneven development: Evaluating built-up area changes in Chengdu based on NPP-VIIRS images (2015–2019). *Landscape, 11*(4), 489.

Liu, M., Yaacob, M. H., Ma, Q., & Ding, S. (2025). Green finance and corporate green innovation: A systematic literature review. *SAGE Open, 15*(3), 21582440251370800.

Li, X., & Gallagher, K. P. (2022). Assessing the climate change exposure of foreign direct investment. *Nature Communications, 13*(1), 1–9. DOI: 10.1038/s41467-022-28975-5 PMID: 35304443

Ljubičić, I. (2025). Tax instruments as a key driver of the green transition. *Journal of Agronomy, Technology and Engineering Management, 8*(1), 45–63.

Lu, L., Zheng, H., Chen, M., & Najam, H. (2022). TACKLING CARBON INTENSITY WITH GREEN FINANCE IN THE COVID-19-ERA: RECOMMENDATIONS FOR OECD ECONOMIES. *Climate Change Economics (Singapore), 13*(3). Advance online publication. DOI: 10.1142/S2010007822400140

Lu, T., & Zhang, Y. (2025). 1 + 1 > 2? Information, humans, and machines. *Information Systems Research, 36*(1), 394–418. DOI: 10.1287/isre.2023.0305

Lutz, C., Zieschank, R., & Drosdowski, T. (2017). Measuring Germany's transition to a green economy. *Low Carbon Economy, 8*(1), 1–19.

Macci, I., Joli, L., Franzoni, G., Rigolio, M., Frassoldati, A., & Micheli, G. J. L. (2022). On the Impact of the Equator Principles Compliance: Supporting the Decision Making in Projects. *Chemical Engineering Transactions, 91*(May), 7–12. DOI: 10.3303/CET2291002

Macve, R., & Chen, X. (2010). The "equator principles": A success for voluntary codes? *Accounting, Auditing & Accountability Journal, 23*(7), 890–919. DOI: 10.1108/09513571011080171

Madrid-Guijarro, A., & Duréndez, A. (2024). Sustainable development barriers and pressures in SMEs: The mediating effect of management commitment to environmental practices. *Business Strategy and the Environment, 33*(2), 949–967. DOI: 10.1002/bse.3537

Mady, K., Battour, M., Aboelmaged, M., & Abdelkareem, R. S. (2023). Linking internal environmental capabilities to sustainable competitive advantage in manufacturing SMEs: The mediating role of eco-innovation. *Journal of Cleaner Production, 417*, 137928. DOI: 10.1016/j.jclepro.2023.137928

Maignan, I., & Ralston, D.-A. (2002). Corporate social responsibility in Europe and the U.S.: Insights from businesses' self-representations. *Journal of International Business Studies, 33*(3), 497–514.

Ma, J., & Chang, C.-P. (2023). The Role of Green Finance in Green Innovation: Global Perspective from 75 Developing Countries. *Emerging Markets Finance & Trade, 59*(10), 3109–3128. DOI: 10.1080/1540496X.2023.2210720

Makhoul, J., Talhouk, N., Loutfi, J., & Al-Madhwahi, A. (2024). Greenwashing by the fossil fuel industry: Impediments to SDGs. *European Journal of Public Health, 34*(Supplement_3), ckae144.420. https://doi.org/DOI: 10.1093/eurpub/ckae144.420

Malamas, V., Dasaklis, T. K., Arakelian, V., & Chondrokoukis, G. (2023). A blockchain framework for digitizing securities issuance: The case of green bonds. *Journal of Sustainable Finance & Investment, 14*(3), 569–595. DOI: 10.1080/20430795.2023.2275212

Manoharan, G., Nithya, G., Razak, A., Sharma, S., & Ashtikkar, S. P. (2024). Challenges and Opportunities in Green Finance: Overcoming Barriers and Scaling up Sustainable Investments. In Misra, S., Jadeja, R., & Mittal, M. (Eds.), *Practical Approaches to Agile Project Management* (pp. 398–413). IGI Global Scientific Publishing., DOI: 10.4018/979-8-3693-3318-1.ch022

Marfo, M., Ofei, E. F., Annan, E., Armah, A. A., Adadevoh, L., Evelyn, B. O., & Asante, C. R. (2025). The impact of competitive advantage on the sustainability of microfinance institutions in Ghana: Assessing the moderating role of capacity building. *SN Business & Economics, 5*(7), 90. DOI: 10.1007/s43546-025-00857-0

Markowitz, H. (1952). Portfolio selection. *The Journal of Finance, 7*(1), 77–91. DOI: 10.2307/2975974

Mavlutova, I., Spilbergs, A., Verdenhofs, A., Kuzmina, J., Arefjevs, I., & Natrins, A. (2023). The Role of Green Finance in Fostering the Sustainability of the Economy and Renewable Energy Supply: Recent Issues and Challenges. *Energies, 16*(23), 7712. DOI: 10.3390/en16237712

Ma, Y., & Zhao, H. (2024). Green technology innovation guiding policies under the synergy of government and financial institutions. *Sustainable Operations and Computers, 5*(2), 88–103.

McKinsey & Company. (2022). *Creating value with ESG in private equity*. https://www.mckinsey.com/business-functions/sustainability/our-insights/creating-value-with-esg-in-private-equity

McWilliams, A., & Siegel, D. (2001). Corporate Social Responsibility: A Theory of the Firm Perspective. *Academy of Management Review*, *26*(1), 117–127. https://www.jstor.org/stable/259398

Mercanti-Guérin, M. (2011). Crisis in the banking sector and portrait of the ideal bank: A study conducted among young consumers. *The Journal of Management Sciences*, *3-4*(249-250), 57–64.

Messomo Elle, S. (2021). Caractéristiques des produits de microcrédit et performance financière des institutions de micro finance (IMFs) au Cameroun. *Recherches En Sciences de Gestion*, *143*(2), 143–170. DOI: 10.3917/resg.143.0143

Mhlanga, D. (2024). FinTech and Inclusive Economic Development in Africa. *Africa Growth Agenda*, *21*(4). https://hdl.handle.net/10520/ejc-afgrow_v21_n4_a3

Mia, M. A. (2024). Loyalty of rural microfinance borrowers: International evidence. *Bulletin of Economic Research*, *76*(1), 67–94. DOI: 10.1111/boer.12415

Miao, Y., Tian, Y., Cao, J., & Yu, X. (2025). Green finance and privatization of green projects in the fossil fuels industry. *Resources Policy*, *103*. Advance online publication. DOI: 10.1016/j.resourpol.2025.105547

Ministry of Mines and Energy (MME). (2021). Renewable Energy Incentive Program. Retrieved from http://www.mme.gov.br/documents/1138775/0/Programa+de+Incentivo+às+Energias+Renováveis/06754788-7409-4f9b-9f8b-1311e7bc92e4?version=1.0

Ministry of New and Renewable Energy (MNRE). (2020). National Solar Mission. Retrieved from https://mnre.gov.in/schemes/decentralized-systems/solar-off-grid-2/

Mitra, R., & Guseva, M. E. (2021). Does Population Ageing Reduce FDI Inflows in OECD Countries? Evidence from Bayesian Panel VAR Estimates. In *Contributions to Management Science*. https://doi.org/DOI: 10.1007/978-3-030-60354-0_6

Mkhitaryan, A. (2022). Critical evaluation of organizational structure and culture impact on the productivity of MFIs within the example of Agroleasing Leasing Credit Company LLC in Armenia. *Review of Applied Socio-Economic Research*, *24*(2). Advance online publication. DOI: 10.54609/reaser.v24i2.239

Mnasri, K. & Ben Romdhane, S. (2024). Towards an Environmental Finance Framework: The Contribution of the Equator Principles. *Bankers, Markets, Investors*, Focus On, 179, December 2024.

Mohajan, H. (2021). Germany is ahead to implement sustainable circular economy. *Journal of Economic Development. Environment and People*, *10*(2), 46–64.

Mohamed, T. S., & Elgammal, M. M. (2023). Are donor funds used effectively? An examination of Islamic and conventional microfinance institutions. *International Journal of Islamic and Middle Eastern Finance and Management*, *16*(5), 1009–1029. DOI: 10.1108/IMEFM-11-2021-0462

Moher, D., Shamseer, L., Clarke, M., Ghersi, D., Liberati, A., & Petticrew, M. (2015). Preferred reporting items for systematic review and meta-analysis protocols (PRISMA-P). *Systematic Reviews*, *4*(1), 1. PMID: 25554246

Morin, M. (2006). *Banking and sustainable development. From communication to action*. L'Harmattan.

Morningstar. (2021). *ESG investing and performance 2021*. https://www.morningstar.com/lp/esg-investing

Muangmee, C., Dacko-Pikiewicz, Z., Meekaewkunchorn, N., Kassakorn, N., & Khalid, B. (2021a). Green entrepreneurial orientation and green innovation in small and medium-sized enterprises (SMEs). *Social Sciences*, *10*(4), 136.

Musa, H., & Chinniah, M. (2016). Malaysian SMEs development: Future and challenges on going green. *Procedia: Social and Behavioral Sciences*, *224*, 254–262.

Nascimento, J., & Loureiro, S. M. C. (2024). The PSICHE framework for sustainable consumption and future research directions. *EuroMed Journal of Business*, *19*(3), 571–611. DOI: 10.1108/EMJB-12-2021-0199

Nasrin, S., Rasiah, R., Baskaran, A., & Masud, M. M. (2018). What determines the financial performance of microfinance institutions in Bangladesh? A panel data analysis. *Quality & Quantity*, *52*(3), 1409–1422.

Nawaz, A. (2010). Performance of microfinance: The role of subsidies. *Savings and Development*, *34*(1), 97–138.

Nenavath, S. (2025). Analysing FDI inflow effects on CO2 emissions: A comparative study of OECD and BRICS nations with PHH and PHE models. *International Journal of Energy Sector Management*, *19*(1), 80–100. DOI: 10.1108/IJESM-02-2024-0006

Network for Greening the Financial System (NGFS). (2020). A call for action: Climate change as a source of financial risk. Retrieved from https://www.ngfs.net/en/call-action-climate-change-source-financial-risk

Network for Greening the Financial System (NGFS). (2021). *Progress report on integrating climate-related and environmental risks into supervision.* https://www.ngfs.net

Network for Greening the Financial System (NGFS). (2022). Climate-related risk assessment practices by financial institutions: A stocktake. https://www.ngfs.net/

Network for Greening the Financial System (NGFS). (2023). *Network for Greening the Financial System: Annual Report 2023.* Retrieved from https://www.ngfs.net

Nhung, D. T. H., & Hang, T. T. T. (2024). Research on Green Finance: A Bibliometric Analysis. *RESEARCH REVIEW International Journal of Multidisciplinary, 9*(7), 01–07. https://doi.org/DOI: 10.31305/rrijm.2024.v09.n07.001

Nooman AlMallahi, M., Al Swailmeen, Y., Ali Abdelkareem, M., Ghani Olabi, A., & Elgendi, M. (2024). A path to sustainable development goals: A case study on the thirteen largest photovoltaic power plants. *Energy Conversion and Management: X, 22*, 100553. https://doi.org/DOI: 10.1016/j.ecmx.2024.100553

Normann, R., & Ramirez, R. (1993). From value chain to value constellation: Designing interactive strategy. *Harvard Business Review, 71*, 65–75. PMID: 10127040

Nuryakin, N., & Maryati, T. (2022a). Do green innovation and green competitive advantage mediate the effect of green marketing orientation on SMEs' green marketing performance? *Cogent Business & Management, 9*(1), 2065948. DOI: 10.1080/23311975.2022.2065948

OECD. (2020). *Developing Sustainable Finance Definitions and Taxonomies.* OECD Publishing.

OECD. (2020). *ESG investing: Practices, progress and challenges.* https://www.oecd.org/finance/ESG-Investing-Practices-Progress-and-Challenges.pdf

OECD. (2021). *Mobilizing Institutional Investors for Financing Sustainable Development in Developing Countries: Emerging Evidence of Opportunities and Challenges.* OECD Publishing. https://one.oecd.org/document/DCD(2021)11/en/pdf

OECD. (2022). *ESG investing and climate transition: Market practices, issues and policy considerations.* https://www.oecd.org/finance/ESG-investing-and-climate-transition.pdf

OECD. (2024). *Development Co-operation Report 2024: Tackling Poverty and Inequalities through the Green Transition*. OECD Publishing., DOI: 10.1787/357b63f7-

Ogbeifun, L., & Shobande, O. A. (2020). Causality Analysis of Disaggregated FDI Inflows on Sectorial Growth in OECD Area. *Studia Universitatis Vasile Goldis Arad. Economics Series, 30*(4), 92–110. DOI: 10.2478/sues-2020-0026

Oliver, C. (1991). Strategic Responses to Institutional Processes. *Academy of Management Review, 16*(1), 145–179.

Omar, A., Al-shari, A., Shah, S. H. A., Erkol Bayram, G., Zameer Rahman, E., & Valeri, M. (2024). Green manufacturing practices and SMEs' sustainable performance: A moderated mediation mechanisms of green innovation and managerial discretion. *European Business Review, 36*(4), 588–609.

Ong, P. (2012). Environmental Justice and Green-Technology Adoption. *Journal of Policy Analysis and Management, 31*(3), 578–597. https://www.jstor.org/stable/41653815

Organisation for Economic Co-operation and Development. (2020). *Developing sustainable finance definitions and taxonomies*. OECD Publishing., DOI: 10.1787/134a2dbe-

Organisation for Economic Co-operation and Development. (2021). *Blended finance in the least developed countries 2020*. OECD Publishing., DOI: 10.1787/57620d04-

Oyebanji, M. O., & Kırıkkaleli, D. (2022). Green technology, green electricity, and environmental sustainability in Western European countries. *Environmental Science and Pollution Research International, 30*(45), 38525–38534. PMID: 36580250

Pacces, A. M. (2021). Will the EU Taxonomy Regulation Foster Sustainable Corporate Governance? *Sustainability, 13*(21), 12316. DOI: 10.3390/su132112316

Palmaccio, M., Galeone, G., Shini, M., & Campobasso, F. (2023). Green finance: Past, present and future studies. *Journal of Financial Management. Markets and Institutions, 11*(2), 1–19.

Parsons, T. (1960). Structure and Process in Modern Societies. *American Journal of Sociology*, 66(5), 344 pages.

Pasquero, J. (2005). Corporate social responsibility as an object of management science: A historical look. In B.-Turcotte M.F. and Salmon A., Corporate social and environment responsibility, *Presses of Québec University*.

Pata, U. K., Si Mohammed, K., Nassani, A. A., & Ghosh, S. (2024). Discovering the sustainable development role of fintech credit and the pilot low carbon project on greenwashing in China. *Environment, Development and Sustainability*. Advance online publication. DOI: 10.1007/s10668-024-04919-5

Pattnaik, D., Ray, S., & Hassan, M. K. (2024). Microfinance: A bibliometric exploration of the knowledge landscape. *Heliyon*, *10*(10). PMID: 38813228

Paul, J., & Criado, A. R. (2020). The art of writing literature review: What do we know and what do we need to know? *International Business Review*, *29*(4). Advance online publication. DOI: 10.1016/j.ibusrev.2020.101717

Pavlidis, G. (2025). Empowering sustainable finance with artificial intelligence: a framework for responsible implementation. In Lee, J., & Darbellay, A. (Eds.), *A Research Agenda for Financial Law and Regulation* (pp. 23–38). Edgar Online., DOI: 10.4337/9781803929996.00009

PBoC. (2016). *Guidelines for Establishing the Green Financial System*. People's Bank of China.

Peck, G., Rosenbaum, H., Hudon, I., Yoon, J.-W., Kamal-Chaoui, L., & Lagarde, P. (2022). Financing SMEs for sustainability. *OECD SME and Entrepreneurship Papers*, *31*, 1–38.

Peñarreta Quezada, M., & Chavez Alvear, N. (2025). Impacto del capital intelectual en el desempeño financiero de las instituciones microfinancieras de Ecuador. *European Public & Social Innovation Review*, *10*, 1–18. DOI: 10.31637/epsir-2025-1588

People's Bank of China (PBOC). (2019). Implementation of Green Finance Policies. Retrieved from https://www.pbc.gov.cn/en/3687297/index.html

People's Bank of China (PBOC). (2020). Green finance guidelines. Retrieved from https://www.greenfinance.org.cn/index.php/Home/Index/englishdetail/id/357

People's Bank of China. (2016). Green Finance Guidelines. Retrieved from https://www.pbc.gov.cn/english/130919/3164453/index.html

Pfeffer, J., & Salancik, G. (1978). *The External Control of Organizations: A Resource Dependence Perspective*. Harper & Row.

Piot-Lepetit, I., & Tchakoute Tchuigoua, H. (2022). Ownership and performance of microfinance institutions in Latin America: A pseudo-panel malmquist index approach. *The Journal of the Operational Research Society*, *73*(5), 1167–1180. DOI: 10.1080/01605682.2021.1895683

Plihon, D. (2010). Global Regulation in the Aftermath of the Subprime Crisis. In CRIFO P., Ponssard J-P. *Corporate social responsibility: from compliance to opportunity*, Editions of the Ecole Polytechnique, 17-26.

Plihon, D., & Rigot, S. (2022). Public financial intermediaries and climate change. Presses de Sciences Po. *Revue économique*, *73*, 243–266.

Popescu, I.-S., Schaubroeck, T., Gibon, T., Petucco, C., & Benetto, E. (2024). Investment funds are responsible for substantial environmental and social impacts. *Communications Earth & Environment*, *5*(1), 355. DOI: 10.1038/s43247-024-01479-4

Porter, M. E., & van der Linde, C. (1995). Toward a new conception of the environment-competitiveness relationship. *The Journal of Economic Perspectives*, *9*(4), 97–118. DOI: 10.1257/jep.9.4.97

Pourasl, H. H., Barenji, R. V., & Khojastehnezhad, V. M. (2023). Solar Energy Status in the World: A Comprehensive Review. *Energy Reports*, *10*, 3474–3493. DOI: 10.1016/j.egyr.2023.10.022

Power, G. J., & Tandja-M, D. C. (2024). Does it pay to be Green? The impact of equator principles on project loans. *European Journal of Finance*, *31*(5), 616–646. DOI: 10.1080/1351847X.2024.2419568

PRI (Principles for Responsible Investment). (2020). *Fiduciary duty in the 21st century: Final report.* https://www.unpri.org/fiduciary-duty

Principles for Responsible Investment. (2020). *Sustainability-linked loans: Connecting finance to ESG performance.* https://www.unpri.org

Principles, E. (2006). *The Equator Principles. A Financial Industry Benchmark for Determining, Assessing and Managing Social & Environmental Risk in Project Financing,* Equator Principles Financial Institutions, Washington, DC. Retrieved from: http://www.equator-principles.com/documents/Equator_Principles.pdf

Principles, E. (2011). *Summary Response by Equator Principles Association to the Equator Principles Strategic Review Report*, Equator Principles Financial Institutions, Washington, DC. Retrieved from http://www.equator-principles.com/resources/ep_association_summary_response_ strategic_review.pdf

Principles, E. (2013a). *The Equator Principles Association Governance Rules.* Equator Principles Financial Institutions, Washington, DC. Retrieved from http://www.equator principles.com/resources/ep_governance_rules_december_2013.pdf

Principles, E. (2013b). *The Equator Principles III.* Equator Principles Financial Institutions, Washington, DC. Retrieved from http://www.equatorprinciples. com/index.php/ep3/ep3

Principles, E. (2014). *The Equator Principles Implementation Note*. Equator Principles Financial Institutions, Washington, DC. Retrieved from http://www.equator-principles.com/ resources/equator_principles_implementation_note_july_2014.pdf

Pupion, P. C. (2013). Sustainable development-CSR: A quest for legitimacy of European banks. Association for Research and Publications in Management. *Gestion, 2000*(30), 39–59.

Purwandani, J. A., & Michaud, G. (2021). What are the drivers and barriers for green business practice adoption for SMEs? *Environment Systems & Decisions, 41*(4), 577–593. DOI: 10.1007/s10669-021-09821-3 PMID: 34155474

Puschmann, T., Hoffmann, C. H., & Khmarskyi, V. (2020). How Green FinTech Can Alleviate the Impact of Climate Change—The Case of Switzerland. *Sustainability, 12*(24), 10691. DOI: 10.3390/su122410691

PwC. (2023). *The state of climate tech 2023*. https://www.pwc.com/gx/en/services/sustainability/publications/state-of-climate-tech.html

Qian, L. H. (2024). An Empirical Study on the Relationship between Urbanization, Transportation Infrastructure, Industrialization, and Environment Degradation in China, India, and Indonesia. *Environment, Development and Sustainability*, •••, 1–27. https://link.springer.com/content/pdf/10.1007/s10668-024-05773-1.pdf

Rabbani, M. R., Khan, S., & Thalassinos, E. I. (2020). FinTech, blockchain and Islamic finance: An extensive literature review. *International Journal of Economics and Business Administration*, *8*(2), 65–86.

Raharjo, K. (2019). The role of green management in creating sustainability performance on the small and medium enterprises. *Management of Environmental Quality*, *30*(3), 557–577.

Ramadugu, R., Doddipatla, L., & Stone, J. (2022). Leveraging Artificial Intelligence and Machine Learning for Sustainable Financial Technologies: Innovations, Challenges, and Future Prospects. [IJSRM]. *International Journal of Scientific Research and Management, 10*(08), 942–959. DOI: 10.18535/ijsrm/v10i8.ec01

Raman, R., Ray, S., Das, D., & Nedungadi, P. (2025). Innovations and barriers in sustainable and green finance for advancing sustainable development goals. *Frontiers in Environmental Science*, *12*, 1513204. DOI: 10.3389/fenvs.2024.1513204

Ramonjy, D. (1997). Contribution to the study of organizational legitimacy: Comparative study of the legitimacy strategies of two fair trade organizations in France. Free Communication presented at the 75th ACFAS congress.

Rani, J. (2025). Cultural and social norms supporting sustainability. In IGI Global eBooks, 43-78. https://doi.org/DOI: 10.4018/979-8-3373-1280-4.ch003

Raza, S. A., Shah, N., & Arif, I. (2021). Relationship Between FDI and Economic Growth in the Presence of Good Governance System: Evidence from OECD Countries. *Global Business Review*, *22*(6), 1471–1489. DOI: 10.1177/0972150919833484

Rehman, R. U., Ahmad, M. I., Belas, J., Battisti, E., & Santoro, G. (2024). Green learning orientation and corporate environmental performance: The mediation role of green knowledge acquisition-management and the moderating role of CEO-gender. *Journal of Knowledge Management*. https://www.emerald.com/insight/content/doi/10.1108/JKM-08-2023-0752/full/html

Renneboog, L., Ter Horst, J., & Zhang, C. (2008). Socially responsible investments: Institutional aspects, performance, and investor behavior. *Journal of Banking & Finance*, *32*(9), 1723–1742. DOI: 10.1016/j.jbankfin.2007.12.039

Reserve Bank of India. (2018). Framework for Sustainable Development Goals Financing. Retrieved from https://www.rbi.org.in/Scripts/BS_PressReleaseDisplay.aspx?prid=44168

Reserve Bank of India. (2019). National Strategy for Green Banking. Retrieved from https://www.rbi.org.in/Scripts/BS_ViewBulletin.aspx?Id=17989

Reserve Bank of India. (2020). Green Finance Cell within RBI. Retrieved from https://www.rbi.org.in/Scripts/BS_PressRele

Reserve Bank of India. (2021). Guidelines on ESG Risk Management for Banks and Financial Institutions. Retrieved from https://www.rbi.org.in/Scripts/NotificationUser.aspx?Id=12006&Mode=0

Reuters. (2018). India's ReNew Power issues $475 million green bond. Retrieved from https://www.reuters.com/article/us-renew-power-bonds/indias-renew-power-issues-475-million-green-bond-idUSKBN1HN12G

Reynaud, E., & Walas, A. (2015). Discourse on CSR in the process of legitimizing the bank. *French Management Review*, *41*(248), 187–209.

Richardson, B. J. (2009). Keeping ethical investment ethical: Regulatory issues for investing for sustainability. *Journal of Business Ethics*, *87*(4), 555–572. DOI: 10.1007/s10551-008-9958-4

Ringel, M., & Mjekic, S. (2023). Analyzing the role of banks in providing green finance for retail customers: The case of Germany. *Sustainability*, *15*(11), 8745.

Rizos, V., Behrens, A., Van der Gaast, W., Hofman, E., Ioannou, A., Kafyeke, T., Flamos, A., Rinaldi, R., Papadelis, S., & Hirschnitz-Garbers, M. (2016). Implementation of circular economy business models by small and medium-sized enterprises (SMEs): Barriers and enablers. *Sustainability*, *8*(11), 1212.

Rohmana, L., & Wulandari, P. (2025). The key determinants of digital repayment performance of ultra-micro entrepreneurs in Indonesia microfinance institution. *Journal of Entrepreneurship and Public Policy*, *14*(2), 207–229. DOI: 10.1108/JEPP-04-2024-0050

Roy, P. K. (2023). Enriching the green economy through sustainable investments: An ESG-based credit rating model for green financing. *Journal of Cleaner Production*, *420*, 138315. DOI: 10.1016/j.jclepro.2023.138315

Roy, S. (1996). Development, Environment, and Poverty: Some Issues for Discussion. *Economic and Political Weekly*, *31*(4), 29–41. https://www.epw.in/journal/1996/4/review-political-economy-review-issues-specials/development-environment-and-poverty

Roy, S., Rautela, R., & Kumar, S. (2023). Towards a Sustainable Future: Nexus between the Sustainable Development Goals and Waste Management in the Built Environment. *Journal of Cleaner Production*, *415*(20), 137865. https://www.sciencedirect.com/science/article/abs/pii/S0959652623020231

Rozman Cafuta, M. (2015). Open space evaluation methodology and three dimensional evaluation model as a base for sustainable development tracking. *Sustainability*, *7*(10), 13690–13712.

Ruan, W., Guo, Z., Yang, J., Gao, L., Dong, Y., & Liu, Q. (2024). Assessing the progress toward achieving energy- and climate-related sustainable development goals under four global energy transition outlooks. *Sustainable Development*, *32*(4), 3695–3707. DOI: 10.1002/sd.2873

Ruggieri, A., Braccini, A. M., Poponi, S., & Mosconi, E. M. (2016). A meta-model of inter-organisational cooperation for the transition to a circular economy. *Sustainability*, *8*(11), 1153.

Sachs, J. D., Woo, W. T., Yoshino, N., & Taghizadeh-Hesary, F. (2019). *Handbook of Green Finance: Energy Security and Sustainable Development*. Springer.

Saeedi, M., & Ashraf, B. N. (2024). The Role of Technology in Promoting Green Finance: A Systematic Literature Survey and the Development of a Framework. *Journal of Risk and Financial Management, 17*(10), 472. DOI: 10.3390/jrfm17100472

Safi, A., Kchouri, B., Elgammal, W., Nicolas, M. K., & Umar, M. (2024). Bridging the green gap: Do green finance and digital transformation influence sustainable development? *Energy Economics, 134*. Advance online publication. DOI: 10.1016/j.eneco.2024.107566

Saha, T., Sinha, A., & Abbas, S. (2022). Green financing of eco-innovations: Is the gender inclusivity taken care of? *Economic Research-Ekonomska Istrazivanja, 35*(1), 5514–5535. DOI: 10.1080/1331677X.2022.2029715

Sajan, M. P., Shalij, P. R., & Ramesh, A. (2017). Lean manufacturing practices in Indian manufacturing SMEs and their effect on sustainability performance. *Journal of Manufacturing Technology Management, 28*(6), 772–793.

Salman, M., Long, X., Dauda, L., & Mensah, C. N. (2019). The Impact of Institutional Quality on Economic Growth and Carbon Emissions: Evidence from Indonesia, South Korea, and Thailand. *Journal of Cleaner Production, 241*, 118331. https://www.sciencedirect.com/science/article/abs/pii/S0959652619332019

Samad, G., & Manzoor, R. (2011). Green Growth: An Environmental Technology Approach. *Pakistan Development Review, 50*(4), 471–490. https://thepdr.pk/index.php/pdr/article/view/2480

Sarfraz, M., Qun, W., Hui, L., & Abdullah, M. I. (2018). Environmental risk management strategies and the moderating role of corporate social responsibility in project financing decisions. *Sustainability (Switzerland), 10*(8). Advance online publication. DOI: 10.3390/su10082771

Sarpong-Danquah, B., Adusei, M., & Magnus Frimpong, J. (2023). Effect of board gender diversity on the financial performance of microfinance institutions: Does judicial efficiency matter? *Annals of Public and Cooperative Economics, 94*(2), 495–518. DOI: 10.1111/apce.12396

SASB. (2021). *SASB Standards Overview*. Sustainability Accounting Standards Board. https://www.sasb.org

Saxena, K., & Singh, M. (2024). Investors reward countries for participating in climate agreements. *Nature Communications, 15*(1), 8908. DOI: 10.1038/s41467-024-53012-y PMID: 39414786

Schmitt, A. (2021). Green fintech: Innovations for sustainable finance. *Journal of Sustainable Finance & Investment, 11*(2), 245–258. DOI: 10.1080/20430795.2020.1857639

Schoenmaker, D. (2021). Greening monetary policy. *Climate Policy, 21*(6), 735–750.

Schoenmaker, D., & Schramade, W. (2019). *Principles of sustainable finance*. Oxford University Press.

Scholtens, B. (2009). Corporate social responsibility in the international banking industry. *Journal of Business Ethics, 86*(2), 159–175. DOI: 10.1007/s10551-008-9841-x

Scholtens, B., & Lammertjan, D. (2007). Banking on the Equator. Are Banks that Adopted the Equator Principles Different from Non-Adopters? *World Development, 35*(8), 1307–1328. DOI: 10.1016/j.worlddev.2006.10.013

Schwanitz, V. J., Paudler, H. A., & Wierling, A. (2024). The contribution of European citizen-led energy initiatives to sustainable development goals. *Sustainable Development, 32*(4), 3313–3328. DOI: 10.1002/sd.2844

Schwartz, M. S., & Carroll, A. B. (2007). Integrating and Unifying Competing and Complementary Frameworks: The Search for a Common Core in the Business and Society Field. *Business & Society, 47*(2), 148–186. https://journals.sagepub.com/doi/10.1177/0007650306297942

Scott, J. (1979). *The Moral Economy of the Peasant*. Yale University Press.

SEACEN. (2024). *Green finance and central banking: Roles, perspectives and experiences of SEACEN members*. The SEACEN Centre. Retrieved from https://www.seacen.org/publications/RePEc/702001-100499-PDF

SEC. (2022). *Proposed rule: The enhancement and standardization of climate-related disclosures for investors*. U.S. Securities and Exchange Commission. https://www.sec.gov

Securities and Exchange Commission (SEC). (2022). *Proposed rule: Enhancement and standardization of climate-related disclosures for investors*. https://www.sec.gov/news/press-release/2022-46

Sehajpal, S., & Sidhu, N. K. (2024). Neuroscience, nursing, and financial innovation: A synergistic approach to optimized patient care and economic well-being. In *Neuromarketing's Role in Sustainable Finance*. IGI Global., DOI: 10.4018/979-8-3693-9117-4.ch008

Sethi, S. P. (2002). Standards for corporate conduct in the international arena: Challenges and opportunities for multinational corporations. *Business and Society Review*, *107*, 20–40.

Setzer, J., & Higham, C. (2022). *Global trends in climate litigation: 2022 snapshot*. Grantham Research Institute on Climate Change and the Environment. https://www.lse.ac.uk/granthaminstitute/publication/global-trends-in-climate-litigation-2022-snapshot/

Setzer, J., & Higham, C. (2022). *Global trends in climate litigation: 2022 snapshot*. Grantham Research Institute on Climate Change and the Environment.

Shajar, S. N., Kashif, M., George, J., & Nasir, S. (2024). The Future of Green Finance: Artificial Intelligence-Enabled Solutions for a More Sustainable World. In Jafar, S. H., Rodriguez, R. V., Kannan, H., Akhtar, S., & Plugmann, P. (Eds.), (pp. 316–328). Advances in Finance, Accounting, and Economics. IGI Global., DOI: 10.4018/979-8-3693-1878-2.ch013

Shandilya, S. K., Datta, A., Kartik, Y., & Nagar, A. (2024). Navigating the Regulatory Landscape. In S. K. Shandilya, A. Datta, Y. Kartik, & A. Nagar, *Digital Resilience: Navigating Disruption and Safeguarding Data Privacy* (pp. 127–240). Springer Nature Switzerland. https://doi.org/DOI: 10.1007/978-3-031-53290-0_3

Sharifi, A., Allam, Z., Bibri, S. E., & Khavarian-Garmsir, A. R. (2024). Smart cities and sustainable development goals (SDGs): A systematic literature review of co-benefits and trade-offs. *Cities (London, England)*, *146*, 104659. DOI: 10.1016/j.cities.2023.104659

Sheehama, A. P. G. (2021). Equator Principles 4-Revised Climate Change Risk: What Does This Mean For Project Financing in Africa Amidst The Ongoing Energy Transition? *Journal of Sustainable Development Law and Policy*, *12*(1), 72–91. DOI: 10.4314/jsdlp.v12i1.4

Shettima, U., & Dzolkarnaini, N. (2018). Board characteristics and microfinance institutions' performance: Panel data evidence from Nigeria. *Journal of Accounting in Emerging Economies*, *8*(3), 369–386.

Shi, L., Han, L., Yang, F., & Gao, L. (2019). The Evolution of Sustainable Development Theory: Types, Goals, and Research Prospects. *Sustainability*, *11*, 7158. https://www.mdpi.com/2071-1050/11/24/7158

Shi, S., & Nisar, A. (2025). The Effects of Circular Economy, Green Finance and ICT Developments on Resource Productivity aimed Ecological Sustainability: Evidence from OECD Countries Using a CS-ARDL Approach; Wpływ gospodarki o obiegu zamkniętym, zielonych finansów i rozwoju technologii ICT na produktywność zasobów ukierunkowaną na ekologiczną zrównoważoność: dowody z krajów OECD stosujących podejście CS-ARDL. *Problemy Ekorozwoju, 20*(2), 223–245. DOI: 10.35784/preko.7059

Siddik, A. B., Yong, L., & Rahman, M. N. (2023). The role of Fintech in circular economy practices to improve sustainability performance: A two-staged SEM-ANN approach. *Environmental Science and Pollution Research International, 30*(49), 107465–107486. DOI: 10.1007/s11356-023-25576-7 PMID: 36735123

Siegel, R., Antony, J., Garza-Reyes, J. A., Cherrafi, A., & Lameijer, B. (2019). Integrated green lean approach and sustainability for SMEs: From literature review to a conceptual framework. *Journal of Cleaner Production, 240*, 118205.

Siegel, R., Antony, J., Govindan, K., Garza-Reyes, J. A., Lameijer, B., & Samadhiya, A. (2024a). A framework for the systematic implementation of Green-Lean and sustainability in SMEs. *Production Planning and Control, 35*(1), 71–89. DOI: 10.1080/09537287.2022.2052200

Siekmann, F., Schlör, H., & Vengaus, S. (2023). Linking Sustainability and the Fourth Industrial Revolution: A Monitoring Framework Accounting for Technological Development. *Energy, Sustainability and Society, 13*(26). https://energsustainsoc.biomedcentral.com/articles/10.1186/s13705-023-00405-4

Sierra, J., Muriel-Patino, V., & Rodríguez-López, F. (2024). A comprehensive framework for understanding microfinance performance evaluation methods. *Humanities & Social Sciences Communications, 11*, 764.

Singh, J., Singh, H., & Kumar, A. (2020). Impact of lean practices on organizational sustainability through green supply chain management–an empirical investigation. *International Journal of Lean Six Sigma, 11*(6), 1035–1068.

Singh, K. (2024). Social performance, financial risk and financial performance in microfinance institutions. *International Journal of Bank Marketing, 42*(4), 768–793. DOI: 10.1108/IJBM-01-2023-0005

Singh, R. K., Kumar Mangla, S., Bhatia, M. S., & Luthra, S. (2022). Integration of green and lean practices for sustainable business management. *Business Strategy and the Environment, 31*(1), 353–370. DOI: 10.1002/bse.2897

Siti-Nabiha, A. K., & Siti-Nazariah, A. Z. (2011). Evaluating social performance: A case study of a microfinance institution in Malaysia. *International Journal of Management and Enterprise Development*, *10*(4), 271–290.

Söderholm, P. (2020). The green economy transition and sustainable technological change. *Sustainable Earth Reviews*, *1*(1), 1–17.

Sohu, J. M., Hongyun, T., Junejo, I., Akhtar, S., Ejaz, F., Dunay, A., & Hossain, M. B. (2024). Driving sustainable competitiveness: Unveiling the nexus of green intellectual capital and environmental regulations on greening SME performance. *Frontiers in Environmental Science*, *12*, 1348994.

Song, J., & Gao, X. (2025). Does China's green credit interest subsidies policy promote enterprises' green technology innovation quality? *Journal of Environmental Management*, *390*, 126366. PMID: 40577875

South African Reserve Bank. (2020). Climate Risk Prudential Practice Guide. Retrieved from https://www.resbank.co.za/Publications/Detail-Item-View/Pages/Publications.aspx?sarbweb=6aa80196-3909-40e8-80d3-b5f698f33564&d=Climate%20Risk%20Prudential%20Practice%20Guide&l=CLIMATE%20RISK%20PRUDENTIAL%20PRACTICE%20GUIDE&per=2020&of=0&sc=0&fl=climate%20risk%20prudential%20practice%20guide

Sreenu, N. (2024). The influence of fintech and financial knowledge on sustainable business success: Exploring the mediating effect of financial accessibility in Indian. *Benchmarking*. Advance online publication. DOI: 10.1108/BIJ-12-2023-0875

Stafford-Smith, M., Griggs, D., Gaffney, O., Ullah, F., Reyers, B., Kanie, N., Stigson, B., Shrivastava, P., Leach, M., & O'Connell, D. (2017). Integration: The Key to Implementing the Sustainable Development Goals. *Sustainability Science*, *12*, 911–919. https://pmc.ncbi.nlm.nih.gov/articles/PMC6086249/ PMID: 30147763

Stern, N., Unsworth, S., Valero, A., Zenghelis, D., Rydge, J., and N. Robins (2020). *Strategy, investment, and policy for a strong and sustainable recovery: An action plan*. Centre for Economic Performance, London School of Economics and Political Science, London, July.

Suchek, N., & Franco, M. (2024a). Inter-organisational Cooperation Oriented Towards Sustainability Involving SMEs: A Systematic Literature Review. *Journal of the Knowledge Economy*, *15*(1), 1952–1972. DOI: 10.1007/s13132-023-01196-x PMID: 40478941

Suchman, M. C. (1995). Managing Legitimacy: Strategic and Institutional Approaches. *Academy of Management Review*, *20*(3), 571–610.

Sule, A. K., Eyo-Udo, N. L., Onukwulu, E. C., Agho, M. O., & Azubuike, C. (2024). Green finance solutions for banking to combat climate change and promote sustainability. *Gulf Journal of Advance Business Research*, *2*(6), 376–410. DOI: 10.51594/gjabr.v2i6.54

Sullivan, R., & Mackenzie, C. (2017). *Responsible investment: Guide to ESG data providers and relevant trends*. International Finance Corporation.

Suri, A. (2023). A Comprehensive Framework for India's Climate Finance Strategy. *Carnegie Endowment for International Peace*. https://carnegieendowment.org/research/2023/03/a-comprehensive-framework-for-indias-climate-finance-strategy?lang=en

Suwandi, S., & Badrianto, Y. (2023). The Role of Competitive Strategy and Green Supply Chain Management in MSME Performance. *Jurnal Multidisiplin Madani*, *3*(10), 10. Advance online publication. DOI: 10.55927/mudima.v3i10.6512

Suzlon Energy Limited. (2021). Wind Energy. Retrieved from https://www.suzlon.com/business/wind-energy/

Taghizadeh-Hesary, F., & Yoshino, N. (2019). The way to induce private participation in green finance and investment. *Finance Research Letters*, *31*, 98–103.

Tang, Y., & Zhou, Y. (2020). Performance evaluation and application of banking industry based on equator principles. *E3S Web of Conferences, 214*(December 2007), 1-5. https://doi.org/DOI: 10.1051/e3sconf/202021402055

Tang, D. Y., & Zhang, Y. (2020). Do shareholders benefit from green bonds? *Journal of Corporate Finance*, *61*, 101427. DOI: 10.1016/j.jcorpfin.2018.12.001

Tao, H., Zhuang, S., Xue, R., Cao, W., Tian, J., & Shan, Y. (2022). Environmental Finance: An Interdisciplinary Review. *Technological Forecasting and Social Change*, *179*, 121639. DOI: 10.1016/j.techfore.2022.121639

Task Force on Climate-related Financial Disclosures (TCFD). (2017). *Final report: Recommendations of the TCFD*. https://www.fsb-tcfd.org/publications/final-recommendations-report/

Task Force on Climate-related Financial Disclosures (TCFD). (2017). Recommendations of the Task Force on Climate-related Financial Disclosures. Retrieved from https://www.fsb-tcfd.org/publications/final-recommendations-report/

Taşkın, Z., & Aydinoglu, A. U. (2015). Collaborative interdisciplinary astrobiology research: A bibliometric study of the NASA Astrobiology Institute. *Scientometrics*, *103*(3), 1003–1022.

Tata Steel Limited. (2021). Sustainability. Retrieved from https://www.tatasteel.com/sustainability/

Tazhibekova, K., & Shametova, A. (2024). Ecological Initiatives and Their Influence on the Competitiveness and Sustainability of Companies: "Green" Strategies of SMEs. *Journal of the Knowledge Economy*. Advance online publication. DOI: 10.1007/s13132-024-02062-0

Testa, F., Pretner, G., Iovino, R., Bianchi, G., Tessitore, S., & Iraldo, F. (2021). Drivers to green consumption: A systematic review. *Environment, Development and Sustainability*, *23*(4), 4826–4880. DOI: 10.1007/s10668-020-00844-5

Thanki, S., & Thakkar, J. J. (2020). An investigation on lean–green performance of Indian manufacturing SMEs. *International Journal of Productivity and Performance Management*, *69*(3), 489–517.

The long path to achieving green economy performance for micro small medium enterprise | Journal of Innovation and Entrepreneurship. (n.d.). Retrieved August 11, 2025, from https://link.springer.com/article/10.1186/s13731-022-00209-4

Thiétart, R.-A. (2007). Introduction. In *Management Research Method*. Dunod.

Thomas, J. R., & Kumar, J. (2016). Social performance and sustainability of Indian microfinance institutions: An interrogation. *Journal of Sustainable Finance & Investment*, *6*(1), 38–50.

Thrikawala, S., Locke, S., & Reddy, K. (2017). Dynamic endogeneity and corporate governance-performance relationship: Lessons from the microfinance sector. *Journal of Economic Studies (Glasgow, Scotland)*, *44*(5), 727–744.

Timbula, M. A., & Marvadi, C. (2023). Digital transformation: Acceptance and use of technology among microfinance institutions in developing country: An application of UTAUT2 model. *International Journal of Information Technology : an Official Journal of Bharati Vidyapeeth's Institute of Computer Applications and Management*, *15*(8), 4459–4468. DOI: 10.1007/s41870-023-01535-w

Tiwari, S., Cheong, C. W. H., See Mey, L., & Saji, T. G. (2024). Does fintech really matter for energy, economy and environment? From the lenses of SDG-7, SDG-8, SDG-13, COP27 and COP28. *Resources Policy*, *98*. Advance online publication. DOI: 10.1016/j.resourpol.2024.105318

Tolliver, C., Keeley, A. R., & Managi, S. (2019a). Green bonds for the Paris agreement and sustainable development goals. *Environmental Research Letters*, *14*(6), 064009. DOI: 10.1088/1748-9326/ab1118

Toryanto, C. J. K., & Indriani, F. (2022). Green Marketing Orientation Towards Competitive Advantage and Marketing Performance of Non-Food SMEs in Java. [IJSRM]. *International Journal of Scientific Research and Management, 10*(02), 02. Advance online publication. DOI: 10.18535/ijsrm/v10i2.em06

Treasury, H. M. (2019). Green Finance Strategy. Retrieved from https://assets.publishing.service.gov.uk/government/uploads/system/uploads/attachment_data/file/791618/green_finance_strategy_web.pdf

Tsamadias, C. P., Pegkas, P., Mamatzakis, E. C., & Staikouras, C. K. (2019). Does R&D, human capital and FDI matter for TFP in OECD countries? *Economics of Innovation and New Technology, 28*(4), 386–406. DOI: 10.1080/10438599.2018.1502394

Tufail, M., Song, L., & Khan, Z. (2024). Green finance and green growth nexus: Evaluating the role of globalization and human capital. *Journal of Applied Econometrics, 27*(1). Advance online publication. DOI: 10.1080/15140326.2024.2309437

Udeagha, M. C., & Muchapondwa, E. (2023). Green finance, fintech, and environmental sustainability: Fresh policy insights from the BRICS nations. *International Journal of Sustainable Development and World Ecology, 30*(6), 633–649.

Ullah, M., Shahid, A., Din, I. U., Roman, M., Assam, M., Fayaz, M., Ghadi, Y., & Aljuaid, H. (2022). Analyzing Interdisciplinary Research Using Co-Authorship Networks. *Complexity, 2022*, 1–13. DOI: 10.1155/2022/2524491

Ullah, S., Nobanee, H., Azim, F., & Khiati, M. (2025). Financial foundations for sustainability: How business sophistication, tax policy, and technology shape ESG in Belt and Road Initiative countries. *Global Sustainability, 8*, e3. DOI: 10.1017/sus.2025.4

Umar, M., & Safi, A. (2023). Do green finance and innovation matter for environmental protection? A case of OECD economies. *Energy Economics, 119*. Advance online publication. DOI: 10.1016/j.eneco.2023.106560

UN General Assembly. (2015). Transforming Our World: The 2030 Agenda for Sustainable Development. A/RES/70/1. https://docs.un.org/en/A/RES/70/1

UNCTAD. (2023). *The Least Developed Countries Report 2023: The low-carbon transition and its daunting implications for structural transformation*. United Nations Conference on Trade and Development. Retrieved from https://unctad.org/system/files/official-document/ldc2023_ch4_en.pdf

UNCTAD. (United Nations Conference on Trade and Development). (2024). World Investment Report 2024. https://unctad.org/publication/world-investment-report-2024

UNEP (United Nations Environment Program). (2011). *Towards a Green Economy: Pathways to Sustainable Development and Poverty Eradication*. UNEP.

UNEP FI. (2019). *Changing course: A comprehensive investor guide to scenario-based methods for climate risk assessment, in response to the TCFD*. https://www.unepfi.org

UNEP FI. (2021). *A new vision of sustainable investing: A holistic approach to ESG integration*. United Nations Environment Programme Finance Initiative.

UNEP. (2016). *Definitions and concepts: Background note for the G20 Green Finance Study Group*. United Nations Environment Programme.

United Nations Development Programme (UNDP). (2020). Sustainable Development Goals Knowledge Platform. Retrieved from https://sustainabledevelopment.un.org/

United Nations Environment Programme (UNEP). (2018). Adaptation Finance Gap Report 2018. Retrieved from https://www.unep.org/resources/adaptation-finance-gap-report-2018

United Nations Environment Programme Finance Initiative (UNEP FI). (2021). Positive Impact Finance: From Theory to Practice. Retrieved from https://www.unepfi.org/positive-impact-finance-from-theory-to-practice

United Nations Environment Programme. (2016). *Green finance for developing countries: Needs, concerns and innovations*. UNEP. https://wedocs.unep.org

United Nations Framework Convention on Climate Change. (2021). *Introduction to climate finance*. UNFCCC. https://unfccc.int/topics/climate-finance

Varchenko, O., Varchenko, O., Drahan, O., Tkachenko, K., Rybak, N., & Zubchenko, V. (2024). «GREEN FINANCE» IN THE POST-WAR RECONSTRUCTION OF UKRAINE: ORGANIZATIONAL AND FINANCIAL ASPECTS. *Financial and Credit Activity: Problems of Theory and Practice*, *3*(56), 75–85. DOI: 10.55643/fcaptp.3.56.2024.4403

Volz, U., Böhnke, J., Eidt, V., Knierim, L., Richert, K., & Roeber, G.-M. (2015). Financing the green transformation: How to make green finance work in Indonesia. In *Financing the Green Transformation: How to Make Green Finance Work in Indonesia*. Palgrave Macmillan. https://doi.org/DOI: 10.1007/978-1-137-48612-7

Voronova, E., Simonova, M., & Yarnykh, E. (2023). "Green" Investments in Renewable Energy in the Context of Innovative Development and Digitalization. In *Digital International Relations*. Springer Nature. https://doi.org/DOI: 10.1007/978-981-99-3467-6_14

Vranovci, S. (2025). Exploring the relationship between client protection practices and sustainable performance in the microfinance sector: A study of Kosovo's microfinance institutions. *WSEAS Transactions on Business and Economics*, *22*, 574–583. DOI: 10.37394/23207.2025.22.51

Vrontis, D., Chaudhuri, R., & Chatterjee, S. (2022). Adoption of Digital Technologies by SMEs for Sustainability and Value Creation: Moderating Role of Entrepreneurial Orientation. *Sustainability*, *14*(13), 13. Advance online publication. DOI: 10.3390/su14137949

Wang, E., Liu, X., Wu, J., & Cai, D. (2019). Green Credit, Debt Maturity, and Corporate Investment-Evidence from China. *Sustainability (Switzerland)*, *11*(3), 1–19. DOI: 10.3390/su11030583

Wang, H., & Liu, F. (2024). Digital finance and enterprise innovation efficiency: Evidence from China. *Finance Research Letters*, *59*, 104709. DOI: 10.1016/j.frl.2023.104709

Wang, R., Destek, M. A., Weimei, C., Albahooth, B., & Khan, Z. A. (2024). Drivers of Sustainable Green Finance: Country's Level Risk and Trade Perspective for OECD Countries. *Journal of Environment & Development*, *33*(1), 125–148. DOI: 10.1177/10704965231217046

Wang, T., Umar, M., Li, M., & Shan, S. (2023). Green finance and clean taxes are the ways to curb carbon emissions: An OECD experience. *Energy Economics*, *124*. Advance online publication. DOI: 10.1016/j.eneco.2023.106842

Wang, Y., & Taghizadeh-Hesary, F. (2023). Green bonds markets and renewable energy development: Policy integration for achieving carbon neutrality. *Energy Economics*, *123*. Advance online publication. DOI: 10.1016/j.eneco.2023.106725

Wang, Y., Zhi, Q., Zhang, H., & Wei, Y. (2022). Can green finance promote sustainable economic growth? Evidence from China. *Journal of Cleaner Production*, *339*, 130652. DOI: 10.1016/j.jclepro.2022.130652

Wan, S., Lee, Y. H., & Sarma, V. J. (2023). Is Fintech good for green finance? Empirical evidence from listed banks in China. *Economic Analysis and Policy*, *80*, 1273–1291.

Watchman, P. (2006). Banks, business, and human rights. *Butterworths Journal of International Banking and Financial Law*, *2*, 47–50.

WCED (World Commission on Environment and Development). (1987). *Report of the World Commission on Environment and Development: Our Common Future*. United Nations.

Weber, O., & Acheta, E. (2016). The Equator Principles: Do They Make Banks More Sustainable? Working Paper, Unep Inquiry, February.

Weber, O. (2014). The financial sector's impact on sustainable development. *Journal of Sustainable Finance & Investment*, *4*(1), 1–8.

Weber, O., & Acheta, E. (2014). *The Equator Principles: Ten Teenage Years of Implementation and a Search for Outcome (24)*. CIGI.

Weber, O., & Feltmate, B. (2016). *Sustainable Banking: Managing the Social and Environmental Impact of Financial Institutions*. Business & Sustainability Series G- Reference, Information and Interdisciplinary Subjects Series.

Weick, K. E. (1995). *Sensemaking in organizations*. Sage Publications.

Weiland, S., Hickmann, T., Leder, M., Marquardt, J., & Schwindenhammer, S. (2021). The 2030 Agenda for Sustainable Development: Transformative Change through the Sustainable Development Goals? *Politics and Governance*, *9*(1), 90–95. https://www.cogitatiopress.com/politicsandgovernance/article/view/4191

Wen, Z., Chen, Y., Liu, H., & Liang, Z. (2024). Text Mining Based Approach for Customer Sentiment and Product Competitiveness Using Composite Online Review Data. *Journal of Theoretical and Applied Electronic Commerce Research*, *19*(3), 1776–1792. DOI: 10.3390/jtaer19030087

Wilbanks, T. J., & Fernandez, S. J. (2014). Climate Change and Infrastructure, Urban Systems, and Vulnerabilities: Technical Report for the U.S. *Department of Energy in Support of the National Climate Assessment*, 1–92. https://doi.org/.DOI: 10.5822/978-1-61091-556-4

Williamson, O. (1993). Opportunism and Its Critics. *Managerial and Decision Economics*, *14*, 97–107.

Wirasedana, I. W. P., Sudarma, M., Andayani, W., & Mulawarman, A. D. (2024). The role of capital in microfinance financial performance and cultural sustainability. *Cogent Business & Management*, *11*(1), 2287770. DOI: 10.1080/23311975.2023.2287770

World Bank. (2019). *Public-private partnerships for sustainable development*. World Bank Group. https://ppp.worldbank.org

World Bank. (2022). *Blended finance: Mobilizing private capital for sustainable development*. https://www.worldbank.org/en/topic/financialsector/brief/blended-finance

World Bank. (2023). FY23 Climate-Related Financial Disclosures. https://thedocs.worldbank.org/en/doc/23a63a4bde452fe676c0843ab879405a-0340022023/original/World-Bank-FY23-Climate-Related-Financial-Disclosure.pdf

World Population Review. (2025). Greenest (Most Eco-friendly) Countries 2025. https://worldpopulationreview.com/country-rankings/greenest-countries

Wright, C., & Rwabizambuga, A. (2006). Institutional Pressures, Corporate Reputation, and Voluntary Codes of Conduct: An Examination of the Equator Principles. *Business and Society Review*, *111*(1), 89–117.

Wu, H. (2023). Evaluating the role of renewable energy investment resources and green finance on the economic performance: Evidence from OECD economies. *Resources Policy*, *80*. Advance online publication. DOI: 10.1016/j.resourpol.2022.103149

Xiumei, X., Ruolan, J., Shahzad, U., & Xiao, F. (2023). Sustainable Innovation in Small and Medium-Sized Enterprises: Environmental Regulations and Digitalization as Catalyst. *The Journal of Environment &Amp. Development*, *32*(4). Advance online publication. DOI: 10.1177/10704965231211585

Xu, J., Xu, J., Zeng, S., & Cui, J. (2023), Green Finance and Corporate Green Innovation: Evidence from the Equator Principles. Available at *SSRN*: https://ssrn.com/abstract=4405067 or

Xu, Y., & Cai, Y. (2024a). Is green finance a motivator for energy transformation investments in the OECD? *Economic Change and Restructuring*, *57*(3). Advance online publication. DOI: 10.1007/s10644-024-09705-x

Yadav, V., & Gahlot, P. (2022). Green Lean Six Sigma sustainability-oriented framework for small and medium enterprises. *International Journal of Quality & Reliability Management*, *39*(7), 1787–1807. DOI: 10.1108/IJQRM-08-2021-0297

Yang, M. (2024). Research on Teaching Methods of Integrating Watercolor Techniques and Information Technology in Higher Education Art Education. *Applied Mathematics and Nonlinear Sciences*, *9*(1), 20242803. DOI: 10.2478/amns-2024-2803

Yildirim, S. (2023). Greenwashing: A rapid escape from sustainability or a slow transition? *LBS Journal of Management & Research,* 21(1), 53-63. https://www.emerald.com/insight/content/doi/10.1108/lbsjmr-11-2022-0077/full/html

Yoon, S., & Ko, J. (2025). The effect of FDI regulatory barriers: Evidence from OECD countries. *Applied Economics Letters*, *32*(10), 1484–1497. DOI: 10.1080/13504851.2024.2308558

Yousaf, Z. (2021). Go for green: Green innovation through green dynamic capabilities: accessing the mediating role of green practices and green value co-creation. *Environmental Science and Pollution Research International*, *28*(39), 54863–54875. DOI: 10.1007/s11356-021-14343-1 PMID: 34018115

Yousef, B. A. A., Obaideen, K., AlMallahi, M. N., Alajmi, N., Radwan, A., Al-Shihabi, S., & Elgendi, M. (2024). On the contribution of concentrated solar power (CSP) to the sustainable development goals (SDGs): A bibliometric analysis. *Energy Strategy Reviews*, *52*, 101356. DOI: 10.1016/j.esr.2024.101356

YPCCC. (2022). Global Warming's Six Americas, September 2021. https://climatecommunication.yale.edu/publications/global-warmings-six-americas-september-2021/

Yu, X., Li, W., Wang, Y., & Chen, H. (2025). The impact of green finance policy on environmental performance of firms. *Sustainability*, *17*(17), 7589.

Zaby, S. (2019). Science mapping of the global knowledge base on microfinance: Influential authors and documents, 1989–2019. *Sustainability*, *11*(14), 1–21.

Zadek, S., & Flynn, C. (2013). South-originating green finance: Exploring the potential. United Nations Environment Programme & Geneva International Finance Dialogues. https://www.unepfi.org/fileadmin/documents/south-originating_green_finance.pdf

Zakari, A., & Khan, I. (2022). The Introduction of Green Finance: A Curse or Benefit to Environmental Sustainability? *Energy Research Letters*, 3(3). https://erl.scholasticahq.com/article/29977-the-introduction-of-green-finance-a-curse-or-a-benefit-to-environmental-sustainability

Zameer, H., Yasmeen, H., Wang, Y., & Saeed, M. R. (2024). Sustainability-oriented corporate strategy: Green image and innovation capabilities. *Management Decision*. https://www.emerald.com/insight/content/doi/10.1108/MD-08-2023-1407/full/html

Zetzsche, D. A., Bodellini, M., & Consiglio, R. (2022). The EU Sustainable Finance Framework in Light of International Standards. *Journal of International Economic Law*, *25*(4), 659–679. DOI: 10.1093/jiel/jgac043

Zhang, A., Wang, S., & Liu, B. (2022). How to control air pollution with economic means? Exploration of China's green finance policy. *Journal of Cleaner Production*, *353*, 131664. DOI: 10.1016/j.jclepro.2022.131664

Zhang, D., & Zhang, Z. (2021). Green finance in China: Emerging trends and policy implications. *Sustainability*, *13*(2), 769. DOI: 10.3390/su13020769

Zhang, D., Zhang, Z., & Managi, S. (2019). A Bibliometric Analysis on Green Finance: Current Status, Development, and Future Directions. *Finance Research Letters, 29*, 425–430. https://www.sciencedirect.com/science/article/abs/pii/S1544612319300765?via%3Dihub

Zhang, D., Zhao, N., & Yang, Z. (2025). The Impact of Green Finance on Rural Green Development: Theory and Evidence. *Finance Research Letters, 107648*, •••. https://www.sciencedirect.com/science/article/abs/pii/S1544612325009079

Zhang, D., Zhao, Z., & Lau, C. (2022). Sovereign ESG and corporate investment: New insights from the UK. *Technological Forecasting and Social Change*, *182*, 121899.

Zhang, J. A., & Walton, S. (2017). Eco-innovation and business performance: The moderating effects of environmental orientation and resource commitment in green-oriented SME s. *R & D Management*, *47*(5). Advance online publication. DOI: 10.1111/radm.12241

Zhang, K. Q., Chen, H. H., Tang, L. Z., & Qiao, S. (2022). Green Finance, Innovation and the Energy-Environment-Climate Nexus. *Frontiers in Environmental Science*, *10*, 879681. DOI: 10.3389/fenvs.2022.879681

Zhang, K.-C., Safi, A., Kchouri, B., Banerjee, A., & Wang, L. (2024). The three greens: Innovation, finance, and taxes—Performance analysis and future implications. *Journal of Innovation and Knowledge*, *9*(4). Advance online publication. DOI: 10.1016/j.jik.2024.100627

Zhang, X., Wang, W., Teng, X., & Yang, L. (2024). Navigating Competitive Intensity: The Role of Digital Orientation in SMEs' Green Innovations. *Journal of the Knowledge Economy*. Advance online publication. DOI: 10.1007/s13132-024-02110-9

Zhang, Y. (2022). How Economic Performance of OECD economies influences through Green Finance and Renewable Energy Investment Resources? *Resources Policy*, *79*. Advance online publication. DOI: 10.1016/j.resourpol.2022.102925

Zhang, Y. (2024). The impact of green finance on the sustainable development of new energy enterprises. *Highlights in Business. Economics and Management*, *4*(3), 59–74.

Zhan, Y., Tan, K. H., Ji, G., & Tseng, M.-L. (2018). Sustainable Chinese manufacturing competitiveness in the 21st century: Green and lean practices, pressure and performance. *International Journal of Computer Integrated Manufacturing*, *31*(6), 523–536. DOI: 10.1080/0951192X.2016.1268721

Zheng, M., Feng, G.-F., & Chang, C.-P. (2023). Is green finance capable of promoting renewable energy technology? Empirical investigation for 64 economies worldwide. *Oeconomia Copernicana, 14*(2), 483–510. DOI: 10.24136/oc.2023.013

Zheng, M., Wu, L., Feng, G. F., & Chang, C. P. (2025). The impact of green finance on sustainable development: An investigation into national ESG performance. *Journal of Applied Econometrics, 28*(1), 2528672.

Zhong, M., Umar, M., Mirza, N., & Safi, A. (2024). Mineral resource Optimization: The Nexus of sustainability, digital transformation, and green finance in OECD economies. *Resources Policy, 90*. Advance online publication. DOI: 10.1016/j.resourpol.2024.104829

Zhou, B., & Wang, Q. (2024). FinTech matters in sustainable finance: Does it redistribute the supply of financial services? *Journal of International Financial Markets, Institutions and Money, 91*, 101913. DOI: 10.1016/j.intfin.2023.101913

Zhu, H., Chen, M., & Zhao, S. (2024). Natural resource rent, green finance, and CO2 emissions from the industrial sector. *Resources Policy, 98*. Advance online publication.

Zhu, R. (2022). Research on fiscal policy support for green finance development in the context of green recovery. *BCP Business & Management, 30*(1), 102–114.

Zournatzidou, G. (2025). Green finance and sustainable development: Investigating greentech ecosystems through PRISMA analysis. *Administrative Sciences, 15*(4), 150.

Zupic, I., & Cater, T. (2015). Bibliometric Methods in Management and Organization. *Organizational Research Methods, 18*, 429–472. DOI: 10.1177/1094428114562629

About the Contributors

Karima Sayari is an Associate Professor in Managerial and Financial Sciences Department at Al Zahra College for Women. She holds a bachelor's degree in international trade, a master's degree in economics and international finance, and a PhD in Finance and Economic Sciences in 2012. Dr. Sayari has over 10 years of teaching experience and has published extensively in reputable international journals indexed in Scopus and Web of Science and served as Reviewer and Editor in various international journals. Her research focuses on economics, finance, banking, and digital finance. She is an active peer reviewer in various academic journals.

Revenio C. Jalagat, Jr. is presently employed in Al-Zahra College for Women in the Sultanate of Oman since 2013 and as Associate Professor in 2023. He had a total accumulated experience of 18 years in both the industry serving as Accountant, Chief Accountant, Finance Manager, and in the Academe as Lecturer, Assistant Professor and Dean in the Philippines. Dr. Jalagat was also a lecturer at Gulf College in Oman for almost two and a half years. He is a Certified Public Accountant (CPA) in the Philippines and graduated Doctor of Management at Capitol University, Philippines. He has published research in internationally reputed journals, including Scopus and Web of Science indexed journals, and served as Reviewer and Editorial Member in various international journals.

Rafat Al Batayneh is currently employed as the Head of the Department and Associate Professor in the Managerial and Financial Sciences at Al Zahra College for Women, Sultanate of Oman. He finished his PhD in Finance in 2014 and worked in professorial capacities in different Universities for more than 10 years in Jordan and overseas. In the field of research, he has published and presented papers in international fora including Scopus and Web of Science indexes as well as serving as editor and reviewers in various international peer-reviewed journals. As an experienced academician, he has also supervised theses and dissertations as proof of his expertise in the field of finance.

***

Nishtha Agrawal is a full-time PhD scholar at the Department of Commerce, CMP Degree College, University of Allahabad, India. Her research interests include financial economics, investor, stock Market, Capital market, behaviour sustainable finance, and corporate finance. She has obtained bachelors in commerce and masters in commerce from the University of Allahabad. She is also an author and has published her research work in International Journal.

Neetu Ahmed, an avid economics scholar, brings nearly 16 years of experience in research and teaching management courses. She is currently an Assistant Professor at the School of Management, GD Goenka University, Gurgaon, Haryana, where she teaches Economics to undergraduate and postgraduate students and guides Ph.D. scholars. Dr. Ahmed has presented her work at various national and international conferences and has published extensively in renowned journals. Her research interests include sustainability, the knowledge economy, and international trade.

Shafqat Ali is a full-time PhD scholar at the Department of Commerce, CMP Degree College, University of Allahabad, India. His research interests include Fintech, Green Banking, Behavioral finance, Sustainable finance, Corporate finance and Investor Behaviour. He has obtained bachelors in commerce and masters in commerce from the University of Allahabad. He is also an author and has published his research work in international journals.

Syrine Ben Romdhane holds a Habilitation to Supervise Research in Finance obtained in July 2022 from the Faculty of Economics and Management of Tunis, and a PhD in Management Sciences obtained in 2011 from the same Faculty. The author is currently Associate Professor at the Ecole Supérieure des Sciences Economiques et Commerciales de Tunis where she teaches Financial Management, Portfolio Management, Financial Mathematics, Advanced Financial Analysis and Financial Diagnosis. She also teaches "Company Valuation", "Startup Finance", and "Financial and FinTech Economics" modules, respectively for students enrolled in the Professional Masters in "Financial Engineering" and "Management of Social and Solidarity Organizations", and Research Master in "Quantitative Economics and Finance". The author also provides supervision for students enrolled in a Research Master and a Professional Master. She taught Finance courses also in private institutes (ULT University, Time University, Central University and ESPRIT). She has published research articles in reputable journals. Her research interests focus on information technology, digitalization, banking efficiency, financial stability, sustainability, green finance, and cryptocurrencies.

Manasi Gujarathi is a dedicated and ambitious MBA student at SaiBalaji International Institute of Management Sciences (SBIIMS), Pune. With a strong academic foundation and a keen interest in business management, she aims to build a successful career in the corporate sector. Manasi is known for her analytical thinking, leadership qualities, and proactive approach toward learning. During her MBA program, she has developed a solid understanding of subjects such as marketing, finance, human resource management, and business strategy. She actively participates in group projects, presentations, and seminars, showcasing her teamwork and communication skills. Apart from academics, Manasi is also involved in extracurricular activities and college events, reflecting her well-rounded personality. Her enthusiasm for innovation, commitment to professional growth, and ability to adapt to dynamic business environments make her a promising future management professional. Her career goal is to contribute meaningfully to the business world by applying her managerial knowledge, problem-solving skills, and ethical decision-making to achieve sustainable success for organizations she associates with.

Shweta Jaiswal is a full-time PhD scholar at the Department of Commerce, CMP Degree College, University of Allahabad, India. Her research interests include financial economics, behavioural finance, sustainable finance, and corporate finance. She has obtained bachelors in commerce and masters in commerce from the University of Allahabad. She is also an author and has published her research work in IGI Global Scopus Indexed Book chapter.

Jipson Joseph has a PhD in Ethics from DVK Bangalore. Currently, he is a Research Scholar at School of Law, Christ University, Bangalore, India. His research interests are in the fields of ethics, gender studies, constitutional law, human rights, human security, environmental justice, SDGs, developmental policies, and global poverty. He has published 6 books, co-edited one book, and contributed scholarly articles to many international and national journals and edited volumes including IGI Global Scientific Publishing's edited books.

Rishikaysh Kaakandikar is a distinguished academician, researcher, and mentor known for his dynamic leadership and unwavering commitment to excellence in management education. With years of experience in teaching, mentoring, and academic administration, Dr. Kaakandikar has made significant contributions to the development of future leaders in the fields of business, finance, and strategy.

Currently serving as a respected faculty member at SaiBalaji International Institute of Management Sciences, Pune, Dr. Kaakandikar is widely admired for his engaging teaching style, insightful case-based learning methods, and his ability to connect theory with real-world business applications. His mentorship has played a pivotal role in guiding numerous students through academic challenges, research projects, and career development. An advocate for innovation and holistic growth, Dr. Kaakandikar is also actively involved in national and international conferences, case competitions, and research publications. He encourages students to think critically, act ethically, and pursue excellence in all endeavors. His dedication to nurturing talent and fostering a culture of continuous learning has earned him immense respect among colleagues and students alike. Beyond his academic roles, Dr. Kaakandikar is a passionate supporter of student-led initiatives and actively promotes experiential learning through events, competitions, and real-world problem-solving exercises. Dr. Rishikaysh Kaakandikar embodies the qualities of a true mentor—knowledgeable, approachable, and deeply invested in the growth of his students.

Gurleen Kaur is an economics enthusiast with around 12 years of experience working as an Assistant Professor in Department of Economics at Sri Guru Gobind Singh College of Commerce, University of Delhi. She teaches Economics to undergraduates and mentors both graduate and post graduate students in their research projects. She has presented papers in International and National Conferences and has contributed acclaimed publications in reputed Scopus indexed journals both National and International. Her opinion-based paper on COVID-19 and the Rise of the New Experience Economy got a special mention in a Forbes article in 2021.

Shital Newase is a seasoned academician and dedicated educator specializing in finance and business studies, with over 10 years of experience in teaching, research, and academic leadership. She has made significant contributions to higher education through her expertise in curriculum development, student mentorship, and scholarly work. She holds a Doctorate (Ph.D.) in Internet Banking, along with a Post Graduate Diploma in Banking (PGDB) and an MBA in Finance. She has also qualified the National Eligibility Test (NET), demonstrating her academic rigor and expertise in her field. Her educational background equips her with a comprehensive understanding of both theoretical frameworks and practical applications in business and financial management. Currently, she serves as an Assistant Professor at the SaiBalaji Education Society's International Institute of Management and Human Resource Development (w). In this capacity, she actively contributes to curriculum design, academic administration, and research supervision, while mentoring students and preparing them for the complexities of the financial and business sectors. Her areas of academic focus include financial planning, investment analysis, corporate finance, and business strategy. She has presented at numerous national and international conferences, authored research publications, and remains committed to advancing innovative teaching methodologies and contributing to the broader body of knowledge in finance and management.

Ananya Pandey is a Research Scholar in School of Law at Christ University, Bangalore. She has her research interests in the field of Constitutional Law, Environment Law, Human Rights, Food Security, Intellectual Property Law and Jurisprudence.

Sonam Prabhakar is a PhD research scholar at the Department of Anthropology and Tribal Studies, Central University of Jharkhand, Ranchi. She has completed her BSc. and MSc. from Dr. Rajendra Prasad Central Agricultural University, Pusa, Samastipur, India with a specialization in family resource management. She has many publications in her name in national and international journals. Her area of research interest is entrepreneurship, gender, and tribal studies.

Anamika Rana is currently working as an Assistant Professor in the Department of Commerce, School of Commerce, Finance and Accountancy, Christ (Deemed to be University).

Jyoti Rani, Assistant professor, school of fashion design and technology. Research and Academic experience. 2 year experience in academics and research. Research area: fashion, textile, natural dyeing, consumer behaviour, AI, merchandising. she has published 28 research paper in refered journal and 5 book chapters.

Ambar Srivastava is working as an Assistant Professor in School of Commerce, Finance & Accountancy at Christ (Deemed to be University), Delhi NCR, Ghaziabad, India. He has qualified for the UGC-NET in commerce and completed a CA (Inter) from the Institute of Chartered Accountant of India (ICAI). Mr. Srivastava is amongst the top 5 in Master of Commerce (M. Com) from Jai Narain Vyas University, Jodhpur, Rajasthan. Besides these, he has taught at the Mohanlal Sukhadia University, Udaipur, Rajasthan. His teaching interests include financial accounting, corporate accounting, financial management, e-accounting, direct & indirect taxation, etc. He has published three textbook titled "Goods & Service Tax", "Income Tax" & "Cost Accounting" published by Choudhary Prakashan, Jaipur. He also published good research papers in reputed journals. His research interests include sustainability reporting, financial performance, corporate governance, taxation issues, etc.

Kumar Vivek is a seasoned Real Estate Professional with 14+ years of total experience in the construction, planning and valuation domain. He has been engaged with real estate appraisal, project and developer due diligence, construction finance and collateral risk assessment for Tier A financial institutions for last 10+ years.

Index

A

C

E

F

R

S

T

www.ingramcontent.com/pod-product-compliance
Lightning Source LLC
LaVergne TN
LVHW080908300926
849162LV00003B/606